THE MANAGING

OF

POLICE ORGANIZATIONS

Paul M. Whisenand, Ph.D.

Chairman, Department of Criminology
California State University, Long Beach

R. Fred Ferguson, M. S.

Chief of Police
Riverside (Calif.) Police Department

PRENTICE-HALL, INC., Englewood Cliffs, New Jersey

Library of Congress Cataloging in Publication Data

WHISENAND, PAUL M
   The managing of police organizations.

   Includes bibliographies.
   1. Police administration. I. Ferguson, Robert
Fred, 1925-   joint author. II. Title.
HV7935. W43   350'.74   72-10322
ISBN 0-13-550749-9

Printed in the United States of America

10 9 8 7 6 5

Prentice-Hall International, Inc., *London*
Prentice-Hall of Australia, Pty. Ltd., *Sydney*
Prentice-Hall of Canada, Ltd., *Toronto*
Prentice-Hall of India Private Limited, *New Delhi*
Prentice-Hall of Japan, Inc., *Tokyo*

To our favorite managers—
Joan Whisenand and Marilu Ferguson

CONTENTS

PREFACE

The Managing of Police Organizations, intended as a contribution to the literature on the criminal justice system, has police
managers—both existing and potential—as its primary target audience.
Although it is relevant to all local law enforcement practitioners
(chief, sheriff, captain, lieutenant, sergeant, or patrolman), obviously
the higher the rank, the more immediately applicable are the ideas
and functions described herein. The text is also meaningful to the
criminal-justice/police student. As the differentiation between police
practitioner and police student grows less and less distinct, we frequently find practitioner-students in local police agencies and colleges. Our goal is to promote a philosophy and style of management
that is beneficial to the police manager, the police student, or both.

We the authors, who both teach and practice law enforcement,
have purposely tried to inject our personal work-related experiences
and education into the design and content of the book, believing that
these are examples of the trend toward the emergence of educator-
practitioners and practitioner-educators in the criminal justice field.
There are two underlying beliefs that motivated us to write this text:
First, we believe that police work, whether it be managing law en-
forcers or the law enforcing itself, can be made more efficient and

more satisfying; that is, law enforcement agencies can be structured and managed so that they are more effective in accomplishing organizational goals and in satisfying human goals. This belief is based on our experience as educator-practitioners. Second, we believe that learning can be maximized in terms of enjoyment and information used and retained, a belief derived from our experience as practitioner-educators.

The text awaits your evaluation; after reading its thirteen chapters, you will be able to judge to what degree it has been successful as a "contribution to the literature on the criminal justice system." We look forward to your assessment.

PAUL M. WHISENAND, Ph.D.
R. FRED FERGUSON, M.S.

Long Beach, California

1

POLICE MANAGEMENT:
The Role
and the Values

Organizational excellence and managerial excellence are one and the same. Consequently, any attempt to improve one automatically involves the other. This book approaches organizational excellence through better management, more specifically, better *police* management. Thus, we focus on the need to increase the manager's understanding of police organizations so that he will be equipped to control and direct them in response to complex human purposes. In terms of concepts, strategies, and skills essential for achieving such managerial abilities, and methods of learning them and then putting them to work, the stage is set. Our text covers the prospects and the need for a modern police management that is capable of directing the modern police organization. *Our major premise is that the police manager is undoubtedly capable of improving his organization so that it can accomplish its particular goals and at the same time meet the needs of its members. Our major hope is that one of the manager's most sought-after goals is within reach; namely, mastery of himself and thereby of his organization.*

The remainder of Chapter 1 is devoted to defining the pertinent concepts and terms, discussing the basic conditions that create the need for a "new" police management, taking a quick look at the manager's future behavior, and giving a brief preview of the style and organization of the subsequent chapters. We believe that the

1

following three recommendations can aid the reader in getting to the heart of the book: (1) The organization's objectives will probably be attained more effectively by so managing the work and the people that their individual needs are met while on the job. We seek to provide the means for making our opening sentences a reality—organizations can achieve excellence by helping their managers achieve excellence. (2) The book should be read as a study of *managerial* dynamics. It should not be read as a study of *individual* behavior. (3) Please keep in mind that the material is primarily for you—the potential or actual *police manager*. Most of the ideas and strategies presented, however, can also be applied in other organizations.[1]

SELECTED DEFINITIONS

Selecting a definition is similar to picking a winning horse at a race track—everyone has his own choice. As for the terms that are defined in this section, your definition may be as good or better than ours. The primary purpose is, therefore, to create some general agreement as to what we mean when certain ideas are discussed. Only those terms central to our thinking are reviewed at this time. Other terms receive consideration in the chapters that focus on their parameters and dynamics.

Let us begin by looking at the term *police*. We use it to identify a particular type of formal organization, and, for our purposes, it is a government organization. Hence, we define *police* as *a formal government organization responsible for enforcing the laws of society and maintaining peace*.[2] Our definition encompasses local (municipal and county), state, and federal policing agencies. It should be noted, however, that our focus is on local police organizations and that we will consider the term *local law enforcement* as being synonymous with the term *police*.

The term *organization*, so prevalent in the above paragraph, is so frequently used in conjunction with the term *management* that the two are often confused. Waldo offers a useful discussion on how to distinguish them:

[1]One of the first accounts of the principle of the universality of management is given in a Socratic discourse as recorded (or imagined) by Xenophon, one of Socrates' disciples. It clearly indicates that even in the fifth century B.C. men were aware of or beginning to be aware of the same principles that would apply in the twentieth century when an effective manager of a soap company could also be an effective head of an automobile concern or secretary of defense. For a highly readable text on the development of management theory and practice, see Claude S. George, Jr., *The History of Management Thought* (Englewood Cliffs, N.J.: Prentice-Hall, Inc., 1968).

[2]For an excellent discussion of the goals of contemporary local law enforcement, see James Q. Wilson, "Dilemmas of Police Administration," *Public Administration Review*, 28 (September-October 1968), 407–16.

Organization is the anatomy, management the physiology, of administration. Organization is structure; management is functioning. But each is dependent upon and inconceivable without the other in any existing administrative system, just as anatomy and physiology are intertwined and mutually dependent in any living organism. We are close to the truth, in fact, when we assert that *organization and management* are merely convenient categories of analysis, two different ways of viewing the same phenomena. One is static and seeks for pattern; the other is dynamic and follows movement.

More precisely, organization may be defined *as the structure of authoritative and habitual personal interrelations in an administrative system.*[3] (Italics added.)

Waldo defines *management* as *"action intended to achieve rational cooperation in an administrative system."*[4] The chapters that follow concentrate on the "action" part of the definition. This can also be referred to as the role of the manager, or the behavior that is expected of him in order to achieve universal cooperation. The role is comprised of a variety of functions or processes that the manager must promote and facilitate. More will be said about the manager's role in the subsequent section.

We are now in position to describe *administration* and *administrative system.* They are *formal groupings deliberately constructed to seek specific goals.* And, organization and management serve as the structure and the processes for arriving at the heart of any administrative system—the attainment of goals. *A goal is a desired state of affairs which the administrative system attempts to realize.* The primary responsibility of the police manager is, therefore, to use the organization as a tool for moving the administrative system toward goal attainment. Since administrative goals are so critical, let us examine them more closely.

The goals of a police organization serve many ends. First, *goals provide direction by depicting a future state of affairs which the organization strives to realize.* Second, *goals also constitute a source of legitimacy which justifies the activities of an organization and, indeed, its very existence.* Third, *goals serve as bench marks by which members of an organization and outsiders can evaluate the success of the organization, that is, its effectiveness and efficiency.*

Modern organizations usually have more than a single goal and tend to rank them in order of significance. Let us analyze the preceding sentence in light of our present-day police organizations. You will recall that we cited the two major goals of local law enforcement as law enforcement and order maintenance. While we advocate two basic

---

[3] Dwight Waldo, *The Study of Public Administration* (New York: Random House, Inc., 1955), p. 6.

[4] *Ibid.*, p. 7.

goals, some lists are a lot longer. For example, a recognized source describes six goals, as follows (note that their listing of goals is prefaced by what they refer to as a "mission," which is another term for major goal):

> The police mission, succinctly stated, is maintenance of social order within carefully prescribed ethical and constitutional restrictions. The mission as currently defined involves:
>
> 1. *Prevention of Criminality.* This activity views the police role in constructive terms and involves taking the police into sectors of the community where criminal tendencies are bred and individuals motivated to indulge in antisocial behavior, and includes seeking to reduce the causes of crime.
>
> 2. *Repression of Crime.* This activity stresses adequate patrol plus a continuous effort toward eliminating or reducing hazards as the principal means of reducing the opportunities for criminal actions.
>
> 3. *Apprehension of Offenders.* This activity views quick apprehension as the means to discourage the would-be offender. The certainty of arrest and prosecution has a deterrent quality which is intended to make crime seem less worthwhile. Additionally, apprehension enables society to punish offenders, lessens the prospect of repetition by causing suspects to be incarcerated, and provides an opportunity for rehabilitation of those convicted.
>
> 4. *Recovery of Property.* This activity seeks to reduce the monetary cost of crime, as well as to restrain those who, though not active criminals, might benefit from the gains of crime.
>
> 5. *Regulation of Noncriminal Conduct.* This aspect of the police mission involves sundry activities that are only incidentally concerned with criminal behavior, such as the enforcement of traffic and sanitary code provisions. The main purpose is regulation, and apprehension and punishment of offenders are means of securing compliance. Other methods used to obtain compliance are education (e.g., observance of laws) and the use of warnings, either oral or written, to inform citizens of the violations without taking punitive actions.
>
> 6. *Performance of Miscellaneous Services.* This involves many service activities peripheral to basic police duties and includes, for example, the operation of detention facilities, search and rescue operations, licensing, supervising elections, staffing courts with administrative and security personnel, and even such completely extraneous things as chauffeuring officials.[5]

In regard to the rank ordering of goals, we can surmise that the above list places emphasis on the law enforcement goals. Interestingly, James Q. Wilson and a few others differ with this priority. They suggest that the order maintenance goals (regulation of non-

[5] James F. Bale and George D. Eastman, "Police Service Today," in *Municipal Police Administration,* 6th ed., ed. George D. Eastman and Esther M. Eastman (Washington, D.C.: International City Management Association, 1969), pp. 3–4.

criminal conduct and performance of miscellaneous services) should be stressed. Wilson argues:

> *First, the police should recognize clearly that order mainte-*
> *nance is their central function—central both in the demands it*
> *makes on time and resources and in the opportunities it affords for*
> *making a difference in the lives of the citizens.* Hunting criminals
> both occupies less time (at least for the patrolmen) and provides
> fewer chances for decisive action. How well disputes are settled
> may depend crucially on how competent, knowledgeable, and
> sensitive the police are; *how fast the crime rate mounts is much*
> *less dependent on the level and nature of police activity.* (As will
> be argued below, other than by reducing the size of the lower
> class *the best way society can affect the crime rate may be through*
> *the court and correctional systems rather than through the*
> *police.*)[6] (Italics added.)

More will be said later about the goals of police organizations.

We now examine a concept that is becoming increasingly more important—*the criminal justice system,* or the *administration of criminal justice.* The administration of criminal justice includes the following six components: law enforcement, prosecution, probation, courts, corrections, and parole. The concept of a criminal justice system is relatively new—it originated in the 1960s. Hence, there is very little literature about it and even less agreement as to its components and parameters.[7] While the phrase *administration of criminal justice* is often used, it is in fact a misnomer. In reality, a loose system of relationships prevails. Ackoff supplied a useful and simple definition of a system when he described it as "any entity, conceptual or physical, which consists of interdependent parts."[8] Dorsey provided a framework for operationalizing systems theory when he defined a system as

> a bonded region in space and time, within which information
> and/or energy are exchanged among subsystems in greater quan-
> tities and/or at higher rates than the quantities exchanged or rates
> of exchange with anything outside the boundary, and within
> which the subsystems are to some degree interdependent.[9]

[6] See Wilson, "Dilemmas of Police Administration," p. 412.

[7] John P. Kenney describes the system of criminal justice in terms of the voluntary partnership that has been established between the local police agencies and the
state in *The California Police* (Springfield, Ill.: Charles C Thomas, Publisher, 1964),
p.111. See also Space-General Corporation, *Prevention and Control of Crime and Delinquency,* report prepared for the Youth and Adult Corrections Agency, State of California (El Monte, Calif.: Space-General Corporation, 1965), p. 14.

[8] Russell L. Ackoff, "Systems, Organizations and Interdisciplinary Research,"
General Systems, 5 (1960), 1.

[9] John T. Dorsey, "An Information-Energy Model," *Papers in Comparative Public
Administration,* ed. Ferrel Heady and Sybil L. Stokes (Ann Arbor, Mich.: Institute of
Public Administration, 1962), p. 43.

An extensive vocabulary of systems theories exists and includes such terms as system, boundary, environment, homeostatic-equilibrium, interaction, interdependent, structural-functional relationship, input-output, exchanges, and open versus closed system. In the complete system block diagram (Figure 1-1), it is possible to identify the numerous interrelationships within the criminal justice system. The diagram makes it readily apparent that those working in criminal justice are placed in the middle of a system of relationships, out of which they must fashion an operating system that assists in accomplishing the objectives of many involved organizations. When local, state, and national law enforcement organizations are viewed as subsystems, it becomes possible to ascertain the basic significance and utility of improving the criminal justice system in total. The Omnibus Crime Control and Safe Streets Act of 1968 is a major step in making what has been called our nonsystem of criminal justice into a *system*.[10]

BASIC CONDITIONS THAT CREATE THE NEED FOR A "NEW" POLICE MANAGER

From an almost unrecognized position in 1900, *management has risen today to be the central activity of our age and organizational society*. And, as we become increasingly more an organizational society, the importance of effective management also grows. Etzioni aptly puts it:

> *Our society is an organizational society.* We are born in organizations, educated by organizations, and most of us spend much of our lives working for organizations. We spend much of our leisure time paying, playing, and praying in organizations. Most of us will die in an organization, and when the time comes for burial, the largest organization of all—the state—must grant official permission.[11]

Management is at one and the same time the determiner of our national progress, the supervisor of our employed, the amasser of our resources, the guide for our effective government, and the molder of our society. *It is the focal point of our social as well as personal activities, and the way we manage ourselves and our organizations reflects with pertinent clarity what we and our society are in the process of observing.*

[10] For an excellent overview of this act, the government organizations it created, and the direction it has taken in order to improve the criminal justice system, see *1st Annual Report of the Law Enforcement Assistance Administration* (Washington, D.C.: Government Printing Office, 1969).

[11] Amitai Etzioni, *Modern Organizations* (Englewood Cliffs, N.J.: Prentice-Hall, Inc., 1964), p. 1.

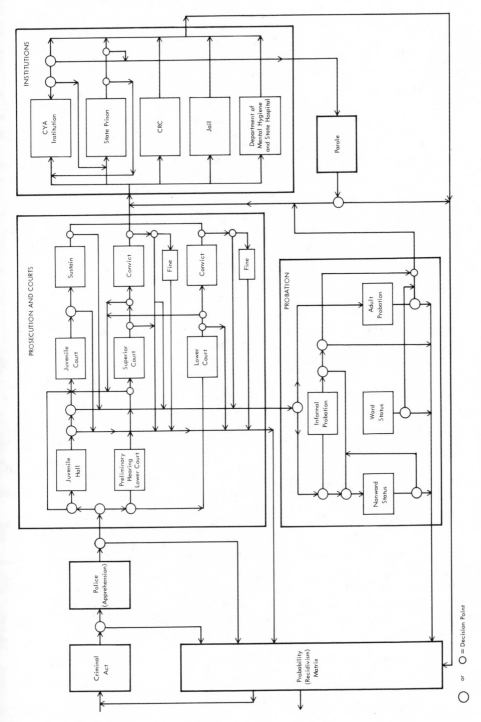

FIGURE 1-1 The California Criminal Justice System: Block Diagram

○ or ○ = Decision Point

7

Despite its importance and omnipresence, however, management is one of the least understood functions, being found in the homes, churches, governments, and economic undertakings of all societies. It is and always has been the crucial tool of a successful leader. But regretfully:

> Accepted theory and conventional wisdom concerning leadership have a lot in common. Both seem to be saying that the success of a leader depends on the leader, the led, and the unique situation. This formulation—abstract and majestically useless—is the best that can be gleaned from over 100 years of research on "leadership."[12]

By implication or explicit recommendation *the current literature suggests to the manager the utility of divergent managerial styles,* organization structures and climates, and types of management training. For the behavioral and social scientists who devote their lives to understanding these topics, the apparent contradictions and ambiguities are confusing enough, but for the practicing manager who is responsible for this new knowledge as a guide in making organizational decisions, the confusion may at times seem insurmountable. If nothing else is understood, however, the manager is certainly aware that *there is no one best way to manage or organize in all situations.* The need for reducing this confusion is vital for one all-important reason. One of the major causes of management's concern with organizational issues is that the technical, social, economic, and geographical conditions facing their organizations are becoming more diverse and are constantly changing. The police are caught up in such diversity and change.[13] And the police may be more affected by it than are most other organizations in our society. Consequently, effective management is all the more critical to their organizations.

The "new" management that we refer to is fundamentally and primarily caused by *change*—change from one state of affairs to another. Our organizational society is experiencing a rapid transition from the bureaucratic form (mechanistic) to the systems form (adaptive) of organizing and managing. There are two primary reasons for this phenomenon. First, the demise of our bureaucratic structures is close at hand. Second, certain factors are shaping our emerging administrative systems. To begin, bureaucracy consists of the following attributes:

1. A precise hierarchy of authority

[12] Warren G. Bennis, "The Leader of the Future," *Public Management,* 52 (March 1970), 13.

[13] In regard to organizational change, see a series of articles entitled "Evaluation of Change Programs," *Administrative Science Quarterly,* 15 (March 1970).

2. A system of rules for dealing with all work activities
3. A detailed division of labor based on specialization
4. Established routines
5. Impersonality in human relations[14]

This form of organization which proved effective in the nineteenth century is under attack by twentieth century conditions. Many leading organizational theorists are predicting that the death of bureaucracy is but a matter of time. Their thinking is derived from the numerous sociotechnical changes that are occurring in our society. In referring to this prediction made in 1965 regarding the pending death of bureaucracy, Bennis now writes:

> Ironically, the bold future I had predicted is now routine and can be observed wherever the most interesting and advanced practices exist. Most of these trends are visible and have been surfacing for years in the aerospace, construction, drug, and consulting industries as well as professional and research and development organizations, which only shows that the distant future now has a way of arriving before the forecast is fully comprehended.[15]

At least four reasons account for the disappearance of bureaucratic organizations, and combined they indicate an overt finding on the part of those wanting to make our organizations more effective—bureaucracy either will not work at all or is highly ineffective in handling our contemporary problems: (1) We are experiencing rapid and unexpected change—bureaucracy, with its precisely defined chain of command, its rules, and its rigidities is ill adapted to the rapid change the environment now demands; (2) we are experiencing constant growth in organizational size and number of activities performed—bureaucracy with its overhead, tight controls, impersonality, and outmoded rules and organizational structures is incapable of meeting the demands of sustained growth; (3) we are experiencing greater degrees of diversity—bureaucracy with its lack of integrating devices fails to interface the completion of modern technology with the competences of modern man; and (4) we are (thankfully!) experiencing a change in management behavior—bureaucracy is not designed to accommodate new concepts of man, power, and human values. For those of you who are seeking more caustic or "gut level" reasons for destroying our

---

[14] Max Weber is considered to be the first to identify the characteristics of bureaucratic organizations. An analysis of his thinking and samples of his writing can be found in H. H. Gerth and C. Wright Mills, *From Max Weber: Essays in Sociology* (New York: Oxford University Press, Inc., 1946).

[15] Bennis, "The Leader of the Future," p. 13.

bureaucratic structures, see the writings of Robert Townsend and Lawrence Peter.[16]

Now let us examine some of the conditions that either are now or in other cases will soon be molding our organizational structures. During your review of the conditions cited below, continually ask yourself, What is their potential impact on management? More specifically, What is their potential impact on *police* management? First, the environment in which the police organization operates is undergoing significant transition. Perhaps the single most outstanding change is the increasing amount of complexity—social, economic, technological, and so on. Environmental complexity places a series of demands on the police organization for dealing with uncertainty and large-scale problems. This, in turn, creates the need for greater interdependence among organizations within and outside the criminal justice system. One example is seen in the number of relationships being established between police departments and data processing firms. Second, the characteristics of the population that the police serve are changing. The higher educational level as well as the growth in the number of educated people in our society is the most distinctive of all such related factors. Look at your own position as an illustration. What was required in the way of an education ten years ago for a police manager? How does it compare with current requirements? Moreover, what does the future indicate? A school *dropout* is now being defined as a person who has not attended an educational or a training program in the last year. The rate of professional obsolescence is considerably faster today. Third, related to the preceding point, is the shift in work values. The increased level of education will change the values we place on work. People will be more intellectually committed to their jobs and will probably require more involvement, participation, and autonomy. Police managers take note! Fourth, the tasks of the police organization will be more technical, complicated, and unprogrammed. They will rely more on intellect and less on muscle. And, in most instances, they will be too complicated for one person to comprehend, to say nothing of control. Essentially, they will call for the collaboration of specialists in a project or a *team* form of organization. Fifth, there will be a greater complication of goals. The police manager is already being confronted with this problem. Wilson provides testimony to this when he writes:

> The dilemmas of police administration arise out of the difficulty confronting a chief who seeks policies which can guide his men

---

[16]Robert Townsend, *Up the Organization* (New York: Alfred A. Knopf, Inc., 1970); and Lawrence J. Peter and Raymond Hull, *The Peter Principle* (New York: William Morrow & Co., Inc., 1969).

in performing the order-maintenance function and a technique which will prove efficacious in serving the law-enforcement function. The conflict over how the police should behave in order-maintenance cases results from differing expectations as to the appropriate level of public or private order and differing judgments over what constitutes a just resolution of a given dispute. In a homogeneous community, where widely shared norms define both the meaning of order and the standards of justice (who is equal to whom and in what sense), the police role is comparatively simple. *But where the community, usually because of differences of class or race, has no common normative framework, the police have no reliable guides to action and efforts to devise such guides will either be half-hearted or sources of important public controversy. The conflict that arises over the performance of the law-enforcement function, on the other hand, arises out of the lack of any technique by which crime can be reduced significantly and without incurring high costs in terms of other values—privacy, freedom, and so forth. The dispute about the law-enforcement function is, unlike the dispute over order maintenance, not over ends but over means.*[17]

Sixth, the social structure of organizations of the future will have some unique characteristics. The key word will be *temporary*. There will be adaptive, rapidly changing *temporary systems*. These will be task forces organized around problems to be solved by groups of individuals with diverse professional skills. "Adaptive, problem-solving, temporary systems of diverse specialists, linked together by coordinating and task-evaluating executive specialists in an organic flux— this is the organizational form that will gradually replace bureaucracy as we know it."[18] Again, police manager take note! Call it what you will. We choose to title these new-style organizations *administrative systems*. Seventh, and finally, administrative systems should increase motivation, and thereby effectiveness, because they generate situations under which the individual can gain increased satisfaction with the task itself. Thus, there should be a supportive relationship between the policeman's need for tasks that are significant, satisfying, and creative and the structure of the administrative system.

In conclusion, the future job requirements that we described are clearly not easily fulfilled. The police manager who decides to "hang-in-there" must anticipate and shape a number of profound changes in the ways he organizes his work and human relations. Change is equivalent to challenge, and that is what management must be prepared to meet and deal with *effectively*.

[17] Wilson, "Dilemmas of Police Administration," p. 408.

[18] Warren G. Bennis, *Organization Development: Its Nature, Origins, and Prospects* (Reading, Mass.: Addison-Wesley Publishing Company, Inc., 1969), p. 34.

THE FUTURE MANAGER

The role of the future police manager will remain essentially the same as it is today (planning, organizing, communicating, etc.). *The strategies for fulfilling the role requirement, however, will drastically change.* To begin with, the role will be best served by a shift in management philosophy. The police manager will need (1) a new concept of man based on increased knowledge of his complex and shifting needs, which replaces an oversimplified, "rational animal" idea of man; (2) a new concept of power, based on cooperation and reason, which replaces a model of power based on coercion and threat; and (3) a new concept of organizational values, based on humanistic-democratic ideals, which replaces the depersonalized, mechanistic value system of bureaucracy. Such a philosophy automatically demands the selection of innovative strategies appropriate to its concepts.

A few progressive police managers have already discerned the need for a new philosophy and have thus taken action on the development of the necessary management strategies. These managers are continually working on the problems of how to develop police departments that can move with changing requirements and can be "proactive" (influencing the environment) rather than reactive. They are seeking ways to establish a work climate in which increasingly complex decisions can be made by personnel with the information, regardless of their location in department. Progressive police managers are looking for ways in which increasingly complex technologies can be managed and in which police officers who have an ever higher sense of freedom and autonomy can be encouraged to want to stay and work in their department. The search for ways of concurrently increasing collaboration among the members of criminal justice organizations and at the same time increasing the rationality of decisions occupies many hours of their time. The primary cause for a new philosophy and resultant strategies stems not from the bookshelf but from police managers themselves. The remainder of this text is devoted to a discussion of the emerging strategies for managing police organizations. To repeat, our major concern is the adoption of management strategies that further the movement toward organizational excellence.

THE OUTLINE AND APPROACH OF THE TEXT

To reemphasize a recommendation made earlier, this book is best read and, therefore, comprehended as a study of managerial dynamics. It is not a text on individual behavior. Furthermore, the basic outline of this volume is straightforward. Each of the following chapters contains one or more learning exercises, some of which have been previously published. Learning exercises include (1) case studies, (2) structured experiences, and (3) miscellaneous material. Each of the lessons has a relatively sharp managerial focus, whether it be on the manager and his role or on the manager and his future problems (or problems with the future). These managerial focuses do not exhaust the field, but they do provide a wide-ranging familiarity with much of relevance to the police manager.

Business (e.g., the Harvard Business School) and, later, public administration discovered that learning exercises such as case studies improved the training experience of their students and practitioners. The development of *case studies* and *structured experiences* is particularly valuable in adding realism about "what goes on out there in the real world." But the training technology in business and public administration has only slowly assimilated the recent advances in the study of human behavior, that is, "what goes on in here." Police literature has yet to fully use the case study or the structured experience approach for training in either environmental or human administrative realities. It appears that this text is an initial attempt to tackle both dimensions; however, with a definite bias toward the human dimension.

Two essential yet often omitted supporting resources are also provided along with the learning exercise. First, each is introduced by a brief essay designed to highlight some of the intellectual learning opportunities offered by each exercise. Hence much attention is given to research findings, innovative practices, and theories that form managerial strategies of significance to police managers. Second, most chapters also contain a suggested learning design on how to best use the exercise. The simple learning design is meant to structure a situation useful for increasing the learner's awareness of what goes on within and outside himself as a police manager. Interestingly, the supporting resources in each chapter may be read before or after the case studies. Experimentation will tell you which is the most effective sequence for your particular training and educational objectives.

Chapters 1 and 2 treat the role and values of the police manager in a general sense. Chapters 3 through 11 analyze the specific job requirements that serve to form the manager's role. In other words, the police manager is expected to plan, communicate, organize, control, make decisions, coordinate, lead, and effectively handle people and machinery. Finally, Chapters 12 and 13 deal with existing and soon-to-be existing challenges to his successful fulfillment of the behavior expected of him to bring about organizational excellence.

2

VALUES AND
VALUE ORIENTATIONS

In short, value differences are sometimes nothing more
than differences in ways of looking at reality. Sometimes
they consist of honest differences in opinion about the most
effective way to achieve mutually agreed-upon goals. Sometimes they reflect fundamental differences in primary
orientation to the world we live in. These differences may
be as simple as a preference for the Martins over the Coys;
they can be as complex as the choice between egoism and
humanitarianism.[1]

If you want to know what makes a competent police manager, ask
the man who is one. In most cases he will not be able to tell you.
Police managers are, after all, men of action; they are too deeply
involved in their daily tasks to introspect and contemplate on what
makes them tick. To be sure, you do get some high-level generalities
and abstractions. Once in a while a police leader does get the time to
write or to articulate his ideas at some conference or other. But, in
general, all that these utterances produce is a somewhat ambiguous
emphasis on such qualities as courage, morality, broad-gauge thinking, and decisiveness—the attributes and symptoms, after all, of any

[1]Robert Boguslaw, *The New Utopians: A Study of System Design and Social
Change* (Englewood Cliffs, N.J.: Prentice-Hall, Inc., 1965), p. 202.

14

emotionally mature individual and certainly not limited to police managers.

A variety of notions about reasons for a manager's successful behavior as compared with unsuccessful behavior has emerged. Some believe that the better manager is a generalist. This thinking proposes that he does not have to be a technical expert—he can hire specialists to perform these functions. His position, therefore, is to direct organizational activities. Some regard him as a coordinator, bringing divergent views together into an integrated set of goals. Others contend that he is a man who gets things done through others. All these viewpoints suggest that the police manager does not have to know anything—that his main responsibility is to coordinate the work and effort of the management team. In contrast, others see the manager as a man of superior intellect, understanding, and analytical ability who makes the ultimate decisions. He functions at the center of an information network and assesses conditions, and he decides accordingly. Still others see him as a man primarily concerned with maintaining the organization—both the work organization and the decision-making organization. Here the assumption is that if the organization is functioning efficiently and effectively, the manager is performing well. Finally, there are some who see the police manager simply as a figurehead who operates in the public eye and in general represents his organization in important community affairs. Obviously there is some truth in all the above-mentioned ideas about what a police manager does to be effective. We can approach the question more systematically, however, by examining his *values*! To this end Drucker writes:

> Direct results always come first. In the care and feeding
> of an organization, they play the role calories play in the
> nutrition of the human body. But any organization also
> needs a commitment to values and their constant reaffirma-
> tion, as a human body needs vitamins and minerals. There
> has to be something "this organization stands for," or else
> it degenerates into disorganization, confusion, and paralysis.
> In a business, the value commitment may be to technical
> leadership or (as in Sears Roebuck) to finding the right goods
> and services for the American family and to procuring them
> at the lowest price and best quality.
>   Value commitments, like results, are not unambiguous.
>   The U.S. Department of Agriculture has for many years
> been torn between two fundamentally incompatible value
> commitments—one to agricultural productivity and one to
> the "family farm" as the "backbone of the nation." The
> former has been pushing the country toward industrial agri-
> culture, highly mechanical, highly industrialized, and
> essentially a large-scale commercial business. The latter has
> called for nostalgia supporting a nonproducing rural pro-

letariat. But because farm policy—at least until very recently
—has wavered between two different value commitments, all it
has really succeeded in doing has been to spend prodigious
amounts of money.[2]

Furthermore:

> The social and personal values of the law enforcement
> officer strongly condition the quality of service he delivers
> to different segments of the populace at large.[3]

Underlying all the chapters in this volume is a basic assumption
that the values, norms, and ideologies of society are important condi-
tioners of managerial behavior. The effective police manager is the
individual who has identified and operates according to a culturally
preferred set of values.[4] For example, in modern democratic societies
humanitarian behavior is much more desired in management than
not. Golembiewski lists five organizational values which should
guide human behavior.

1. Work must be psychologically acceptable, nonthreatening.
2. Work must allow man to develop his faculties.
3. The task must allow the individual room for self-
   determination.
4. The worker must influence the broad environment
   within which he works.
5. The formal organization must not be the sole and final
   arbiter of behavior.[5]

Modern students of management, of course, follow Weber in
emphasizing the importance of organizational values and norms for
understanding the managerial process, but less attention has been
paid to the relation of these to the values of the whole society.[6] Im-
plicitly it seems to be assumed that in the long run, organizational
values can continue successfully at odds with societal values. *We
firmly believe this assumption is in error.* Moreover, we believe that
professional skills, human empathy, and even the values of his or-

---

[2] Peter F. Drucker, *The Effective Executive* (New York: Harper & Row, Publishers, 1967), p. 56.

[3] Jacob Chwast, "Value Conflicts in Law Enforcement," *Crime and Delinquency*,
11 (April 1965), 152.

[4] For one example, see Everett G. Dillman, "Impact of Culture on Management
Practices," *Public Personnel Review*, 31 (April 1970), 114–17.

[5] Robert T. Golembiewski, *Men, Management, and Morality: Towards New Organizational Ethics* (New York: McGraw-Hill Book Company, 1965), p. 73.

[6] For details, see H. H. Gerth and C. Wright Mills, *From Max Weber: Essays in
Sociology* (New York: Oxford University Press, Inc., 1946).

ganization unit are seemingly not enough to guide the action of the manager in the police department. Police management in our modern world is stagnated and at times threatened by organizational ideologies inappropriate to the goals of the whole society. Even the successful application of human relations knowledge requires identification with the goals of the organization and of the society. The point is the old one that administrative units do not act in isolation, but within a distinct cultural environment. An awareness of societal values and ideology constitute an additional and vital knowledge for *all* police managers. Boguslaw indirectly implies the central role of values when he writes that

> The point, of course, is simply that values are not derived either scientifically, logically, or intellectually. They are simply prime factors.[7]

The remaining sections of this chapter deal, in turn, with (1) definitions, (2) the values of management, (3) the manager's value systems, and (4) a learning exercise.

A FEW BASIC DEFINITIONS

We designate *values* as those sentiments, or ethical principles, regarded as ultimate. Such values cannot be criticized concerning their appropriateness. A society as a whole may affirm certain values as its implicit assumptions, but so, too, do all the myriad of organizations within that society. Commonly, however, administrative units tend to affirm only some of the same values found in the larger society. Their values may be in partial conflict with those of the society and with one another (the learning experience exemplifies such a situation).

Norms are derived from the ultimate values as rules of conduct applicable under specified conditions. The distinction between norms and values is often a vague one in practice. The distinction rests on the assumption that it can be demonstrated that the norm is a rule of conduct derived from an ultimate value.

Ideology is a set of interrelated norms. Therefore, ideology becomes the mode of action for the individual.

POLICE MANAGEMENT AS VALUE LADEN

Among the most outstanding values in American culture of the twentieth century are *progress, efficiency, science, rationality, goal achievement* (effectiveness), and *success*. These values have helped·

[7] Boguslaw, *The New Utopians,* p. 198.

to produce a highly dynamic society—a society in which the predominant characteristic is *change*. More specifically, they have served as both an ideology and a stimulus to action for our police organizations and their managers. By citing the above values, we are not recommending that organizations or managers "fall in line." We simply feel that there may be more appropriate and less appropriate values, and a police manager who would be effective would do well to be aware of such differences. Hence, it is not suggested that the manager adopt the societal ideology as his own; rather, he and his department should attempt to recognize that they must operate within the framework of societal values. It is more than a request to be aware of the "public interest"; it requires the organization and the manager to be aware of the relationship between their actions and societal values.[8]

> If this is the case, it would seem of cardinal importance to examine the nature of police values so as to comprehend better the specific ways in which they affect police work. This is especially imperative since, in dealing with the diverse peoples they encounter, the police might be projecting values which may be either totally or partially inappropriate, or, at least irrelevant to such encounters.[9]

We would be more than a little presumptuous in telling *you*, the police managers, what *your* values are or ought to be. But at the same time we encounter a fairly well recognized general set of managerial values that are either in fact or in fantasy influencing the behavior of many managers today in a variety of organizations. Let us repeat those mentioned earlier:

Progress
Efficiency
Science
Rationality
Success
Goal achievement (effectiveness)

Which is paramount? Well, preferably it would be that of "goal achievement," for the others are dependent on it for their very existence. Hence, "we shall term appropriate an ideology of administration which, if followed by an administrator, yields a high probability of achieving both organizational and societal goals."[10]

---

[8] For a comprehensive examination of the public interest, see Glendon Schubert, *The Public Interest* (Chicago: The Free Press of Glencoe, 1960).

[9] Chwast, "Value Conflicts in Law Enforcement," pp. 152–53.

[10] Charles Press and Alan Arian, eds., *Empathy and Ideology: Aspects of Administrative Innovation* (Chicago: Rand McNally & Co., 1966), p. 9.

The above list is sorely remiss in a critical way—*it fails to indicate the manager's "human" empathy for "humanity"*—humanity in the dual sense of people within (the employees) and outside (the clientele) the organizational boundaries. Consequently, to the list we now add

Human empathy

The literature in support of this managerial value is vast, convincing, and growing at a rapid pace.[11] Regretfully, some managers approach the values of progress, efficiency, and so forth as being incongruous or, worse yet, in direct conflict with those of a human bent. This is not only wrong, but it can significantly impede goal accomplishment! According to Bennis:

> This is the paradigm: bureaucratic values tend to stress the rational, task aspects of the work and to ignore the basic human factors which relate to the task and which, if ignored, tend to reduce task competence. Managers brought up under this system of values are badly cast to play the intricate human roles now required of them. Their ineptitude and anxieties lead to systems of discord and defense which interfere with the problem-solving capacity of the organization.[12]

In a more concrete manner, he went on to state that a concern for the individual can be put into practice by:

1. Improvement in interpersonal competence of managers.
2. A change in values so that human factors and feelings come to be considered legitimate.
3. Development of increased understanding between and within working groups in order to reduce tensions.
4. Development of more effective "team management," i.e., the capacity for functional groups to work competently.
5. Development of better methods of "conflict resultion" rather than the usual bureaucratic methods of conflict resolution are to be sought after.
6. Development of organic systems. This normative goal, as outlined

---

[11]Obviously a citing of references in this regard would require thousands of pages. For those interested in a short but broad overview of the human factor in organizational settings, see Timothy W. Costello and Sheldon S. Zalkind, eds., *Psychology in Administration: A Research Orientation Text with Integrated Readings* (Englewood Cliffs, N.J.: Prentice-Hall, Inc., 1963); Leonard R. Sayles and George Strauss, *Human Behavior in Organizations* (Englewood Cliffs, N.J.: Prentice-Hall, Inc., 1966); and Edgar H. Schein, *Organization Psychology* (Englewood Cliffs, N.J.: Prentice-Hall, Inc., 1965).

[12]Warren G. Bennis, *Changing Organizations*, (New York: McGraw-Hill Book Company, 1966), p. 116.

by Shepard and Blake, is a strong reaction against the idea of organizations as mechanisms, which, they claim, has given rise to false conceptions (such as static equilibria, frictional concepts like "resistance to change," etc.) and, worse, to false notions of social engineering and change, e.g., pushing social buttons, thinking of the organization as a machine, etc.[13]

Three rather obvious though difficult managerial tasks result from the above thinking. Here is what must be done to assure *yourself* that *you* have a comprehensive set of values—organizational and individual. First, recognize that the most vital resource within a police department is its people—sworn and civilian. Second, recognize that these people have social and individual needs that, if met, allow them to experience greater job satisfaction and increased levels of work output. As Argyris puts it:

> In order to experience psychological success, three requirements are essential. The individuals must value themselves and aspire to experience an increasing sense of competence. This, in turn, requires that they strive continuously to find and to create opportunities in which they can increase the awareness and acceptance of their selves and others.
> The second requirement is an organization that provides opportunities for work in which the individual is able to define his immediate goals, define his own paths to these goals, relate these to the goals of the organization, evaluate his own effectiveness, and constantly increase the degree of challenge at work.
> Finally, the society and culture in which he is embedded can influence the individual and the organization. It can influence the individual, through the process of acculturation, to place a high or low value on self-esteem and competence. The process of acculturation, in turn, is a function of the society's norms and values as well as its economic development.[14]

Third, through your position as a manager and your personal capacity for leadership, lead the organization in the direction of improved goal achievement and individual happiness. You have a responsibility to yourself, your department, and those who work for you to do both. If you disagree (and we doubt that you do), perhaps it is time to compare your values with those expressed above. Better still, compare your values with those of other managers who you deem to be successful.

The next section discusses how and where managerial values are generated.

[13] *Ibid.*, p. 118.

[14] Chris Argyris, *Integrating the Individual and the Organization* (New York: John Wiley & Sons, Inc., 1964), pp. 33–34.

VALUE SYSTEMS

What is good for General Motors is good for the Nation.[15]

Societal values, norms, and ideologies vary from place to place and from situation to situation. Even within a society, institutional, organizational, and individual values, norms, and ideologies may differ. But if the police manager is to be effective in his efforts, he must attempt to forge an ideology that will synthesize the values and norms of his organization and society. The values that the manager must cope with are derived from a number of areas or systems. They are societal, historical, institutional, departmental, structural, professional, and personal.

Societal Values

If the police manager functioned like the TV detective of yesteryear, insisting only on "the facts, ma'am," he would be demoted to walking a beat. The most important value system in which the manager operates is that of society. A manager is a creature of our society; he operates in an organization that is a segment of our society; he is part of our ongoing history. He has risen to a key position in one of our most important social institutions. The decisions he makes will have important repercussions throughout society even though he may see them as affecting his own community alone.

Currently there is great concern over the influence of law enforcement, particularly that of large-scale police organizations, on the emerging social character of our urban centers. This is an important value consideration because the ultimate test of the usefulness of any organization lies in the kind of services it provides and the people it produces.

Historical Values

Today's police manager operates not only within the evolving values of our own time but also within a historical framework of past values that have become embodied in our institutions. His forebears were often deeply religious men who saw in work, in organization, and in use of capital the practice of God's will on earth. Formal organizations in this country are in a very real sense the institutional embodiment of the Puritan mind. Even though they may not be conciously aware of the origins of their beliefs, many police managers are deeply convinced of the essential morality of discipline,

---

[15] Attributed to Charles Erwin Wilson while testifying before a senate committee, *New York Times*, January 24, 1953, p. 8.

service, efficient organization, and work. We are not saying this is wrong or right, but merely drawing it to the attention of the reader. (However, if asked, we would be quick to defend such an ethic.) It is therefore important to recognize that the police manager operates in this kind of value environment whether he is aware of it or not. The decisions he makes, whether they come out of his own thinking, the *FBI Bulletin,* or the International Association of Chiefs of Police, all have ethical implications. He may not know it, but as he guides his department in its task of improving laws and maintaining order, he is shaping the history of his community and the nation.

Institutional Values

The police manager is usually aware that he differs from other institutions in our society—religious and educational institutions, unions, government, communities, and so on. He may see some of these other institutions as obstacles. Society is characterized, however, by a web of institutions that represents a network of differing values as well as cooperative relationships. Each institution is constantly striving to promote its own values. Each institution, in a sense, views society from its own value system and seeks to universalize its objectives, ideologies, and functions. Moreover, police departments have taken on more functions than they ever dreamed of twenty-five years ago. In fact, most departments today perform the functions not only of law enforcement but also of general community service. Many are now wondering whether all the time being spent by departments in this manner might not better be used to bolster our existing organizations (social welfare, recreation, counseling service, etc.).

This is not the place, however, to enter into arguments about the functions of the various institutions in our society. It is enough to make the point that interinstitutional differences constitute an important environment in which the police manager functions and one with which he must come to grips. He must have a broad understanding of the way a great society runs and the roles and functions of the various institutions that comprise it, and a statesmanlike knowledge of the special values and place of local law enforcement in the "big picture."

Departmental Values

A fourth important value system in which the police manager operates is the culture, or character, of his department. Each police organization has a way of doing things—a set of conventions, customs, and social habits that constitutes its unique character. Managerial development in many police organizations represents a kind of socialization whereby the new officer is taught how this particular department functions—what its philosophy is, what its character is, what kinds of things it will do, what kinds of things it positively will not do, what its policies and common values are.

The difference between the new employee, the fellow who does not know his way around, and the older one is often simply a difference in the degree of socialization that has occurred.

The culture of a department and the understanding that police managers and employees within the organization have of this culture are important controls.[16] As a consequence, determining the character of a police organization, which really means determining who you are, where you are going, and how you operate in this complex world, is likely, and rightfully so, to absorb a great deal of the attention of the management team.

Structural Values

Related to the departmental value system is that of structural values, particularly in its hierarchical character. Every organization is a hierarchical system in which each individual operates within an interacting triad of relationships in which some people are viewed as being in higher positions to him, some as being in lower, subordinate positions, and some as being at the same level. Dealing with these various levels and modifying behavior in appropriate ways in terms of the hierarchical system is one of the important skills of the police manager. He has to learn how to get things done through the boss, how to approach him at the right time, how to avoid getting a definite *no*, how to sell ideas to him, how to motivate him, and so on. The police manager who lacks these skills fails to get much done. Every individual has to be a promoter of ideas; he has to be "selling" all the time.

The manager also has to learn how to deal with subordinates as well as with those at his own level. With his subordinates he has to learn how to sell the sometimes unpopular notion of work and change; he has to learn how to translate organizational values into goals that have meaning to those under him; he has to learn to balance the impersonal values of the organization against the personal values of his people.

Consequently, one of the major problems of police management is achieving some kind of integration of the myriad of values that are being pushed by the various members of the management team and the subordinate personnel. Nothing is more stultifying than the neat balance that some uninspired (or retired on-the-job) managers achieve.

---

[16] One authority recently focused on the issue of department values. See Herman Goldstein, "Who's in Charge Here," *Public Management*, 50 (December 1968), 305–7.

We believe that a dynamic imbalance is best. At least there is movement; at least some are motivated and pleased, even if others may be
dissatisfied. Perhaps their disaster function will serve as an impetus
to "try harder."

Professional Values

The police manager also functions within a professional value
system. Such values are most obvious in the so-called professions of
the medical doctors, engineers, scientists, and others. These men owe
allegiance not only to an organization of which they are a part but
also to their profession.

Many occupational groups strive for professional status as a kind
of way out—a means of achieving the security or recognition that
would normally come from their particular organizations. It is suspected that some of these efforts toward professionalization are the
result of the employee's not getting this kind of recognition from his
organization, or in any event, not getting the degree of recognition he
expects. Under such circumstances, a man finds the recognition he
needs, the sense of colleagueship and support, the feeling of understanding, of status, and of worth in his professional group.

Even those police managers who do not see themselves as members of professional groups often think of themselves as professionals.
A profession is more than a function; it is frequently a way of life. It
directs the interests of those engaged in it, shapes their values, determines their relationships with others, and pulls people of similar
interests and often similar personalities together and thus enhances
the interaction among them. The manager often identifies with his
job. He is not merely Captain Blayback, police manager; he is a leader,
a controller of resources, a personnel man, an instructor. An attack on
his speciality is an attack on him. Moreover, he tends to generalize
the special interests and values of his field and wonders why others
are so ignorant and so impervious to his philosophy. For example, the
police manager is dedicated to goal fulfillment—goal fulfillment with
efficiency, rationality, and so forth. The police officer, however, is
dedicated to goal fulfillment but usually cares less about efficiency. In
other words, the manager would say, "Catch the crook at *so much*
cost," while the policeman would say, "Catch the crook at *all* costs."
Simply put, the manager is primarily "hung up" on economy, efficiency, and rationality of operation. The police officer continues to
focus on getting the job done, "hang the expenses." The reason for
renouncing the above thinking is simple, but pertinent—police managers and police practitioners (while members of the same department) possess similar and *dissimilar* values. Thus, we find that police

managers and police officers frequently differ in their thinking on not *what* but *how* the job ought to be done.

Personal Values

At this point we have little to offer in the way of advice or comments because personal values are exactly that—personal. Your heredity, early learning experiences, and general environment have caused you (or us) to be shaped in certain ways that tend to be reflected in job relationships and task orientation. Sufficient at this point is the knowledge that we—all of us—have certain values. And, by recognizing them, we find that "to thine own self be true" becomes a reality and an invaluable help in solving our daily problems. Although we would welcome the invitation to continue with our analysis of what *you* ought to cherish or value, we feel it not only proper but circumspect to stop here. Hence, let us proceed with the learning exercise.

LEARNING EXERCISE

Learning exercises or case studies are especially useful for re-examining an individual's or an organization's values, as noted above, and the following selection attempts to sensitize the reader to this very significant perspective of the job of the police manager. At its best, the approach to police management as an applied social science can simply suggest ways to achieve what it is the manager values by understanding and appropriately manipulating his environment. But if an applied social science provides useful tactics and a working idea of what the world is like, an enormous question remains unanswered: What should the "good" administrative state be? In dealing with immediate subordinates, similar to formulating policy for others, the police manager is forced to consider his values and those of others. This requirement cannot be avoided. Therefore, no alternative exists to facing and working through the difficult and frustrating personal and institutional issues of value.[17]

The following learning exercise clearly shows that the problems in police work reside not so much in the statutes or in the tacit norms controlling police management and enforcement as in a "value confrontation" between one form of management (police) and another (city manager).[18] As Sherwood states:

[17] Robert T. Golembiewski, ed., *Perspectives on Public Management: Cases and Learning Designs* (Itasca, Ill.: F. E. Peacock Publishers, Inc., 1968), p. 10.

[18] Socialization plays a highly influential part in determining how the actor—in this case the manager—is going to behave. It is also the cause of differing values and, therefore, interpersonal conflicts. For a more comprehensive treatment of this subject, see Mark Abrahamson, *The Professional in the Organization* (Chicago: Rand McNally & Co., 1964), pp. 19–20.

1. Unlike a number of other municipal functions, the *administration* of the police service inevitably involves community value questions. The manager must realize that norms other than efficiency enter into these behavior patterns. It is also of some interest that the manager often enjoys a certain degree of flexibility with regard to his role in these matters; and in this sense his own value system may determine his perception of his responsibilities.

2. The guildism of the police, which is the product of a great many factors, is to be seen in a variety of ways. Even where closed promotions are not prescribed, the community desire for a "local boy" in this sensitive position places important limitations on the manager's ability to deal with the police department as "cleanly" as he can with others. From the standpoint of the theory, these experiences seem to indicate how difficult it is to legislate human behavior. It may suggest the desirability of a more flexible organization structure to permit greater accommodation to the demands of the individual situation.

3. Finally, it is important for the manager to recognize that simple occupancy of the top of an administrative hierarchy does not automatically accord him the power capacity required to wield effective authority. The municipal government is an open system; power is obtained outside as well as inside the structure. The police chief is one of the most powerful figures in city government, but such informal factors of the authority relationship do not normally appear as a part of traditional council-manager theory.[19]

Basically, the case, a true story, portrays a value conflict situation between two managers—one city and the other police.[20]

A CITY MANAGER TRIES TO FIRE HIS POLICE CHIEF

Frank P. Sherwood

INTRODUCTION

In 1956, the year City Manager Singer fired Police Chief Black, or tried to, the population of the City of Valley had risen to about 25,000.[21] Within a two-hour drive from Los Angeles, Valley was the center of a large citrus farm

[19] Frank P. Sherwood, "Roles of the City Manager and the Police," *Public Management*, May 1959, p. 113.

[20] Reprinted with the permission The Bobbs-Merrill Co., Inc. (ICP Case Series: Number 76, 1955).

[21] The names of persons and local jurisdictions used in this case are entirely fictitious. Because of the author's departure for an overseas assignment, portions of this case—particularly those dealing with the political background—have been prepared by the editor.

area. The green orchards which dotted the hillsides south of the city relieved the semi-desert brownness of the landscape. Valley was also the site of a sizable college supported by a Protestant denomination.

For years, going back to World War I, Valley had held a reputation as one of Southern California's most pleasant and peaceful communities. Before 1940 its population had been composed of four main groups: citrus owners, and leaders of associated service firms (packing company owners and managers, and the like); downtown businessmen, realtors, and professionals; the college people; and the Mexican-American laborers. The town had always been heavily and quite seriously Protestant; the Baptist and Methodist congregations were two of the largest groups in the city.

The Setting

Railroad tracks running from east to west bisected the community. High ground and hills rose to the south. With the exception of the college, which formed its own little enclave of green lawns and architectural confusion, the area north of the tracks was the poorer part of town. Here the houses were older, the people less well-to-do, less educated. Here one was more apt to find a Democratic voter. Also in this northern section was the Mexican-American community, predominantly Roman Catholic, which tended to be isolated socially from the rest of the city. Rising south of the tracks were the leading hotel, the banks (units of state chains, which appointed the local managers), the City Hall, and the business district. Also to the south was the country club, which had the reputation of being a gathering place for the prestigeful, the old families, and the better-off, although some of the more austere or fastidious among the eligible families chose not to frequent it. Still farther south, up in the hills, were the luxury homes.

By 1956 there had appeared a new element in Valley's population—one that could not be as neatly categorized as those that had been familiar for over forty years. Valley was gradually becoming a "bedroom city." The new people were the product of the rapid growth of the nearby Xerxes metropolitan area. They lived in Valley, but they worked close by in the larger urban centers. These new residents spread throughout the community. Many moved into housing developments on the north side. The wealthier ones erected homes up on the hills. Religiously, the newcomers seemed to include more Catholics and fewer Methodists and Baptists than the pre-existing population. Economically, socially, and politically it was not clear just where they would fit. Although Valley had often been regarded by outsiders as hostile to newcomers who might disturb the peace and order of its settled ways, the newcomers were absorbed without visible eruptions. Up to 1956 observers had not detected any real impact by the newcomers on the politics of the city.

Politically, Valley had always been a city of predominantly Republican voters. Xerxes, the county seat, a railway center with a population three times the size of Valley's, was a Democratic city, and since the mid-thirties the County Board of Supervisors and the county administration had usually been under Democratic control. California state law required non-party local government elections, but most informed people in Valley knew who the infrequent Democratic candidates for the City Council were and whether a Republican or a Democrat had been elected to speak and vote for Valley on the County Board of Supervisors.

By and large, Valley's citizens were not intensely interested in party politics or in city government. From the well-to-do citrus families there had usually come a leading element of support and influence in the Valley Republican organization, but much of the party work and many of the candidates willing to devote time to local government came from the ranks of the more established local businessmen, realtors, and professionals. Some of the downtown businessmen and professionals, meeting regularly and separately for luncheon in different local chapters of six different national service organizations (Rotary, Kiwanis, and the like), some of the country club people, some of the leading laymen in the church congregations, and the (Republican) publisher and editor of the daily *Valley Times* were usually aware of political and governmental events. But beyond this circle were the majority of citizens who seemed uninterested in governmental affairs as long as things ran smoothly and quietly—which up to the 1950s they almost always did.

The "Lemon Street Gang"

Among those who were quite well-informed, an almost legendary element in the city's political history was the Lemon Street Gang. Most people in Valley did not know of its existence, and among those who claimed to, its membership, its political influence, or even its continued existence were often guessed at or disputed. The men alleged to be in the group denied that such a group existed or that they worked together; they were just friends of long-standing and intimate acquaintance. But most insiders believed that the group operated informally and secretly to wield influence in local government and politics.

No hard evidence has been found that the Lemon Street Gang played any part in the events of 1956 that form the subject of this study, but some of the principal participants suspected that the Gang was active behind the scenes.

Actually, the group had started as an informal personal association of a half-dozen Valley war veterans—not sons of high-status families—after they had returned from military service in World War I. They had found it difficult to get jobs and discovered that they were not the only returning veterans who were not well-regarded by potential employers. They resolved to work together at influencing affairs in Valley to see that deserving veterans were taken care of, despite the unsympathetic attitudes of Valley's leading citizens and the existing Republican organization. Many of the men who were associated with the group proved to have considerable ability in politics and government. Some were sons of small tradesmen who, in the twenties, were far down from the top of Valley's informal social ladder.

Some members of the group organized a formal veterans organization that spread throughout the county and beyond. One of the leading members became an extremely effective precinct worker for the local Republican organization. The group bargained its voting influence in order to secure jobs for veterans in local and county government. The more jobs it obtained for veterans, the greater its political bargaining power became. Its leaders began to operate increasingly at arms length from the older, more conservative, and more socially established men who acted as leaders of the local Republican organization. Finally, in the middle thirties, one of the leading political figures in the group, dissatisfied with the recognition offered by the county and local Republican organizations, helped secure the election of the first Democrat as County Supervisor from Valley. He stayed on the Democratic side of the fence and formed the first Democratic organization in the city and in the county. During the Depression the political efforts of the Lemon Street Gang to win jobs for veterans were not disturbed by the fact that some were in the Democratic camp and others were Republicans. The members of the group moved below the level where the public tends to pay attention to politics (which in Valley was not deep) to place their protégés, using whatever means their ingenuity could devise. Most often, it was admitted, the men they placed in government jobs proved to have the necessary ability.

The Lemon Street group had its greatest successes in the thirties, when Valley operated under a modified commission form of government, which was then traditional in California. By 1945, some of the leaders in the original group had moved out of Valley to careers in county, state, and even federal government. In the early postwar years the remaining members of the group succeeded in getting the city to set up a veterans bureau with a paid staff. One of the leaders of the group helped to secure necessary Council support for Valley to accept an extensive public housing project, against the inclinations of several local realtors. The group also allegedly secured the appointment of an extraordinarily able and dedicated man to serve as director of the housing project. Some of those who benefited from these projects—including the Mexican-Americans—were alleged to be sufficiently appreciative to vote as the group's leaders suggested when the Lemon Street men wanted to muster support behind some particular local candidate or issue.

The Introduction of a City Manager

The postwar period also brought to Valley a growing pressure from civic-minded citrus families, professionals, and local businessmen in favor of more efficient municipal government under centralized management. A public services director was appointed in 1946 and given many of the powers of a city manager. Under the leadership of Mayor Cassius Bolt, a temperate and respected local businessman who was a deacon in the Methodist congregation, the council-manager plan was adopted by Council ordinance in 1949. Bolt had been moved to devote time to local government by a sense of duty. He took no part in local political party organizations, although, like most respectable people in the city, it was assumed that he voted Republican in state and national contests. Among those strongly supporting the plan was Councilman Antrim Heald, one of the few Democrats ever elected to the Council. Heald was a planing mill owner and a leading figure in the local Democratic organization. Widely-respected, Heald was not connected with the Lemon Street group, although one of the leaders of that group remained active in the Democratic organization and presumably helped to get votes for Democratic candidates.

It was believed by some of the leading supporters of the council-manager plan that during the 1950s the leaders of the Lemon Street group found the existence of a city manager a threat to their continued influence in local government—particularly in the placement of protégés. Hence it was believed by the council-manager adherents that any event that appeared to embarrass the manager or hinder the success of centralized management in local government had been caused by the secret manipulations of the Lemon Street Gang. It appeared to some outsiders that by the mid-1950s the Lemon Street Gang had lost influence and, to some extent, had lost interest in municipal affairs. The movement of some of the group's members to higher echelons of government, the increasing age of those who remained, and the fact that city jobs were no longer as highly sought after as they had been during the

Depression were all reasons for less intense involvement in local affairs. But when they wanted to, the remaining Lemon Street men could produce votes and could use extensive personal connections. And there was some evidence that the group was still sufficiently interested to fight selected rear-guard actions against the advance of unsympathetic city managers. Its members still mobilized occasionally to support certain Council candidates who were personally sympathetic, Republican or Democrat. And it resisted efforts of city managers and "good government" supporters who sought to turn certain elective posts such as city treasurer into positions filled by managerial appointment. Whatever it actually did or did not do, whether it was still intensely active or declining in influence and interest, or even whether it still existed as a group, the Lemon Street Gang was still seen in the 1950s as a potent harassing force, working secretly and deviously for patronage and against city manager government. It was seen this way only by those few insiders in Valley who supported manager government and who were sufficiently acquainted with local affairs to have heard of the Gang's alleged activity. Since the friends who reputedly made up the Lemon Street Gang never acknowledged publicly that they worked together, much less had an organization, it was hard to tell just what the truth was.

THE EARLY DAYS OF MANAGER SINGER

Jack Singer became Valley's third City Manager in July 1952. He was a lean six-footer in his mid-thirties who had formerly been manager of a smaller California city. He had become a manager by progressive municipal experience rather than by a university education for the profession. He had once served as an elected town clerk and had become quite an expert in sewage problems. (Valley was about to undertake a sewage project at the time.) Singer heard of the opening in Valley at a district meeting of city managers. Attracted by what he knew of the city, he applied even though the salary offered was below that prevailing in cities of similar size. He was selected.

In talking with his predecessor, Singer found that Valley's council-manager system was reasonably typical for California. As state law prescribed, the City Council had five members elected at large. The Manager served at the pleasure of the Council. At variance with orthodox theory, however, was the Manager's limited power over appointments of department heads other than the City Treasurer and City Clerk, who were elected. In Valley these key administrative appointments were recommended by the Manager but required Council confirmation. Dismissal of these officials was handled the same way. From the Model City Charter standpoint, these requirements represented a significant infringement on the Manager's "right to manage." But Valley's Manager did have considerable discretion in personnel matters because there were no formal merit system, no civil service tenure, no written appeals procedures, no provisions for probationary service. The lack of these formal procedures and regulations broadened the power of the Manager over city employees, but it also placed heavier burdens on him, since he had no laws with which to justify his actions.

Singer's early conversations also yielded some consistent opinions about the style of administration that Valley's leading citizens felt suitable for their town. He was given to understand that Valley had its own quiet ways of community living and that it would not accept as Manager anyone who pushed for changes too strongly or too rapidly. He learned that one of his predecessors had aroused much personal opposition by being too severe in his rigid devotion to efficiency and management principles. He had been gruff with citizens and allegedly had not treated people in a friendly manner. Irritation with him had become so strong that several Council candidates known to oppose him (but not the manager form of government) had been elected. He had thereupon resigned to take another post. Getting on well with people had always been one of Singer's strongest qualities, and he gathered that this had been one of the things that had been given weight in his selection.

Singer came to value highly the advice he received from former Mayor Cassius Bolt who had been instrumental in passage of the Council-Manager Ordinance in 1949. Bolt had retired as Mayor, but he was still well-informed. From Bolt and from Councilman George Simpson, a well-to-do orange grower and real estate man, Singer learned that the manager form of government was safely established in Valley but that it was not immune from attack if a Manager did not perform acceptably.

Councilman Simpson, who had played a considerable part in the hiring of Singer, had lived in Valley most of his life and came from a local citrus-owning family. He was widely respected on all sides as an able, intelligent man. He held all the essentials for full membership in the community: long residence, conservatism, Protestant church affiliation, and prosperity. He had a firm commitment to the manager form of government, and he was critical of some of the men connected with the Lemon Street Gang.

Singer also learned about Hector and Homer Smith, the brothers who were publisher and editor, respectively, of the *Times,* Valley's only daily newspaper. It had to compete for local circulation with the *Xerxes Clarion,* the nearby metropolitan daily that inserted a Valley page in papers delivered there. The Smith brothers had inherited the *Times* from their father. Hector, the publisher was active in Republican politics in the city and the county. Homer, the editor, was nobody's man, but was willing to give advice, orally or editorially, about almost any community matter. The brothers' policy was that any local controversy should be thoroughly aired, if not inflated, in the *Times* more rapidly and more extensively than in the competing Xerxes daily.

The Kelly Affair

According to Singer's comments in 1960, many of the problems of the Valley government of the fifties arose from events of the past. Valley had been like many other small communities—a government of privilege. Building regulations had been winked at for friends; various public utilities, such as street paving and water lines, had been installed to help the "right" people; and other favors had been financed out of public funds. This same general pattern had been found in the Police Department. "I think it is fair to say," Singer said, "that the appointment of Chief Jason Kelly in 1951 marked the first time that the law was *really* enforced in Valley."

Chief Kelly's appointment in 1951 had followed a heated community controversy about the effectiveness of the police. On that occasion hearings before the Council had been held, and the previous Chief had resigned. Some insiders alleged that he had been too susceptible to the wishes of the Lemon Street Gang. There was internal dissension, several policemen had resigned, and, said the *Times,* "public confidence had been shaken."

The new Chief brought a spirit of friendliness to the Valley police operation. "A good-natured Irishman," Kelly, who had retired as a Lieutenant from the force of the city of North Beach, particularly wooed the downtown business community and regularly dropped into the stores of local merchants to exchange pleasantries. When Singer took over as City Manager several months later, he and Kelly became fast friends. They mixed socially and were regular golf competitors at the country club. As Kelly made friends in the community and with top management, his Police Department settled into an easy routine. Kelly himself was not demanding. "There's enough sordidness in police work without making it tough on the boys," he once commented. He joked with his secretary, other girls in the office, and the members of the thirty-man force; and he found little interest or enthusiasm for the paper work of the operation.

Into this good-natured environment, however, trouble finally descended. It came not from the community but from some of the members of the Department, including the Deputy Chief. They criticized the "country club atmosphere," raised questions about the Chief's alleged relationships with his secretary, and charged that he was not giving full time to his job. These accusations were ultimately brought to public attention through two members of the Council in the late fall of 1954. The Chief first resigned, then agreed to stay when City Manager Singer's investigations led him to conclude that the attacks had been inspired by a few men in the Department. And behind these men, Singer felt sure, stood the Lemon Street Gang.

Singer and some councilmen, including Simpson, believed that the men who had instigated the charges against Kelly had been protégés of the Gang. Some of them had consulted with one of the best known members of the Gang about their complaints and about how to present their charges. The two councilmen who had introduced the charges were also believed to be close to the Lemon Street group. One was Joe Rodriguez, the first Mexican-American and the first Catholic to serve on Valley's Council. Born in the Mexican-American section, he had moved to the richer south side. Rodriguez was a complicated person. He had a law degree, had been a school teacher, and was an escrow officer in a large Xerxes firm. Politically liberal, Rodriguez had generally allied himself with the interests of the less well-to-do and the less powerful in the community. Yet he was a registered Republican. Rodriguez' election in 1954 had caused some surprise. He had been supported strongly by a principal member of the Lemon Street Gang, who had been a personal friend of his father. Rodriguez had made much in his campaign of the fact that he was a World War II veteran. Soon after his election he became a critic of Manager Singer, whom he considered ineffective and "always doing what the downtown businessmen wanted."

The Councilman who had joined with Rodriguez in introducing the police charges against Chief Kelly was Mayor Crispin Lloyd, believed by Councilman Simpson and some others to have won a Council seat in 1952 because of the support of the Lemon Street Gang. Lloyd worked as a handyman in a local store.

Rodriguez and Lloyd were regarded by some local observers as two councilmen who were opposed to domination of city affairs by the Manager or by the well-to-do families of the south side. Often opposed to them were Simpson and Councilman Frank Jones. Jones was one of the largest property owners in the downtown business area. The fifth man on the Council was Ralph Jennings, professor of political science at the local college, whose faculty he had joined in 1949. Jones, Rodriguez, and Jennings had all been elected for four-year terms in April 1954. A Democrat and a liberal, Jennings, like Rodriguez, had run well in the public housing area, but he had received a good number of votes on both sides of town. He supported the council-manager system, but had voted with Rodriguez to elect Lloyd Mayor, while Simpson and Jones had abstained. Jennings saw himself as the "swing man" on the Council, with Rodriguez and Lloyd on one side and Simpson and Jones on the other. Jennings had not heard of the Lemon Street Gang until he became a Councilman. As time went on, he developed an increasing respect for Councilman Simpson, despite the latter's conservatism.

When Manager Singer opposed accepting the resignation of Chief Kelly at the meeting at which Lloyd and Rodriguez introduced the police statement of charges, both councilmen sought to override his suggestion. Nevertheless, the City Manager stood his ground, rejected the Chief's resignation, and stoutly defended Kelly. By a four-to-one vote, the Council went along with the Manager in refusing the resignation.

Shortly thereafter the Deputy Chief was demoted to Lieutenant and at least two other officers were fired. These actions against the individuals who were presumably the central figures in the attack on the Chief caused more disquiet in the community. It could not be ignored by the Council. At the insistence of Lloyd and Rodriguez, joined by a number of citizens including one of the Lemon Street leaders, the Council finally agreed to an investigation. The hearings were closed, but the press was invited and permitted to report in detail. One of the Lemon Street men contributed to pay for a lawyer for the discharged and demoted policemen. A citizens committee was also appointed to play a watchdog role and insure that procedures at the hearings were fair to both sides.

In the newspapers the community read of (1) the Deputy Chief's withdrawal of his original charges, (2) accusations that some officers had sought to force the Chief's secretary to lie about the closeness of her relationship with her boss, (3) allegations that the Chief's accusers had planned all succession arrangements favorable to themselves once the Chief had been forced to resign, and (4) evidences that the Chief had apparently not run a tight administrative organization. Emotion in the community was very high; the City Manager, his behavior, and the form of government he personified did not escape criticism from the defenders of the discharged policemen. It was clear that Singer had trusted Chief Kelly to run his own department. The Manager had not known much about what was happening in the Police Department until the investigation. (From this point on, he kept a close eye on it.) At the conclusion of the hearings one of the Council members emphasized that the only question with which the legislative body had to deal was whether it had lost confidence in the Manager because of the dismissals and other problems in the Police Department. If so, he should be fired. Otherwise the Council should sustain the Manager. In the vote that followed four councilmen supported Manager Singer. The fifth abstained.

On the surface the police problem was settled. Yet the effects remained. There were people in the community who felt that the prevarications of police officers could cut both ways. Was it not just as possible that the Deputy Chief and the other police officers had capitulated to the Manager and to the other leaders in order to hold their jobs?

Four months after what the *Times* called the "marathon police investigation," Chief Kelly left Valley to accept a position as Chief of Security in a private industrial organization at "twice the pay." His resignation was reluctantly accepted by City Manager Singer as of March 15, 1955, and the Manager's search for a new Chief began.

THE SEARCH FOR A NEW CHIEF

William Black was a retired Lieutenant Commander in the Navy. In the spring of 1955 he was teaching at the University of Southern California, as a one year replacement for the University's professor of police administration who was in Iran. However, Black did not plan to stay in teaching and was interested in engaging in more active police work. When the Director of the University's Delinquency Control Institute told him about the opening for a Police Chief in Valley, Black was interested. He immediately dispatched a letter to Valley expressing his availability and thus became one of about thirty applicants for the post, which paid approximately $550 a month. The letter in which City Manager Singer acknowledged Black's application reported that there were no major police problems. Particularly striking to Black was the statement that "the present department is in top working efficiency, as the former Chief retired voluntarily to go into private industry." The letter, mimeographed and obviously sent to all applicants, was dated March 23, 1955.

By the time Black had heard about the opening and made his application, City Manager Singer had taken a number of steps to fill the vacancy created by Kelly's resignation. First he reviewed the personnel situation in the Department and decided that none of the officers in the organization "looked too strong." Since he was under no pressure to appoint a local person, Singer determined to recruit a new Chief on a California-wide basis. The absence of a formal civil service system meant that there was nothing to block such a recruiting program. Singer inserted an announcement of the vacancy in *Western City Magazine,* and wrote to a number of cities in California soliciting applications.

Because he recognized the appointment of a new Chief to be one of the most important steps he had taken in his more than four years in Valley, Singer was determined to make the selection system as foolproof as possible. Therefore, he appointed a Screening Board composed of the City Manager, the Assistant Administrative Officer, and the Chief of Police of three different cities in Southern California. Of the thirty applicants for the position, ten were interviewed by this Board at a meeting attended by Singer. Although several chiefs of smaller departments were among those screened, the professor from USC, William Black, was the unanimous choice of the Board. Singer, too, was greatly impressed. Black had strong recommendations from the University. He "interviewed well," and he seemed to be just the kind of person needed to compensate for Kelly's laxity in administrative routine. While the Manager felt some hesitation about Black because he had not had actual experience as a Chief of Police previously, members of the Board agreed that the professor's technical competence outweighed his lack of experience and made him first choice. Singer decided to recommend the appointment, which was tantamount to selection. Council confirmation had become, as in many other centralized management cities, largely perfunctory. Despite all the previous police problems, Council members did not actively involve themselves in the selection process for the new Chief. Jack Singer was being given a chance to run his own show without interference from the Council. Black was "his" man.

The new Valley Chief of Police first heard of his appointment in a telephone call from a reporter on the *Los Angeles Examiner,* asking for a comment. Then Manager Singer called Black to say that he had been hired and to ask when he could start. The date agreed upon was June 13, 1956. After the hiring, Black journeyed to Valley to meet the Council. It was a friendly occasion. As Black recalled, he was particularly impressed with the words of Mayor Crispin Lloyd, who said, "We have made you Chief because we want a firm law enforcement program." It was the kind of statement Black was pleased to hear. It became a charter for his future actions. Crew-cut and muscular, active in amateur wrestling, Black had about his whole being an air of authority. He also had a strong commitment to the professionalization of the police and felt that too frequently police officers themselves failed to pay a proper respect to the important work they had undertaken. He viewed the police function as important to the maintenance of an organized society, as technically demanding, and as requiring the highest moral and intellectual integrity. William Black was now anxious to prove himself equal to the task.

The first day on the job, June 13, Black spent with Manager Singer, who also emphasized that he wanted a rigorous enforcement program. Much of the time on that day was spent in discussing the people in the city government and in the community. Singer for his part believed that he was introducing the newcomer to the mysteries and subtleties of the city government. He was anxious to keep Black from making an early slip. But as Black recalled the talk, the Manager produced a picture of the members of the Department taken in 1954 and talked about each man on the force. Particularly striking to Black was the fact that a number of the men in the photograph were no longer in the city's employment. At this time, he had little knowledge of the Kelly affair, and he was struck by the high attrition rate. Black says he left the meeting somewhat worried. He felt that Singer demonstrated a "suspicion of everyone who was not on his side."

THE RIFT BETWEEN BLACK AND SINGER

William Black was Police Chief in Valley for just about a year. Nearly every event during that year was seen and interpreted differently by Black and Singer, and the passage of more years has not made any easier the assembly of a set of facts acceptable to both sides. From the day of their first meeting in June 1955 a gulf widened between the City Manager and his new Police Chief despite the fact that both men had every reason to desire a successful and satisfying relationship.

Singer's Background

Jack Singer was very familiar with the ways of the small town. He had had several years of successful experience as a Manager and as an elected City Clerk. Valley embodied a style of life he accepted, enforced, and understood.

Singer's particular view of the responsibility of the manager seemed to be rooted more in the concept of responding to community expectations and wishes than to hewing rigidly to city manager professionalism. He saw the Manager as the *interpreter* of citizen and Council desires, which he was obliged to satisfy. This orientation, along with his background, led Singer to be more sensitive to the play of forces of power and influence than most city managers might have been. On almost any matter, Singer was acutely aware of his friends and enemies, and of the forces at play. He had, for example, argued strongly and successfully for Council action to carry out more street improvements in the poorer sections of town, and to do it wholly at city expense (with no street assessments), an unusual thing in Valley. On another matter, when a planning officer had aroused protests for pushing a plan some groups thought too rigorous and advanced, Singer had ordered the plan modified so that it was less perfect from a planner's standpoint but more acceptable to those affected. Since his arrival in 1952, Singer had been highly successful in carrying through city planning and capital development programs. He won community approval for such efforts, which were often neglected in other cities of Valley's size.

Within the city administrative hierarchy, Singer believed strongly in the Manager's right to manage. He expected to be held responsible for the functioning of the various departments, and he demanded the authority necessary to meet these obligations. This meant that each department head was distinctly his subordinate and that it was the Manager's prerogative to take whatever fact-finding steps appeared necessary to check on performance in these various units. Nevertheless, the Manager and the employees generally had gotten on well together. On the whole, Singer was proud of the governmental performance of Valley. Despite the events of the previous fall, he did not believe that there was a "mess" in the Police Department, but he knew that the Department was still much in the public eye.

Personally, Singer was happy in Valley. He liked the people and the community. His job, though carrying a compensation somewhat under that paid in other similar-size cities, still returned him a comfortable income. It was a pleasant life which he, his wife, and school-age children enjoyed. He belonged to the country club and to one of the Protestant congregations. Only a very substantial increase in salary could have moved him to another city.

Black's Background

Black's experience and outlook were different from Singer's. His police experience had come in Evanston, Illinois—some of it while studying at Northwestern University. He had had a long career in Navy security. While he had served in the Navy, on the Evanston Police Department, and in academic positions at Northwestern and at the University of Southern California, there nevertheless had been the tangible unifying thread of law enforcement. It was to the profession of law enforcement and its values that Black felt his basic responsibility, not to the city. As he explained later to an interviewer:

> We in police worry so much about how people are going to feel about what we do that we lose sight of our basic responsibility.
> In Valley there was a disrespect for the law. Thus the basic problem was the rebuilding of that respect for the laws of the community and the enforcers of those laws; then would have been the appropriate time to worry about public relations. It is also my conviction that in order to engage in law enforcement you must at times be harsh; but that doesn't mean it is ever necessary to be nasty.

This sense of the profession also seemed to permeate Black's perception of the Police Chief's role in council-manager government. As he saw his responsibility, it was to give the community the best possible law enforcement, judged by his professional standards. Political or community squabbles were matters for higher echelons.

Emerging Differences

Chief Black had been on the job only a few days when he began to see things that upset him. Within the Department, he found no written rules and regulations, inefficient procedures, and oddly arranged shifts. When he asked why things were being done in a certain way, Black said the men had no good answer. In addition he felt that morale was poor, the men inadequately trained, and their general appearance not up to his standards. Nor was Black satisfied with the deployment of the men. He found that the small Department was still using two men in patrol cars in the predominantly residential town. To Black this was a particularly indicative sign of ineffective management. Though a lot of old-timers still preferred two-man cars to the one-man variety, Black laid this resistance to a lack of knowledge of modern police doctrine. Thus the use of the old system in Valley not only revealed a great waste of manpower to him; it also meant that the Department had not had imaginative and progressive leadership in the past. For this failure he blamed not only the former Chief but also City Manager Singer.

In the community as a whole the general disregard of the law that was most striking to Black was in the traffic field. (Black's graduate work had made him something of a specialist in traffic problems.) "Nobody paid any attention to stop signs," he recalled. Speed limits were not observed, and there was no selective enforcement in those areas of the city where accidents were most likely to happen. Parking signs and restrictions were not properly obeyed. A good share of the central district's parking spaces were occupied by local merchants and professional people who "nickeled the machines to death."

Black's answer to these problems was tighter enforcement all along the line. He took a personal hand in sharpening procedures and organization, spending the greater part of his first ninety days writing a policy manual, the first the force had had. There were reassignments, new training programs, redesign of forms, and many other changes.

As a result of Black's policies, the men on the force began to hand out an increasing number of citations for parking and traffic violations. The effect of this stringency was magnified when the *Valley Times* began to print a column listing the names and addresses of those who had received tickets. The irritation of citizens at getting citations for driving and parking practices that had previously not drawn police action was exacerbated when their names and offenses were printed in the *Times* for their neighbors and all others to see. Black publicly congratulated the *Times* for initiating the column. As Black's campaign for better parking and traffic enforcement continued, some policemen carried tape measures and allegedly used them when issuing citations for drivers who parked a greater number of inches from the curb than the city ordinance permitted.

The Chief found another practice he opposed: the issuance of special treatment cards or badges to influential citizens. A request for such an item was made shortly after he came on the job, and he discovered that the practice had long been followed in Valley. Badges or cards had been issued since the twenties to large fruit growers to give them some authority in policing their groves, some of which were in remote sections. Black refused to issue more cards and called the others in. "In two months we picked up about 100. I don't know how many more we didn't get," he recalled.

While thus busily engaged, Black found he had no time to follow his predecessor's practice of visiting the merchants in the downtown business section. Nor did he have an interest in doing so. "I personally think the former Chief engaged in these kinds of activities to the detriment of law enforcement in Valley," Black said later. Some of the downtown businessmen were displeased with Black's policy of strict enforcement of parking meter regulations.

Criticism Reaches the City Manager

Criticisms of Black's approach to his new job almost immediately reached City Manager Singer. Irritation was expressed that he was not a friendly, jocular sort. More indignant were those who had run afoul of the new look in Valley's law enforcement activities. Most significant, however, were charges of increasing belligerence and antagonism on the part of police officers. Singer reported that much of the criticism was directed squarely at Chief Black, who was said to have been stopping people himself. He was accused of having an approach to violators which "was sadistic, officious, and out of proportion to the violations committed."[22] To these attacks Singer at first paid little attention; but the increasing volume of complaints caused him to move to the defense of the Chief by personally urging press and public leaders to help him across a "difficult period of adjustment."

Much of the difficulty, Singer felt, was that Black had not brought the community along with him. A new regime of law enforcement had suddenly descended on Valley without warning. In Singer's mind it was the Chief's responsibility to "sell" his program. He felt it was a mistake for Black to spend his time in his office. He urged him to invite and accept speaking engagements, which the Chief said he did at the rate of two to three a week. Singer has reported he did not question the policy of firm law enforcement Black had inaugurated.

Even at this early stage, communications between the two men seemed to have been strained by two events. The first had to do with an order issued by Black prohibiting officers from discussing police business with anyone. This, he said, was a standard procedure for most police agencies and was included in his manual of rules and regulations which the City Manager approved. The intent was to keep data on investigations restricted to as few people as possible and was not really directed toward administrative matters. Insofar as the councilmen and the Manager were concerned, Black said he instructed his men to answer any questions but to let him know about such conversations, a procedure he felt was normal for any organization which had a formal chain of command.

---

[22] On this point Black has commented: "My officers leaned over backward and were so nice it was almost sickening to watch and listen to. *But* those who had previously talked their way out of arrests or used their influence could no longer do so. When this happened to them for the first time, they reported the officer as belligerent and antagonistic whereas he was nothing of the kind. Several investigations on my part proved this point. In one case an officer said, "No madam" and "Yes madam" only. She reported him to Singer as insulting. She treated the incident as a light joke until she saw she was going to get a ticket for a 50 mph violation; then she became indignant and insulting. To the law violator it might appear that the officer was sadistic, officious, and out of proportion to the violation committed, but it is the result of losing the immunity from arrest that caused the great flareup among a small group of special privileged people. With regard to traffic violations, I have seen every type kill an individual; therefore it is proper and justifiable to treat each violation the same, but with courtesy and firmness."

The order was perceived in quite different terms by Singer. Since the Kelly incident of the previous year, Singer had taken a greater interest in the operation of the Police Department and had come to know a number of the policemen. Soon, however, he found that these men refused to talk to him, even those of long acquaintance. He was told Black had issued an order that the men were not to talk to Singer. If they did, they must report the conversation back to the Chief. The order irritated Singer greatly. Yet nothing was ever said to Black, and he did not realize how a directive which he considered routine had antagonized his superior.

At about the same time another incident occurred. In this instance it was Chief Black who felt he had been "used" by the City Manager to avoid political fire. Among his other duties, Black was the city's official pound-master. It was a nominal title because one man in the employment of the Department did all the work. Up to that time dogs had run relatively free in Valley, and a considerable problem had been created. At the request of the Council, City Manager Singer drafted an animal regulation ordinance and gave it to the Police Chief to introduce at the Council meeting. He said it was within the police responsibility, and the proposed law would perhaps have more acceptance coming from that source. Although he knew that dog laws were almost always controversial, the Chief agreed, because "I really thought it was a good thing."

Then, "all hell broke loose." The citizens of Valley who had let their dogs run free for many years were up in arms. They accused the Chief of something worse than inhumanity—a hatred of dogs. "I took to riding the streets of Valley with my big setter to prove to people that I really loved animals." After much furor, the effort to pass the ordinance was abandoned. What upset Black was that never during the controversy did the Manager make a major public defense of the proposed ordinance.

Meanwhile, Black was making speeches as the Manager had suggested, but they seemed only to deepen the problem. Members of his audiences charged that the newcomer was too free in his criticism of their community. Although Black declares he had never used the word, a story spread among parents and school officials that he had typified Valley youth as "rotten."[23] His appearances before the local civic associations and clubs, according to the editor of the *Times*, probably did more to destroy his support in the substantial segments of the community than any other single factor.

Singer Gets More Complaints

By fall, three to four months after Chief Black had come to Valley, Singer was getting so many complaints that he had to take them seriously. There were many besides those who complained of harsh personal treatment by police enforcing traffic violations. A number of middle-class mothers told the Manager that Black's policies were making their children speak of policemen as enemies rather than as friends. They expressed concern that their sons were talking of stoning police cars, and compared this to the pre-Black days when, they said, police in patrol cars would often stop and chat with teenagers, even those who had been in minor scrapes with the law. The mothers

[23] Black has commented: "This was one of the false stories spread about town by the 'Hate Black' group. I never said this. Actually the man who started the rumor was never at the speech where it was supposed to have been said. He had been arrested previously for speeding—his first time as a local bigshot and was unable to get the officer to let him go."

attributed the trouble to the tough manner used by the police with teen-agers since Black had assumed office.

Another complaint, Singer recalled some years later, had come from the officer who dealt with juvenile delinquents. Several months after Black arrived, this officer reported to Singer that the load of juvenile offenses was rising enormously. This was attributed to the increased stringency of police enforcement.

Singer also received complaints from local insurance men (who were often also realtors and who were one of the occupational groups active in following and influencing city affairs). Black, the Manager recalled later, "had tangled with insurance men who were trying to get the facts on traffic accidents. They needed information for their clients and for their reports to their companies. This sort of information is routinely made available to prop-erly qualified investigators as provided in the Vehicle Code." Black, the in-surance men had complained, had arbitrarily decided to withhold some of the data from them. Black's position was that certain items in the reports should be confidential; these were the things he withheld.

Singer also stated later that he had received some reports that Black had had difficulties with other police jurisdictions. The County Under-Sheriff had paid an unannounced courtesy call shortly after Black had arrived in Valley, but Black had been too busy to see him. A school safety patrol had taken the number of a private car that had gone through a crossing zone near the high school. The teacher in charge had forwarded the license number to Sacra-mento. It had turned out to be the number of a car of a member of the force, and this had led to Black being cautioned by a member of the State Highway Patrol. Black had complained to higher headquarters of the Highway Patrol, denying the charge and criticizing the pettiness of the action.

Another complaint, Singer recalled later, came from the parents of two girls of high school age who were exceeding the speed limit in town one night and were chased by a pair of off-duty policemen who were riding in a car with out-of-state license plates. The policemen sought to force the girls' car to the curb. The girls, allegedly not realizing these were policemen, went even faster and drove toward the deserted areas of town before they were stopped. Their girls, the parents complained to Singer, had been fright-ened almost to the point of hysteria.

These incidents and others arising from tougher parking and traffic en-forcement came to Singer with increasing frequency. In the late fall or early winter, Singer recalls, a former Democratic councilman asked him how long he was going to keep the Police Chief. He suggested that if Singer delayed getting rid of Black, the public would force the Council to act. He allegedly told Singer that if Singer waited too long, public resentment might even cost the Manager his own job.

Black's View

If Valley's problem of adjustment to Black was difficult, so was Black's adjustment to it. He saw himself making compromises difficult for a man of his professional background and ethics to accept. There was the failure to book the homosexual son of a prominent citizen. "After the withdrawal of that complaint," he said, "I felt like I had a sin on my soul. So far as I know, that man is still walking the streets and is not even registered as a sex deviate. Whatever harm befalls him or others, I will certainly have to assume part of the guilt."

In another instance the wife of a prominent official of a nearby newspaper was charged with hit and run. Black said she had knocked down a brick wall with her auto and left the scene of the accident. Her license number was traced, however; and her attorney came to Valley to make a settlement. Black refused to negotiate. Later that same day, Black said he got a phone call from the City Manager asking him to delay arrest until the following day.[24] By that time the warrant had been withdrawn by the court and the Chief was left powerless in the situation. He never said anything further about it, but he often asked himself what would have happened if the offender had been a Mexican, rather than the wife of a prominent newspaper man. As one observer put it, Black had difficulty learning that there are "somebodies and nobodies" in every community. To that Black has agreed.

In January 1956 occurred the "Mr. X" case, which later received considerable attention because of its relationship to compromise and the community elite. Mr. X was a well-to-do citrus man, over sixty, and long influential in Valley. He had the same last name as one of the councilmen. It was alleged that he was driving drunk, had turned a corner and run head on into another automobile. As Black later reported, "Mr. X was drunk. He did not know who I was that night. He said he would get my job for this. He threw money around the street and said he ran Valley. . . ." Actually the arresting officer had been fearful that he was a councilman and had called both the Manager and the Chief when he got him to the station. Black says Manager Singer took a look in the window, said, "I don't know the man. . . . Do what you want with him." As a consequence the Chief gave the order to "treat him like any other drunk." At midnight an attorney for the drunken man came to the jail and asked to post bond for his release. While it was against departmental policy to free booked people before the following morning, the Sergeant was more aware of the standing of the man in the community than Singer or Black and so released him. Black said later that if he had been at the station, he would not have permitted the Sergeant to take such an action. At any rate, Black said that the next morning at 8:00 he got a call from the City Manager wanting to know what could be done about the case. According to Black, a city Councilman was reported as interested in seeing that the charges were either reduced or quashed. However, Black told Singer that the case was already out of his hands, charges having been filed, bail posted, and the man released. It was now up to the courts. The Chief thought that Singer was clearly irritated by this departure from routine and indicated he thought the steps had been taken to thwart any "arrangements." The man was found guilty and fined $350. Later, in public hearings, Singer disputed the Black version and called it a "classic distortion." He reported

> I was met in the parking lot and told that—sure enough, the man
> they held was not Councilman X. I was told also that the "Mr. X"
> they had in custody had been picked up drunk, abusive, and most
> certainly in no condition to drive. I told them to lock him up, and
> I drove home and went to bed. The next morning the man's family,
> worried and concerned, made inquiries. Among others, they asked
> Councilman Jones to find out what had happened to the man.
> Jones asked me, I got the information, and Jones relayed the facts
> to the family. There was no discussion concerning the disposition

[24] One Councilman disagreed strongly with the Black story. He has noted: "This is Black's version, and an example of giving a sinister import to a fairly simple matter. Black considered any request for information to be an attempt to intervene."

or handling of the case. To this day I have never met or talked to—
nor could I recognize on the street—the man who was arrested and
who—the next morning—pleaded guilty and paid a fine.

An incident occurring in March again dramatized the gulf growing between Manager Singer and his Chief. It involved a relatively minor traffic case
in which the wife of a well-to-do professional man was arrested for speeding.
Infuriating to her, however, was the fact that the citation was written outside
her home. By the next morning she and her husband had called a number of
neighbors, with the result that a delegation visited the Manager the following
day to urge the Chief's resignation on the grounds that his men were rude and
arrogant. "I was called into the City Manager's office," Black later reported,
and "he was very much upset. He said he might have to ask me to resign. 'I
had a committee visit me,' he went on, 'and they are upset about your enforcement program.'" Black said he thought the charge was probably untrue and
asked that he be permitted to talk to the woman before any decisions were
made. As a result of a later conversation with the woman, the Chief concluded
that she was angry simply because she got a legitimate ticket. He informed
Singer that he would take no disciplinary action against the officer. Although
the Manager said nothing more, Black felt that his superior was not happy
with the decision.

The Peters Case

However, it was the Peters case, which occurred later in March, that
caused Singer to decide to dismiss Black. A police car in pursuit of an automobile speeding through town at seventy miles per hour collided with a vehicle driven by elderly Phil Peters, who was thrown on the pavement and
killed. The police car was running without flashing light or siren, which was
a violation of a state law specifying the use of such equipment "when necessary" in exceeding the speed limit. The police officer, said Black, had fastened
his safety belt but had not yet had time to open up the various warning devices on the car. At the Coroner's inquest these facts were laid before the
jury; and it was also discovered that the elderly man's driver's license had
been suspended two years earlier. The jury concluded the police officer was
not guilty of negligence. Valley's insurance carriers, however, did settle any
possible claims by making a payment of about $3,000 to the widow.
During the Coroner's inquest on the Peters case, an official in the District Attorney's office told Singer that Black had been angry and had wanted
to testify in the hearing that the officer was simply following the policy of the
Department. Since such a policy would have been in direct violation of the
state law, the official told the Manager, Valley would have been liable for a
huge damage suit. This report was a shock to Singer, and a conference with
Black on the matter did not ease his mind. As a result the Manager himself
issued an order requiring the Department to conform to the state law. Singer
later wrote on the importance of this incident to his final decision,

> I maintained hope that Black still could continue as chief and
> that in time he might come to wear this authority a little more
> comfortably, both for himself and for the people he was brought
> here to protect. But suddenly it was demonstrated that the com-
> munity was actually threatened by the attitudes he held toward
> his job.

I refer to the tragic death of Mr. Phil Peters out on Brookside
Ave. Two conclusions were inescapable concerning the way that
Black intended to carry out his job. One had to do with the quality
of his judgment, and the other again—with his real attitude toward
the citizenry of Valley. Under Black's direct and personal instruction, the police vehicle was violating both the laws of the State of
California and the tenets of generally accepted good police practice. And in so doing was creating as great—if not a greater hazard
to life and property than was the vehicle being pursued.

Section 454 of the California Vehicle Code provides that whenever conditions required that a police vehicle be operated in
excess of legal speed limits that the operator shall use both his
red light and siren. Black had ordered that neither be used until
the officer had clocked the speeder. Had Black, himself, been
driving the fatal police car, he could and should have been booked
for manslaughter.

In discussing with him the possible liability the city had in-
curred by reason of this incident, Black's position was indefensible. The substance of his reaction is covered by the phrase,
"Nothing to get excited about—if you're going to get convictions,
you're going to have to take chances and somebody may get
killed."[25]

*As I sat there listening to him talk, I was forced into the reali-
zation that the city could no longer be exposed to the threat imposed by Black's inexperience, bad judgment and his persistent
refusal to recognize human considerations in carrying out his job.*
[Emphasis added.]

Chief Black has disagreed with Singer's understanding of the events
surrounding the Peters case. He has denied, in the first place, the truth of the
story told by the official of the District Attorney's office to Singer. Furthermore, he has declared he never issued such an order to the Department.
"For heaven's sake, I certainly knew what the State law was," he has commented. He has pointed out that it was his custom to put all general Department orders in writing and that no such command was ever issued.

At the Coroner's hearing, Black said, the District Attorney had asked
the defending police officer, "Do you usually run without a red light?" The
man answered, "Yes, as do most other Departments." Chief Black said he was
much concerned that his officer was leaving the impression that this was Departmental policy, whereas he was really trying to indicate that practice
almost universally did not accord with the state policy. Therefore Black got
up and asked the District Attorney, "Would you like to have me tell you what
the policy is?" The District Attorney said no, and Black made no further
remarks.

Problems of Communication

With so many points of conflict, it would seem appropriate to describe
what the Manager did to alert Black to his deficiencies. Even here, however,

[25] Black's comment: "Here is what I really said. 'We could expect further and
more deaths in the future if proper enforcement tactics are not carried out.' . . . I never
said any such thing [as statement in the text above] to Singer; a man would be crazy to
say anything like that. . . ."

there is dispute between Singer and Black. The Manager has declared that he tried regularly to counsel Black in meetings occurring two or three times a week and lasting 30 to 45 minutes. The Manager did not feel, however, that the Chief ever really listened with an open or receptive mind. Whenever he raised questions or complaints, Singer said, the Chief either denied them or would retort, "Well, you either want a good law enforcement program or you don't." Furthermore, Singer felt that in their conversations Black never perceived that he might have made a mistake. The Manager kept no record of these conversations and was unable later to indicate precisely what was discussed on the various occasions.

Totally different was Black's perception of his contacts with Singer. He said that most of their business was not conducted orally but by written memo. The Chief revealed he also felt ill at ease in talking to the Manager because he kept a recording device in his office. The Manager had told him, Black said, that the recorder could be set in operation without a warning signal. Seldom, said Black, did they discuss the way he was performing his job, although in March 1956, after the angry housewife's delegation had paid its visit, Singer had told him, "These people have put so much pressure on me, I am afraid I am going to have to ask you to resign." Yet even in this situation, Black did not feel that he was being given any clear picture of where he might be making his mistakes. This, incidentally, was a point that Black made continually later in the controversy. He said that he had not knowingly disobeyed any of Singer's orders. If he had done the wrong thing, it was only because the Manager had not made clear to him what the policy was.

To some degree, at least, the channels through which City Manager Singer received his information affected communications between the two men. In almost every instance Singer had to rely on reports, rather than firsthand observations. These came from citizens, school officials, realtors, other policing agencies, and some members of the Police Department. It is possible, as Black contended, that these complainants were not in all cases unbiased; and it is also to be noted that the statements from other governmental agencies, such as the schools, could not be verified officially. These people refused to state their accusations publicly, a problem which became quite acute for Singer later in the case. As a consequence it was someone else's word against the Chief's. From Black's perspective, each of these reports meant that he was "called on the carpet" and decisions made before the facts were in. He did not think he was given the backing a subordinate might expect from his chief. The City Manager had so little confidence in him, or was so fearful of a mistake (and Black thought this was the real problem), that the Chief was never given the discretion and freedom from interference the job required.

Except for parking, where Singer did urge some relaxation, the level of enforcement was apparently never raised as an issue between the two men. Nevertheless, Black always felt this was the heart of the problem. He saw himself as a professional law officer—one who put effective law enforcement above all other considerations, and who in so doing, inevitably had to alienate certain segments of the community. That was the price to be paid for a program that benefited the citizenry as a whole. Singer contended, on the other hand, that the problem lay not in *what* was being done but *how* it was being done. "You can have firmness with courtesy," as he put it. The Department led by Black was playing "cop" too much, and people were resentful not so much of the tickets they got as the way they were treated. Thus the grounds upon which Singer based the dismissal were elusive and difficult to pin down. Black's technical competence, industry, dedication, and general ability were not questioned; he was really not charged with insubordination. In Singer's view, Black's sin lay in certain subtle factors of attitude, approach and judgment, that distorted an otherwise sound program.

In his own mind, Singer was certain that dismissal of Black was the only answer. But how effectively could he communicate his reasoning to the City Council and the public? It was a question that began to answer itself the day William Black was dismissed.

THE LEAK ABOUT BLACK'S DISMISSAL

While the City Council listened to a discussion of a supermarket re-zoning issue on the evening of May 1, 1956, Manager Singer's mind was already dwelling on what lay ahead that night. He had made up his mind to dismiss Police Chief Black and to ask the councilmen for their approval.

Singer's timing, which was later criticized, may have been connected with the fact that the April Council elections and the Council's election of the new Mayor were now over.

Singer had been particularly heartened by the April elections for two Council seats. George Simpson, his firm supporter, had been swept back into office, and his tireless antagonist, former Mayor Crispin Lloyd, had suffered a humiliating defeat. At the first Council meeting after the election, Simpson had been chosen as the new Mayor. Elected in place of Lloyd was a jeweler from the downtown business center, Andy Carter. He was so new on the Council—and to municipal government generally—that it was unlikely that he would raise any questions. The three continuing members of the Council, who had been elected to four-year terms in 1954, included Jones, the big property owner who usually voted with Simpson, and Jennings, the Democratic college professor, who had proved reasonable and who supported the manager system. That left the third continuing member, Joe Rodriguez, who had opposed Singer on the Kelly affair and who had never masked his disapproval of the Manager and many of his policies. Singer, like Simpson, thought he saw behind Rodriguez and the defeated Lloyd the influences of the Lemon Street Gang.

After the regular meeting Singer asked the five councilmen to go to his office for a closed personnel meeting.[26] Singer's expression, recalled one Councilman, indicated that he had a serious problem on his mind, but none of the legislators knew what it was. After they sat down, the City Manager told them perturbedly that he wanted to fire Police Chief Black. He recounted in some detail the events and complaints that had led him to his decision. "I have tried everything conceivable," he reported. "I have held one conference after another and gotten nowhere. I can see no alternative but to ask Black for his resignation. I want you to know about this and the reasons because I am going to need your support." Singer then suggested that Black be given an opportunity to resign. If he did not, he would be dismissed.

Simpson, Jones, and Jennings had expected that such a recommendation might be coming but had not known when. Rodriguez did ask some questions. Most of the time, however, he stared at the table in front of him. The others were clearly unhappy. "The last thing we wanted," one recalled later, "was trouble in the Police Department." Singer then asked if he had the Council's

[26] Under California law, only meetings of legislators having to do with personnel matters may be closed to the public and press.

support. Two or three said, "Well, if it has to be, it has to be." There was no formal vote, and Rodriguez did not register his specific disagreement with the tacit decision. Singer went on to say that Black was out of town for the week, and it was important that the meeting be held in strictest confidence until he had had a chance to see him. The Manager did not want it to appear that he was firing the Chief while he was away. There was no further comment on this strategy, and the meeting broke up shortly after midnight.

The newcomer, Councilman Carter, the downtown jeweler, was not taken entirely by surprise. He had noted that "Bill [Black] was never around the community . . . and we had been accustomed to a man that was a part of the town."[27] Carter also said that even in his short tenure he had had a number of complaints about Black's way of doing things. There was more than one manner of arresting a person, the new Councilman said, and Black could not do it "like a gentleman." Nevertheless, it "came as a jolt to me that Black was to be fired. I didn't think he had been given enough of a chance," he concluded.

One Councilman's View

Simpson, Jones, and Jennings had been in closer touch with City Manager Singer and were more familiar with the problem. One of them explained his general understanding of conditions at the time of the meeting with Singer in this way:

> After Black was appointed, he began a vigorous campaign of traffic enforcement and put much pressure on the men for arrests. Once he took us Councilmen on a tour of the station and showed us a chart of the number of arrests each officer was turning in weekly. We were given to understand that he expected them to come through with a certain amount each week.
>
> No one was really antagonistic to any part of Black's program. It was the extreme pettiness that got them down, for example, the carrying of a tape measure to check on the distance of cars from the curb. People got to feeling that if they were caught in a violation, they would really get the book thrown at them. Black used to cruise around himself and seemed to take great delight in hauling someone down and giving him a tongue lashing. A prominent minister told me he had gone through this, that Black had started out, "Haven't you got better sense. . . ."
>
> I was getting quite a few complaints, and it got to the point where people were asking, "How long are you going to keep this guy around here?" I think we all tried to defend him, saying we wanted vigorous law enforcement. We either took that position or we said nothing when the complaints were made to us.
>
> I believe, too, that we were all aware of these problems. Two or three months after Black arrived, I remember encountering Mayor Lloyd, who asked me, "Are you getting a lot of complaints about this new Chief?" I answered I was. Lloyd's comment was, "Jack Singer's really pulled a boner on this guy."
>
> Actually, the Council was not filled in on Singer's day-to-day

---

[27] Carter meant, presumably, that Black did not socialize much with the downtown merchants in the Kelly pattern. Black lived in Valley in a north side development.

problems with Black, nor what efforts he was making to solve
them. We were aware, however, that the Manager was holding
meetings with the Chief in an attempt to straighten him out. As to
how he was going about this, I don't think we considered it our
problem.[28]

Thus, as of 1:00 a.m. Wednesday, May 2, it appeared that Singer's
proposal to dismiss the Police Chief would have the rather strong support of
at least three members of the Council. One was disposed to go along with
some misgivings, and only one might be in direct opposition. The Manager
had not attempted to present a full dossier of facts on Black that night. He had
relied on the councilmen's general knowledge of the Chief's behavior and
had pointed out that some of the more important causes of dismissal involved
information and complaints whose sources could not be publicly identified.
There was not a great deal of concern at the time as to whether a good public
case for the dismissal would have to be developed. It was apparently hoped
that Black would take the easy course and resign.

Any possibility of a tidy handling of the affair, however, reckoned without the reaction of Councilman Rodriguez. Since he commuted to Xerxes, he
did not talk often with the other councilmen or with the Manager; and though
his colleagues insisted he had been present, he did not remember that the
Manager had ever discussed his problems with the Council before. As a consequence, Rodriguez could not escape the feeling that the "whole thing had
been caused by a couple of big guys being arrested." Secondly, he was perhaps more mindful than his colleagues of the public response to a dismissal
without reasons given. "Personally," he said, "I thought it was only decency
that Black be given a chance to speak."

Councilman Rodriguez first made known his strong feelings the next
afternoon in a discussion with Mayor Simpson. He said then that he would
have "no part in firing Black." The Mayor was conciliatory and unperturbed,
Rodriguez recalled. He told Rodriguez, "Black will resign, and that will be
all there is to it."

The *Times* Breaks the Story

At 10:00 the next morning (Thursday, May 3) Rodriguez got a call from
the *Valley Times*. Was it true, a reporter asked, that Black was being dismissed
as a result of the Manager's recommendation to the councilmen at the closed
session Tuesday night? The indignant Rodriguez replied, "Yes." (The reporter did not tell Rodriguez where he had gotten his information. Singer and
others later suspected that it had come from former Mayor Crispin Lloyd, the
Manager's long-time critic, and that Lloyd might have heard of the dismissal
originally in personal conversations with Rodriguez, his former ally on the
Council.)

The *Times* published the story that afternoon. Councilman Rodriguez
was quoted at length:

> The City Manager asked the Council to agree on two proposals.
> (1) To ask the Chief's resignation and (2) an outright firing backed
> by the council if the chief refused to resign.
> On the basis of the facts presented to us, I cannot see sufficient
> reason for the move. The reason given was "poor public relations"

[28] Chief Black declares that these charges are essentially untrue.

on the part of the chief, but no particular facts to substantiate these reasons were presented to the council.

I was unaware of any problems in the Police Department until the personnel session last Tuesday, and can say I was definitely shocked.

In my opinion the law enforcement program we now have is commendable in many ways. I understand the morale in the police department is now as high as it ever has been. . . .

Chief Black was highly recommended by the city manager as to background, character, police knowledge, and personality. Now, less than a year later, we are informed things are not as they were supposed to be at that time.

I, for one, do not want to see another upheaval in the police department unless it is for the betterment of the community.

There has been no written report of reasons presented to the council, and I think there should be. I further think that Chief Black should be given an opportunity to have his say.

If the chief has failed in his duties, then the council has the right to know all the facts. Persons reporting unfavorably on his conduct should be identified and the facts investigated. The public and the chief should know what the reasons behind this are.

The *Times* reporter had also telephoned the news to Chief Black, who had been in Los Angeles for the week, serving as an official in the wrestling tryouts for the 1956 Olympic team. The *Times* quoted Black as having said on the telephone:

For some time I have been well aware that a group of people who I know have been seeking to get me replaced. I wrote a statement to this effect last week, but in view of the fact that I was going to be out of town for seven days, I decided not to release it until I returned.

The *Times* story noted that City Manager Singer and other councilmen had had no comment for the press.

Publication of the story while Black was out of town put the Manager in a disadvantageous position. Rodriguez' decision to talk was viewed by his colleagues and the City Manager as an unpardonable breach of confidence. They felt he was basically responsible for the ensuing community conflict. Some erroneously believed at first that Rodriguez had been the person who had first leaked the story to the *Times* reporter. Why had Rodriguez confirmed the report? There were doubtless many reasons: his dislike for Singer and his opposition to the downtown business interests. But perhaps the most important was that he had felt no commitment to his Council colleagues to maintain a silence. He believed that Singer had purposely called the meeting late at night to rush through the dismissal. "I didn't know why they were taking the action, and it was too late to argue. I had to work the next day. I just didn't feel they could bind me to silence in such a casual and arbitrary way."

Some of those on the Manager's side felt that the *Times* should have killed the story and avoided plunging the community into another police controversy. The *Times* publisher later expressed a different view: "This wasn't the dismissal of a clerk-stenographer but just about the most important man in our government. Furthermore, it wasn't a question of *if* he was to be fired but *when*. He had alienated too many important publics in town to last.

We were just doing our job." Moreover, some *Times* men pointed out later, the competing Xerxes daily might have published the story first if the *Times* had not.

Singer Sees Black

After Singer received his message from the newspaper, he hurriedly contacted Black, found he was too late, but went ahead and made a date to see the Chief at 4:30 p.m. in Hollywood. By noon he and his assistant were on their way to urge Black to resign.

The call from the *Times* that morning had not surprised Black. The developing pressure, particularly since the Peters case in March, had caused him to set down, before leaving for the Olympic trials, some of the reasons why he believed certain people in the community were trying to have him dismissed. He had written the statement for publication in the *Times* and had personally taken it to the editor. The two men had discussed its content and decided that it would certainly stir things up. But the editor suggested Black "hang on to it for awhile."

When Singer and the Assistant City Manager arrived at Black's Hollywood Knickerbocker suite about 4:00 p.m., little time was lost in getting down to the point. The Chief was shown the proposed resignation, which was typed on City of Valley stationery. Black's name was included, ready for signature. The text was,

> Personal reasons make it necessary that I submit my resignation as Chief of Police of the City of Valley, effective at the earliest possible date.

The Manager explained that it would be better all around if the Chief signed the statement. The city would avoid embarrassment and Black would not have the problem of a discharge on his employment record. Black then asked, "What if I don't sign it?" Then, the Manager said, he would have to institute dismissal proceedings. "What have I done wrong?" Black queried. Singer said there would be no point in such a discussion and urged him to resign. The meeting lasted about 45 minutes, with Black telling the Manager of "20 to 25" improvements that had been made in the Department. He suggested Singer was really submitting to pressure from a small group in the town. Singer said nothing. Ultimately, the Chief declared he would not sign the resignation. He wanted time to consider.

Statements in the Press

The *Times* the next day carried a banner headline that Black had been fired and was demanding a hearing before the Council. Three statements were given prominent display. The first was from City Manager Singer, who said:

> I regret sincerely the extremely unfavorable publicity that has been created by the ill-advised and premature release of information concerning the proposed resignation, or termination, of Chief Black at a time when he was out of town. . . . Because of the premature release of the information it was my desire to contact Chief Black in Los Angeles at his earliest convenience, in order to ex-

plain to him that I had no intention to handle the matter behind his back.

Since Chief Black has decided that he will not submit his resignation, his termination papers are being processed today, because he has not come up to the expectations of the City Manager's office. . . .

This office and the members of the City Council do not disapprove of a firm law enforcement program and firm police department discipline and there will be no efforts made to change these particular programs in any way.

The second statement was from Chief Black. It said in part:

I now request a fair and impartial hearing before the City Council during which time the City Manager would have an opportunity to bring his charges and reasons for asking for a resignation or discharge.

Also, it would give those persons who have charges to make against the Chief [an opportunity] to bring their cases openly before the City Council.

I would also like to bring before the Council police officers so that they may testify as to the present conditions within the department. I am confident that the good people of this community and the members of the police department are desirous of having an honest and efficient administration of the police department. I believe that I have given them such an administration.

I came to Valley to do the best job possible in good law enforcement at the request of the City Council and the City Manager. If the City Manager and present Council desired any change in that policy, or wished a new policy, I would have been most happy to have carried them out. . . .

The third statement came from former Mayor Crispin Lloyd, who made two basic points. The first was that the Council shared responsibility with the Manager for the firing of Black. Valley's elected representatives "have, and should have, a part in such decisions." The former Mayor's second point sounded a theme that was to re-echo in most pro-Black arguments throughout the remainder of the controversy: "We either will have impartial law enforcement, or we can again bow to the privileged few." Lloyd continued:

. . . This action was taken without any opportunity for him [Chief Black] to present his side of the story or defend himself in any manner.

To my knowledge, his only crime is the rigid enforcement of our laws—laws, in many cases, made by the City Council. Admittedly, Chief Black has made some mistakes, as will anyone endeavoring to satisfy the public regarding law enforcement.

Valley is growing and the days of Sacred Cows are rapidly passing. These Sacred Cows are the ones making the strongest complaint. . . . Shall we have a chief of police willing to work and enforce our laws, or shall we have a coffee-drinking, hand-shaking figurehead who takes his office and duties with a detached attitude?

With the Lloyd and Black statements, the pro-Police Chief side assumed the offensive. Black hammered at a point that would recur many times. He had done what he was told. Without warning he was now fired and no specific reasons were given. The Lloyd statement represented a blanket refusal to let the Council off the hook. Since the ordinance required the Council to confirm all appointments and dismissals of department heads, Lloyd charged the Council with responsibility for making a full investigation. There was no question, too, but that Lloyd's raising of the fair and equal treatment question was quite a boon to the Black cause. As one Councilman later remarked, "How can you argue against fair and equal treatment? It's like sin and mothers. And the person who accuses you first has the big advantage. All you can do is deny the charge and claim you're not that bad."

On May 4 City Manager Singer appointed the Deputy Chief as acting head of the Police Department and ordered him to continue to follow the policies laid down by his predecessor. Over the weekend the councilmen were mum. Black was still in Hollywood officiating at the wrestling tryouts and due back on Monday. But the newspapers kept the story going.

Pressure for a Public Hearing

From this point on, the telephones in the homes and offices of the councilmen began an intermittent ringing that was not to cease for almost six weeks. The Black affair aroused citizen feeling as no previous civic matter ever had. The volume of telephone calls, sidewalk conversations, and efforts to register opinions with councilmen or their families was unprecedented. And so was the indignation and vituperation with which the citizens communicated their views to their elected representatives. As the Black affair grew hotter, the phone calls came at all hours of the day and night, and before the controversy ended, many of the councilmen felt considerable strain and fatigue.

At the beginning, the extravagant newspaper coverage and the charge that the Manager had acted because some unnamed, but presumably influential, people in Valley did not want tough law enforcement applied to themselves, made the whole affair "look rather sinister," one Councilman recalled. It indicated to him that people were always ready to believe the worst when it came to governmental matters. "Black," this Councilman said,

> was playing the part of the sincere, conscientious Chief who treated everyone fairly and never knowingly did anything wrong. By assuming this role, he made the rest of us seem as if we did not want such a person in the job. Though in my opinion it was never the issue, he made it appear that the real question was whether we wanted to support Singer's attempt to protect his "friends."
>
> There was no question about the impact of this approach. I got calls from constituents saying "We want you to know that we think it is a good thing to have active law enforcement. Lives can be saved that way."

On Monday Mayor Simpson and all the councilmen except Rodriguez declared that there would be no public hearing. "We intend to be firm on this thing," he said. "A public hearing . . . accomplishes little . . . does much harm to the families of the principals involved . . . is too time consuming . . . is very expensive." The situation was different, the Mayor declared, from the "last Police Department flareup. At that time there were some charges of malfeasance in office." In addition to his oral remarks to reporters, the Mayor also issued a rather lengthy statement, which, however, dealt more with the method taken by the Council in arriving at its decision than the reasons. Among the questions Mayor Simpson said he felt people were asking were:

> ... whether this means a less active law enforcement program; whether the action taken was arbitrary and based on a snap judgment, or whether it resulted from some individual's encounter with local law enforcement officers. To all of these, the answer is definitely NO.
>
> 1. All members of the Council and the City Manager have strongly supported the program of vigorous law enforcement and will continue to do so. . . . Good law enforcement, in the long run, is good public relations, not bad. . . .
>
> 2. While the Council had not been filled in on all details of existing problems until recently, the Manager informs us that he has discussed them repeatedly, and at length, with Mr. Black . . . the decision to take this action was made slowly and reluctantly. It was no sudden decision, and had no reference to any single specific incident.
>
> 3. A number of very fine technical improvements . . . have been made. . . . The problems, without going into unnecessary detail, have apparently been in the area of judgment, personal psychology, relations with other law enforcement agencies, relations with juveniles, etc.
>
> There has been no malfeasance in office, merely a case of resolute incompatibility. It was never intended that the Chief should be dismissed in a manner to prejudice his future employment. . . . Unfortunately the unwise and premature disclosure, before the Manager had a chance to discuss the matter with the Chief, placed both of them in an awkward position. . . .
>
> *It is unhappily true that a small group of perennial trouble makers that enjoy behind the scenes activity in our community will seize upon a problem of this sort to exploit community division.* Issues should not be decided in that setting. Every effort will be made to handle this fairly and properly, and we ask your patience and confidence. . . . [Emphasis added.]

That same day the *Times* published its first editorial on the "Chief Black Affair." It said that the community was deeply disturbed. Conceding that the Chief had been tactless and had moved too fast in his law enforcement program, the newspaper also noted the furor of the previous few days had revealed that a large number of people considered his performance "vigorous, firm, and impartial."

> The majority of the Council and the manager made a mistake in the naive assumption that a highly controversial decision could be made on a Tuesday night, and not leak out before the anticipated Singer-Black conference six days later.
> Having made that mistake the council was then unprepared for the public reaction that followed. All members except Joe Rodri-

guez have been placed on the defensive. They may have excellent reasons for supporting Singer against Black, but the public is unaware of them. They have placed themselves in the position of seeming to have bowed to pressures which they have not explained.

Far more than the council, the people are blaming the city manager. Perhaps it was all right for him to seek council approval of the firing of Black while the chief was out of town for a week. But it doesn't look like fair play to a lot of people.

They are holding the city manager to accountability for his judgment. Only a year ago, they observe, Mr. Singer found Mr. Black to be the best qualified candidate among many. Now he has reversed his opinion and fired the chief.

If he did not like the policies of the Chief of police, then why didn't he issue a different set of instructions, they want to know? Why wasn't Black given a chance to defend himself?

In the first round of the controversy, Mr. Singer has certainly lost, by failing to justify his position publicly. Mr. Black has proved to be an articulate champion of his own position. . . .

What the public wants now is information. . . .

The Council Agrees to Hear Black

Meanwhile, a woman whom Black "had never heard of" began to circulate petitions asking the Council that he be given a hearing. By midmorning of the first day the lady had obtained 43 signatures, and the *Times* printed each name and address. The petition asked that Black be given a chance to state all the facts "regarding his summary dismissal . . . and present to the people of Valley his admirable record in fulfilling his duty, and the just reasons for his reinstatement." The lady said that people were anxious to sign and some thought that the manner of the firing was "un-American." Although it never came out publicly, the circulation of the petition brought the issue of religion into the controversy. Though Black was a Protestant, the woman circulating the petition was a Catholic and most of the early signatures she obtained were those of Catholics. Hence there was some feeling that the Catholic people, who represented about twenty percent of the population and were growing in proportionate number, were using the problem to secure political power in the community.

Spurred by the newspapers, citizen interest grew in extent and in intensity. It was reported that City Manager Singer's home was visited by a mysterious prowler on Monday night and a rock with a threatening note attached was hurled through his garage window on the preceding evening.[29]

It was becoming increasingly clear to the Council members that their hope of avoiding some kind of public unfolding of the issue would be impossible. Five days after Black had been fired, on May 10, the Council passed unanimously a motion by Rodriguez to allow Black to appear before it at the next regular Tuesday meeting. Mayor Simpson said Black had never really been denied the right to appear at a regular meeting. However, he noted the Council "was, and still is, against a lengthy drawn out hearing such as we had a year ago."

---

[29] The note said: "You have lost the best chief of police you ever had or ever will have. You have made the worst mistake you ever will make. Now you can live with it. The window is nothing. Just wait."

Thus the Council bowed to a strong public sentiment. Councilman Jennings particularly felt that the Manager's public relations had been poorly handled. He believed that it was necessary under the circumstances for the City Manager to state as "fully and frankly" as possible his reasons for dismissing the Chief. Until this was done, Jennings did not believe the clamor would subside. Jennings had suggested this step to Singer, and Singer had agreed to prepare such a statement. The expectation that the Manager would have such a statement in time for the next Council meeting was one reason why Rodriguez' motion to grant Black "a fair opportunity to speak before the Valley City Council . . ." had been passed unanimously.

Singer Issues His Statement

The day before the Tuesday, May 15, hearing, City Manager Singer issued the statement Councilman Jennings had requested. It was not specific; rather it was an attempt to create the tone that Singer felt was important to an understanding of the reasons for the dismissal. A major portion of the statement follows:

> Tomorrow the former chief of police will have his say.
> He has asked why he was discharged. You, the people of this sensitive community, have asked also.
> I have been accused of protecting so-called Sacred Cows and yielding to political motives. Am I protecting anyone? Of course. And I fear I must always do so, public hearing or no.
> But I offer no protection to Sacred Cows or other vested interests. They not only do not ask my help, they do not need it. They hire legal counsel or go to a higher power than I.
> You ask to know why a man who has contributed much to the police administration of this city should be tossed aside. Was not his duty that of enforcing laws? Has he not done it more forcefully than any other chief Valley has had in past years?
> Very true. No one has argued that point. We did say, however, that he lacked "good public relations." This meant little to most of you.
> What we should have told you was that he lacks something far more important. That precious quality of human kindness . . . a genuine liking for people and an interest in you, as individuals.
> More high sounding talk? No, rather the reflection of the forlorn look in the eyes of those who have come away from a visit to the former chief, troubled and humiliated.
> These are not people of means and influence. These are people, who, because they lack means and influence, came to me since they had no other place to go. These are the little people. These are the ones who brought the downfall of ex-Chief Black.
> They came alone or in groups of two or three. They came apologetically, sometimes a little fearfully. They ask for no favors or relief from violations of the law. They came humbly, asking only for a courteous audience and perhaps an explanation. They had talked with Black. But he had lost himself in the hard printed words of written law. Laws which after all, were made by people, for people—not against people.
> Black's downfall came not from a lack of professional knowledge or ability. It came not from any one tangible incident. It

came rather from those who spoke softly but from the heart. They cannot step forward and identify themselves "for investigation." They cannot, because they do not even know that their soft words were added month by month to many other soft words, eventually creating a roar which I could no longer ignore. They do not know this, these little people . . . and they never will unless they recognize themselves here.

I did not fire William Black. Nor did the City Council. William Black fired himself.

This was the general situation, the City Manager reported. He went on to say more specifically that there was a "serious, growing friction" between the local schools, the insurance agents, the other law enforcement agencies, and the Valley police, "caused by lack of cooperation or lack of judgment on the part of Mr. Black." Because of their "public positions," however, these agencies and their representatives could not speak openly. Singer concluded:

Yes, other problems exist. In my humble opinion some still should not be discussed. However, you are interested in good government and you have asked, "Why has Black been discharged?"

I have tried to briefly answer this and point out that the step was taken as much to protect the future of the people of this community as for what already occurred.

BLACK DOMINATES THE COUNCIL HEARINGS

Judging by the turnout and the mood of the people at the hearings the next day, Singer's statement had not quieted many citizens who were displeased with the dismissal of Chief Black. Councilman Jennings, who had publicly requested the statement, was not satisfied, either. "You couldn't answer those petition-happy people with high-sounding words. I was well aware of the great difficulties in getting the people who had complained about the Chief to come forward. But . . . I felt we had come to the point where much had to be spelled out and people identified if possible. . . . For example I talked to the school people too. They generally confirmed what the Manager had said to us, but 'couldn't get the schools mixed up in this.' Where did that leave Singer and us?"

The hearings, which began Tuesday, May 15, were "gruesome," as one Councilman put it. Originally scheduled for the Council Chamber in the basement of the City Hall, the appearance of some 300 people forced the removal of the session upstairs to the auditorium. The day was hot, 92 degrees, as some 250 found seats and the others stood around the walls. Chief Black appeared with his attractive wife and teen-age son and daughter. It was a pro-Black audience. Some 1,400 signatures had been obtained on the petitions asking for the hearings, and it looked as if a good number of the signers were present. None of the persons who had previously complained about Black to the Manager could be seen in the audience.

Mayor Simpson was in the chair flanked by all his colleagues except Jennings, who missed the session. The Mayor stated that the proceeding resulted from Chief Black's written request for a public hearing at the regular Council meeting. Black then took the floor and began to read a three-page prepared statement as City Manager Singer sat poker-faced. On this occasion, and in the hearings that followed, the Chief proved to be a highly effective speaker, capable of moving a large audience on his own behalf. Black declared, first, that he was not seeking reinstatement to his position. He said he was still Chief until action had been taken by the Council, "elected to that office to do the will of the majority of the people in keeping with city ordinances." He had refrained from performing his duties since his "illegal" discharge from office because he did not "wish to cause turmoil and upset among the people of Valley." Since no charges had been filed and he had been unable to confront his accusers, Black stated that his dismissal was a violation of the Sixth Amendment of the Constitution of the United States. "I am here to ask the people of Valley to make known to me, through the City Council, the reasons why I should be discharged from the police department," he said, concluding his typewritten statement amidst applause and cheers.

Black then suggested that a motion to restore him to office would be in order. Councilman Rodriguez said, "I so move." But the motion died for lack of a second. Later on Rodriguez tried a second time, but again there was no second.

Black's Speech

No longer reading from notes, Black started a lengthy speech in which he concentrated on four major points: (1) the improvements that he had brought about in the Department ("the first professional administration . . . the Valley police department . . . has ever had"); (2) his insistence on impartial enforcement of the law which had really lost him his job ("it was implied that I would have to adjust to 'the Hill' and to 'the other side of the tracks.' He [Singer] had the wrong man to talk to because I live on the other side of the tracks."); (3) a categorical denial that he failed to co-operate with other agencies ("falsification," he said, producing letters and calling witnesses from the California Highway Patrol and the Valley Police Department); and (4) a view of City Manager Singer as a nice but ineffectual person caught in the squeeze of pressures on his office. (He and Singer "had never had a harsh word" until the current trouble came up.) The witnesses Black called supported his statements, one former officer testifying that he, too, had been warned about the difference between the people on "the Hill" and those "on the other side of the tracks."

At one point in the session Councilman Rodriguez also hurled at Singer the charge that he was not informed equally with the other councilmen about the case. He said he had known nothing of Black's shortcomings before the meeting, and he read from the Manager's Handbook that administrators should "deal frankly with the Council as a unit rather than as individual members."

The meeting ran long over time, but Black was still not finished. The audience by this time was intensely and angrily pro-Black. No one on the Manager's side had commented to any extent. It appeared that the hearings might drag on indefinitely, exactly what the Council had originally sought to avoid. Three of the councilmen—Jones, Rodriguez, and Carter—said that under the circumstances they would not be prepared to vote until "all statements are made." Thus, the Council agreed to convene on Thursday at 3:00 p.m. to continue the hearing. Some young Black supporters moved toward the Manager with jeers as he and the councilmen sought to leave the crowded auditorium, but a newspaper man, fearing violence, headed them off.

The hearing had been a trying experience for City Manager Singer, mindful of the *Times* editorial suggesting that he too was on trial. He had spoken only once when he became angered by Rodriguez' comments, firing back that an example of the Manager's trouble in handling personnel was the hearing, which arose from premature release of information on Black's pending dismissal. "When the end of the meeting came," Singer recalled, "I really felt in physical danger. I'll have to give Black credit. He really stirred up the people in that room."

Singer Faces a Hostile Audience

On the second day of the hearings the atmosphere was, if anything, even more highly charged with intense pro-Black feeling. The crowd numbered at least 350 persons. "Black's supporters applauded him, and moves they considered fair or favorable to him, and were audibly hostile to City Manager Jack Singer," the *Times* reported. This time City Manager Singer was allowed to speak first by Mayor Simpson, even though Chief Black insisted that he still had the floor and should be allowed to continue.

Singer's delivery was mumbling and ineffective compared to the Chief's oratory. In his remarks the Manager was more specific in treating his reasons for dismissing Black. He stated his version of the problem with the schools, with the insurance agents, of the Peters traffic death, and of failures of cooperation with other law enforcement agencies. Against Black's observation the previous Tuesday that the Manager in Valley had too much power over employees who "lived in fear of their jobs" because there was no formal civil service system, Singer made a spirited statement in defense of the council-manager plan. He said

> Mr. Black was familiar with our form of government when he came here. The people of Valley adopted it by vote in 1948. I believe the city has progressed and prospered under it. I feel sorry that Mr. Black believes our form of government has done him an injustice.
> I am shocked to learn from Mr. Black that the department heads and the employees of the city government are constantly in fear of losing their jobs. I can only say that in my four years as city manager, I have dismissed but one department head . . . Mr. Black.

Singer declared that he did not propose to "refute, point by point," Black's allegations but called Acting Chief Ken Boyer and asked him about "discriminatory arrests." Boyer, who had been on the force nearly sixteen years, scoffed at the charge, saying he "never heard of it." Black, then getting permission to speak, asked if Boyer was ever present when Singer interviewed new officers. Boyer admitted he was not.

Jennings Sees a Way Out

During the hour or so that the hearings had been under way that day, Councilman Jennings had become increasingly concerned about where the whole controversy might lead. He felt the hearings were getting out of hand and that Black might want several more days to talk about his side of the case.

The audience was becoming more inflamed, and no one could see any end to them other than increased passion and community discord. Moreover, Jennings was afraid of what Black would do when he had the chance to reply to the Manager's fumbling remarks. "I felt that Black, clever as he is, would tear into it."

Groping for a way out, Jennings recalled a conversation he had had the previous evening with the Reverend Richmond Jackson, pastor of the State Street Christian Church. The minister, who knew Black well and had provided spiritual guidance to him at times, was much disturbed by the affair. Like others, he felt the violent controversy was beginning to tear the community apart. He had talked to Black as he had to Jennings, about finding some more appropriate basis for mediation. Black had approved of Jackson's proposed intervention.

Jennings asked for the floor. Before asking Jackson to speak, Councilman Jennings first observed that there had been a "welter of charges, and counter charges, which are almost impossible to sort and prove or disprove. . . ." He then continued, "I am concerned by what this does internally to a community and by the problems that arise from it." Declaring that in such an environment the quest for a solution to the problem was futile, Jennings asked for a new approach, which would involve the application of Christian ethics to a social situation. He then asked the Reverend Mr. Jackson to speak.

Everyone was taken by surprise. Jennings himself did not know the details of the proposal Jackson would make.

The minister said the hearing as presently operating was dividing the community. There could be no satisfactory conclusion. He suggested a private conference between Black, Singer, the Council, with a committee of ministers attending. In such an atmosphere perhaps a real "Christian reconciliation" could take place:

> Christian reconciliation that would heal this hurt in the community would be my hope. If invited by the Council, I would be very happy to serve.

For the Jackson statement, the *Times* reported, there was "moderate applause." Councilman Jennings then offered a motion that "this Council invite Mr. Jackson, and four or five other ministers of this community, possibly one of the Catholic priests, in for that kind of a conference." The motion was interrupted from the floor on a point of order on the assertion that Black still had the parliamentary right to speak first. The Mayor said the Chief would be given time, and then Councilman Jennings asked Black for his reaction to the proposal. Actually, of course, Black had already given his approval to Jackson's idea. He later wrote, "I purposely feigned reluctance in not wanting to appear overly-enthusiastic. Jackson felt this was the way to bring Singer to terms. . . ."

According to the *Times*, Black replied:

> "This puts me on the spot. I think it is unfair at this moment."
> He then interpreted it as a move that would cause him to lose the floor. He said that the city manager had not said anything new in his prepared statement. Then he said he would have to agree that Jackson did have a point.
> Looking toward the full-house audience, he said, "I don't

know what these people came here to hear. I think they want to know more of what goes on in this community."

This touched off loud applause which continued until the mayor rapped the gavel to restore order.

The Mayor asked Black if he would agree to concluding his remarks in a "reasonable time" and then go "into the personnel session with the ministers. . . ."

Black said Mr. Jackson had an excellent thought, although the proposal came prematurely in the hearing. . . .

Close to "Mob Rule"

Chief Black then resumed his speech. He refuted a number of the points in Singer's statement, talked of a "whispering campaign" by people "who don't have the guts to say those things directly to me." He spoke mainly to the audience, intermittently firing sharply barbed accusations at the City Manager. At one point cries of "fire Singer" were heard from the audience, as the intensity of feeling brought the affair close to "mob rule." Black concluded, saying, "I am forced to the conclusion that some persons are bringing pressure on some members of the city, or city council, or that they have committed themselves to someone. That is the reason for your stony silence. Whatever shackles are binding you, throw them away." The Chief sat down to loud cheers and long applause.

It was then after 5:00 p.m., and a procedural wrangle began. Mayor Simpson said the Jennings motion had been seconded and was before the house. To Councilman Carter's comment that the motion might lead to interminable hearings, the audience shouted, "Vote now." Soberly Jennings said he still felt that Christian social ethics should be applied, adding that the aim would be "to resolve the problem," but with the Council making the final decision. However, Councilman Rodriguez was cheered loudly when he asked for "one last attempt to settle this question, openly, fairly, justly, here in this open meeting as we were elected to do." He saw no reason why Black and Singer could not get along together, and he asked Jennings to withdraw his motion so he could move "for the last time, that we reinstate Black." But he added he would have to go along with the Jennings motion if there were no other choice.

Jennings said the Jackson approach was the only answer and insisted on his motion. The *Times* then described the final events of the afternoon:

> . . . A call for the question brought shouts of "no, no" from the audience. Rodriguez then defended his colleagues saying that they were in a tough spot and deserved the consideration due to members of a deliberative body.
>
> "If Black would cooperate would Singer forgive and forget?" Rodriguez asked, and sought an answer from each.
>
> Black said, "Yes." Singer said he would prefer the Jennings-Jackson approach and added that Rodriguez was out of order, a motion being before the house.
>
> Jennings, asked if the conference would be open to the press, replied, "Yes—that was included in the motion."
>
> . . . At 5:23 the Jennings motion was put to a roll call vote and was carried unanimously, all members being present and voting.

The hassle involving Black and Singer having been referred, in part, to a committee of ministers, the *Times* inquired about their religious affiliations. Both Black and Singer said they are Protestants.

Although the motion was carried unanimously, the degree of support was not as strong as might have been assumed. Not only was Rodriguez strongly opposed; Mayor Simpson also was unsympathetic to the approach. He did not like the idea of "mixing church and state" and wanted to get "hard-boiled" and make a decision to dismiss the Chief. Since he was chairing the meeting, however, Simpson did not put forth his views aggressively.

Thus, after over five hours of meetings, Black's blistering attacks had so excited the community that the Manager and the Council were now clearly on the defensive. Moreover, Singer felt that the reconciliation proposal had lost ground for his position. As he recalled his uncomfortable feeling later, "This just compounded the already existing community feeling that Black and I were engaging in some kind of personal fight. The real principles were being lost sight of. I should have refused to go along. But how do you object to being prayed over?"

IN A "SPIRIT OF CHRISTIAN RECONCILIATION"

The next noon four Protestant ministers met immediately after lunch and hastily drew up the ground rules for the session, which was to begin in two hours with the Council, the Manager, and the Chief of Police. Besides the Reverend Mr. Jackson, the others were pastors of the First Methodist Church, the First Baptist Church, and the Lutheran Church. They were a completely informal body, nominated by no official process, and participating only to create the atmosphere in which Singer and Black might patch up their differences. When the meeting began, these four were joined by the pastor of Valley's Second Baptist Church (a Negro) and two Catholic priests.[30]

The four Protestants developed three principles, which they suggested should govern the tense conference. These were later accepted by the other clerics.

> 1. We propose as a basis for our participation in this conference that we are not going to express a judicial opinion as to the right or wrong action of this case, due to our lack of evidence.
>
> 2. Having no authority in this government, we are unwilling to be responsible for acts which are of necessity the sole responsibility of the duly elected governing officials.
>
> 3. As representatives of some of the religious groups in this community, we are willing to express a concern for the total welfare of the community, and realizing that the final judgment rendered by the Council will leave many persons disappointed,

[30] Black had a strong basis of support in this last group. He had earlier consulted with the Catholic fathers at the church in the Mexican-American community as to the availability of a good young Mexican-American for police service. The Department had one Mexican-American at the time, and Black had given him a more responsible assignment in traffic. The Chief had also talked to church people in the small Negro community about the possibility of putting on a Negro officer. He felt at the meeting that these representatives of the minority groups were basically in sympathy with him.

that whatever decision is arrived at by his duly elected Council, it be accepted by the citizens of this community and that we live up to the ideals of brotherhood and understanding through it.

That afternoon, May 18, 1956, all the members of the Council, the ministers and priests, Singer and Black, and members of the press gathered in the small parish house room of the First Evangelical Lutheran Church. The atmosphere was greatly different from the two previous public meetings. "Affirming the presence of God," the group carried on its discussion amicably over a four-hour period. Members of the clergy and the councilmen did the talking. Black and Singer, sitting only two chairs apart, said very little. When they did talk, they spoke quietly and did not argue. Both men, admitting they had made mistakes, stated their grievances in rather general terms. Singer held that the Chief had attacked his honesty, character, and judgment. Black insisted he was fired without specific charges and without an opportunity to confront his accusers.

The councilmen particularly took the opportunity to express their positions and to confront Black with some of their own questions and grievances. Mayor Simpson said that, based on complaints told him, Black had acted unwisely at times, was dogmatic and belligerent in his approach, and rubbed people the wrong way. "These are some of the intangibles," he said. "That's why we tried for a closed hearing right from the start." He said Valley was a "sensitive town."

Councilman Fred Jones, who had said little earlier declared that he heard many compliments for Black's program. However, he had also been kept aware of the difficulties the Manager said he was having. ". . . When Singer said that he could no longer keep Black subordinate, I agreed. . . . If Singer and Black can agree—then Singer must remember he must have assurance from Black that he will submit himself to constituted authority. . . . If we put him [Singer] in a position where every employee went to the people, it would be untenable."

Councilman Andy Carter also took advantage of the occasion to express his criticism of the Chief. He reminded the group that the problem with the insurance agents had not been resolved. Carter then asked:

If Singer ordered you to work, do you feel in your heart that you could work with the City Manager and the Council? Would you try your best to keep from creating a situation such as we have had? And further, would you throw open your office doors and try to be a likeable citizen?

Black answered, "Yes, sir." Carter then went on:

We would want to know that you would not only obey orders but do so willingly, not grudgingly. You inferred at the hearing that my idea for downtown parking was to give four hours. It actually was for only two hours in the courtesy parking plan. Suppose it doesn't work? If our local Lions club is willing to furnish the nickels and if the Council does act on it, would you instruct your department willingly to go along with these clubs? Maybe it isn't a good plan, maybe it won't work, but if a civic group wants to do something, and you don't want to, then it would be time to resign.

To this Black responded, "I did not say I was opposed to the plan. I was only trying to point out some things. I will certainly do what the Council asks." The Chief, one Councilman later recalled, "was more humble than I ever saw him."

Among the clerics, the general tendency was to emphasize their community responsibility to the actors in the drama. However, one of the Catholic fathers—he came from the nearby estate of a religious order and at least two councilmen had no idea who had invited him—was particularly vigorous in insisting that a decision be reached that would restore Black to duty. Directing many of his remarks to Manager Singer, the priest was sufficiently scathing to cause one Councilman to suggest that he had been "briefed" by Black supporters. Singer was saved from answering the father's query whether he would put Black back to work "tomorrow morning" by several who said that the purpose of the meeting was not to force a decision on the Manager. Black thought Singer would have reinstated him had he not been interrupted by the ministers.

At 6:00 p.m. the meeting broke up. Black said he thought the meeting had been fair. Singer announced the session was "wonderful" but "some things have gone unanswered which I feel must be answered. I don't think the breach can be healed in four hours. There are some things I must do and some you must do." Then, apparently swept up by the "spirit of Christian reconciliation," Singer added, ". . . I now hold a totally different position than when I first came here. I trust we'll clear up every point. I know I certainly will try." On this basis the two principals decided to meet two days later, Monday, May 21, to search out a possibility of resolving the bitter dispute.

The immediate reaction of the community was enthusiastic. One of the councilmen said he had felt "the presence of God at the meeting. Sometimes I lost the feeling but it kept coming back." A reporter for the Xerxes daily enthusiastically reported that the session "bared some souls" and the "new approach" appeared to offer its own "happy ending." The *Times* also provided a happy version of the affair. Black and Singer were shown together in earnest conversation, and six smiling ministers were posed in another picture. Over the pictures the *Times* ran a bold headline, "Black May Be Restored As Chief."

The Monday Morning Conference

Actually, City Manager Singer did feel that the reconciliation meeting had had an effect on him, not perhaps as great later as he had thought at first. Over the weekend Singer was reasonably certain that Black would be reinstated. "The pressure was terrific," he has said, "and it was clear that the only possible villain in the reconciliation picture would be me if I failed to make peace with Black." His only price for a reversal of his decision, Singer said, was some acknowledgement of human frailty by Black: "If Bill would only say he had made some mistakes and would try to correct things, I thought I could get along."

However, as soon as the pair started talking in City Hall on Monday morning, the City Manager said he realized that Black had not changed. The meeting opened with Singer reviewing some of the problem areas that needed correction. Black took notes. On all the critical issues, however, the Chief refused to concede that he had made any errors. "Actually it was his attitude more than what he said," Singer recalled. "I just had the feeling that if there were going to be any changes made at all, I would have to make them. I couldn't buy that. After about two hours, and when I realized the complete hopelessness of the situation, I just said, 'Well, Bill, I guess that's about all.'" At that time Singer did not indicate to Black that he had no further hope of reconciliation.

According to Black's report of this meeting, the moment he walked into the Manager's office Singer said: "I agreed last Friday to a reconciliation, but since then I have talked to certain people and I am not going along." According to Black, the session from that point on was dominated by Singer, who pointed out problem areas and indicated what he would expect of the Police Chief. However, Black perceived these points as "nothing of real importance —little individual things."

At the conclusion of the session the two men issued a statement to the press. Singer said, "We have covered a great deal of ground regarding our own personal reconciliation and we are now in the process of discussing the problem as it exists as a result of the activities during the past two weeks." Black agreed that Singer's comments were "fair and correct," and they both said they would "probably" meet again that same afternoon to continue discussions. Actually, nothing had been said about a future meeting. There was no conference that afternoon or the next day.

It was the following day (Wednesday) at 11:15 that City Manager Singer made public his decision to oppose the return of Black. He summoned the Chief to his office, as well as press representatives, and made the announcement. Black said only, "O.K." and had no comment for the press. As soon as Singer finished, the Chief left. In a statement written in advance of Singer's official announcement, Mayor Simpson declared that a meeting of the Council would be called to "bring the Black matter to a conclusion at the earliest possible time." However, Councilman Carter was in Monterey for the rest of the week attending a conference for new legislators sponsored by the League of California Cities.

Singer's statement was biting and direct:

> It was proposed that Mr. Black and I might attempt some sort of reconciliation. What sort of "reconciliation" I am not sure. I have met in good faith with Mr. Black. This meeting only made it more clear to me that this issue had nothing to do with any personal reconciliation. Reconciliation has nothing to do with the problem of Mr. Black's qualifications to be Police Chief for all the people of Valley.
>
> I have nothing personal against Mr. Black. . . .
>
> Nothing that has happened . . . has in any way changed that condition. It is even more evident to me (and I am sure it is to the people and their Council) that Mr. Black is incapable of being the Chief of Police of the City of Valley. The Council has been able to verify all of the reasons which I gave them in support of my recommendation for dismissal.
>
> It has been, and still is, the responsibility of the Council to act on my recommendation for the dismissal of Mr. Black. I have again notified the Council that I wish their action as soon as possible.

CHIEF BLACK IS REHIRED

By the time Councilman Andy Carter had gotten back to Valley from the Monterey meeting of new city legislators, he was convinced that it would be an error to fire Black. He was deeply disappointed at City Manager Singer's insistence that his action be upheld. With Councilman Jones, he later reported, he went to the Manager's office "with tears in my eyes" and "practically got down on my knees" begging Singer to keep Black on the job.

Finally, Councilman Carter decided that the Council would have to take the initiative itself. He proposed that the City Manager be required by Council action to take back the Police Chief for ninety days. If, in that time, Black failed to work out, it would be agreed in advance that the Council would support the dismissal. Something had to be done, Carter felt, to prevent the complete disintegration of community morale and pride.

(By this time the charges of Black and the leaders of the Black petition movement—charges that the firing on the south side for special treatment—were cutting deep crevices of controversy and suspicion into Valley's customary cohesiveness and orderliness. This was beginning to worry some leading citizens more than the issue of the dismissal of Black.)

Carter frankly admitted that he had changed his mind. Even though he had investigated Singer's charges and felt they had been substantiated, he nevertheless believed that Black's voiced willingness to change at the reconciliation meeting entitled him to another chance.

Excited by the prospect that his compromise would remove the Council from a very uncomfortable hook, Carter consulted with all his colleagues except Rodriguez. He talked with Mayor Simpson for a considerable part of the day. Carter heard the Mayor say he did not think he would "go for it"; but he still felt the Mayor was not completely negative. Actually Mayor Simpson thought he had been arguing against the proposal. He told Carter to see what the others said. "We were in such a turmoil," Simpson recalled, "I didn't want to discourage anybody." While Jones agreed to go along, Councilman Jennings found the idea completely unsatisfactory and reported that his conversation with Carter went something like this:

> *Carter:* "I have talked to George Simpson and I think I have a plan which should be satisfactory to everybody. I will move that Black be reinstated for ninety days. If he doesn't work out in that time, he can be dropped."
> *Jennings:* "Andy, do you realize what you're doing? What you are proposing in effect is to fire Singer."
> *Carter:* "No, I don't want to do that."
> *Jennings:* "You are voting no confidence in the Manager and you are voting to dismiss him."

But Carter protested that his proposal cast no reflection on the Manager and would not affect his position in the least. "While at Monterey," he said, "I came to realize that not only must the councilmen back up their City Manager, but also our City Manager should back up his Council."

Carter Moves a Ninety-Day Trial

The Council meeting was announced late on Monday, May 28. Scheduled for 5:00 p.m., it was 4:00 before the date was given to the public. Nevertheless, about thirty spectators quickly assembled and were present as the deliberations began. Some of them were city employees. Black, who knew nothing of the Carter compromise, later said he thought sure this would be the time when the firing would be made official. Action started quickly when Carter introduced his motion that Black be given another chance and be restored to duty on a ninety-day probationary basis. It was Councilman Jones, sitting next to Carter, who seconded the motion, supported by Rodriguez. The plan had a majority.

Even though the decision was clearly made, it did give most of the councilmen an opportunity to read into the record some of their attitudes toward the whole affair. The most intense was Jones's reaction. The large property owner had been a strong supporter of the Manager. He said he felt that Singer was completely justified in his action. "Black," he said, "has failed from a public relations standpoint. . . . He was abrupt and not well received. . . . Here at home, I've found people have complained. I, too, agreed that Black should go."[31]

Nevertheless, Jones said he was "amazed, actually amazed" that the people who had complained to Singer about Black now refused to come forward and state their positions publicly. This failure had been particularly irritating to the nervous Jones, who had been subjected to anonymous threats and, under the barrage of constant telephone calls, felt himself under terrific pressure. He was, as one of his colleagues said, "boiling mad." As a consequence, Jones said, "I told these people who were against Black that they should come and stand beside me, not behind me. These people apparently haven't felt that this was important enough to stand by Singer. This morning I talked with Singer. I knew his position. He must have the respect of all department heads and employees. I said I'd not ask him to take Black back. I would be willing to take action over his head. . . ." In short Jones was angry enough at the lack of support given the Council by the pro-Singer people in town to put Black back.

The third member of the majority, Joe Rodriguez, was not completely satisfied with the motion. He saw no reason why Black should be placed on probation. "Black," said Rodriguez, "has successfully refuted the charges made." He suggested that if Black went on probation, Singer should too. At this, the *Times* reported, the small pro-Singer audience cried, "No!"

Councilman Jennings also had his say. He read a three-page statement in which he declared that the Police Chief had "handled facts loosely in the hearings and artfully managed to give a sinister implication to a number of things which were not sinister and even questionable." Jennings characterized Singer as honest and conscientious. "Independent" investigations indicated that the "Manager did have grounds for his decision"; but both Manager and Council had handled their public relations poorly.

Then Jennings emphasized his underlying theme. By its action, the Council would either support or undermine council-manager government in Valley. He said:

> Realistically, our only choice now is to either confirm the discharge of Mr. Black or perhaps in effect force the resignation of the City Manager and Assistant City Manager (and possibly lose some other valued city employees as well). We are not supposed to decide whether as individuals we would have acted in identical fashion. Reduced to the basic issue, the Council must decide whether it believes the Manager had any reasonable grounds for his action. If he did, we confirm; if he did not, we ask his resignation. Whether or not we might have preferred another approach, it seems clear that he had grounds. I certainly could not honestly

---

[31] Chief Black says Councilman Jones once told him, ". . . use me as a reference any time."

and conscientiously conclude that Mr. Singer had no reasonable
basis for his decision.

Singer Threatens to Resign

Before the vote was taken, Singer asked for his chance to talk. He said
that the "basic facts in the Black case have not been altered. . . . I feel that I
must urge the City Council to ratify the recommendation that Mr. Black be
terminated." Failing this, he said the Council could order his own termination and accept the responsibility for a decision he did not wish to be "associated with." After applause for Singer's statement died down, the question
was called, and Carter's motion for a ninety-day reinstatement passed by a
three to two vote. The pro-Singer audience felt the defeat keenly. After the
vote, a number of city employees came up to Jennings, two of them women
with tears running down their faces. They thanked him for his vote in support
of the Manager. One department head, in thanking Jennings, referred to
Singer as "the best boss I ever worked for."

Black, quickly shaking Singer's hand after the session, told him, "Jack,
I think I can do it. . . ."

"You'll have to do it without me," Singer shot back.

Within an hour after the close of the meeting, both Singer and the Assistant City Manager had submitted their resignations, effective in thirty days.
Singer said to obey the order would have put him in an "untenable position."
During the month he was still to be on duty, he would take no responsibility
for the Police Department. He declared that administrative authority had
been badly undermined, that the effect was one of electing a Chief to office
by a "small minority of skillfully influenced people," and would result in the
creation of an "autonomous police department." Actually, Singer was saying
a considerable portion of this for public consumption. He was still hopeful
that his departure from Valley might be averted and consequently handed his
resignation to the mayor, rather than the City Clerk. If it had been given to
the latter, it would have been official. As it was, the resignation simply lay in
the Mayor's hands until Singer desired to pass it on to the City Clerk.

The Council decision caused the *Times* to editorialize at considerable
length the next day on Singer and his approach to his job. It pointed out that
Black had become a symbol of impartial but firm law enforcement and therefore his potential support had not been recognized by the Manager and the
Council.

It was Mr. Singer's ideal of professional conduct, however, that
finally put him in an untenable position. He felt that it was only
necessary to do what he sincerely believed was right. He did not
believe that it was incumbent upon him to justify to the people the
correctness of his action. This left many individuals who dealt
with the manager's office with the feeling that they were not getting a sympathetic hearing, that the city was being run "by the
book." When this same philosophy was applied to the Black affair,
it proved to be fatal to the manager.

Black had a large public following—as subsequent events
proved—and any plan for his dismissal had to allow in advance
for answering to that public. Without that planning, a public
clamor ensued and Mr. Singer took the position that it was not up
to him to give a prompt and full accounting to anyone other than
the five members of the council.

In Utopia it may be possible for city managers to remain silent to the public they serve, but here and now a manager can continue in office only so long as he is understood by the public. . . .

THE PROSPECT OF NO GOVERNMENT

By the next morning the condition of Valley's government approached complete chaos. Not only were the resignations of the two top administrative officials submitted, but Mayor Simpson called in the press at 11:00 a.m. to announce that he was quitting, too. (Jennings had made desperate efforts to dissuade him.) Simpson characterized the previous day's action as "a step backward to ward-heeling days" and said that he and Councilman Rodriguez had "diametrically opposite opinions and standards as to methods and approaches to the solution of city problems." He said he wanted "no part of that system."[32]

Unknown to Simpson, Councilman Jones had also made up his mind to resign. He appeared two hours after Simpson's press conference at the City Clerk's office to make the action official, in contrast to the Mayor's presentation of his resignation only to the press. His wife said he had been awake and sick all the previous night. The Councilman declared he could not "take any more of it. I retired from business because of nerves many years ago. . . . My position on the Council has been a lot worse than I thought." That left the city with three councilmen. One was Councilman Jennings, who had applied for a Fulbright Fellowship in The Netherlands the previous September and was expecting to hear at any time about whether he would get it.

Administrative operations, too, were in a state of turmoil. For weeks little work had been done at City Hall. Thirty-five employees signed a statement registering their confidence in the City Manager, and the Planning Director publicly announced he would resign with Singer. In his statement he made an obvious reference to the Lemon Street Gang and its involvement in the situation, saying,

In the past few years there has developed in Valley a small political group that works under cover—a group that follows the old line—Stir up unrest, grasp any incident to create situations that appeal to the emotions, disorganize government. To create these situations they work through the weakest member of the Council [an apparent reference to Councilman Rodriguez] with the hope of weaving a web dragging the sincere members of the Council into a trap from which it is difficult to extricate themselves. This was demonstrated in the Kelly episode. Fortunately for Valley trying as it was, those undercover artists were sent back to their holes.

Now the same old strategy is being used—this time they have succeeded in disorganizing city government. However, I believe there is still time for the sincere Councilmen to extricate themselves from the present trap. In spite of the acute proportions to which this grandstand play has developed, I believe the good

---

[32] Before the Black affair, Mayor Simpson had not given any consideration to resigning from the Council, even though he had been planning a six-week trip to Hawaii for some time. He felt, however, the time had come for a change. "If I couldn't get the job done, we needed some people who could," he said later. A secondary reason, Simpson declared, was his disinterest in "taking any more punishment."

citizens of Valley will rally and again bring organization out of chaos.

Black's status, too, was up in the air. He had gone back to work. Yet Singer, who was still Manager and still Black's boss, had told the Council he would not take the responsibility of putting Black back on the job. He did not order Black back on the payroll. Insofar as Singer was concerned, Black still was fired. Council confirmation or not, Singer took further steps. He said he had checked with the city's insurance carrier, and there was some question as to the municipality's liability should Black make an arrest or get involved in an accident while driving a public vehicle. Therefore, he ordered that Black do neither of these things.

In the atmosphere of crisis, the *Times* again inserted its editorial voice, suggesting that the council-manager form of government was perhaps at fault.

> In theory, the police department is just another department of government, along with cemetery, streets and water. The manager can supposedly deal with the water superintendent and the police chief alike.
> But law enforcement is by its nature a highly controversial subject. . . .
> The oldest question in the book is: Who shall police the police? "the City Manager shall." At least that's what the citizens thought who constantly ran to Jack Singer in an effort to make Chief Black change his policies or his ways.
> This puts the city manager in the political position of having to interpret the wishes of the people and to supervise the police department accordingly. Political decisions are for elected officers —not appointive ones, and that's where our city managers have found themselves in hot water that was not of their own choosing.

A Meeting of Some Leading Citizens

It appeared that a resolution of the conflict would depend in great part on the future composition of the Council. Under California law, Council vacancies could be filled by appointment by remaining members without calling an election. It seemed possible, with Jones and Simpson leaving, and Jennings possibly leaving, too, that Valley would soon be governed by an appointive City Council in which Rodriguez and Carter would be the dominant figures. This prospect alarmed a number of citizens in the community: realtors, businessmen, persons active in clubs or church societies, prominent country club members. These persons included men who had formerly been active in city government, but many were persons who had been content to let the Manager and the Council majority run things. They were concerned at the division caused in the community by the Black affair and by the intense controversy provoked by his charges that his dismissal had been the result of not granting lenient treatment to a favored few. Now the Manager was resigning, and it appeared that there would soon be no Council majority. To some appeared the prospect that there would soon be no government at all.

Because of this prevailing feeling of concern and alarm, Vice Mayor Jennings had no difficulty in bringing together on short notice thirty of Valley's leading citizens. They met in the Mayor's office. A *Times* reporter commented later: "I was near the City Hall at lunch time, and within fifteen

minutes I noticed people going up the steps. It seemed as if almost every-
body who was anybody was going in. . . . These were the people who were
accustomed to giving the time and leadership to clubs, church groups, the
community chest" and the like. Included in the group were several former
councilmen.

During the short session, many of the citizens said they had not realized
the pressure under which the councilmen had been operating. They offered
greater help for the future and public support for the City Manager. As a result, the group was able to stave off Mayor Simpson's threatened resignation.
"As long as we're going to have chaos in city government," Simpson commented, "we should at least have orderly chaos." Councilman Jones, however, had already turned his resignation in to the City Clerk. His resignation
was irrevocable, according to the City Attorney's ruling. One vacancy on the
Valley City Council remained to be filled.

The Selection of a New Councilman

With the pro-Black citizens still extremely active, it might have been
expected that the appointment of a Councilman to succeed Jones would have
led to a considerable struggle. Black had one solid supporter on the Council
in Rodriguez. Singer had two in Simpson and Jennings. The fourth member,
Carter, the downtown jeweler, had said that Singer had had good reasons to
fire Black but had wanted—and obtained—another chance for the Police
Chief. Thus, the appointment of a new Councilman might have been a close
thing. Despite this, it did not appear that the significance of the impending
appointment was appreciated by the community at large, particularly those
on Black's side.

A few days after the meeting in the Mayor's office, former Mayor Cassius
Bolt, the respected Methodist lay leader and businessman who had been
instrumental in bringing city manager government to Valley in 1949, convened an evening meeting of leading citizens at his home. Jennings was the
only Councilman invited. (Simpson was out of town.) Present were leading
businessmen and realtors, club leaders, some former councilmen (including
the Democratic one), some leading church laymen, and some substantial
citrus men who had taken an interest in civic affairs. The purpose of the meet-
ting was to find a suitable person who would be willing to serve on the Council, so that his name might be suggested for appointment. It had been customary in previous years for groups of civic leaders to suggest names when
vacancies occurred.

Because of the strains and difficulties that the incumbent councilmen
were facing, it was not easy to find someone who was willing to serve. The
group, by design, did not include anyone who was "in opposition" on the
Black-Singer matter. Nor did it include anyone who could not be trusted to
work without publicity. Thus Carter had not been invited, nor had the editor
or publisher of the *Times*. The group was looking, first, for some eligible
person who would be willing to serve. No known supporter of Black would
have been considered. Neither would anyone already publicly committed
to Singer.

Several meetings were held before Norman Chandler, manager of the
Valley Citrus Exchange, was selected. Chandler was a former president of
the Valley Rotary Club, a post of respectability in the community. He had
once served as Mayor of the nearby city of Circe. His appointment would
have the additional public relations advantage that he lived on the north side.

Chandler's name was given to Carter, who moved his appointment at the Council meeting on June 5. The motion was unanimously approved. Rodriguez had played no role in the filling of the appointment, nor had he or Black's other supporters done anything to nominate their own candidate. "I didn't see any point in suggesting anybody, because it was obvious that the other three would make up their minds together," Rodriguez said. When Carter nominated Chandler, he said the Council was "full of trouble" but that Chandler was "willing to accept the responsibility." When Chandler was asked if he would like to come forward to be sworn in, he commented, "No, but I will."

A Police Commissioner?

With the legislative body back to full strength, it was late in the session before the problem of Black's status was raised again. It was not, incidentally, on the agenda. However, Councilman Carter tried to make a motion to restore Black to the payroll and name a Council member as police commissioner; he was interrupted twice. Manager Singer, who had refused to accept responsibility for the Department, pointed out that the ordinance specifically required councilmen to work through the Manager.

Then the City Attorney said that the motion to put Black on the payroll was not necessary. He was still on it until the Council ratified the ouster, a point that was supported by a bulky legal document. Furthermore, said the Attorney, he could not interpret Councilman Carter's motion of the week before, because it did not ratify or reject Singer's action. Carter declared he simply wanted to postpone the ratification ninety days.

Carter then said he was much concerned about the exercise of supervision over the Police Department. "I don't want to be police commissioner. I just want Singer to address correspondence to Black as Chief of Police." Singer stated he would resume responsibility and said he had issued a memorandum ordering Black not to drive police cars. However, Black had continued to do so. "There is certainly no indication of any cooperation between Black and my office," the City Manager said.

"Will you direct correspondence to him?" Carter asked.

"I directed this to him and he didn't comply," Singer responded.

The City Manager agreed, however, that he had no alternative but to exercise control over the police. He reiterated that his resignation "still stands under those circumstances. . . ." This statement caused Councilman Rodriguez to ask where the resignation was. (Earlier in the meeting the City Clerk had presented petitions signed by 468 people, asking the Council to accept Singer's resignation.)

The Mayor said he had the resignation . . . but it was not for long. Irked by Rodriguez' question, Singer walked over to Simpson, picked up the resignation, saying, "On second thought I withdraw my resignation and give the Council the opportunity to fire me if they wish!" The Mayor then remarked, "Looks like we're back to status quo. Black is restored to duty for ninety days, and we have no resignation from the City Manager." Shortly thereafter the meeting ended.

As things stood at this point Singer and Black each appeared to have the support of two members of the Council, with Chandler the unknown quantity. While Rodriguez' antagonism to the Manager was long standing, the Manager's refusal to go along completely with the Council's order to reinstate Black had particularly nettled him. "What do you do when the Manager refuses to accept a Council order?" he asked. This intransigence had also irritated Carter, although it was not clear how he would have voted in a show-down. Not even Rodriguez, however, was prepared to force the issue. Little as he would have objected to Singer's leaving, he realized that the Manager had a "lot of friends in town." He didn't think it wise to press the matter.

Singer Assumes Control of Police

Thoroughly angered, Singer the next day reasserted his control over the Police Department with a vengeance. On the bulletin board was the follow-ing order to the Police Chief:

> Until further notice from this office you are to obey the following orders: (1) Any orders from you to the police department, or any of its members, shall first be submitted in duplicate to the office of the city manager for approval. No order or instruction by you shall be effective unless it has such approval. (2) In the absence of the city manager or the assistant city manager you shall submit such orders to the assistant chief of police for approval. (3) In the case of emergency all orders will be issued by the assistant chief of police or that officer who is in charge of the current shift. . . .

In response Chief Black signed and posted the following statement: "Since I am unable by this directive to issue any orders I suggest to all mem-bers of the police department that they comply."

Providing his own kind of harassment, Black followed the order scrupu-lously, sending something for approval to the Manager "every fifteen min-utes," with a duplicate to each Councilman. Furthermore, as the *Times* re-ported, Black's strategy was to suggest three orders covering "certified hot potato issues." He proposed that the Department return to one-man patrol cars instead of the Singer-ordered two-man cars; that a selective enforcement program be reinstituted; and that an officer be reassigned to a regular parking enforcement beat. About the last item, Black commented, "They took the parking patrol man off his beat in May and gave him other duties . . . parking has become commonly improper throughout the city."

To these proposals, the Assistant City Manager responded for Singer with just eight words. "Not approved. Present procedures will remain in effect." The next day Black came back with the same type of proposals, and so the battle went.

A Challenge to the "Old Guard"?

As Black and Singer continued their tug of war, the *Times* on June 7 published an editorial that stirred many in the community. Provocatively titled, "Who Owns Valley?" it fed fuel to Black's claim that he was fired for enforcing the law equitably. The editorial declared:

> What is being challenged is the Old Guard—the people who have been here for decades, if not generations, by the people who have only been here for years (not decades).
> This controversy is being waged with symbols. As the ele-phant is the symbol of the Republican party, City Manager Jack Singer has been cast as the symbol of the Old Guard. As the don-

key is the symbol of the Democratic party, Police Chief Bill Black has become the symbol of the challengers.

. . . As the *Times* had noted before the storm ever blew up, Valley was trying to make up its mind as to how much traffic law enforcement it wished to have. As the publication in the *Times* of the weekly "honor roll" of traffic violators showed to all, there were no sacred cows in the book of Bill Black. North side, south side, speeders, and stop jumpers all looked alike to him.

. . . Sympathetic to the Council many citizens interpreted the pro-Black movement as a junior-grade revolution. They did not understand that what was wanted was fair play for all hands. And they began to fan the very flames which they sought to put out.

They used such terribly ill-advised words as "rabble." They implied that only long-time residents are true citizens of Valley and that newcomers are like children—not really entitled to vote. Some who should know better even used epithets which in a bar room would be strong enough to start a free-for-all brawl.

. . . The calm will finally come when the people generally, are convinced that equality before law is truly the settled policy. It will quiet when the newer citizens finally demonstrate that they are a constructive force in the community—as they are. It will be history when all of the older residents say—and mean it—that Valley belongs to everyone who lives in it.

The editorial, penned by the *Times* editor himself, was bitterly criticized. The newspaper was accused of stirring up controversy. City Manager Singer did not feel that these were the real issues, and most of the councilmen were resentful. (However Councilman Simpson did say the community was "sensitive" and Carter that it was "clannish.") On the other hand, the *Times* editorial provided aid and comfort to the Black forces. The point was almost exactly that which Black had been making. The *Times* editorial helped to keep the Black controversy fierce and flaming. This in itself caused the *Times* to be severely criticized by (1) those concerned with the ugly spectacle of a fiercely divided city, and (2) those who supported the Manager.[33]

A few days later Professor Jennings learned that he had received a Fulbright grant. He was to go to The Netherlands for a year, leaving in August. Jennings got the announcement on Saturday, June 9, and immediately informed the newspapers that he would submit his resignation to the City Clerk on Monday. He pointed out that his resignation would not come as a surprise to his colleagues. He had told them the previous September of his application for the grant. "While we shall not be leaving immediately," he said, "I feel it is imperative that a full council be able to consider a replacement in the near future. Beginning soon one or perhaps occasionally two members at a time will be away on vacation."

[33]Asked in 1958 if he had any second thoughts about the editorial, the *Times* editor said he considered it to be generally valid. He reported that there was no question the "somebodys" were treated differently than the "nobodys," as he thought was true in every community. In the editorial he had sought to point out to the "somebodys" that privileges carried responsibilities as well.

One councilman has labeled the editorial "hogwash." The "Old Guard vs. New Guard business was a nice simple answer, but far too simple. . . . I think the *Times* bears a good deal of responsibility for the way this whole thing developed. I don't blame them for breaking the story when they got it. I do blame them for deliberately promoting community divisions with this kind of talk, north versus south, etc."

RESIGNATIONS AND A DISMISSAL

The nearness of summer made it necessary for Valley's Council to settle the Black case quickly. Councilman Carter was to be gone throughout July, and Mayor Simpson had scheduled a trip to Hawaii for six weeks in June and July.

Two days after Professor Jennings had announced his resignation, the Council filled his position. The new appointee was suggested by the same group of citizens (convened by Cassius Bolt) that had put up Chandler. He was a resident of 37 years, Allen Campbell, a former Councilman and a real estate man. (Black said sometime later that of the groups who opposed him, none was so powerful and bitterly antagonistic as the real estate people.) The nomination of Campbell, who by his background certainly seemed to fit the Old Guard mold described by the *Times,* was made by new Councilman Chandler. The nomination was seconded by Carter, and these two were joined by Mayor Simpson in the vote. Councilman Rodriguez was absent because of the death of his father-in-law. If he had been present, however, Rodriguez would not have opposed Campbell's appointment. He had grown up with Campbell, talked to him about Council problems, and privately felt that Campbell might be on his side.

The supporters of Black again did nothing to advance a candidate of their own. It happened that Black was the personal leader and symbol of a new and hastily organized group of people who were not really close to the city government's power centers. As one Councilman recalled, "I had never seen the people who supported Black at a Council meeting before. I think that was the first time they had ever thought about city government." Some of these persons were the new commuters.

The Pressure on Rodriguez

Who could provide the leadership for the Black supporters that would enable them to rival the Council majority? Rodriguez was the most conspicuous possibility. However, there were two reasons why he was not particularly interested in assuming such responsibility. In the first place, he was not as heavily committed to the Black cause as his public utterances might have suggested. He thought the method of dismissing Black was wrong and was prepared to support his opinion with his vote. Having professional responsibilities outside Valley, however, he was not interested in waging the all-out fight necessary to keep Black in his position. "If they had simply taken the vote to dismiss at the public hearing, I would have voted my way and that would have been that," he later commented. "I wouldn't have made a further fight."

Second, Rodriguez himself was feeling tremendous pressures from the other side. "People I had never seen before in the community told me I was public enemy no. 1," he recalled. His wife, a city school teacher, felt a change in her treatment. And the Xerxes land title firm for which he worked was visited by a delegation of Valley's real estate men threatening to withdraw their business unless Rodriguez was dismissed. He was not fired. The firm's President had said, "I won't *ask* you to quit." But there were no salary increases.

That left Black the obvious man to take the leadership. However, he was still an administrative officer of the city. Even though he was involved in one of the biggest political fights of the town's history, this status imposed certain restraints on his behavior. He could not, he believed, engage actively now in a struggle over Council appointments, and he did not.

Singer Resigns

The Black affair was resumed shortly after Allen Campbell assumed his seat on the Council at 2:14 p.m., June 13. City Manager Singer reopened the problem himself when he reminded the Council that Black's status was not yet legally clear. The City Attorney then said that it would be necessary for the Council to take a definite action on the Manager's recommendation of dismissal, either approving or disapproving. He felt that the Carter compromise ought to be rescinded and direct action taken.

Singer then reported to the Council that the situation in the Police Department was "unhealthy" and that a "material split within the Department" was developing. He said two officers would be willing to appear before the Council and that there were rumors six planned to turn in their badges. "I don't enjoy making this request again, nor do I enjoy anything about this whole situation. I do not take this as a stand or a pressure move, but I am seriously concerned with what is happening to the Police Department," he continued. He said that he and the Assistant City Manager were resigning again.

Singer did not feel physically capable of continuing. Furthermore, the controversy was having an effect on his entire family. His child had been threatened in school; and he was not prepared to make further personal sacrifices, though he was still reluctant to leave Valley. In his formal statement, Singer declared that it was "evident" that no effort was to be made to resolve the "personnel problem that exists and becomes more serious with passing of time." He said his work could be of "little effect or benefit under existing circumstances." The Assistant City Manager simply asked that his resignation be effective in thirty days.

However, the request for definite Council action got nowhere. Mayor Simpson declared that any decision would have to await the return of Councilman Rodriguez. Speaking to Singer, Councilman Chandler said he had hoped the Manager would give the Council "a little longer—at least until all the Council members return from their vacations." But Singer said, "I live with this 24 hours a day. The phone is busy all day at the office and doesn't stop even after I go home. I cannot physically or constitutionally live with it any longer." Newly-seated Councilman Campbell said he and others had appreciated Singer's efforts. Would it be possible, he asked, for the Manager to take a month or six-week vacation and let the Assistant assume responsibility? Singer said he wished he could accept but he felt that the budget and other items of business had been delayed too long. Furthermore, he declared that he could not ask the Assistant City Manager to stay. The Assistant, he reported, had been "literally living on dietary supplements and high potency shots—he has not been able to eat or sleep for some time."

Thus the session ended with no decision. This time Singer and his Assistant filed their resignations with the City Clerk.

Black Challenges Singer

Police Chief Black lost no time issuing a statement the next day. He denied that there was a significant split in the Department and said, "Even assuming the accuracy of Mr. Singer's statement, more than eighty percent of my department is solidly behind the policies which I have attempted to institute. . . ." Black went on to say that he had begun again a training program with "police courtesy" a part of the curriculum, had gotten in contact with the president of the local insurance adjusters association to straighten out the records problem, and had attempted to be "co-operative" with the City Manager and "obedient to every order."

The next day, Thursday, Singer was completely discouraged, and he began to clean out his desk at City Hall. During the day he had gotten a phone call telling him his eighth grade daughter had been slapped and roughed up by boys in a school bus coming home on the final day of school.[34] She was near hysteria but uninjured. For Singer this was a final straw. His main interest was simply to get away and forget the whole affair. That included a budget session of the Council, which was scheduled for Friday night. Budget preparation was about six weeks behind schedule, but neither Singer nor his Assistant had any desire to participate further in city matters.

On Friday City Manager Singer did not go up to his office. During the day, however, he was visited at home by a group of citizens, led by new Councilman Allen Campbell. The meeting was relatively brief. Campbell said, "Jack, we don't ask for anything more right now. We just want you to be at the Council meeting tonight. That's all. Will you do that?" Singer remonstrated but finally agreed to go to the meeting.

Final Decision

The extent to which the new appointments had been decisive in settling the Black affair was seen at the Council meeting that night. Mayor Simpson was insistent that there be a final resolution of the problem, as he was leaving the next day for his month and a half in Honolulu. No elaborate preparations had been necessary. Simpson, Chandler, and Campbell met briefly before the session, as Mayor Simpson recalls; the principal question was who would introduce the resolution supporting the Manager. Chandler said he would do so. Campbell said he would second. Councilman Carter, who had nominated Chandler and who seconded Campbell's nomination, was not consulted and knew first about the changed outlook when Chandler spoke in Council meeting.

That night the Council Chamber was filled to capacity. Police guards turned away others who sought to enter.

As planned, Councilman Chandler took the initiative. After explaining that he lived on the "north side" and that his interest was in preserving Valley, he declared that he had come to conclude that the real issue, "regardless of who the Manager is," was the council-manager form of government in Valley. He emphasized that he brought little personal emotion to the situation, as he had seen neither the Manager nor the Police Chief before the previous week. Primarily he felt that the council-manager form was worth fighting for, as it was the only kind of government "capable of handling an area that is growing rapidly like Valley is." Chandler reminded the audience that he had served as Mayor in a town operating under the commission form of government, "and you wouldn't want it."

The Council's duty was reasonably clear, Chandler continued. As in a

---

[34] Chief Black says this did not happen. "An investigation by the Assistant Chief . . . showed that this was not the case. Singer's daughter had been one of several children struck on the head by books in the hands of other youngsters celebrating the last day of school. . . . This is an example of the great distortion which took place. . . ."

business, the Council held the Manager responsible for the operation of city affairs. As long as the Council had confidence in its Manager, it had the obligation to stand behind his handling of personnel matters. "The Council," he said, "approved the Manager's recommendation before—please, let's have no applause or boos—I think the Council should ratify the Manager's recommendation." He then made the formal motion endorsing the dismissal of Police Chief Black, who was in the audience with his attorney.

The new cut of the Council was indicated when Councilman Campbell, the man who had led the delegation to Singer, took the floor. Declaring his great respect for Councilman Chandler, Campbell went on to say that he too felt the Council had an obligation to back the office of City Manager, regardless of the occupant. He said he recognized the effectiveness of the Police Department's work in protecting "lives and property" in Valley. Yet, Campbell stated, "I don't believe . . . in the Chief of Police telling the Council what to do," an obvious reference to Black's oratory in the earlier hearings. "I'm sure Black is making every effort to do his best, and I believe he's a man who will probably go far—somewhere but not in Valley. . . . I'm going to second the motion." Campbell's second sealed the Police Chief's defeat. Mayor Simpson's vote would give the Singer position a three-to-two majority in the Council.

Before the vote was taken, however, Councilman Carter again stated his feeling that he wanted to keep both the Manager and the Chief. The Council had agreed to dismissal, Carter said, "only if . . . Black failed to mend his ways. So far there has been nothing but improvement," he asserted. The City Attorney again emphasized that the Carter compromise had not been satisfactory in that it neither ratified nor rejected the Manager's action.

Black's attorney then spoke. The lawyer declared that there was no need for Council action, because the Manager had not formally dismissed the Chief but had merely appointed an acting Chief. At the very least, he said, new hearings were required because of the change in the membership of the Council and the new allegations made against Black. The City Attorney responded that since personnel rules in the city were not formalized by law, it was unnecessary for the Manager to follow any specific procedure, and on the same grounds it was not required that the Council hold further hearings. Some of the conflict might have been avoided, the Attorney observed, if the dismissal steps had been spelled out in greater detail. Nevertheless, "we must operate within the framework of these laws."

In the two votes that were taken, the Singer victory was complete. First, the ratification of Black's dismissal was voted by Mayor Simpson and the two new members of the Council; then, by the same majority, the resignations of Singer and his Assistant were refused.

After the meeting, Black commented that "the city government of Valley now consists of Jack Singer."

AFTERMATH

Although the three-to-two decision of the Council marked the end of Black's tenure as Valley's Police Chief, it was almost a year before the issue— and the former Chief—receded from public attention.

Almost immediately after Black's dismissal his supporters began to organize formally a Better Government League, which was to be a "non-profit continuing citizen group." As the president of the League later said, the organization was created as a counter-balance to the "very few" who held political power. The president also said:

New people have come to our town who owe no allegiance,
social or otherwise, to the families long entrenched. A few efforts
have been made to right some of the wrongs, but they lacked the
proper organization to accomplish anything.

The incident which triggered the formation of the Better Government League was the dismissal, rehiring and again dismissal of
William Black as chief of police. It is not important whether Black
was a good or bad chief—it was the manifest injustice of the whole
thing which made a few people band together in an honest effort
to bring about a better government. Our name means exactly what
it says.

Perhaps the best-known personality in the new League was former
Mayor Crispin Lloyd, who was named Chairman of the Board. The membership of the new organization included a number of the newer residents and
some older residents who had taken the lead in circulating petitions for Black
when his dismissal had first been announced.

The core members of the group had little connection with either of the
local political party organizations. Most had taken little part in civic affairs
before. One of the members was an automobile salesman; another had a soft-
water service route. Several wives were active in the group.

The League embarked on a strenuous program to secure its first objective, "fair treatment" for Black. It retained an attorney to press the case for the
deposed Police Chief in the courts. At the attorney's suggestion, the League
also went directly to the people by circulating petitions for an initiative election on a civil service ordinance. The ordinance would have established a
standard merit system requiring formal charges and procedures for employees, whose dismissal could only be effected on specified grounds. Such
civil service protection against discharge was to be conferred on all city department heads who had been in office on May 1, 1956, the day Black's dismissal had first been raised with the Council by the City Manager. The proposed legislation would thus have the effect of putting Black back in office
and giving him the job security of civil service rules and procedures.

The ordinance proposed was one modeled after that in operation in
Bakersfield, California, whose Chief had taken a special interest in Black's
problem. He appeared before the League, explained what he considered to
be civil service advantages, and urged the League membership to push for
its adoption. However, it was two months after Black's dismissal before the
circulation of petitions finally began. Since direct legislation procedures in
California require that fifteen percent of the registered electorate sign petitions for an election on such a proposal, it was anticipated that 1,300 signatures would be needed. Later, the total registrations proved to be 10,456 and
1,569 signatures were necessary. There was hope that the required number
could be obtained quickly, inasmuch as about two months were required to
arrange for the actual election once the petitions had been certified. However, it was six months later, the middle of January, before the Better Government League finally qualified the measure for an April 2, 1957, ballot.[35]

---

[35] The *Times* published the names of all the signers and made an analysis of their
residences. "The Country Club might be considered the center of social status and
power in the community," the *Times* editor has said, "and as one moved north from that
point, the number of signers picked up from zero proportionately with the distance
traveled. There were some modest exceptions, of course, but we were very much struck
with the relationship we discovered."

Meanwhile the circulation of the petitions was not lost on the City Council. During August it had the City Manager conduct a secret poll of Valley's 204 municipal employees to find out their attitudes about the Better Government League's proposed ordinance. While the League argued that "the public should decide," the councilmen said the people most concerned were the employees themselves. The councilmen opened the ballots and found that an overwhelming majority of the 174 voting opposed the ordinance. Twenty-nine favored it. Later, a Municipal Employees Association was formed. Its Board of Directors campaigned actively against the proposed ordinance.

In the intervening months, Bill Black played an active role in the initiative campaign. Shortly after his return from a trip East, he made the first of several appearances at the Council, speaking as a "private citizen." He made several efforts to secure the election of new councilmen (to replace the three appointees). He made speeches at Council meetings for the dismissal of City Manager Singer. On one occasion he accused Singer of lying, spreading false rumors, committing felonious acts, and of incompetency. The statement was so hot that the newspapers would not print it for fear of libel. Nevertheless, the former Chief did have many of his statements published in the local press. He was by all odds the most quoted man before the April 2 election. The Manager made no statements on the election. As to the reasons Black stayed in Valley to fight, he said in statements that he did not want to be a "deserter." He continued:

> The Better Government League came into being to promote fair government for the citizens; I did not give birth to the BGL, but I have nurtured it since it came into our midst because it is the tangible expression of the minds of people for impartial government.
> A Chief of Police is a public figure; he can do things to improve a city, to help the citizens; that is the reason, and only that, for my remaining in Valley. I am not asking for benefits or privileges; I am asking for myself and the people only the rights guaranteed by the Constitution of the United States. To obtain, guard, and defend these rights, our just heritage, I have stayed in this City.

As long as Black stayed in Valley and carried much of the fight for the passage of the initiative ordinance, it was almost inevitable that opposition should center on him.[36] Two organizations were created specifically to fight the proposal. One, the April Second Committee, included three ex-Mayors in its membership and was well financed. The other, coming into battle later and playing a lesser role, was the Young Guard.

Both groups declared the issue was the former Police Chief and that the proposed ordinance was in his interest and not those of the city employees. The Chief, furthermore, was characterized as a "demagogue." In the frenzied activity, the anti-Black groups did pick up temporarily the support of Councilman Andy Carter. Friend of Black on both the critical votes in the Council, Carter said a few days before the election that he had changed his mind and was no longer on the side of the former Chief. He said Black's "wild and intemperate utterances" had demonstrated that he was "unfit to

---

[36] Many people in Valley, incidentally, felt that Black lost a great deal of community support because of his free-swinging political activity. Among these people was Councilman Rodriguez, who did not participate at all in the campaign.

lead any City Department, let alone a quasi-military organization such as the Police Department." He would vote against the ordinance, Carter declared, first, because he had no confidence in Black, and second, because "our present form of Council, City Manager government is the best for our city."

By April 2, 1957, the charges and counter-charges were flying thick and fast. Many on both sides were extreme, emotional, and provocative. But there was no question of citizen apathy. The newspapers ran thousands of inches of argument, dutifully quoting any of the principal spokesmen and printing scores of letters, the majority of which seemed to be in opposition to Black. So saturating was Valley's first experience with direct democracy that the *Times* commented on election eve that the experience had been "exhausting." Yet the newspaper also said that the consequence had been a complete discussion of the issues and "nothing like it could have been had in any other way." The editor added that the people were now "ready for the question."

The election brought the largest turnout in the city's history in a purely local contest, with 62 percent of those eligible voting. No other proposition or office was contested. The civil service initiative was defeated 4,312 votes to 3,090, with the Better Government League winning in only one of seven precincts. An analysis of the votes in the city again suggested that, in political terms, the split between the north and the south had some significance. How much of it had been caused by the election campaign and by Black's resistance was impossible to determine. At any rate, one of the north side precincts which had its polling place in a public housing project was the lone supporter of the proposition by a margin of 425 to 319. The initiative's worst defeat occurred in a distinctly south side precinct where the vote was 627 against, 108 for. Another south side precinct registered a four to one vote against, whereas the four other precincts in the city were more evenly divided.

The former Chief's own feeling was that the election occurred too late to provide any accurate index of the nature of his support at the time of dismissal. "If the election had been held within ninety days or so of my final discharge, I think I would have won. As it was, the matter dragged on, and interest and indignation deteriorated," he commented later.

The Court Fight

In the latter part of August 1956, the attorney for the Better Government League obtained a writ of mandate from the Superior Court demanding that Black be reinstated or that a proper hearing be granted. To that the city filed a demurrer. A series of lengthy court actions ended with a decision favorable to the city. Black decided in 1959 "to let the matter drop since it would cost a considerable amount of money to press it further, and, too, one of my ardent [Valley] sponsors passed away . . . her will was never found, yet I took her to her attorney so she could make some changes in it. An interesting and mysterious case well fitting into the intrigues of the community as I so well knew it."

Later Events

Manager Singer's appointee as Acting Police Chief continued in charge of the Department until the defeat of the civil service proposal provided assurance that Black would not be returned to his job. Singer then moved rapidly to select a new Chief. Again he went outside the Department, appointing a man who had been serving as Assistant Chief in a neighboring city of 50,000.

Singer said he believed the second recruitment program had yielded a better group of men. As with the Black appointment, a Screening Board was used. This time, however, the Council joined the interviewing sessions and thus participated directly in the selection of William Black's successor.

In June 1962 the new Police Chief was still serving in Valley, and so was City Manager Singer. Things were calm in the Police Department, and the Manager's record of getting along well with city employees—and almost everyone else—was more conspicuous with the passage of six more years.

The Better Government League had disappeared. Following the high point of community conflict over Black in 1956, there had been six changes on the City Council in eleven months, all vacancies being filled by appointment. Chandler became Mayor and proved to be somewhat stronger in his management of Council meetings. When the former Chief made one of his later "private citizen" appearances before the Council to read a lengthy prepared statement, Chandler, after a few minutes, gaveled for silence and told Black to file the rest of his prepared statement with the Clerk. It was the first time that Black's oratory at Council meetings or hearings had been treated this way. Occupying the seat of former Mayor Simpson was the operator of a service station "across from City Hall" who was also a director of the Chamber of Commerce, a member of a Protestant congregation, and a member of the Elks and Rotary. He had been appointed against the wishes of the Better Government League, which, making its first effort to advance a candidate for appointment, had suggested former Mayor Lloyd.

Realtor Campbell, a Rotarian like Chandler and like Simpson's successor, announced his resignation as Councilman in April 1957, after the civil service initiative proposal had gone down to defeat. Council membership had been too great a drain on his time, he said. Campbell emphasized that he was leaving the city in sound condition again and in the hands of three good men in whom he had "all the confidence in the world." Specifically omitted from his statement was the name of Councilman Joe Rodriguez.

Within a week Councilman Rodriguez submitted his resignation. Senior member of the Council by virtue of three years service, Rodriguez said that the pressures directed against him and his family had been too great. "People in Valley, and I suppose other towns as well," he observed, "tend to let a man's actions in the role of councilman influence their relationships toward him as an individual and toward his family. This creates hardship on a councilman's family and affects friendships of long standing." Shortly after his resignation, Rodriguez received a promotion. Appointed to succeed Rodriguez and Campbell were another Mexican-American and a retired resident of the north side. In April 1958 regular municipal elections were held. The Better Government League supported a slate against the appointed incumbents. Its slate was defeated by three to one. Shortly after this, the Better Government League, dwindling in size, became involved in a divisive controversy over a freeway location. By 1962 it no longer existed.

Lasting Scars

Some of the leading supporters of Black in 1956 would carry lasting scars as a result of Valley's most intense civic controversy. It was considered unlikely that the attorney who had acted for the Better Government League would ever develop a substantial practice in the city. The automobile salesman's prominent connection with the pro-Black forces apparently raised the possibility that some citizens would be less inclined to buy cars from his employer, and he lost his job and left town for a time. The pro-Black leader who operated a soft-water service route ran into difficulties at the height of the controversy when one of two south side housewives reported to his employer that they would not let such a man as he enter their homes.

Black himself reported troubles in finding another job. In May 1958 he commented: "I'd be working right now if I had signed that resignation paper at the Hollywood Knickerbocker. Chiefs who have been complete busts on their jobs and have resigned have been appointed in other cities at higher salaries. I know because I have competed against them . . . and lost. I chose to fight something I considered wrong and now no manager wants to touch me." He finally got only a six-months' temporary assignment in a California city of 10,000 to reorganize a small department. The City Manager there later praised his work highly. "He did everything I asked of him, and we had a most pleasant relationship," he said. In 1959 Black accepted a professorship of police science at a state college in the west.

By June 1962 Valley's turbulent days seemed far away. But many leading citizens of Valley still shuddered when they recalled the 1956 controversy about Chief Black. Even to men who had not been strongly active on either side, it seemed in retrospect as if the community and its government had been threatened with disintegration by the intensity of the fight and by the nature of the charges and counter-charges. People who had lived together and accepted one another for years had begun to look at one another with hostility and suspicion, it was claimed. Even the small, comradely reportorial staff of the *Times* had felt the impact of the community's split on the issue, some reporters treating others with the reserve necessary when associating with a member of an enemy force.

Some citizens maintained that the editor and publisher of the *Times* had also felt the whip of public indignation from the affair that the newspaper had had a hand in creating. Originally "playing" the controversy for all it was worth in news value, the *Times* had drawn increasing criticism from the pro-Manager side for irresponsibly encouraging a bitter community dispute that at times had seemed about to lead to outbreaks of violence. The newspaper's treatment of the later phases of the matter had been more subdued, and some former councilmen said in 1962 that the editor and publisher had never since sought to whip up unnecessary controversy about governmental affairs.

City Manager Singer believed that some of the leading citizens of Valley had also learned something from the Black controversy—something about the cost of keeping silent on controversial public questions and letting the Manager and the Council bear alone the brunt of running the government. Singer reported in 1962:

> The Chamber of Commerce is now working in active cooperation with the City Council and the City administration, and has stated to the public several times that it would never again allow such a thing to happen in this community. It would stand in support of the City and the administration to prevent a recurrence.

3

PLANNING:

Coordination for Tomorrow

Planning, Long-Range:
A Happening

Planning is best handled by the boss and
his key men (*see* Marketing, for how).

Once I was asked to head up a new long-range planning effort. My
wife listened to my glowing description of my new job. Next evening she blew the whole schmeer out of the water by asking:
"What did you plan today, dear?" Bless her.[1]

In this chapter we emphasize *planning* rather than the resultant
plan. In other words, we are primarily concerned with the process—
not the output. Few would doubt the central nature of planning to the
management of an organization. Ample evidence—theoretical and
practical—is available to show just how vitally important planning is
to the overall success of an organization. Of the many authorities who
have offered witness to the significance of the planning process, Gardner is clearly an advocate. He writes:

[1] Robert Townsend, *Up the Organization* (New York: Alfred A. Knopf, Inc., 1970),
p. 146.

> Every individual, organization or society must mature, but
> much depends on how this maturing takes place. A society whose
> maturing consists simply of acquiring more firmly established
> ways of doing things is headed for the graveyard—even if it learns
> to do these things with greater and greater skill. In the ever-re-
> newing society (or police department) what matures is a system or
> framework within which continuous innovation, renewal and re-
> birth can occur.[2]

Contained in the above statement is a partial reason or purpose for planning, "continuous innovation, renewal and rebirth" of individuals and organizations—in our case *police organizations*. We would add a second part to complete the primary purpose of this management process—*the continuous innovation, renewal, and rebirth of individuals and organizations in order to more effectively accomplish their goals.*

Let us reflect for a few moments on some of the early and not so early writings about planning. First, Sun Tzu wrote in approximately 500 B.C.:

> Now the general who wins a battle *makes many calculations in
> his temple ere the battle is fought.* The general who loses a bat-
> tle makes few calculations before hand. It is by attention to this
> point that I can see who is likely to win or lose.[3]

Second, and more plainly stated, is the following writing by Cyrus in early Greece:

> ... not to adopt such plans only as you have been taught, but to be
> yourself a *contriver of stratagems* ...[4]

Similarly on planning we should remember his statement:

> Consider at night what your men shall do when it is day; and
> consider in the day how matters may be best settled for the night.[5]

With due regard for space, we jump many centuries to the eighteenth where the value of careful and explicit planning began to be recognized. Although the industrialists of the era did not seem to realize the extent to which planning could be utilized and did not attempt to plan the details of company and office operations as is often done to-

[2]John W. Gardner, *Self-Renewal: The Individual and the Innovative Society* (New York: Harper & Row, Publishers, 1963), p. 5.

[3]Thomas P. Philips, *Roots of Strategy* (Harrisburg, Pa.: Military Service Publishing Co., 1955), p. 23.

[4]J. S. Watson and Henry Dale, trans., *Xenophon's Cyropaedia and the Hellenics* (London: G. Bell & Sons, Ltd., 1898), p. 42.

[5]*Ibid.*

day, at least two planning techniques were successfully used in this period which remain among the most productive: plant location and payback computations. As early as 1759 we find clear evidence of location planning in the Carron Ironworks in Scotland, where "everything, even the site, was planned with a view to the greatest efficiencies of production and transportation in the smelting and casting of iron."[6] Adam Smith, understanding the need for payback computations, outlined a method for their application in machine acquisition and replacement. His explanation was that "when any expensive machine is erected, the extraordinary work to be performed by it before it is worn out, it must be expected, will replace the capital laid out upon it, with at least the ordinary profits."[7]

It was also during the eighteenth century that of the five generally accepted functions of management at that time (planning, organizing, staffing, directing, and controlling), several economists began to consider planning as the most important. Laughlin gives the reasoning behind this when he says:

> He who controls a large capital actively engaged in production can never remain at a standstill; he must be full of new ideas; he must have power to initiate new schemes for the extension of his market; he must have judgment to adopt new inventions, and yet not to be deceived as to their value and efficiency.[8]

Some of you might enjoy paraphrasing the above quotation to fit your particular organization. For example, substitute the words *public activity* for "capital," *law enforcement* for "production," and *service* for "market." The Prussian General Carl von Clausewitz appeared to concur with this thinking, since he stressed that careful planning was a necessity for the managing of a large organization, with the first requisite being to define one's goals.[9] Note the last term in the preceding sentence—*goals*. For the general was quick to point out the explicit relationship between planning and an organization's goals. He also emphasized that all decisions must be based on probability, not on logical necessity, as commonly believed at the time. Of course, his idea of probability was not as detailed as our current statistical probability, but the theory of trying to prepare best for what might

---

[6] Frederick C. Dietz, *An Economic History of England* (New York: Henry Holt and Company, 1942), p. 34.

[7] Adam Smith, *An Inquiry into the Nature and Causes of the Wealth of Nations* (London: A. Strahan and T. Cadell, 1793), III, 154.

[8] J. Lawrence Laughlin, *The Elements of Political Economy* (New York: American Book Company, 1896), p. 223.

[9] For details on his concepts of management, see especially Carl von Clausewitz, *On War* (New York: Barnes & Noble, Inc., n.d.); and *Principles of War* (Harrisburg, Pa.: Military Service Publishing Co., 1832).

happen is the same. Of all his pronouncements, perhaps Clausewitz's major contribution to management was that managers should accept uncertainty and act on the basis of thorough analysis and planning designed to minimize this uncertainty.

Finally, it is time that we view the twentieth century and planning as it specifically relates to the police department. Obviously the vast majority of contemporary police managers are in support of more and better planning. Paradoxically, however, of the hundreds of pages comprising the Crime Commission's *Task Force Report: The Police*, only two dealt with police planning.

> There are two vital needs of police departments which can be served by areawide, coordinated planning. One is crime and modus operandi analysis, which calls for areawide planning because of the regional nature of certain crimes and criminal activity. The other assistance on administrative and operational matters, in which many small departments lack competence and facilities. Both are functions which should be performed on a metropolitan or statewide basis.
>
> Crime analysis is a planning function regardless of the organizational unit in which it is placed. The primary purpose of crime analysis is to study daily reports of serious crimes in order to determine the location, time, special characteristics, similarities to other criminal attacks, and various significant facts that may help to identify either a criminal or the existence of a pattern of criminal activity.
>
> Modus operandi, or method of operation, refers to the criminal's individual peculiarities—his methods, techniques, and the tools he uses in the commission of a crime. Modus operandi analysis is concerned primarily with persons, whereas crime analysis relates principally to events although they are interrelated.
>
> Sound police organization and procedures depend upon good planning. Frequently, the emergency nature of police work and the constant attention that must be given to day-to-day operations do not leave enough time for effective planning. Much planning is done daily in all police operations, but, primarily, it is to serve an immediate need. Most police administrators seek to improve their organizations, but many do not know how or do not have enough time to correct deficiencies in organization and faulty procedures.[10]

While somewhat disappointing, the quotation does provide additional weight—this time by police authorities—to the rapidly rising awareness of the critical organizational requirement for an adequate planning process in local law enforcement. The police are not alone in their recognized absence of a planning mechanism because, in general, organizations engage in opportunistic decision making rather

[10] The President's Commission on Law Enforcement and Administration of Justice, *Task Force Report: The Police* (Washington, D.C.: Government Printing Office, 1967), pp. 77–78.

than in planning: rather than explain courses of action that will lead the way to the attainment of their goals (and in some cases identify new goals), they extemporize, handling each crisis as it emerges. Thus the challenge becomes all the more obvious—the police need a process (planning) for generating, on a continual basis, *plans*.

The remaining sections of the chapter cover the following topics. Based on the logical connection between planning and organizational goals, we first turn to an examination of the goals of our local police department, keeping in mind that it is the goals of an organization that underpin any rationale for planning. Second, we will discuss the part (role) that the manager plays in the planning process. Also in this section is a short review of the interdependency existing in planning, plans, and policy formation. Third, we will describe one of many structural techniques (as compared with scientific or functional) to enhance the quality and quantity of the end product—a plan(s). Finally, the reader will experience a learning exercise that constitutes a "plan" for planning. More will be said later about the extent and content of the exercise. Let us proceed with our analysis of the goals of a police organization.

GOALS: A FUTURE DESIRED STATE OF AFFAIRS

The managerial role of planning is one of identifying the organizational goals and then creating the policies, programs, procedures, and methods for achieving them. The planning role is essentially one of providing a framework or mechanism for integrated decision making in terms of keeping the organization pliable (yielding to constant renewal and change) and viable (striving toward goal accomplishment).

GOALS: IN A GENERAL SENSE

The goals of an organization serve many uses. Etzioni asserts that

they provide orientation by depicting a future state of affairs which the organization strives to realize. Thus they set down guide lines for organizational activity. Goals also constitute a source of legitimacy which justifies the activities of an organization and, indeed, its very existence. Moreover goals serve as standards by which members of an organization and outsiders can assess the success of the organization—i.e., its effectiveness and efficiency. Goals also serve in a similar fashion as measuring rods for the student of organizations who tries to determine how well the organization is doing.[11]

The fundamental reason for an organization's existence lies in its

[11] Amitai Etzioni, *Modern Organizations* (Englewood Cliffs, N.J.: Prentice-Hall, Inc., 1964), p. 5.

goals. Although once the goals are decided upon, organizations frequently generate unforeseen needs (for example, providing job satisfaction to their employees in order to retain them). In such instances, organizations usually reduce their attention on their primary goals in order to handle their acquired needs. At times organizations go so far as to abandon their initial goals and pursue new ones more suited to the organizations' needs. We will return to this and other problems concerning goals in a few moments. First, let us look at what organizational goals are, how they come into being, and their benefits.[12]

What is a goal? "An organizational goal is a desired state of affairs which the organization attempts to realize."[13] The organization may or may not be able to create this hoped-for image of the future. For example, it is very unlikely that our American police system will ever be able to attain its principal goal of maintaining social order at all times. But if a goal is attained, it ceases to be a guiding image for an organization and is either dismissed or replaced with another. Actually, a goal never exists; it is a state that we seek, not one we have. We should distinguish between *real* and *stated* goals. At times they are one and the same, but we are often able to detect that an organization is moving in a direction different from that expressed as its goal. The reasons for this vary from a lack of awareness that this is happening to hiding the real goal so that it can be more easily achieved. The real goals of an organization are those future states toward which a majority of the organization's resources are committed, as compared with those that are stated but receive fewer resources. The distinction between real and stated goals is crucial because they should not be confused with the important difference between intended and unintended consequences. Real goals are always intended. Stated goals can be intended or not.

How are goals derived? All formal organizations have recognized, usually legally specified, means for creating goals and also for changing them. Regardless of the formal means, in practice goals are usually established in a complicated power play involving (1) organizational subdivisions (groups), (2) individuals, and (3) environmental influences. The outcome of the three-cornered power play provides direction for (1) sharpening and clarifying goals, (2) adding new goals, (3) shifting priorities among goals, and (4) eliminating irrelevant goals. In summary, goal formation is the result of policy making. Policy making involves planning which, in turn, draws upon numerous decision centers in order to reach the final choice—in this case, which organizational goals to retain or modify.

What are the benefits of goals to an organization? We can list

---

[12] Most of the remainder of this section on organization goals is taken from Paul M. Whisenand, *Police Supervision: Theory and Practice* (Englewood Cliffs, N.J.: Prentice-Hall, Inc., 1971), pp. 73–79.

[13] *Ibid.*, p. 6.

the primary benefits of a goal or a set of goals as providing a vehicle for—

1. Presenting the general purpose and ideology of the organization,
2. Guiding and supporting organizational decision making,
3. Developing and maintaining a useful information system,
4. Performing the control function,
5. Motivating the people in the organization,
6. Delegating responsibility,
7. Integrating the activities between the operating subunits within the organization, and
8. *Targeting the planning process.*

Let us continue with a discussion of multiple goals, goal displacement, and goal succession. First, most organizations have *multiple goals*. Argyris's "Mix Model" defines one of the essential properties of organization as "the achievement of goals or objectives."[14] As an illustration, besides apprehending offenders, the police also act to prevent offenses. Interestingly, the latter goal seeks to make the former unnecessary. One final comment in regard to multiple goals—organizations that serve more than a single goal do so more effectively than single-purpose organizations of the same category. The reasons for this are twofold: (1) serving one goal often increases the achievement of another goal, and (2) there is a much improved recruitment appeal because the nature of the work provides more variety and, therefore, enhanced job satisfaction.

Second, with respect to *goal displacement* we find that the attainment of a goal or goals is vastly increased when goal displacement is kept at a minimum.[15] Briefly, goal displacement happens when an organization substitutes for its legitimate goal some other goal for which resources were not allocated, and which it is not known to serve. Since goal displacement is injurious to the effectiveness of an organization, what can be done to avoid it? Making the goals more tangible is the simple answer, for goal displacement is minimized when goals are tangible. Gross, however, takes exception to the importance of goal tangibility in his "Clarity-Vagueness Balance" when he writes that

> there is no need to labor the need for clarity in the formulation of
> an organization's objectives. Precise formulations are necessary
> for delicate operations. They provide the indispensable frame-
> work for coordinating complex activity . . . yet in the wide enthu-

[14]Chris Argyris, *Integrating the Individual and the Organization* (New York: John Wiley & Sons, Inc., 1964), p. 150.

[15]*Ibid.*

siasm for "crystal-clear goals," one may easily lose sight of the
need for a fruitful balance between clarity and vagueness. . . .[16]

Gross again supports the merit of vagueness by writing:

> If all points on a set of interrelated purpose chains were to be
> set forth with precise clarity, the result would be to destroy the
> subordination of one element to another which is essential to an
> operating purpose pattern. The proper focusing of attention on
> some goals for any particular moment or period in time means that
> other goals must be left vague. This is even truer for different pe-
> riods of time. We must be very clear about many things we aim to
> do today and tomorrow. It might be dangerously misleading to
> seek similar clarity for our long-range goals.[17]

Gross's thinking leaves us in somewhat of a quandary. Should we
create tangible goals in order to better accomplish them or vague
goals in order to be more flexible? The solution to this apparent dilemma is not perfectly clear. Perhaps it lies in better and more frequent organizational analysis—if an organization will subject its
goals to periodic study and evaluation, the opportunity for changing
them is improved. Hence, the necessity of vagueness becomes less
because the tangible goals are kept updated and relevant through the
planning process. At the same time, the overall mission or philosophy
of an organization can remain vague to facilitate adaptation and innovation. For example, the police philosophy "to protect and serve"
leaves considerable room for creating and changing the more tangible
goals of a police department.

Third, not only do modern organizations usually have multiple
goals and experience goal displacement, but they also tend to find
new goals when the traditional ones have been attained or cannot
be attained. This latter tendency on the part of an organization is
known as goal succession. Therefore, *goal succession* is the replacement of a goal or goals with another goal or goals, or merely the acquisition of new goals. The police organization is a case in point. To the
more traditional goals of arresting and recovering stolen property
have been added those of maintaining public order. Initially, the
newer goals, and this holds true for the police, are justified in that they
improve the accomplishment of the traditional goals, but they often
become equal in importance. We have arrived at a point where it
appears appropriate to focus the discussion of goals on those of police
organizations.

[16] Bertram M. Gross, "What Are Your Organization's Objectives: A General Systems Approach to Planning," *Human Relations*, 18 (August 1965), 213.

[17] Bertram M. Gross, *The Managing of Organizations* (New York: The Free Press
of Glencoe, 1964), p. 497.

GOALS: IN A POLICE SENSE

We can draw from any number of sources for a list of police goals. Most listings contain a strong orientation toward law and enforcement. We approach the police organization as having three basic goals:

    Law enforcement
    Order maintenance
    General government services

Evidently the police are actually functioning in three related but different ways. The manager is directly involved in the planning for all three.

Law enforcement is clearly the more venerable goal of our policing agencies. In attempting to meet this goal, the police play an integral part—along with the prosecutors, the probation departments, the courts, the parole agencies, and the correctional organizations—in the operation of the criminal justice system. At this point you should note that the police are members of two governmental systems: (1) local government—fire, finance, recreation, personnel, etc., and (2) criminal justice—prosecution, probation, etc.) As the front-end agency in the criminal justice system, the primary responsibility of the police is to initiate criminal action against those who violate the law. This responsibility is well defined by statutes and court decisions and is subject to strict departmental controls. In the fulfillment of this goal, police officers must arrest offenders, recover stolen property, prevent criminal acts, and handle civil disorders.

By *order maintenance* we mean the handling of disputes (or behavior that tends to produce disputes) among people who disagree on what is morally right, misconduct, or assignment of blame in a situation. A family quarrel, a street disturbance by teen-agers, and a disagreement in a tavern exemplify community problems that require police intervention. The police are called upon to maintain order (keep the peace) without making an arrest. They must resolve human conflict—a task all of us realize is not easy. First of all, when a policeman intervenes, someone is likely to feel wronged, outraged, or neglected. Though a law may have been broken, as in a husband's assault on his wife, the policeman cannot simply compare a particular behavior with a clear legal standard and then make an arrest if the standard has been violated. For one thing, the legal rule is vague in many order-maintenance cases. "Breach of peace" implies a prior definition of "peace"—a matter on which people commonly disagree. For another thing, even when the legal standard is clear enough, as in an assault, the "victim" is often not innocent (indeed, he may have called for the police because he was losing a fight he started). Thus the question of "blame" may be more important to the participants than the question of "guilt," and they will expect the officer to take this into account. Second, most order-maintenance situations do not result in an arrest; the people involved want the officer to do something that will solve the problem, but they do not want that solution to be an arrest. Third, if there is an offense, it is likely to be a misdemeanor, and thus in most instances the patrolman cannot make an arrest unless the illegality was committed in his presence or unless the victim is willing to sign a complaint. As a result, the officer cannot expect a judge to dispose of the case; he himself must decide on a solution that will make order out of disorder. In due regard for the complexities surrounding order maintenance, Tamm states:

> But the social climate of our times has immensely broadened this concept to where the police find themselves the arbiter between rival social factions, where they find themselves involved in the most delicate problems of human relations in the rapidly changing social structure of our modern society. It is no exaggeration to say that the type of duties normally performed by social workers occupy as much as fifty percent of the long day of both police administrators and line officers.
>
> To meet these demands requires abilities, training, and understanding far beyond what was ever conceived as necessary police characteristics in the not-too-distant past. Today any plan of action must be carefully considered from the standpoint of the human factors involved. . . .
>
> Most police executives recognize this problem and are actively eliminating the basic cause through increased emphasis on sociological training and developing expertise in human relations among the personnel under their supervision.[18]

And according to former Los Angeles Police Chief Thomas Reddin:

> Times change and we must change with time. The policeman of the future will be more effective and will function at a more personal level than in the past. He will be much more sociologist, psychologist, and scientist than his present-day counterpart. He will have many more scientific and technological aids to assist him.
>
> In short, he will utilize space-age techniques of the physical sciences coupled with a type of police work that draws upon the best lessons learned from the social scientists.[19]

The third and final goal—the provision of *general government services*—includes everything else that the police department is asked to do by its clientele. Its personnel must abate nuisances, con-

---

[18] Quinn Tamm, *The Police Chief*, 33 (November 1966), 6.

[19] Tom Reddin, "The Police, the People, the Future," *Los Angeles Times*, May 19, 1968, Sec. G, p. 4.

trol traffic and crowds, administer first aid, furnish information, and provide a wide range of other miscellaneous services.[20]

In summary, when relating the goals of a police organization to the two systems that it belongs to we find the following:[21]

Law Enforcement ⟶	Criminal Justice System
Order Maintenance ⟶	Criminal Justice System +
General Government Services ⟶	Local Government System

Of the three goals, which is most important? We will let you, the reader, argue which is more vital. Keep in mind, however, that all three are being served at present. Hence, all three must be *planned for* irrespective of how the argument goes.

THE ROLE OF A PLANNER: ACTIVITIES, POLICY FORMATION, AND PROBLEMS

To generate an individual and a collective climate conducive to cooperative participation, every police manager must perform several recognizable roles. He must, for example, decide what the goals of the department are, how they should be accomplished, and when plans should be implemented. Making these decisions involves a conceptual look at needed future action—be it tomorrow or five years from now. It thus requires looking ahead, conceptualizing about the future, and planning today so as to adequately meet the future.

Obviously, planning is, in most instances, not a separate recognizable function. It is usually interlaced with other managerial activities. A police manager does not typically give a directive by mere impulse or reflex. On the contrary, even a casually written or oral communication about needed action may well involve some planning along with the message itself. To reemphasize, *every managerial act, mental or physical*, is inexorably intertwined with planning. Although we are able to conceptually separate planning for the purpose of theoretical discussion and analysis, we must remember that in practice it is neither a distinct nor a separable entity. For analysis, let us theoretically extricate the managerial planning function from the others to see how it is involved in the managing of a police department.

Planning, as a conceptually separate managerial role, consists of looking ahead, "systematically" predicting, and anticipating probable future events and the actions needed to cope with them. Planning may result in nothing more than a simple plan for police employee vacations next year in relation to the variations in the probable

[20] People are increasingly referring to the police as a service agency. See Thomas E. Bereal, "Calls for Police Assistance," *American Behavioral Scientist*, 13 (May-June and July-August 1970), 681–91.

[21] Herman Goldstein, "Police Response to Urban Crisis," *Public Administration Review*, 28 (September-October 1968), 420.

workload, or it may produce a plan of action to reduce stranger-to-stranger crime and thus minimize the impact of criminal activity eighteen months hence. Whatever the area of consideration, police managers in the performance of the planning function systematically analyze the problem in light of probable future events and therefore make decisions *now* in order to deal more effectively with a constantly changing environment.

Before discussing some of the problems that are currently harassing the full utilization of a planning vehicle, it seems best to provide a definition to what *we* mean by *planning*. A *plan* (the output of planning) is a rational decision with regard to a course of action. The rational selection of a course of action, that is, the making of a rational plan, includes basically the same procedures as those of any rational decision: Most, and if possible all, the courses of action must be identified, the consequences of each course must be predicted, and the courses having the preferred consequences must be selected.[22] Hence the planning process is comprised of the following activities:

> Analysis of the situation (problem identification)
> Goal setting (desired future state of affairs)
> Design of courses of action (alternative approaches to goal attainment)
> Comparative evaluation of consequences (predicting the result of each alternative)
> Final selection of course of action (decision making)

It should be recognized that each of these activities is not only interrelated but actually overlaps the others. Also, all the activities can vary as to the type and the number of scientific tools employed. For example, an analysis of the situation might well include such scientific methods as operations research, mathematical modeling, survey research, and DELPHI and statistical inferences. The enormous data processing power of a computer can also be used in support of these methods. Now—what is planning? *Planning is a dynamic process that involves a number of activities and methods for generating plans that provide an organization with sustained renewal and change in terms of more effective goal accomplishment.*

A basic problem for police organizations in urban America concerns their policy with respect to planning. Police agencies, once past a critical point in the accumulation of sufficient resources, have grown at an ever-accelerating pace. Through their development, services not available to our citizens a half century ago have become necessities for American society. Police services move in many directions: toward improving the physical security of life, toward restoring peace,

---

[22] An excellent discussion of the relationship between decision making and planning can be found in Amitai Etzioni, "Mixed Scanning—A Systems Approach," *Public Administration Review*, 26 (January-February 1969), 3–15.

toward solving community problems, and toward bettering the quality of life. And the rapidity of societal and technological change, and the diversity of existing and potential police services, put a premium upon the anticipation and direction of these changes through systematic planning. "Any (police) organization which does not have a four-, or five-, or ten-year plan is risking destruction or a series of continuing crises in its operations."[23]

The planning process can be operated through two auxiliary or staff functions, one to develop specific alternative courses of action for anticipated changes in the environment, the other to gather predictive indicators about community changes and reactions to police programs. Both these functions are generally combined in a single staff group or an endeavor to the great neglect of the indicator function. Guesswork replaces exact knowledge of community trends. The planless extreme is currently illustrated by those universities which lack a planning staff and have been overwhelmed by the tremendous increase in demand for their services (trends that everyone knew about but were not anticipated in building or staffing programs). Many other city departments have been in the same situation, and have not planned for zoning, traffic, water, and sewage services. They are now paying the price for the old policy of day-to-day opportunism —the police are not alone in their lack of planning and plans!

Once the policy question has been answered affirmatively—that is, that there will be in fact a planning process—still another automatically arises. The police manager is confronted with a decision about the levels of detail and comprehensiveness that the planning process should include in the plan(s). In this case, the manager must rely on the process itself to generate significant plans. Hence, the planning process should be capable of handling various levels of complexity and scope. In other words, from the very narrow and highly detailed plans, the process ought to be able to produce those of a broad and general nature. A plan that is overly narrow, or overly broad, frequently fails to meet its intended objectives. Of the two failings, inappropriate broadness is the more common. Such grandiose but impractical plans are actually a *very* common phenomenon, particularly among managers entrusted with long-range planning. For example, "city planners are notorious for designing master plans that call for absurdly unrealistic behavior on the part of other agents (such as massive expenditures on parks and nearly perfect law enforcement)."[24] Downs refers to this too broad approach as the *superman syndrome*.

[23] Daniel Katz and Robert L. Kahn, *The Social Psychology of Organizations* (New York: John Wiley & Sons, Inc., 1966), p. 272.

[24] Anthony Downs, *Inside Bureaucracy* (Boston: Little, Brown and Company, 1967), p. 218.

All managers engaged in planning process actions have some incentive for indulging in the superman syndrome. It is much easier to make theoretical assumptions about how others will behave than to negotiate with them and base plans upon what they are actually likely to do. In theory, every manager can assume that others will perform their functions and responsibilities in the way he himself regards as most efficient. The actual behavior of these people, however, will be heavily influenced by their views of what is efficient as well as by self-interest. Both of these elements are often difficult to foresee. Superman planning is intellectually more satisfying than realistic planning. Unfettered by reality, planners can develop far more original, daring, sweeping, and internally consistent visions of what should be done than if they actually have to deal with the disenchantment of conflicting interests in the real world. The superman plans produced by a police department often serve specific functions as targets or aspirations that are in fact unattainable (at least in the time proposed) but nevertheless provide utility to their beholders. For example, planning for the use of a helicopter in routine patrol operations normally contains a statement in the plan that crime *will* decrease by a significant percentage. For the above reasons, superman planning is the great temptation of all managers faced by the immense complexities of attempting to design appropriate maneuvers in policy space. They tend to yield to this temptation in direct proportion to the breadth of their operations and the absence of restraints forcing them to create realistic plans.

Planning for Planning

Although all the managerial functions are interrelated and the police manager performs each at one time or another, any given phase of organizational activity must begin with planning. As mentioned earlier, planning is the process by which the police department adapts it resources to changing environmental forces and achieves its goals. It is a highly dynamic function and must be carried out effectively so as to provide a *solid* foundation for the remaining managerial activities. The planning function in the police organization can be considered as an integrated decision system which establishes the framework for the activities of the organization.[25] It is the responsibility of management planning to plan an integrated planning system that will enhance organizational performance. In other words, planning for planning.

Managers on all levels of the police organization are engaged in

[25] Such a system is described in Sherman C. Blumenthal, *Management Information Systems: A Framework for Planning and Development* (Englewood Cliffs, N.J.: Prentice-Hall, Inc., 1969).

all the basic functions of the management process. As the police manager moves up the organizational structure, however, he will or should spend relatively more of his time planning, as compared with other managerial functions. At the upper levels there is also an increased amount of time spent on planning for various time periods in the future. Upper management not only should devote most of its time to planning but must be dedicated to the creation of processes for long-range plans. It is the manager's responsibility to define the desired role of the organization in the future, to relate the organization to its environment, and to perceive the goals that the organization can fulfill. No one else within the police department is equipped to define the desired role of the department. Together with an internal definition must come an external one that is derived from the city management, the community, and the related criminal justice organizations. The character of the agency must be established, and its goals must be set forth explicitly as guidelines to decision making throughout the entire police organization. Clear statements of expectations, along with both external and internal premises for planning, help focus the effort of all police personnel toward common objectives. The outcome of effective planning is accurate decision making throughout the department.

In regard to planning, first, the manager must refrain from treating it as an entity in itself. Planning should be geared to obtaining, translating, understanding, and communicating information that will improve the rationality of current decisions that are based upon future expectations. Expectations are developed through the process of forecasting and predicting the future. Much effort is being devoted to refining predictive techniques to enable police departments to forecast their social, political, legislative, and tactical environment. Police agencies are becoming more interested in broad environmental data such as social indicators and are relating departmental services to the overall social community outlook. Second, the police manager must also refrain from acting as if forecasting were planning. While forecasting provides a basis for understanding and formulating expectations, management must go beyond this orientation stage by developing and implementing action plans designed to optimize the department's total performance. Since these plans themselves may alter the future—not only of the department but of the total environment—forecasts, no matter how rigorously developed, are not completely significant. The impact of any forecast resides in its insertion into an *action plan* that is *implemented*.

Three levels of plan. The selected planning process should be capable of generating plans that are targeted toward three levels of complexity:

The environmental plan—sets forth the broad social, cultural, political and legislative parameters in which the department must operate

The tactical plan—describes the service demands, criminal justice relationships, and agency-clientele relationships for the particular community in which the department operates.

The internal organization plan—indicates the organizational structure, objectives and policies, and functional relationships which distinguish one department from all others.

PLANNING TEAMS: EXPLOITING THE POTENTIAL FOR IMPACT AND QUALITY

Depending on the size and structure of the department, management first divides itself into a number of planning teams. Let us assume that there are three such teams: Uniform Investigation (UI), Sustaining Activities (SA), or staff, and General Management (GM). The GM team is the top team and provides overall coordination and direction for the others. One or more of the members on the GM team also serve on one of the other teams. Thus, there is overlapping membership, which tends to facilitate coordination and communication. It is the job of the GM team representative to aid the members of one of the three teams in organizing themselves, in acquiring the skills necessary to create and maintain a planning process, and in supporting them in their attempts to implement the resultant plans. In essence, the GM team member eventually acts as a stimulus and conversion quarterback. The UI and SA teams contain a number of middle managers and supervisors who represent the total divisional membership. Considerable rotation among the members ought to occur so that fresh ideas are constantly inserted into the process. The planning and research unit should be given the responsibility for facilitating, researching, developing, and implementing the ideas of the teams. Thus this unit acts as staff to the planning teams.

The actual work of planning teams cannot be defined specifically until the divisions of this particular department are marked out and clearly identified. A design that would be optimal for policing an urban center, for example, is likely to be far different from that for a rural area. *Each organization has its own character, its own problems, its unique potential.* Despite these differences, planning teams concentrate on elements that must be included in any planning process.

The planning teams are to be evaluated according to their output—*plans*. If the plan is viable and implemented, then one can assume that the processes being used by the teams are sound. Broadly speaking, the plans and the processes that they represent can be judged as follows:

Excellent—rigorous logic is being applied and has resulted in a written description of a generalized plan and of specific action plans; they are widely understood and supported and have strongly influenced both effectiveness and development, as they are revised on a scheduled basis.

Average—a strategic plan exists in that the character of the agency and the broad outlines of its probable growth are understood; it has not been evaluated against criteria of rigorous logic; there is no scheduled basis for plan review, though review of police operations and results does occur.

Unacceptable—there is no plan to set the character or the direction of the agency; the department's operations are best pictured as evolving from tradition or as responses to community conditions in an opportunistic way.

To repeat, "good planning is a part of good management."[26]

LEARNING EXERCISE

The following learning exercise is actually a grant application recently submitted by the Los Angeles Sheriff's Department (LASD) to a funding agency. Its intent is quite clear and its argument very cogent. An award is being requested in order that a planning process —a process for constant renewal and planned change—can be built and subsequently maintained. It furnishes the reader with a proposal design and suggested framework for creating such a process. By the time this text is in print, the process will perhaps be a reality. (As of this writing, the grant has been made to the LASD and by 1974 a long-range planning capability will be in existence.)

APPLICATION TO CALIFORNIA COUNCIL ON CRIMINAL JUSTICE: A GRANT TO DEVELOP THE LAW ENFORCEMENT LONG-RANGE PLANNING PROJECT

Peter J. Pitchess

I. PROJECT SUMMARY

The ability of American law enforcement to perform its responsibilities well is a function of executive ability to make appropriate and accurate long-range decisions.[27] This process requires the availability of the best possible

---

[26]Thomas H. Roberts, "How to Strengthen the Planning-Management Team," *Public Management*, 51 (December 1969), 12.

[27]Permission to use the grant proposal was provided by Peter J. Pitchess, sheriff, Los Angeles County, California.

knowledge about the consequences of allocative decisions which often commit vital public resources for many years to come. To perform his responsibilites well, the administrator must have the capacity to measure the operational results of police managerial decisions against expectations of effectiveness through systematic feed-back.

The Los Angeles County Sheriff's Department proposes in this application to come to grips with the planning problem as it prepares to meet demands of a new decade. There is no doubt that demands for public safety services, many of which are provided by the Department and which are only minimally related to law enforcement, will continue to rise at an even greater rate than they have during the last decade.

The ability to identify problems, define goal priorities, and allocate needed resources of law enforcement in an urban environment as diverse and complex as Los Angeles County involves careful and thoughtful planning. In Los Angeles County, with a total population of nearly eight million, a major share of this planning naturally falls upon the Sheriff's Department as a direct responsibility. The Department therefore seeks to prepare itself functionally, procedurally, organizationally, and behaviorally to meet law enforcement problems of the future. In terms of economic and demographic growth, Los Angeles County represents one of the most important urban concentrations in the country. A failure by law enforcement to anticipate and prepare for the effects of this growth would cause a crisis of national proportions.

The purpose of this project is to design, demonstrate, and evaluate a prototypical long-range planning process in the Los Angeles County Sheriff's Department which will enable it to make long-range decisions with an improved knowledge of the future effects of such decisions.

Important project benefits will include:

Development and description of a comprehensive goal set for the Department.

Identification and consideration of environmental factors which may impact upon its missions and roles.

Examination and evaluation of current and prospective, automated or manual information systems insofar as they support planning activities.

Demonstration of an advanced staff activity unique to contemporary law enforcement.

Comprehensive project documentation which will of itself form a significant contribution to the law enforcement literature.

To develop this ability the Department intends to seek the assistance of a contractor experienced in sophisticated management analysis and planning technology to function as an integral part of a joint project team which will develop and demonstrate a comprehensive process for Long-Range Planning in a law enforcement setting.

II. PROBLEM BACKGROUND

The ability of a Police Department to estimate and meet demands for services placed upon it in the future is increasingly dependent upon its capacity to plan effectively in the present. In common with other law enforcement agencies throughout the country, the Los Angeles Sheriff's Department has been seeking to provide services in the face of a dilemma which underlies

all American police activities, that of satisfying simultaneously the requirements for maintenance of order and enforcement of law. This dilemma is as
much a planning problem as it is a bureaucratic problem. As one writer
expresses it:

> Policymaking for the police is complicated by the fact that, at
> least in large cities, the police department is an organization with
> at least two objectives (maintenance of order and enforcement of
> the law), one of which produces conflict and the other of which
> cannot be attained. The dilemma facing police administrators
> arise(s) out of their inability to obtain agreement on what consti-
> tutes satisfactory performance of the first objective, and their dif-
> ficulty in finding a strategy which would permit realization of the
> second.[28]

The difficulty in satisfying simultaneously the requirements for meeting
these two objectives is a planning problem that must no longer be ignored.

Within Los Angeles County, the Sheriff's Department supplies contract
law enforcement services to twenty-nine incorporated cities in addition to
services provided to the entire population remaining under its general con-
stitutional jurisdiction. The Department therefore plays a major role as an
integral part of the County Criminal Justice System, the effectiveness of
which depends in large measure on the quality of planning in the Sheriff's
Department and the extent to which this reinforces the planning of the other
criminal justice agencies.

Organizing a planning process adequate to satisfy this dilemma is not
a simple matter. It is constrained by a natural subservience to the past. Almost all criminal justice activities are based on traditional, time-proven assumptions, concepts and methods. Current Department planning is often
nothing more than a linear extrapolation of operational data gathered and
classified according to the tenets of an unchanging *modus operandi* and an
unchanging organization. Nevertheless, these tenets are applied to a dynamic
environment that *is* changing and growing and of necessity should be continually re-examined.

This project will develop a set of procedures enabling the Department
to cope with its changing environment and in particular to interface more
effectively with companion agencies in the Los Angeles County Criminal
Justice System.

III. PROJECT OBJECTIVES

The purpose of this project is to design, demonstrate, and evaluate a
long-range planning process which prescribes what a large law enforcement
agency should be doing today in preparation for an uncertain tomorrow. The
implementation of such a process will support those areas of current decision-
making by senior management of the Los Angeles County Sheriff's Department which should reflect the future consequences of present programs.

This section will describe the three objectives of this long-range planning project and some associated project benefits to be realized upon its
successful completion.

[28] James Q. Wilson, "Dilemma of Police Administration," *Public Administration
Review*, September-October 1968, p. 407.

A. Project Objectives

1. To establish, within the Los Angeles County Sheriff's Department, an advanced, long-range planning capability by developing and demonstrating a prototypical planning process to support management of the Department's operations on a permanent basis.
2. To define planning methodologies sensitive to broad sources of knowledge which describe, in a logical and systematic way, the rapidly changing social, legal, and political environment in which the Department must operate, thereby providing continual input, flexibility and responsiveness, essential to the process.
3. To train appropriate Sheriff's Department personnel to understand, use and develop the planning capability on a continual basis so that planning within the Department may become self-sustaining and no longer in need of consultant services.

Performance of the project will yield an awareness of necessary planning changes and improvements in an organizational setting, along with methodologies for achieving them. Tasks related to the project objectives will identify short-term as well as long-term constraints, define the Department's general long-range goals, and exercise the planning methodologies as part of a systematic process. Tasks related specifically to Objective 3 (Training) will identify the necessary personnel skills required for the planning staff, clarify the kinds of data that should be maintained on a regular basis, and incorporate useful analytical techniques which may be developed during the course of the project.

B. Associated Project Benefits

Important benefits to be derived from the design and demonstration of the long-range planning process in the Los Angeles Sheriff's Department are:

1. Development and description of comprehensive organization-wide goals, in order of priority for the Sheriff's Department; this effort has never before been undertaken deliberately and systematically.
2. Comprehensive identification and consideration of environmental factors (social, behavioral, legal, political, technological and economic) which impact upon the missions, roles, and philosophy of the Department and, to an extent, of any law enforcement agency.
3. Evaluation of the utility of current information systems within the Sheriff's Department and the Los Angeles County Criminal Justice System insofar as they support long-range planning goals, including the corollary to this evaluation which is the specification of additional information requirements needed to support the planning process.
4. Practical (real world) demonstration of an advanced staff activity unique in law enforcement and which can serve as a model for other police agencies.
5. Comprehensive and concise documentation of the progress of the project which, in addition to the four final Phase reports, will make

a significant contribution to the management literature of criminal justice institutions.

IV. APPROACH FOR ACHIEVING THE OBJECTIVES

The rationale underlying the approach is best understood by briefly examining the project's evolution. Accordingly, this section will be divided into two parts, the first presenting an historical review of the project, the second being an overview of the selected work program.

A. Project Evolution and Rationale

The Sheriff's Long-Range Planning Unit (LRPU) originated in the Administrative Division of the LASD in 1969. Unit guidelines at the time were of necessity quite broad and generally acknowledged the innovative, indeed experimental, nature of such an undertaking. Subsequent efforts of the LRPU, interacting with Department executives, served to clarify its responsibilities. The mission to be performed was twofold:

1. To stimulate Departmental planning at all operational levels, and
2. To lend technical direction to Departmental planning operations over an extended period of time.

In order to fulfill this mission, the LRPU assumed the following responsibilities:

1. Review of the philosophies and techniques of long-range planning as used by private industry and governmental agencies.
2. The forecasting of required LASD resources five to twenty years into the future.
3. The development of a master plan to assist the Department in best organizing its operations to meet projected County-wide needs.
4. Consideration of long-term effects of policies, objectives, and programs of the Department, rendering frequent recommendations to administrators.
5. Liaison with other agencies interfacing with law enforcement planning.

Because of the experimental nature of LRPU and the responsibilities perceived at its inception, it was decided that these guidelines should be tentative, thus affording the Unit flexibility of action enabling it to modify its goals and functions as its members became aware of failures, successes and limitations.

Incipient study led to the development of a work plan based upon a self-generated master plan to determine where the Department is today and where it should be going. This initial plan hypothesized that Departmental work loads were created by a number of environmental factors within Los Angeles County. The problem was to identify those factors, measure them, estimate their future consequences, and then to evaluate their impact upon the Department. Accordingly, the Unit began to gather data.

In addition to factors outside the Department's control, the plan also recognized the need for data within the Department that more accurately reflected operational activities. As a result, research efforts were initiated to improve a reporting system capable of more effectively monitoring patrol and related activities.

The results of these early planning activities were disappointing. The collection of masses of general data of questionable value together with the absence of a rigorous analytical framework indicated that the original development plan was somewhat naive and impractical. That data would be required was not the point. Dissipation of the Unit's limited resources in gathering huge data samples without regard to how data were to be used forced a re-evaluation of the role of the LRPU.

The knowledge gained as a result of these experiences led to the conviction that before the LRPU would be in a position to perform its functions with any sophistication, it should first develop and evaluate a systematic process for long-range planning. It became evident that the requirements for this process, or set of procedures, should be established at the outset; planning techniques would have to be analyzed for their applicability and relevance; expert opinion concerning the existing and perceived role of police would be needed; personnel at all levels of Departmental management who may be expected to participate would require orientation and training.

As the Sheriff's Department does not now possess the resources to undertake a program of this nature without such assistance, it was decided at this juncture, that the Department should seek external assistance in the form of a contractor experienced in sophisticated management analysis and planning technology. The role of the LRPU therefore developed into one which, with contractor support, coordinates the creation of a comprehensive long-range planning capability to serve the executive and managerial levels of the Department on a permanent basis.

From this new role, based upon knowledge gained from previous experiences of trial and error, the approach selected for this project evolved.

B. Overview of the Work Program

The work program for the project is divided into four phases and nine tasks, and is presented as a block diagram in Figure 1. The phases are predominantly sequential although Phases III and IV do overlap (a time-dependent schedule is presented in Section V Part B).

Use of the systems approach as an underlying philosophy in the work program is particularly relevant and necessary in a planning project of this nature. In the first phase, the status quo is assessed in terms of:

Current Departmental planning procedures and capability, decision-making methods, organizational flexibility, and degree of interaction with other county criminal justice agencies (Task 1).

A state-of-the-art survey of philosophies, methods, and techniques both for long-range and for operational planning in use by the private sector and by governmental agencies at all levels (Task 2).

In Phase II, the long-range planning process is first developed and exercised. Development of the process entails:

The preparation of a preliminary scheme and detailed schedule for the long-range planning process (Task 3).

The identification of short-term and long-term constraints (Task 4) in each of the following six dimensions:

the Department's charter, people, and organization
the criminal justice, law enforcement, and legislative environments
the Department's current and future resources
the political environment
the demographic and social environment of the communities the Department serves, including those cities which contract for its services
technological advances

The development of a comprehensive and hierarchically-structured goal set for the Department reflecting an awareness of the real constraints identified above and the Department's sense of its own priorities (Task 5). The DELPHI or other method of elicting relevant expert opinion will be used in this task.

Exercising the long-range planning process (Task 6) means developing and analyzing data in support of one strategic decision at a time. Because subgoals in the goal set have been ranked in an approved order of priority, the most important one will be addressed first: What are the feasible strategies or options open to the Department for achieving this particular goal? In other words, what should the Department *do*? Alternatives will be identified, cost-benefit analyses performed, and a strategy recommended. This information, prepared by adhering to or refining the planning process, is submitted to top management for a strategic decision.

In Phase III, the chosen strategy must then be put into effect by transforming it into an operational plan. First, a preliminary process is designed to do this (Task 7) including a detailed schedule and work assignments. Next, the process is exercised (Task 8). Depending on the strategy, many people and a large phase-in time period may be involved. Thus, control, coordination, and optimal use of available resources are prime considerations in this task, and the extent to which they are facilitated by the operational planning process will determine its success.

Finally, a set of procedures for keeping both planning procedures complementary and responsive to changing needs will be developed in Phase IV (Task 9). Exercising both processes in an organizational setting on a permanent basis will generate many kinds of feedback information, and this task will ensure that such information serves to refine, up-date, and otherwise maintain the planning processes in their most effective state.

Formal project documentation will consist of four major reports, one at the end of each phase, documenting the results and critical evaluations of the work performed, and monthly progress reports.

V. STATEMENT OF WORK

In this section the tasks necessary to achieve the project objectives are described along with their interactions both from a standpoint of information feedback and concurrency of execution. Following the task descriptions, a time-phased schedule, and pertinent information about the staffing arrangements for the project are presented.

A. Task Descriptions
B. Schedule
C. Staffing Arrangements

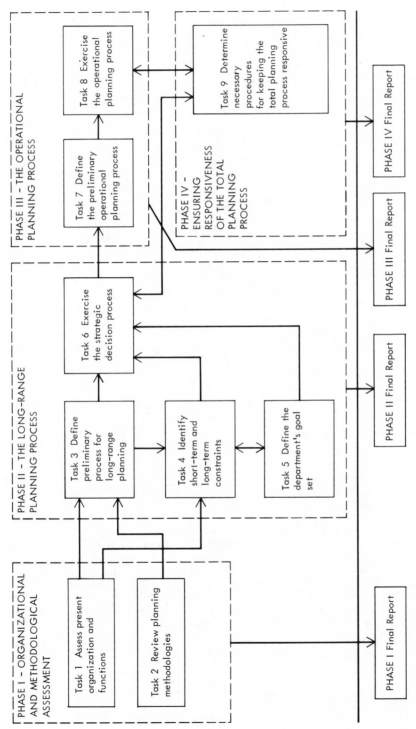

No time dependencies are implied in this diagram.

FIGURE 1. **Overview of the Work Program**

105

A. Task Descriptions

Phase I Organizational & Methodological Assessment. *Task 1. Assess Present Organization and Functions with Emphasis on Planning Mechanisms and Capabilities.* As with the police agencies across the nation, the size, scope and complexity of the Los Angeles Sheriff's Department's operations have increased over the last few years, particularly in harnessing the benefits (and problems) of advanced technology. Although the Department has been successful in accommodating many of the increased demands for its services, it remains almost totally reactive to changes occurring around it.

Decision-making in the Department has been traditionally delegated, to a large degree, to competent men who must make decisions in the course of their regular duties. However, development of an overall picture of decision-making in the Department has never been attempted. This is a necessary prerequisite to any work involving planning activities. That assessment will form the focus of this task, with special emphasis placed on current planning procedures and capabilities.

This work will lean heavily on personnel interviews with key officials and analysts in the Department and will include an investigation of budget-formulating procedures. Of particular interest will be the supporting data developed and used to justify the soundness of decisions having significant implications for future Department action.

The output of this task will be knowledge and written descriptions of:

the basic decision structure, its relationship to the organization of the Department and functions within it.

current planning mechanisms to distinguish between the more successful and worthwhile practices and marginally useful ones.

perceptions within the Department of long-range planning and potential problem areas.[29]

constraints currently in effect which explain some of the difficulties associated with planning (treated in detail in Task 4).

the means by which the Department incorporates plans of the other agencies into its own plans.

Task 2. Review Planning Methodologies of Selected Public and Private Organizations. The purpose of this task is to place the findings of Task 1 into perspective by answering the following questions: To what degree are the problems and constraints experienced by the Department uniquely a function of the Department? What problems are common to other public and private organizations? How are they attempting to solve them, if at all?

The basis for organization selection will be a comprehensive search of the literature, such as the military, progressive public corporations, research firms and universities, and progressive law enforcement agencies.

The output of this task will be a description of those methodologies

---

[29] In this respect, the results of a survey recently carried out for the Los Angeles County Sub-Region Advisory Board by Public Systems Research Institute of the University of Southern California will be useful. The scope of their survey encompassed law enforcement agencies in Los Angeles County.

and techniques found to be particularly adaptive and beneficial to law enforcement planning.

This step is necessary to ensure that the design of the planning processes in Tasks 3[30] and 7[31] makes the greatest use of applicable methodologies proven elsewhere and adaptable to the law enforcement setting.

Phase II   The Long-Range Planning Process. *Task 3. Define Preliminary Process for Long-Range Planning.* The objective of this task is to arrive at an exercisable preliminary[32] long-range planning process whereby the Department can make long-range planning decisions. The process must be devised within the constraints (identified concurrently in Task 4) imposed internally and externally upon the Department, and should be guided by the hierarchical goal set to be developed in Task 5. The nature of long-range planning thus involves analytical processes which not only constitute an integral part of the *process* but also serve to guide and constrain it. For this reason, Tasks 4 and 5 proceed concurrently with Task 3.

Although by its very nature, long-range planning is broad in scope and basically qualitative, the *process* for accomplishing it will necessarily be as specific as an implementation plan, replete with planning task assignments, responsibilities, and schedules. The process will consist of a set of procedures which are to be followed by selected individuals in specific sequences.

The process will be developed around the following three considerations:

a knowledge of the elements and techniques of strategic planning.

a knowledge of the current planning and decision-making processes within the Department and the degree to which change can be introduced.

the degree to which necessary cooperation can be obtained between the Department and all other involved groups.

It should be emphasized that particularly at this stage, in order to minimize the degree of compromise in the design of the process, the preliminary process should be conceived independently of the personnel who will exercise it, the kinds of strategic planning decisions addressed, and the availability of data to support those decisions. During the initial exercising of the process in Tasks 4 through 6, these latter considerations will increasingly exert a modifying influence on the mechanism, thus tailoring it to the peculiar needs and characteristics of the Department.

The output of this task will be a clear and concise interim working paper describing the preliminary long-range planning process. Documentation of this task should be used as a communicating and learning device for affected personnel during their involvement with the process. The need is envisaged for a number of semi-formal orientation seminars in addition to the distribution of this written information.

Evaluation of the preliminary process will take place during Tasks 3 through 6 (to be discussed under Task 6). Modifications of the preliminary

---

[30] Preliminary definition of Long-Range Planning Process.

[31] Preliminary definition of Operational Planning Process.

[32] Necessarily so at this stage, but to be refined through various kinds of feedback when the mechanism is exercised in Tasks 4 through 6.

process mentioned earlier will in fact be the result of this on-going evaluation.

Task 4. Identify Short-Term and Long-Term Constraints. Effective planning *cannot* be performed in isolation either from other parts of the organization or from the greater environment. The objective of this task is to identify the time-dependent constraints imposed upon the Department as a result of factors that are fixed and thus beyond Departmental control, those that might be susceptible to limited Departmental influence, and those factors subject to direct control by Departmental management. The search for these factors will encompass a comprehensive examination of the following areas as they relate to operations of the Department:

  its charter, organizational behavior, and philosophy.

  its personnel resources.

  its relationship to criminal justice, law enforcement, and legislative environments.

  its economic resources.

  its political environment.

  its social environment (Los Angeles County and the Los Angeles Basin in general).

  its capacity to utilize technological advances.

Knowledge of these constraints will enable parallel and subsequent planning system development to be guided toward realistic concepts and solutions.

To a large degree, this task defines limiting factors and freedoms which serve to bound the current project. Special attention will be given, where possible, to the propensity for and direction of change which might occur with time in any of the constraints identified. Thus, where a long-range 5–10 years) constraint is identified which is not also identified as a short-range (less than five years) constraint, evidence of the probability of the occurrence of certain events or actions supporting that belief will also be provided.

One of the most critical short-term constraints worthy of special mention here is the Department's ability to understand the nature of the long-range planning process, and to eventually manage, direct, and maintain the planning processes developed in this project.

The two methods to be used to identify these constraints are personal interviews with key personnel (to be carried out when interviewing these same people in Task 1 activities), and analysis of outputs from Tasks 1 and 2.

The output of this task will be a document delineating, in each of the aforementioned categories, the constraints and freedoms (or "constrained options") within which subsequent planning processes are to be limited and which will input modifications to the preliminary process being designed concurrently in Task 3. The goal set to be developed next in Task 5 will recognize these constraints particularly in the shorter-term goals, but again we must emphasize that the nature of long-range planning inherently allows the planner to conceptualize and even to set his goals *beyond* short-term constraints. Thus, one definition of a short-term constraint is a limitation which might be removable within five years, assuming that the desirability for such action and the necessary resources allocated for that purpose exist. This definition correctly implies iterative feedback to and from Task 5.

Task 5. Define the Department's Goal Set. This task is central to the entire project, and its success rests on the comprehensiveness, clarity, and realism with which the Department's goal set is formulated. In order that the following discussion may be better understood, some definitions are in order to clarify frequently misconceived notions regarding organizational policies, goals, and plans.

> a policy may be described as a stable condition under which the organization has elected to function.

> a goal, or objective, represents an attribute or state, the achievement of which is desired by the organization.

> a plan sets down the precise method by which the organization is to achieve its goal.

Plans should seek to set out in detail[33] the preferred courses of action that an organization should take to achieve particular goals, leading to the achievement of some overall goal or desired condition, the process being governed by a set of policies. Short- and long-range goals are simply early and late "milestones" in the plan. Where such milestones are sequential in time, we say that the later ones represent goals which are hierarchically superior to the earlier ones. Thus, as in a PERT[34] network, where certain milestones must be achieved before others, so do lower-order goals have to be achieved before higher-order ones. And just as milestones have to be set at the time a plan is first drawn up, so must a hierarchy of goals, or *goal set*, be developed at the time the planning process is initiated.

This task specifically addresses the important and crucial activity of developing a hierarchical and ordered goal set. This goal set also constitutes the output of the task.

As with PERT planning, long-range planning establishes hierarchy of goals and, for goals on the same hierarchical level, their order of importance so that:

> progress through the goal set can be measured by following the successive achievement of objectives.

> the effect on the goal set can be seen should one or more goals be changed.

> tighter control in steering the organization toward its ultimate objective or higest-level goal can be accomplished.

> more accurate forecasting of future resource requirements can be established.

> probable effects of goal changes on the budget can be determined.

The analogy between the tasks or activities directed toward the achievement of a milestone in a PERT network and the optimal[35] method for achieving each goal is a good one, and is further discussed in Tasks 6 through 8.

---

[33]Long-range plans, by contrast less detailed, are often thought of as strategies, and provide the necessary framework upon which detailed plans are built.

[34]PERT (Program Evaluation and Review Technique) is an analytic management control tool. Using PERT a complex group of activities is represented by means of events (nodes) and activities (connecting lines) or a network in sequential form with time estimates.

[35]Best method given real constraints.

Formal goal setting techniques have been successfully used by the military, the Apollo Space Program, and more recently by large corporations and some state governments. Although there are differences in these techniques, the common denominator has been a method of eliciting a *consensus opinion from a group of experts* regarding aspects of goal setting such as:

the desirability of the goal, reflected in priority rankings.

the probability of achieving each goal, and the corresponding time lag.

the probability of overcoming likely technological or other deficiencies in order to achieve certain goals.

It is proposed to use a method, for example the DELPHI technique developed at the RAND Corporation,[36] to develop a hierarchical goal set for the Sheriff's Department.

A by-product of this activity, particularly useful for exercising the process in Task 6, is the identification of possible future events which will have a more than even chance of impacting upon the Department's operations.

The output of this task will be documented in the final Phase II Report, and will describe in detail the procedures undertaken to develop the goal set as well as a narrative and diagrammatic description of the goal set itself. Rationales will be provided justifying the goals selected, their levels in the hierarchy and, for those having the same level, their priority rankings.

Task 6. Exercise the Strategic Decision Process. This task has two closely related but distinct purposes: To refine the preliminary mechanism developed in Task 3, and to demonstrate the feasibility and utility of the refined planning process. It is proposed initially that the demonstration effort should involve specifically addressing at least two of the most significant goals as selected by the project management team with the approval of the Grant Review Authority (GRA),[37] taking them one at a time and analyzing which strategy should be adopted that would most effectively and most economically achieve each goal. This process of selecting and adopting a strategy is what may be termed making a strategic decision; at least two strategic decisions will be addressed while exercising the process in this task.

Implicit in the above description of the task activities are several points which need special emphasis:

a. This task is, by its nature, a continuum. For the purposes of this project, however, at least two strategic decisions will be addressed.

b. Analytical support for subsequent strategic decisions will become procedurally easier as the learning curve for project personnel levels off. *Note:* Although feasibility of the long-range planning process in a law enforcement setting is well founded, it has never been attempted before, and new kinds of technical and organizational problems will have to be faced continually.

c. Analyzing and selecting optimal strategies will be extremely complex. Feasible alternatives or options have to be generated and then,

---

[36] Theodore Gordon and Olaf Hehmer, "Report on a Long-Range Forecasting Study," RAND Corporation, P–2982, September 1964.

[37] Part C, Section 5 contains a detailed description of the composition, role, and functions of this important committee of department executives.

cognizant of the constraints set down in Task 4, analyzed in terms of:

> expected costs.
>
> expected benefits.
>
> expected "forcing-events."[38]
>
> expected trends in relevant technologies, social behavior, politics and government, legislation, activities of related agencies, and other factors.

    d. Controls will be developed to ensure that assignments are carried out properly and on time, that deadlines are met, and that any problems encountered are brought to the attention of appropriate members of the project team.

During this task, the long-range planning process (after constraint and goal set definition) will be exercised basically as follows:

    a. Definition of group roles (applicable to affected groups such as the Long-Range Planning Unit, Management Staff Services, Research and Development Bureau, Division Chiefs, Project Consultants, etc.).

    b. Orientation briefings.

    c. Task assignments, predominantly to identify and to collect specific data related to the particular strategic decision to be made.

    d. Development of feasible strategic options to meet the goal being addressed.

    e. Analysis of each feasible option in an effort to determine the "futurity" of the decision—expected costs, benefits, and likely forcing-events.

    f. Preparation of a report listing and summarizing the analysis of each option, and recommending an optimal choice to meet the particular goal being addressed. Such reports will become an important source of information supporting top level decision-making in the Department.

As stated earlier, work in this task will continue indefinitely and will be evaluated by the project management team (a combination of Department personnel and consultants) and, more importantly, by the GRA. Together, many separate facets of the work can come under close scrutiny, such as the quality of data, feasibility of strategic options,[39] and behavioral, organizational, educational, technical, and economic aspects.

There are two outputs from this task, and the task is considered formally

[38] Future events likely to have a significant impact on the mission and operations of the Department.

[39] The current plan to construct a new enlarged combination LASD/LACFD Communications Center in East Los Angeles is a good example of a strategic option having been chosen in pursuit of the (broad) goals of improved communications, reduction in call response time, and eventual lower cost per call processed. However, under the auspices of a formal strategic planning process, the following two considerations might have (or not) affected this decision: 1) Future merging of all L.A. County (or even L.A. Regional) law enforcement agencies. 2) Increased risk of centralizing communications facilities given the current rather violent trends in civil disturbances.

complete for the purposes of this project when the first of these[40] is documented and approved. In order, these outputs are:

1. A final Phase II Report containing a description of the long-range planning process undergoing its several refinements, a description of it in its final GRA approval state, and a critical evaluation of the process.

2. A report in support of each strategic decision addressed, representing tangible evidence of the process having been successfully exercised.

In addition to evaluating the activities and outputs of this task, the work performed in the earlier Tasks 4 and 5 will receive particularly careful evaluation.

The constraint identification work carried out in Task 4, utilizing as it does outputs from Phase I, is evaluated by both the GRA and the project team against criteria of comprehensiveness, reasonableness, degree of perception shown in recognizing the more subtle constraints, degree of interaction among goals and constraints, and the time-dependence of constraints (How long are they to be considered constraints?).

The goal set work of Task 5 will also receive on-going evaluation by the GRA and the project team regarding the following points:

the process used to derive the goal set,

the cognizance demonstrated of the constraints,[41]

the hierarchical structure of the goal set,

the priority rankings of goals,

the identification of forcing-events,

the documentation of Task 5 work.

At this stage of the project, an attempt will be made to assess the impact upon the Department as a whole.

Phase III. The Operational Planning Process. *Task 7. Define the preliminary Operational Planning Process.* Operational planning is the mechanism whereby a strategy designed to accomplish a goal is translated into a course of action comprising a number of specific tasks to be performed in certain time sequences. During the period the plan is to be put into effect, the resources required are precisely determined in subsequent operational planning, i.e., providing program type inputs to the budgetary process. Operational planning is, therefore, at the same time a very broad coordinative function and a very precise quantitative process. An example is the choice and installation of telecommunication equipment in patrol cars.

---

[40] The nature of the decisions may not allow the preparation of final reports to top management in the time formally allotted to this task. The time and effort estimated is designed to allow sufficient time primarily to "debug" the *process.* Once it is found to operate effectively and efficiently as an integral element within the organizational structure of the Department, the project will move on to the next task although the mechanism will continue to be exercised.

[41] Including the corollary: The degree to which reasonable goals are set *in spite of* current constraints.

The purpose of this task is to define the operational planning *process* which will be exercised during the next task, just as it was the purpose of Task 3 to define the long-range planning process which will be subsequently exercised in Tasks 4 through 6.

The task of defining the process implies a thorough understanding of what is involved in operational planning. For example,

> The preliminary plan should be a written document, reducing ambiguity to facilitate communication among those who are involved.
>
> Operational planning should be done, in large measure, by those who will be required to carry out the plans. Hence, these people must be identified at this stage, and interaction among them incorporated into the planning process.
>
> Operational planners should be aware of the degree of current organizational flexibility, along with all current budgetary and nonbudgetary constraints.
>
> The operational plan should be specific enough in terms of responsibilities and functions assigned so that its performance can be measured and closely controlled. In law enforcement, this may prove to be very difficult.
>
> The process, whereby the estimated additional resources required to carry out the plan are incorporated into the current and future budgets, should be included in the plan together with a contingency plan in the event of a smaller budget appropriation.

The operational planning process will be developed in a rational way and might well be based on the following skeletal framework:

1. Understand the strategic decision and the reasons for selecting the preferred strategy to accomplish a particular goal.
2. Guided by the requirements imposed by the selected strategy, determine the particular groups and supervisory personnel who will most likely carry out the plan.
3. Arrange meetings with these supervisory personnel and receive their cooperation and inputs, such as staff availability.
4. Resolve conflicts or problems apparent at this stage.
5. Coordinate all elements in the plan, specify roles of personnel involved, change procedures and schedules of task assignments. Ensure that each assignment has a clear purpose and a specified degree of freedom in carrying it out.
6. Estimate costs for each element in the plan.
7. Arrange a second round of meetings to obtain approval for the cost estimates and task assignments of the preliminary operational plan.
8. Resolve conflicts or problems apparent at this stage.
9. Issue copies of the approved preliminary operational plan to affected personnel.
10. Submit cost estimates for inclusion into the budget.

The output of this task will be a written document describing the preliminary operational planning process. Evaluation of the efficacy of the process, while on-going, becomes more telling the more the process is exercised and refined during the next task.

Task 8. Exercise the Operational Planning Process. The more diligently the planning process is defined in the previous task, the easier it will be to develop sound operational plans. To be sure, operational problems and conflicts will have to be resolved particularly where differences in opinion exist between operational entities regarding methods to be used, personnel assigned, or resources allocated. But these kinds of problems are not new, and the Department already has mechanisms to resolve them.

It warrants repeating that the plan should:

be in writing.

be specific regarding responsibilities, procedures, functions, assignments, schedules, etc.

use currently available resources or justify the use of increased resources in future fiscal periods.

be feasible (within given constraints).

be capable of effective control.

Exercising of the process which occurs in this task will be characterized by several iterations of trial and error (in the form of unforeseen delays and conflicts) until the process of operational planning has been sufficiently refined, the organizational impacts considered and minimized, and the appropriate personnel oriented and trained. Once the process has matured, the task will be considered complete notwithstanding the fact that it may not be possible for a complete operational plan to have been produced when the task is finished. This again emphasizes the fact that the focus of the project is the development and inculcation of *planning processes and attendant capabilities* in the Department, rather than the nature of specific decisions and the production of specific plans. However, it is highly likely that at least one operational plan will be produced before the end of the project to sufficiently demonstrate the quality and utility of the process.

Evaluation here involves an examination of the work accomplished in this task with respect to:

the adequacy and effectiveness of intra-departmental communications and the consequent common understanding of the goals, strategies, and plans.

the clarity, conciseness, and precision of the document describing the operational planning process.

the simplicity and effectiveness of the process.

the control procedures imbedded in the process, and the provisions for management override or procedural change included therein.

The output of this task, in addition to an effective set of procedures for operational planning, will be incorporated into and form the major substance of the final Phase III Report. The document will describe the operational planning process and the several refinements it has undergone as a result of its having been exercised in this task. Particular attention will be given to a comparison of the final refined process to the pre-project method hitherto followed by the Department.

Phase IV. Ensuring Responsiveness of the Total Planning Process. *Task 9. Determine Necessary Procedures for Keeping the Total Planning Process Responsive.* Different stages of the process will occur simultaneously for different goals, even though the basic planning process of goal definition, determination of strategies to meet those goals, and operational plan formulation to carry out those strategies occur sequentially for the same goal. For example, consider the activities being simultaneously pursued when goal D is being addressed: The strategy for goal C is being analyzed, operational plans to achieve goal B are being developed, and the plans to achieve goal A are being carried out, all at the same time. Consider even the more complicated situation further down the line when goal number 37 is being addressed, several of the earlier goals having already been achieved, operational plans for goal number 36 are being developed, several other plans are being carried out, and a new goal set is being developed. Essential as it was to develop the strategic and operational planning process separately in the first instance, it is equally essential to develop procedures for controlling the interaction between the several planning activities for each goal as well as similar activities for other goals being addressed simultaneously.

This task is carried out simultaneously with the previous task and has two related and interdependent purposes. The first evaluates the interaction between the long-range and the operational planning processes as they begin to be exercised together, demonstrating the facility with which procedures can be changed in response to changing needs.

The second purpose is to develop new procedures which relate to both processes, testing the new procedures, and documenting the approved versions.

This task for the first time in the project addresses the smooth and effective functioning of the entire planning process, and seeks to remove any impediment judged to interfere with the overall process by altering existing procedures to improve their effectiveness or by instituting new ones. In fact, this is a second process refinement step, treating both long-range and operational planning processes together in contrast to the first refinement which treated each process separately.

Besides evaluative feedback from the GRA to the project team, the methods used will be a series of meetings with affected groups to discuss their particular problems, reactions, preceptions, and attitudes. Where these are related *procedurally* or *organizationally*, as opposed to kind and quantity of data, for example, then some procedural solutions will be suggested, discussed, and the better ones approved for immediate trial. Not only will the new procedures now become an integral part of the formal planning process if they are found to be an improvement, but the procedures for developing them will also be evaluated, adopted, and documented if found to be effective.

It is essential that this task become an integral part of the ongoing planning process and continue beyond the duration of this project. Therefore, for the purposes of this project, the *task* will be considered complete once the total planning processes have matured and in the judgment of the GRA are operating smoothly and effectively. The task output, in addition to a smoothly functioning set of planning processes, will be a description of the procedural and evaluative work carried out in the task, and will be incorporated in the final Phase IV Report.

B. Schedule

The time-phased schedule for the two-year project is shown in Figure 2. Also shown is the schedule for each of the four major Phase Reports to be generated during the project.

Four tasks together comprise 86% of the project effort for the contractor, reflecting both their importance and their difficulty. These are the definitions of the Department's goal set, Task 5; the exercising of both the long-range and the operational planning processes, Tasks 6 and 8; and the final highly integrative Task 9. The latter three tasks continue to be performed by the Department long after the project is formally completed.

C. Project Staffing Arrangements

The management and staffing arrangements for this project recognize the continuing need for broad interfaces with other criminal justice agencies while maintaining close direction and control of the project's progress.

Central to the arrangement, as shown in Figure 3, is the Grant Review Authority (GRA) which will provide a top level interface between the project team and both the Executive Office of the Sheriff and the California Council on Criminal Justice. The primary purpose and function of the GRA is to *review and approve project progress.* It has therefore overall decision-making authority with respect to the project, and should resolve any problems or conflicts brought to its attention by the Project Director, subject to any constraints imposed upon it by the Los Angeles County Board of Supervisors.

The GRA is also established to be the focal point for external inquiry, particularly by the CCCJ, the Los Angeles Sub-Regional Advisory Board, and by other criminal justice agencies. In turn, where vertical or horizontal interfacing is necessary to further the objectives of the project, such interfaces will be arranged and coordinated by the GRA.

The GRA will consist of a minimum of five members to be appointed by the Sheriff from Division Chiefs, one of whom will act as chairman. These key people would be chosen less on the basis of their Departmental functions and more on their personal qualities of judgment and administrative capability.

The GRA will receive and evaluate monthly progress reports from the project team and convene monthly to receive an oral presentation in support of each progress report by the project team (LASD personnel together with appropriate contractor staff). The GRA is at liberty to invite whomsoever it wishes to attend these meetings, depending on either the relevant expertise. of the invitees or the degree to which they are required to interface with the project team. In turn, after such a monthly presentation, and when the monthly progress reports and phase completion reports are approved, by the GRA, appropriate documentation of project progress will be forwarded through the Project Director to the CCCJ.

The Project Director will be the Sheriff. Personnel assigned full-time to the project shall be from the Long-Range Planning Unit, supplemented as required by other staff personnel from groups such as the Career Develop-

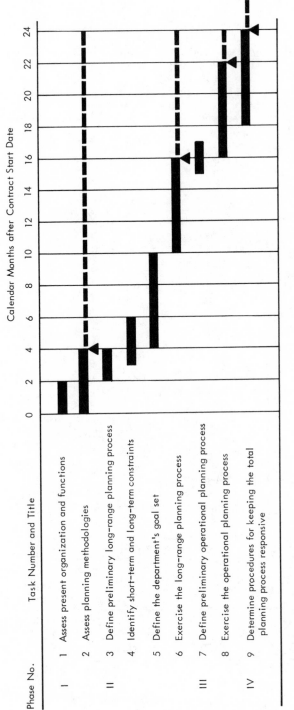

Figure 2. **Project Schedule**

Monthly Progress Reports not shown.

117

ment Bureau, Research and Development Bureau, and Management-Staff Services Bureau.

Participating personnel will consist of a variety of Departmental executives and managers. These personnel will be involved intermittently throughout the project to provide them with actual experience of goal setting and plan formulation. In this manner, their participation will help to ensure "real world" validity of the planning process as it develops and will also serve the third project objective (training) as they learn to utilize the process to support actual long-range decisions.

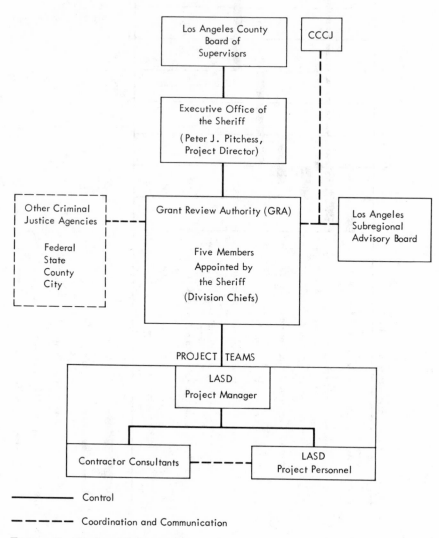

FIGURE 3. **Project Management**

Roles of Departmental personnel assigned to this project or interfacing with it in any way will be:

> to learn and understand the processes developed during the project, and to interact with consultant personnel in ways that will further the objectives of the project.
>
> to provide essential feedback to consultant suggestions, particularly during the tasks where the long-range and operational planning processes are exercised.

Functions of the consultants chosen for this project will be to assist with:

> an objective assessment of current Departmental decision-making as it relates to planning.
>
> an assessment of planning methodologies transferable to law enforcement agencies.
>
> the identification of preliminary long-range and operational planning processes.
>
> the orientation and training of affected Departmental personnel enabling them to utilize the processes without continued guidance.

The role of the project team, composed of assigned Sheriff's Department personnel and consultants will be to:

> identify short-term and long-range Departmental constraints.
>
> develop an integrated hierarchically-structured goal set with which the GRA concurs.
>
> develop iterative procedures which will help to keep the planning flexible and responsive.
>
> perform on-going objective task evaluations to aid the GRA.
>
> prepare monthly progress reports and assist the Department's project manager in monthly presentations to the GRA.
>
> prepare interim training reports and the four final phase reports.

VI. PROJECT EVALUATION

Project success is directly dependent upon the quality of thorough evaluation. Thus, it will be required in the Request For Proposal (RFP) that the contractor furnish a comprehensive and objective evaluation mechanism built into services he provides. This mechanism may involve advanced forms of simulation modeling, game theory or other techniques designed to bridge the time gap between long-range decisions and long-range reality.

Through critical evaluation of documents, oral presentations by the project team, and direct observations of the process, the GRA will be able to subjectively evaluate the work as the project progresses.

To augment evaluation by the GRA it is proposed that a separately contracted, non-competitive agency with research experience be retained possibly from available private universities or government funded institutions. The sole purpose of such a contract would be to evaluate work of the prime contractor and input the GRA and project management with an independent analysis of the work product at the completion of Phases II and III (the critical research components of the project). The evaluation contractor would evaluate work in those phases in terms of technique and results, advising project management as to the validity of all work performed and suggesting ways and means to improve or test their products.

As proper subjects for evaluation, the following aspects of the project are listed in order of their currently perceived sensitivity to the ultimate success of the project:

> the demonstrated understanding of the nature of planning by Departmental personnel involved in the activity.
>
> the efficacy and flexibility of the planning processes as demonstrated in the Department's operations.
>
> the substantive improvement in quality of the Department's long-range and operational planning as a result of the institutionalization of the process.
>
> the resulting impacts upon the Department and, to an extent, upon other criminal justice and planning agencies.
>
> the sensitivity of the planning processes to the goals and decisions addressed and environmental constraints impacting achievement of those goals.

Because of its innovative nature there exists no similar model upon which to base comparative judgements. Furthermore, as the work of each task becomes successively dependent upon the validity of previous accomplishments, it therefore becomes increasingly important to thoroughly evaluate critical phase effort before proceeding too far into the succeeding phase.

Sheriff's Department personnel will furnish police system expertise toward evaluation of the process as it develops. This is necessary to ensure its practical utility to the needs of the Department and to law enforcement generally. The GRA, as ultimate managers of the project, will be in a position to make many evaluations relative to these needs. They cannot, however, make evaluations which are technical and outside the scope of police training or general expertise. The prime contractor performing the work should not be the sole evaluator of his own work in those specialties unfamiliar to members of the GRA, or other members of the project team. Hence the need for an independent evaluation contractor.

Evaluation by a separate agency will, in effect, create a check and balance system composed of three spheres of examination and evaluation: first by the joint Sheriff's-Contractor Project Team prior to submission of their work to the GRA; second by GRA personnel representing the administration of the Department; and third by an independent evaluation contractor retained for that purpose.

Methods for fulfilling the evaluation component of this project are at this time flexible. Two alternatives are suggested, both of which would adequately meet the requirements enumerated.

The first method calls for funding a separate evaluation component in conjunction with the work program, the approximate equivalent of one consultant man-year. Requests for Proposals would be issued to fill this component. Responses could then be assessed and a contract let to the respondent best meeting the requirements stated.

A second alternative would require participation of the Los Angeles County Sub-Regional Advisory Board. This Board currently has before it a proposal to establish a sub-committee on County-wide long-range planning in Criminal Justice. Should this group be formed within that body, it might consider acting as an evaluation or advisory board to fulfill the evaluation component of this project.

THE MANAGEMENT
OF COMMUNICATIONS
AND THE COMMUNICATIONS
OF MANAGEMENT

> I know you believe you understood what you think I said, but I
> am not sure you realize that what you heard is not what I meant.

Communication is the vehicle for managerial planning, and the police manager is a key person in developing and maintaining effective organizational communications as he interacts with subordinates, peers, superiors, and members of the community. To succeed in this task, he must communicate in many directions for the basic purpose of exerting his influence and control. A large part of our consideration of police management, therefore, deals with the subject of communications. Excellent testimony to the importance of *good* management as it relates to *good* communications is expressed in the following statement:

> But good government [police work] requires more than good
> people. It requires good management of these good people. And
> too often, managers tend to spend great time and effort on their
> program responsibilities and their monetary resources while
> leaving their people-management responsibilities and oppor-
> tunities to take care of themselves. This type of imbalance must be
> corrected.
> Our greatest single obstacle is poor communication. We are

engaged in a rebuilding of the federal personnel system [police system] to better serve the needs of management and employees in the 70's. But we have to communicate what we are doing and why.[1]

A message system, or in terms of organizational setting a communications system, provides the means by which information, statements, views, and instructions are transmitted through a police organization. Although one often speaks of the "flow" of information, this flow actually consists of a series of discrete messages of different length, form, and content. These messages are transmitted through certain channels (or lines of communication), which make up the communications system or network. Each message is sent by a transmitter (an individual, a group, a division, a computer) to a receiver or several receivers. It may stimulate action or a reaction in the form of a countermessage or both. Every individual or division in a police organization acts as a sender and a receiver, though not for the same messages. Some individuals, depending on their position in the police organization, send more than they receive; others receive more than they send. Significantly, the manager's day is filled with a heavy volume of transmissions and receptions.

Communications can be viewed as occurring in a variety of ways and, in an organizational sense, at a number of levels—interpersonal, group, and systemic. This chapter covers the relevance of communications to the police manager, types of communication channels, direction of communication, volume and types of messages, cybernetics, the computer, basics of effective communication, and two learning exercises. Only brief reference is made to such technological systems of police communications as the police radio and teletype.[2] Our discussion of communications is thus built around the internal organizational transmitting and receiving of messages by managers.

WHY COMMUNICATE?

Why communicate? First, and most important, a police manager makes decisions (or should be making decisions) based on information received in conjunction with previously developed plans, procedures, or rules. Consequently, the communication process is necessary be-

[1] Robert E. Hampton, "Special Feature—Dialogue for the 70's," *Public Personnel Review*, 31 (October 1970), 295.

[2] For those interested in information pertaining to the technological aspects of police communication systems, see the President's Commission on Law Enforcement and Administration of Justice, *Task Force Report: Science and Technology* (Washington, D.C.: Government Printing Office, 1967); and selected articles in S. I. Cohn, ed., *Law Enforcement Science and Technology II* (Chicago: Port City Press, Inc., 1969).

cause the flow of proper information to the decision points throughout the police organization is such a vital requirement for goal accomplishment. In fact, if managing were thought of primarily as decision making and if the decision process were considered essentially a communication process including a network of communications systems, then the act of managing could be witnessed as a communication process. Thus the several concepts—communications, planning, control, information, and decision making—are interwoven. Plainly, the closer we look at influence, control, and planning, the more we become aware of the basic features of information exchange. Wiener aptly writes in support of this thinking.

> Information is a name for the content of what is exchanged with the outer world as we adjust to it, and make our adjustment felt upon it. The process of receiving and using information is the process of our adjusting to the contingencies of the outer environment, and of our living effectively within that environment. The needs and the complexity of modern life make greater demands on this process of information than ever before, and our press, our museums, our scientific laboratories, our universities, our libraries and textbooks, are obliged to meet the needs of this process or fail in their purpose. To live effectively is to live with adequate information. Thus, communication and control belong to this life in society.[3]

The term *information-decision system* may be used to emphasize that available information should be transmitted in light of the decisions to be made throughout the police organization. Thus an information-decision system is a communication process relating the necessary new inputs to the already stored information and the desired decisional outputs. It is likely that decisions at a given stage in the organization represent output from one communication process and input information for another decision at the same level, a lower level, or an upper level. The total information flow is a *communications system* with many interdependent elements and subsystems.

A police manager communicates so as to send or request information for the making of a decision on the direction and coordination of departmental "resources." Hence, we design communications systems to carry the requisite information for decision making to fulfill the provision of task-oriented direction and coordination.[4] The system may be formal or informal or both, and it may be manual or auto-

[3]Norbert Wiener, *The Human Use of Human Beings: Cybernetics and Society,* 2nd ed. (New York: Doubleday & Company, Inc., 1954), pp. 17–18.

[4]For an excellent description of the relationship between communications and information systems, see Sherman C. Blumenthal, *Management Information Systems: A Framework for Planning and Development* (Englewood Cliffs, N.J.: Prentice-Hall, Inc., 1969).

mated or both. Specifically, then, why does a police manager depend on the quality of a communications system? The answer is that goal attainment is achieved through communications. We find that the system's degree of success is based on its doing five things: (1) providing sufficient information to accomplish assigned tasks—this communication function may be satisfied through a variety of forms, such as periodic training, provision of technical reference manuals, daily coaching, and orders; (2) communicating clarified perceptions and expectations of responsibility—organization charts, job descriptions, work plans, schedules, routes, performance ratings, orders, and other devices may serve this function; (3) facilitating the *coordination* (now and in the future) of men and materials in achieving specific objectives; (4) making possible organizational problem solving (task oriented) and conflict resolution (interpersonal problems); and (5) furnishing general direction not only on what to achieve but also on how to achieve it. Johnson, Kast, and Rosenzweig provide a fitting ending for this discussion when they write:

> Throughout history the transmission of information has been a key to progress. Efficient communication is important in all fields of human endeavor.[5]

MULTIPLE COMMUNICATION CHANNELS

Various channels of communication are available to the police manager for exchanging information. A communications system can be categorized into formal and informal channels. We choose to change this list by dividing the informal communication channels into three subclasses: subformal, personal task directed, and personal nontask directed.[6]

Formal Communication Channels

All organizations develop formal communication channels as a response to large size and the obviously limited information-handling capability of each individual. The formal channels comply with the recognized official structure of the organization and transmit messages expressive of the policy nature of authority. Hence, one typically sees formal orders and directives, reports, official correspondence, standard operating procedures, and so on. Those persons who emphasize going

---

[5] Richard A. Johnson, Fremont E. Kast, and James E. Rosenzweig, *The Theory and Management of Systems* (New York: McGraw-Hill Book Company, 1963), p. 87.

[6] This classification is suggested in part by William M. Jones, *On Decisionmaking in Large Organizations* (Santa Monica, Calif.: The Rand Corporation, 1964).

through channels are doing so in adherence to the unity-of-command principle within the formal hierarchy.

Rigid compliance with formal channels can be harmful. The injuries are mainly in terms of time, creativity, and experience. First, it takes a long time for a formal message from a police manager in one division to pass to a manager in another division. Second, formal messages are on the record and thus restrain the free flow of thoughts. Third, in practice, a formal communications system cannot cover all informational needs. Informational needs change quite rapidly, while the formal channels change only with considerable time and effort. Therefore, the most urgent need for *informal communication channels is to "plug" the gaps in the formal channels.*

Informal Communication Channels

Although some consider formal communication channels the only way to send information necessary to the functioning of the police organization, this theory is no longer as sacred as it was in the past. Not only are we witnessing an interest in obtaining a better understanding of the informal organization, but along with it has come an awareness of its potential use. This interest and awareness logically leads to a different perspective on the structuring of communication flow. This perspective does not delimit organizationally useful communications to purely formal channels. It encompasses all the social processes of the widest relevance in the functioning of any group or organization. Therefore, we now recognize informal and personal communications as a supportive and frequently necessary process for effective functioning. The unofficial communication channels also become a prime means for researching the formal organization. In fact, police managers are often expected to seek information through channels not officially sanctioned or recognized.

A large number of informal channels means that formal channels do not fully meet the important communications needs in a police department. Therefore, it is futile for police managers to establish formal channels and expect that those channels will carry most of the messages. Ironically, the more restricted the formal channels, the greater the growth of informal ones. Although the informal system seeks to fill the gaps in the formal one, the leaders of a police organization can severely curtail the development of the former by simply directing subordinates not to communicate with each other, by physically separating people, or by requiring prior clearance for any communication outside a certain division. In doing so, the number of significant messages is sharply reduced, thus affecting the general effectiveness of the organization.

We next proceed to an analysis of three kinds of informal communication channels. The first two are task, or goal, oriented, while the third is oriented toward the *individual*.

Informal communication channels: subformal. Subformal channels move those messages arising from the informal power structure existing in every police organization. Every member of the department must know and observe informal standards and procedures about what to communicate and to whom. Such norms are seldom written down and must be acquired by experience and example, a necessity that causes difficulties for newcomers.

Subformal communications consist of two types: those that flow along formal channels, but not as formal communications; and those that flow along strictly informal channels. Both types have the definite advantage of not being official—they can be withdrawn or changed without any official record being made. Therefore, almost all new ideas are first proposed and tried as subformal communications. Would anyone refute the statement that the vast majority of communications in police organizations are subformal?

As mentioned above, subformal channels of communication develop whenever there is a need for police personnel to communicate but no formal channel exists. Formal channels are usually vertical, following the paths of the formal authority structure. Thus, most of the gap-filling subformal lines of communication are horizontal, connecting peers rather than subordinates and superiors. This characteristic is one reason that police managers find subformal channels so vital in their job. Through subformal communications a police manager can interrelate his work unit and their efforts to others. Even when subformal channels are used by the police personnel of different ranks, the informality of the information exchanged reduces the distinctions in organizational status. Subformal communications supply a way for subordinates from all levels to speak more freely to their superiors—the managers!

While in general it has been shown that subformal channels meet the communication requirements not met by formal channels, they become all the more necessary under certain conditions. First, the greater the degree of interdependence among activities (e.g., patrol and detectives) within the department, the greater the number and use of subformal channels. Second, the more uncertainty about the objectives of the department, the greater the number and use of subformal channels. Third, when a police organization is operating under the pressure of time, it tends to use subformal channels extensively, since there is often no time to use formal channels. Thus, police managers stretch out for information wherever they can get it from whatever channel is necessary. Fourth, closely cooperating sections rely primarily upon subformal communications. Conversely, if the divisions of a police organization are in competition, they tend to avoid subformal channels and to communicate only formally. Obviously, rivalry has significant communications drawbacks (vice vs. detectives). Fifth, subformal communication channels are used more often if departmental members have stable, rather than constantly changing, relationships with each other.

Informal communication channels: personal task directed. A personal task-directed communication is one in which an organization member intentionally reveals something of his own attitude toward the activities of his own organization. While personal, this communication is also targeted toward the goals or activities of the organization. Thus we can refer to it as task directed. It possesses the following characteristics: (1) Task-directed personal channels are nearly always used for informing rather than for directions; (2) before a person acts on the basis of information received through personal channels, he usually varies that information through either subformal or formal channels; (3) the channels transmit information with considerable speed because there are no formal mechanisms to impede its flow; and (4) because task-directed personal messages are transmitted by personnel acting as individuals, they do not bear the weight of the position generating them. To this extent, they differ from subformal messages, which are transmitted by individuals acting in their assigned capacity—but not for the official record!

Informal communication channels: personal nontask directed. As suggested by its title, this form of communication *apparently* does not contain information related to the tasks of the organization. Note the emphasis on the word *apparently*. Paradoxically, this channel may handle information on occasion far more valuable to the achievement of organizational goals than any other channels, including the formal ones. An example of this channel is the manager's learning through a loyal subordinate the reasons for growing job dissatisfaction. A discussion of its characteristics will provide an explanation of its benefits: (1) non-task-directed channels furnish a vehicle for an individual to satisfy his social needs, (2) this channel provides a way for an individual to "blow off steam" over things that disturb him, (3) non-task-directed channels frequently supply useful feedback normally comprised of unexpected information not obtainable in any other way, and (4) personal channels offer the best medium for a person to become adjusted to his organizational setting (unwritten standards, group values, and "the way we do things here" are conveniently expressed through non-task-directed channels). In conclusion and to reemphasize our contention:

The efficiency of a large formal organization is sizably enhanced when its own chain of command or decision or communication is tied into the informal network of groups within the organization, so that the network can be used to support the organization's goals.[7]

COMMUNICATIONS: DOWNWARD, UPWARD, AND HORIZONTAL

Traditionally, communication flow was viewed as being exclusively downward and identical with the pattern of authority. The pattern of authority provides, of course, the structure of an organization, but almost invariably it is found to represent an overly idealized notion of what the organization is like, or what it should be like, and this is why students of organization theory constantly need to analyze the informal structure for other directions of communication flow. A message can flow in one of three directions: downward, upward, and laterally (horizontally).[8]

Downward

Communications from superior to subordinate are of five types:

1. Specific task directives: *job instructions*
2. Information to produce the understanding of the task and its relation to other organizational tasks: *job rationale*
3. Information concerning organizational *procedures and practices*
4. *Feedback* to the subordinate officer about his performance
5. Information to instill a sense of mission: *indoctrination of goals*

The first type of message is most often given first priority in police organizations. Instructions about the job of police officer are communicated to the person through direct orders from his manager, training sessions, training manuals, and written directives. The objective is to insure the reliable performance of every individual in the organization. Less attention is given to the second type, which is designed to provide the police officer with a full understanding of his position and its relation to similar positions in the same organization. Many police personnel know *what* they are to do, but not *why*. Withholding information on the rationale of the job not only reduces the loyalty of the member to his organization but also makes the organization rely heavily on the first type of information, specific instructions

---

[7] Bernard Berelson and Gary A. Steiner, *Human Behavior: An Inventory of Scientific Findings* (New York: Harcourt, Brace & World, Inc., 1964), p. 370.

[8] This particular section is drawn from Anthony Downs, *Inside Bureaucracy* (Boston: Little, Brown and Company, 1967), pp. 235–47.

about the job. Some city and police administrators are in favor of reducing the policeman's behavior to that of a robot; others want to use
his intelligence by having him act on his understanding of the total
situation. It can be seen, therefore, that the benefits of giving fuller
information on job understanding are twofold: If an officer knows the
reasons for his assignment, he will often carry out his job more
effectively; and if he has an understanding of what his job is about in
relation to the overall mission of his department, he is more likely to
identify with its goals. Third, information about organizational procedures supplies a prescription of the role requirements of the organizational member. Fourth, feedback is necessary to insure that the
organization is operating properly. Feedback to the individual about
how well he is doing in his job, however, is often neglected or poorly
handled, even in police organizations in which the managerial
philosophy calls for such penetrating evaluation. Fifth, the final type
of downward-directed information has as its purpose to emphasize
organizational goals, either for the total organization or for a major
unit of it. Consequently, an important function of a police manager is
to describe the mission of the police department in an attractive motivational sense.

Upward

Communications about or from subordinates to the police manager are as follows:

1. Information about his *performance* and *grievances*
2. Information about the *performance* and *grievances* of others
3. Feedback regarding organizational *practices* and *policies*
4. Feedback concerning *what* needs to be done and the *means* for
    doing it
5. Requests for *clarification* of the goals and specific activities

For a variety of reasons, however, there are great barriers to free
upward communication. Most prominent is the structure itself. Simply
stated, bureaucracies or highly formalized organizations tend to inhibit upward informal communications. In doing so, a tremendous
amount of important information never reaches the upper-level decision centers. Other factors also adversely affect the upward flow of
messages. Managers are less in the habit of listening to their subordinates than of talking to them. And because information fed up the
line is often used for control purposes, the manager's subordinates
are not likely to give him information that will lead to decisions
affecting them adversely. They tell the manager not only what he
wants to hear but also what they want him to know. How many of

you, readers and managers, have detected this in your conversations with those over whom you exert power? Moreover, is it your fault or theirs?

Horizontal

Communications between people at the same organizational level are basically of four types:

1. Information necessary to provide task *coordination*
2. Information for identifying and defining *common problems* to be solved through cooperation
3. Feedback from co-workers which fulfills *social needs*
4. Information needed to provide *social* (not organizational) *control* for a group so that it can maintain the members' compliance with its standards and values

Organizations face one of their most difficult problems in procedures and practices concerned with horizontal communication. In essence, a working balance must be found between unrestricted and overrestricted communications among co-workers in an organization. Unrestricted communications that are horizontal can detract from maximum efficiency because too much nonrelevant information may be transmitted. At the opposite extreme, efficiency suffers if an employee receives all his instructions from the person above him, thus reducing task coordination. Our position here is that some lateral communication is critical for an effective police organization. The type and amount of information that should be circulated on a horizontal basis is best determined by answering the question, Who needs to know and why? An interesting "hang-up" in horizontal communication occurs when people overvalue peer communication and neglect those below and above them. Lieutenants talk only to lieutenants, and captains only to captains. The problem resides in the word *only*, for they should be interacting in all directions.

MESSAGES: NUMBER AND KINDS

Communication is expensive! Every message involves time for deciding what to send, time for composing, costs of sending the message (which may consist of time, money, or both), and time for interpreting the message. Not only do messages take time and money, but they can also seriously hamper an individual because they subtract time from his working day. Obviously, the more time a person spends in searching or communicating, the less he has for other types of activity. Every individual has a saturation point regarding the amount of information he can usefully handle in a given time period. If he should become overloaded, he will be unable effectively either to comprehend the information given to him or to use it. All of this means that the particular methods used by a police organization to collect, select, and transmit information are critically important determinants of its success. First we take a closer look at the number of messages; second, at the kinds of messages.

Number

The frequency of messages in a police organization is determined by six basic factors:

1. The total number of members in the organization
2. The nature of its communications networks (downward, upward, or horizontal)
3. The sending regulations controlling when and to whom messages are sent
4. The degree of interdependence of the organization's various activities
5. The speed with which relevant changes occur in its external environment
6. The search mechanisms and procedures used by the organization to investigate its environment

High message volume usually results in "overloading." Attempts are automatically made to reduce any overloading. Police managers can react to this situation in one or more of the following ways. They can slow down their handling of messages without changing the organization's network structure of transmission rules. *But*, this action will cause the police department to reduce its speed of reaction to events and will thereby lessen its output. *Or*, they can change the transmission procedures so that their subordinates screen out more information before sending messages. *But*, this reaction will also reduce the quantity of the department's output. *Or*, they can create more channels in the network to accommodate the same quantity of messages in the same time period. *But*, this reaction will provide more opportunities for message distortion and will be more expensive. *Or*, they can relate tasks within the organization so that those units with the highest message traffic are grouped together within the overall communications system. *But*, this action will reduce the volume of messages sent through higher levels in the network and will facilitate the coordination of effort. *Or*, they can improve the quality of messages in order to reduce the time needed for receiving, composing, and transmitting them. In addition to improving the content and format of the messages, the manager can decide on better methods for handling them.

Kinds

Messages vary in content and form. There are reports, statements, inquiries, questions, accounts, comments, notes, records, recommendations, rejoinders, instructions, and so on.[9] Each message may have a different purpose and may thus lead to a different response. Messages can be transmitted either formally or informally in one of three ways: (1) written communication, (2) oral communication in face-to-face meetings of two or more individuals, and (3) oral communication in telephone conversations.

Written messages. Samuel Eilon groups written messages into six categories: routine report, memorandum, inquiry, query, proposal, and decision.

Routine report. A routine report is a message that supplies information as part of a standard operation. A report can be generated in two ways: (1) time triggered—a report called for at set time intervals (for example, a police manager is required to send weekly reports on the activities of his subordinates), and (2) event triggered—a report called for when certain tasks are completed (for example, a report is to be sent when a case is finished, or when certain training has been provided to a manager's subordinates). Remember that in this case the initiative to make a report does not lie with the manager —the circumstances under which a report is issued are clearly specified by organizational procedures; and the manager is required only to determine that the circumstances conform to the specification.

Memorandum. A memorandum also furnishes information, but not as part of a routine procedure. A memorandum can be (1) a *statement of fact,* submitted in response to an inquiry, to assist in evaluating a problem or to prepare plans for action; (2) a *statement that is event triggered,* released when circumstances have changed in an unprescribed manner, calling for some initiative by the sender in drawing attention of others to the change so that a plan of action can be developed; or (3) a *comment,* made in response to some other statement to information or to give a different interpretation of data. This does not mean that all routine reports are devoid of initiative, whereas all memorandums are not. If a memorandum is made in response to a request, then the intitiative for generating the memorandum lies with the requesting individual, not with the person who created the

---

[9] Most of this section is drawn from Samuel Eilon, "Taxonomy of Communications," *Administrative Science Quarterly,* 13 (September 1968), 266–88.

memorandum. And although event-triggered routine reports do not call for any initiative to create them, initiative may be exercised in determining their content, while event-triggered memorandums may not call for a great deal of initiative with respect to content. Moreover, the creation of a message containing information (report or memorandum) may include one or several of the following activities: (1) extracting data from records; (2) processing data, including computations and analysis, on a routine basis; (3) collecting data as needed; and (4) processing data as needed. In the case of reports, activities are mainly confined to the first two, while memorandums may include all four.

Inquiry. An inquiry is a message requesting information to aid in evaluating a given problem, usually before making recommendations for action. The response to such a request would be a memorandum, which would involve a statement with the necessary information and an analysis of the data. An inquiry normally includes information not contained in reports, unless the reports are time triggered and the information is needed before the next report is due. Also, an inquiry may meet with a comment, which asks for clarification or points out the difficulties in providing certain information in the time specified.

Query. A query is a message defining the characteristics of a problem and asking for instructions or plans about courses of resolution. A query is often made by a subordinate concerning problems not fully discussed in standing regulations, either because of the novelty of the situation or because of ambiguities or inconsistencies in procedures.

Proposal. A proposal describes a course of action the writer feels should be taken. It can be the result of several exchanges of queries, inquiries, reports, and memorandums. It may be generated by a subordinate, on his own initiative or at the instigation of a manager; or it may be created by a manager seeking to test the reactions of his peers or subordinates. A response to a proposal may take the form of a comment or a counterproposal. The absence of a reaction to a proposal is usually viewed as tacit approval.

Decision. A decision states the action to be taken. This message may be of two kinds: (1) a decision that affects repetitious events—which provides direction on how to handle not only the particular event that caused the discussion before the decision but also similar events in the future, and (2) a decision on an *ad hoc* problem—which does not formally affect future procedures. A decision can take a number of forms. It may start with a request to review the causes for making a decision to resolve certain problems; it may continue by outlining alternative courses of action and explaining the reasons for the rejection of some; it may go on to specify what has been decided and how the decision is to be implemented; and it may then express what feedback is expected to keep the decision maker informed of progress in implementation.

Oral messages. Oral messages are of two types: meetings (face-to-face) and telephone conversations (ear-to-ear).

Meetings. A meeting is a discussion involving two or more persons. Meetings have four purposes: (1) to provide a vehicle for exchanges to take place quickly, (2) to provide a job environment in which members are stimulated to new ideas by the rapid exchange of views, (3) to lessen the degree of semantical difficulties through face-to-face interaction,[10] and (4) to get the members attending the meeting committed more strongly to given plans or procedures than they would be otherwise.

There are two types of meetings: *routine meetings,* such as those of permanent committees, and *ad hoc meetings,* those called to discuss particular issues. The distinction between a routine and an *ad hoc* meeting is similar to that between a routine report and a memorandum. Like a routine report, a routine meeting can be either time or event triggered, while an *ad hoc* meeting may either be called in regard to a request to consider a particular problem or be event triggered. A meeting can also result from the issuance of any one or several of the messages listed earlier: a report, a memorandum, an inquiry for further information, a request for instructions, a proposal, or a decision. Significantly (as most police managers can attest to), a meeting can also fizzle and end inconclusively.

Telephone Conversations. Most of the remarks made on meetings are relevant to telephone communications. The distinction made earlier between routine and *ad hoc* communications may be useful here. There are, however, some noteworthy differences between these two types of oral messages: (1) A telephone conversation is generally confined to two participants, and (2) it lacks certain unique characteristics of interaction which take place in a face-to-face exchange. (Simply stated, if you want to influence someone—do it in person!)

CYBERNETICS: WHAT'S A CYBERNETIC?

Since the latter part of the 1940s a new technology has taken hold in our modern social organizations, one so new that its significance is just now beginning to be understood. While many aspects of this

[10] The importance of semantics for a manager is explained in Gerald H. Graham, "Improving Superior-Subordinate Relationships through General Semantics," *Public Personnel Review,* 30 (January 1969), 36–41.

technology are yet unclear, it has moved into the management scene rapidly, with definite and far-reaching impact on our formal organizations. In this and the next section we first explain and then conjecture about this new technology. We refer to this new technology as *information technology*. Implied in this title is our major concern, communications. Information technology is composed of several related components. One includes the machinery and techniques for processing large amounts of information rapidly. A second component is in the offing, though its applications have not yet emerged very clearly; it consists of the simulation of higher-order thinking. A third component centers around the application of statistical and mathematical methods to decision-making problems; it is represented by techniques like mathematical programming and by methodologies like operations research. A fourth component is the control and communication of information for the purpose of feedback. These last two components frequently use computers. We now focus on the fourth component, *feedback*, after which we will discuss the *computer*.

First we take time to justify our review of information technology. Broadly speaking, it is certain to have a significant impact on police management. Information technology either will be or is (1) placing more responsibility for planning on the manager, (2) requiring the manager to be innovative in performing his role, (3) freeing the manager from red tape, and (4) asking the manager to put this new technology to work solving his problems.

Feedback and cybernetics are often considered as being one and the same. The distinction between them, however, is significant. To explain, certain aspects of communication imply that organizations have a built-in capacity to correct their errors, enhancing their potential for effectiveness. *Cybernetics* (a word coined from the Greek *kybernetes*, "steersman") focuses strongly upon the role of feedback in the learning process. *Feedback* is defined by Norbert Wiener as a means for controlling an organization by reinserting into it the results of its past performance.[11] He further described cybernetics as "the entire field of control and communication theory, whether in the machine or in the animal."[12] Wiener explained his rationale for linking communication and control into cybernetics as follows:

> When I control the actions of another person, I communicate a message to him, and although this message is in the imperative mood, the technique of communication does not differ from that of a message of fact. Furthermore, if my control is to be effective, I must take cognizance of any messages from him which may indicate that the order is understood and has been obeyed.[13]

[11] Wiener, *The Human Use of Human Beings*, p. 61.

[12] Norbert Wiener, *Cybernetics* (New York: John Wiley & Sons, Inc., 1948), p. 19.

[13] Wiener, *The Human Use of Human Beings*, p. 16.

Feedback is extended here to mean any information that influences an organization's or an individual's current action. Cybernetics denotes both the process by which feedback is furnished (communications) and a special purpose for feedback (control). The computer fits neatly into this picture because, by being hooked up with electronic data processing machines, the new communication-control systems are able to respond more quickly and accurately to changes in a large-scale environment. Hence, the most obvious impact of cybernetics has been in the acceleration of technological change through new machines that can replace routinized mental labor.

One word of caution—some erroneously seek to use cybernetics in shaping human organizations, in other words, change our organizations to operate like machines. This concept envisions a self-steering network composed of receptors, transmitters, and feedback controls. Such thinking refutes what we feel or should feel about the purpose, will, consciousness, autonomy, integrity, and meaning of man and his organizations. Simply, its mechanistic doctrine looks like what we might call "robot" management. Please remember that the control function over people is best exercised by people, not by machines. Machines can select and process information. *It remains for man to act upon it.*

ENTER THE COMPUTER

The electronic computer is essentially for imputing, judging, and otherwise processing or usefully modifying knowledge. (See Chapter 11.) Thus it expands brainpower as other man-made machines enlarge muscle power. Like man, the computer expresses knowledge in terms of symbols. Man's symbols are letters and numbers; the machine's symbols are electromagnetic impulses that represent letters and numbers. There are two categories of computers: (1) the analog, which measures and compares quantities in one operation and has no memory, and (2) the digital, which solves problems by counting precisely and sequentially and has a memory. The analog computer is about fifty years old, enjoys a big and growing use in simulation and process control, and is "hybridized" with digital computers in some applications. But it accounts for a very small percentage of the overall computer market, and its potentialities at present are not so universal as are those of the digital machines. Most police managers fully understand the benefits of digital computers. First let us briefly discuss the machinery; later we will examine some of its uses.

Automatic data processing (ADP) encompasses both electronic data processing (EDP) and electric accounting machines (EAM). EDP means the type of automatic handling of information that is done by the million-operations-a-second electronic computer, as compared with the limited mechanical handling done by EAM. The five major phases of any information system are *input,* acquisition of data and placement into the system; *storage,* to file data either temporarily or permanently; *processing,* to manipulate data according to specified rules; *output,* to present the results of the processing or the status of data stored in the system; and *communications,* to transmit the data from one node in the system to another. A very important sub-phase, especially to those in local law enforcement, is *inquiry.* An integrated law enforcement information system is highly dependent on remote inquiry and receiving devices. An inquiry involves both the input and the output functions at a single location.

A survey made of police ADP systems provides us with an appreciation of computer usage by police organizations.[14] Note that the findings are limited to city police departments and, therefore, do not supply data on county, state, or federal policing agencies. In 1968 all municipal police agencies servicing cities with populations over 25,000 were questioned regarding both present and future automated police data processing systems, and existing or planned-for applications. Of the 592 city police departments sent questionnaires, 252, or 43 percent, responded with a complete set of answers. To ascertain the effects of city size on the responses, the population was divided into five subpopulations as follows:

City Size (Population)	Total Number of Cities	Number of Cities That Responded
500,000 or over	27	19
250,000–500,000	27	15
100,000–250,000	96	48
50,000–100,000	153	66
25,000– 50,000	289	104
Total	592	252

The response to the questionnaire was related to city size (67 percent of the cities with populations over 500,000 responded, while only 36 percent of cities with populations under 50,000 responded), as was the use of ADP. Of the police departments responding, 110, or 44 percent, indicated that they were using some form of automatic data processing. The proportion of cities using ADP in the five categories ranged from 100 percent of the cities of 500,000 population or more to only 18 percent of the cities with populations under 50,000. The police departments were also asked if they had plans to implement a data processing system in the next three years; an additional

[14] For further details, see Paul M. Whisenand and Tug Tamaru, *Automated Police Information Systems* (New York: John Wiley & Sons, Inc., 1970).

49, or 19 percent, indicated that they had plans firm enough to allow them a year for installation.

The basic results of the survey as related to ADP use can be summarized as follows:

1. Of the police departments responding (252 of 592, 43 percent), a group of 110, or 44 percent, indicated that they were using automatic data processing.
2. By 1971 this group should have increased to 159, or 63 percent of the departments responding.
3. A vast majority of the ADP equipment being used are computer systems (84 percent) as compared with electronic accounting machines (16 percent).
4. The trend is definitely in favor of computer systems, although the proportion of computers to EAM will remain about the same.
5. The use of ADP is directly related to city size, with larger cities more likely to use ADP than smaller ones, as would be expected.
6. There seems to be no definite trend at this time that establishes a pattern of control, operation, or location of ADP equipment. Some 50 percent of the departments reported that they operate their own equipment, and the sentiment in law enforcement is absolutely in favor of police control of their own systems.

The computer is performing still another service to local law enforcement—that of linking the numerous separate police ADP systems into a unified, or integrated, network. The local ADP system is becoming a building block for a nationwide computer-based police information system. California's Law Enforcement Telecommunications Systems (CLETS) is one example of an effort to put together a total statewide ADP system. It is also an example of highly important federal-state linkage. It permits any urban or rural law enforcement agency to transmit messages to any other agency in the state and to receive instant information on wanted persons, stolen or lost property, and firearms. Any agency will be able to send a message to all other agencies within the state or to any combination of agencies. The state's law enforcement agencies will be tied to computers at the California Department of Justice, the California Department of Motor Vehicles, the California Highway Patrol, and the Federal Bureau of Investigation's National Crime Information Center and Project Research in Washington, D.C. Computers, switching center personnel, and the backbone circuitry with one terminal point per county are being provided by the state. Each local agency will provide the circuitry and equipment to link itself to its county terminal point. When CLETS is fully operational, a police officer, in a few seconds, will be able to ask for and receive information from a statewide data base that contains facts on persons, vehicles, property, and firearms.

The computer looms large in the "present" of a police manager. Basically, the computer will upgrade the status and the responsibilities of the manager's role in the police organization and will permit him more time for personal contact. In other words, the computer will assist the manager in accomplishing one of his primary duties, organizational control. Simultaneously, it will free him for performing another primary duty, planning. For those police managers who have stayed on the sidelines while their co-workers have increased their physical and intellectual accessibility to the computer, it seems inevitable that they will become immersed in the computer progress and problems of their department.[15]

EFFECTIVE COMMUNICATIONS: SOME SUGGESTIONS

The importance of maintaining effective communications is as vital as it always has been. Every human act or thought within a police organization depends in some way on communication. Although it is a vital part of every police manager's job, communication remains a highly personal art. Human beings have been communicating with each other by gestures and signs since the origin of the species, by spoken words for perhaps half a million years, and by some form of writing for more than four thousand years. We should be experts at it by now, but unfortunately we are not. The major problem today is not that we are not experts at communication but that the demands now being placed on human communication threaten to exceed its capacity. Since communication is a human activity, even though machines may be used to help man in "talking," we emphasize a fundamental principle: The effectiveness of communication tends to be directly proportional to the degree to which both the sender and the receiver regard and treat each other as "human," in the personal context of the event.[16] The following techniques or basics for effective communications should be evaluated and (perhaps) implemented with these thoughts in mind.[17]

Many techniques have been developed whereby police managers may remove or circumvent the blockage at each point in the communication process. The major techniques may be broadly classified in terms of the blockage they remedy. There are five areas where blockage might occur in a communications system: (1) sender—one who initiates a message, (2) message—the device for transmitting in-

[15] A provocative discussion of the importance and relationship between intellectual and physical accessibility to computers can be found in Herbert H. Isaacs, "Computer Systems Technology: Progress, Projections, Problems," *Public Administration Review*, 28 (November-December 1968), 488–94.

[16] Edward E. Marcus, "The Basis of Effective Human Communication," *Public Personnel Review*, 28 (April 1967), 111.

[17] For a comprehensive discussion on communications-organization, management, and interpersonal relations, see Lee Thayer, *Communication and Communication Systems* (Homewood, Ill.: Richard D. Irwin, Inc., 1968).

formation, (3) symbol—the content and format of the information, (4) channel—the means for interchanging messages, and (5) receiver— one who accepts a message. The major techniques for surmounting the impasses are as follows (take note, manager):

Sender blockage	Special positions or units whose function is to disseminate information inside or outside the organizations
	Formal and informal reporting systems
Message blockage	Standards for the preparation of reports
	Summarization of long or complex messages
Symbol blockage	Improved style
	Training in use of special terms
	Visual aids
Channel blockage	Liaison officers and special intermediaries
	Routing, screening, and clearance procedures
	Reeducation of hierarchic levels and number of intermediaries
	Exploitation of informal channels and polyarchic relations
Receiver blockage	More use of face-to-face communication
	Indoctrination in common frame of reference

The application of such techniques is obviously, by itself, no promise of better communication. Any one of them, in helping to cope with one source of blockage, may cause still another kind. If many of them together resulted in much more communication, the end product could be a serious increase in the information overload. The correct use of well-known techniques and the invention of new ones are rooted in the broader understanding of police managers who have developed an interest in the communication process and the ability to communicate. The manager with an interest in communication is one who, instead of taking communication for granted, is always alert to the possibility of blockage at any point. Perhaps of greatest importance is that police managers comprehend the communications systems in their organization. They must become familiar with the strengths and the weaknesses of both formal and informal communication channels in the organization's structure. They learn through their analysis of the communication process about personal judgments and values, the meanings that individuals place on certain facts, and self-enforcing group attitudes. Even poor managers develop some skills of oral or written presentation. The more successful managers, however, also develop the skills of listening, thereby facilitating their entry into two-way communication interchanges. Both types of skill reach the level of art only when the police manager as sender-receiver is able to regard and treat others as "human" in the personal context of the event.

LEARNING EXERCISES

This chapter presents two learning exercises on the value, role, and use of establishing and maintaining effective communications. The first lesson is a case study that relates how a city (the study also has meaning for city police departments) designed and implemented a far-reaching public information program! Basically, it describes an attempt on the part of the city to build a supportive climate for its program within the community. Hence, it reports on an "internally" oriented effort. The second case is an "internally" directed effort to free-up communications. As compared with the first case, it suggests an analytical plan for reducing message distortion and blockage. The case has been modified to more clearly reflect the interpersonal dynamics as they might occur within a police department.

PR —HOW IT WORKS IN DAYTON

James E. Kunde and Melvyn Weinberg

Local governments are recognizing the unique importance of providing information to their citizens—swiftly, accurately, and fully.[18] They regard this service as essential to the understanding of every other service they perform.

The city of Dayton, Ohio (pop. approximately 250,000), has become a leader in its use of public relations to inform and involve its citizenry. Dayton keeps firmly in mind the informal definition of public relations: "Do something right, and get caught at it."

PR in Dayton is by no means a low priority item of municipal service. News dissemination is recognized as a daily operation, necessary for the smooth working of every aspect of city administration.

It hasn't always been this way. In former years, city publications, for example, tended to vary confusingly from one edition to another. Little consistent use was made of radio or television. Press conferences rarely took place, with the result that media coverage of city accomplishments was spotty, unrelated, and noncomprehensive. As for citizen involvement, it consisted largely of "name" committees formed at times of tax support campaigns.

In January, 1969, all this changed. Then City Manager Graham W. Watt appointed Dayton's first public information officer (PIO), a new position created by action of the city commission.

This officer is charged with certain well-defined responsibilities:

> To develop widespread knowledge and understanding of the city's programs, needs, resources, and accomplishments.
>
> To create a climate of confidence, encouraging acceptance of city programs and policies.

[18] Permission to reprint this case granted by the International City Management Association. It originally appeared in *Public Management*, 52 (December 1970), 15–17.

To overcome voter apathy by stimulating interest and support.

To open channels of communication through exchange of ideas.

To establish and reinforce feelings of citizen pride in Dayton.

To meet these objectives, Public Information Officer Melvyn Weinberg has instituted a number of PR programs, all of them with thorough documentation back-up.

Dayton issues several kinds of reports to its citizens, spelling out progress on various levels. An annual report tries for widest possible readership and circulation. A financial report goes to the financial community of interested citizens, business leaders, and investors. Other special publications report the growth and progress of city-involved projects.

One unusual publication is a directory of city services, with a handy list of names and phone numbers to call for further information. It covers recreation, clinics, and rumor control centers as well as more standard municipal services.

Schools are informed on how to arrange guided tours of city facilities. A monthly in-house publication, *Facet,* presents an attractive image of the helpful people who man city positions and services. Supplied to all media as well as to city personnel, it generates widespread interest in addition to news articles and broadcast features.

Radio and television stations receive the public information officer's consistent attention, and they receive news stories, feature leads, and audiovisual material acceptable for public service announcements. Dayton's morning and evening newspaper reporters are also given every possible cooperation in their search for news among city departments.

Should "static" develop—when, for example, a department news source prefers to retain information that a newsman wants—the establishment of a special temporary procedure is helpful. For the period of the crisis, all news from that department is released only through the public information office . . . a practice which ensures accuracy and tends to "bury the hatchet" for all contending parties.

At this point, the PIO puts himself in the middle and absorbs the heat, resulting in the appearance of fewer editorials headed, "Health Department's Job Not To Protect Violators."

Since it was organized two years ago, Dayton's Office of Public Information has explored several innovations in communication. Its 1969 Annual Report (issued in January, 1970) is a case in point. Something special was needed to reach the Greater Dayton audience which includes 300,000 people who live outside the city limits but who work in Dayton and pay city income tax.

It was determined that a special magazine supplement delivered to the 750,000 readers of the *Dayton Sunday News* would have the necessary reach and impact. The result was a full-color, 24-page tabloid, called "Faces of the Changing City." In it, important city services were described in typical magazine format, with each article accompanied by appropriate illustration.

Involvement of local commercial artists was arranged by invitation of the project art director who paid each artist a modest fee and strongly stressed the honor of being asked to contribute. More than 100 Dayton school children also participated, with the winning second-grader's effort appearing on the report's back cover. An added PR benefit was achieved by the exhibition of the young artists' masterpieces in the salon of the city's leading department store.

Entered in regional competition sponsored by the Dayton Advertising Club, the report won first place against the area's best corporate reports. National attention followed, and the public information office has received many congratulatory comments from municipalities all over the country.

The broadcast media have not been overlooked. "City on the Air" currently programs 10 shows each week over area stations. Titles of the programs vary from "Action City and You," to "Inside City Hall," to "Model Cities Profile," to "Soul Beat Car No. 158."

Urban problems are examined and solutions proposed. Program formats range from interview, moderator/panel, to listener telephone-in. The public information officer hosts a weekly radio and TV show, both pretaped. Other hosting chores and guest appearances are handled by uniformed and civilian city employees. Audience response has been excellent.

In line with many municipalities, the city staffs a speakers' bureau to answer requests by program chairmen. Something different, yet logical, is the new listeners' bureau established by City Manager James E. Kunde. To fulfill this vital part of the PR function, the manager assigns top-level officials to attend neighborhood and community meetings. The result is that grassroots organizations are learning that the city "cares enough to send its very best." And community needs are quickly known at city hall.

Involvement and feedback are key factors in several city actions designed to improve its public relationships. The welfare department has become the department of human resources. The workhouse has become the rehabilitation center where strong emphasis is placed on a program of high school courses offered to the inmates.

The city manager has initiated a neighborhood grant program setting aside $200,000 for neighborhood improvements to be selected by the citizens of the neighborhoods, another indication of enlightened public relations at work. Finally, an ombudsman program has been approved by the city commission as a means of providing a mechanism to increase government's responsiveness to its citizenry.

To channel news effectively, it is recognized that a stable working relationship must exist between the city manager and his public information officer. Accordingly, Manager Kunde holds a weekly meeting with his executive staff at which the PIO is able to gather and discuss material for press releases and conferences.

In a similar way, the public information office is able to keep in touch through staff meetings with all departments, and act as a clearinghouse for ideas and PR techniques. Each department learns about and adapts from the successes of another department in the city's public information activities. Dayton's experience indicates it serves a useful purpose to have the public information officer immediately adjacent to the city manager's office and conference room. Because news often "breaks" here, it can be delivered "hot" to media men without delay, a circumstance that pleases almost everyone.

The public information staff consists of one full-time secretary and two part-time, college-level communications "interns." Area universities can also provide bright students on assignment in the particular field of their studies. On occasion, local advertising agencies or agency personnel are retained for special campaigns. The annual public information office budget is $71,000.

One of the public information office's most sensitive areas is the reluctance of many officials to discuss projected plans and policies with newsmen. As one official said, "Everything we say gets translated or condensed or twisted into what comes out as a bold, condemning headline!" Reporters hold an opposing viewpoint.

To ease conflicts and anxieties the public information officer discusses each problem topic with department heads, and editors and reporters, working toward accommodations that, hopefully, will suit everyone concerned. While this isn't always possible, the city is convinced that the success of government lies in mutually helpful cooperation between the city administration and the news media.

Naturally, city hall tries to put its best foot forward, but also keeps communication channels open for media people to find news on a day-to-day basis. There is no question but that many a reporter's discovery has resulted in bringing a community problem into constructive focus and has led to an effective solution.

For Dayton, and for any city, the PR goal is always fairness and accuracy, with the ideal result stated in the slogan of a great newsgathering organization: "The truth well told!"

A CASE OF CHANGING COMMUNICATIONS AND INFLUENCE PATTERNS

This case illustrates a strategy for developing trust and effective communication between staff/line and headquarters/field groups.[19]

BACKGROUND

The organization in this case is a large, extremely effective urban police department, with a rather extensive community relations program. There are geographical divisions (stations) located in various parts of the city.

The managers (captains) of these divisions report to higher managers (inspectors) who are physically located in the central headquarters. These managers (in turn) report to a bureau chief.

To service the geographical divisions, there are a number of staff divisions located at headquarters. There is a management systems staff which furnishes methods improvement, work study, organization analysis, and information systems. There is also a human resources staff which is concerned with training, management development, recruitment, and employee and labor relations.

The staffs in the police headquarters had had continuing problems in the past of acceptance in the divisions, and of introducing their techniques and technologies to their operations. Such techniques and technologies were not always welcomed by the field police managers. There was also a certain amount of competition between the various staff units, particularly those concerned with introducing organization change.

THE NEED

The need for this particular organization-wide change effort was originally felt by one of the headquarter managers (inspectors). He had received a lot of input from his geographical divisions managers about the poor relationships between the divisions and the headquarters staffs. Field managers complained of a lack of service and inadequate support from the central headquarters. Simultaneously, a need was reported for better coordination of

[19]Adapted from an actual case described in Richard Beckhard, *Organization Development: Strategies and Models* (Reading, Mass.: Addison-Wesley Publishing Company, Inc., 1969), pp. 87–92.

efforts among the management systems, and the human resources staffs. The inspector checked with his counterparts and found similar attitudes existed with their captains. He contacted the heads of the various staffs. Working with an internal consultant (a member of the top management staff whose function was to facilitate organization-improvement efforts) he developed an overall strategy. Outside consultant help was brought in to assist with the diagnosis and change program.

INITIAL DIAGNOSIS AND STRATEGY

The analysis indicated the following:

1. A need for establishing intergroup collaboration and a better working relationship between the human resource development and the management system groups.

2. A need for the examination of the system of rewards to both these staff groups. The rewards had been pretty much for services rendered in their own specialty. No rewards were given for collaborative work with another unit.

3. A recognition that there was a lot of capability in both staff organizations and that many of the skills overlapped. An agreement that a team approach with a combination of operations-research and behavioral-science capabilities could, in many instances, do the best diagnosis and give best assistance to field problems.

4. A need for upgrading the personnel or human-resources function in the field stations to decrease the dependency on the headquarters.

5. A need for division station managers and inspectors to examine their own styles relative to the management of human resources.

6. A need for some joint problem-solving by the field managements and the headquarters staffs.

7. A possible need for some new forms of organizing the way services were called for and provided.

From this analysis the following strategies were developed:

1. There should be some internal team-building efforts within the staffs to get their own self-images clear.

2. There should be some intergroup work between human resource development and management systems to search for common goals and ways of increasing collaborative effort.

3. There should be some further information-collection from station managers on their needs and problems.

4. The inspectors should examine the quality of the personnel function in the stations as a basis for developing improved capability in each geographical division.

5. There should be some joint activity between representatives of station and top management (inspectors) and representatives of human resources development and management systems (captains) to work on the issues between the groups and to look for ways of improved collaboration and service.

6. Top line management (inspectors) and top staff management

(inspectors) should periodically review the state of the relationships and the work.

ACTIONS

The following actions occurred:

1. The human resources development group held a couple of team-building programs to work on their own interpersonal relations and team effectiveness.
2. Members of this team attended advanced programs in training and/or organization development to upgrade their technical capability.
3. Members were started on a regular communications basis between the heads of the human resources development group concerned with organization development and with the heads of the management systems staff.

    Several joint meetings were held with an outside consultant and the total membership of both groups, to examine their relationships and problems, to work on the development of common goals, and to improve work methods.

4. One station manager (line) at this regular semiannual management meeting devoted the majority of the meeting to an assessment of the problems and obstacles toward improved performance that grew out of the relationship between the field division and the staff units at headquarters. The output of this was shared with the other field managers and the inspector and with the head of human resource development.
5. A three-day off-site meeting was held between human resource development and line management. Attending were the head human resource development which included the managers of the employee relations, training and development, and recruitment; and three of the four division managers, inspectors and seven of the sixteen station managers (captains).

    At this meeting the field people shared their image of, and attitudes about, the human resources development staff. Conversely, the staff people expressed their frustrations and problems with the line people. A list of priority issues was produced and ways for handling each of the issues were developed. The outputs of this meeting included:

    a) A major reorganization of the services to the field from within the human resources development group, the employee-relations people were designated to have liaison responsibility with a specific number of stations. Their major mission was redefined as: to be available to field management for the diagnosis and development of priority concerns for improvement within the station and for the provision of appropriate technical support from both the human resource development and the management systems staffs.

b) To help prepare the employee-relations people for this change role, a specialist who was highly skilled and trained in organization-development was assigned full time to this group to help them upgrade their technical capability, and to be available as a consultant to them in their relations with the field.

c) Steps were undertaken to upgrade the quality of personnel in that role.

d) Follow-up meetings were arranged between the various groups. A timetable was developed for introduction of these changes, station by station.

6. One inspector, in order to facilitate the organization-development program, assigned a number of managers (both line and staff) to be "change agents." Their assignment was to provide help to units of the station engaged in various change efforts. They were to assist in team-development activities, improve intergroup collaboration, and improve planning. This group is engaged in an intensive self-development program, using behavioral-science consultants from a university staff.

7. More members of the management systems and the human resources development staff are attending advanced-training programs in this field.

8. A coordinating organization composed of line people representing four levels of management, plus the leadership of the various staff organizations, has been created. It functions as a task force to maintain perspective on, and continue the forward development of, the entire change effort in local law enforcement. This group meets quarterly with two behavioral-science organization consultants.

SUMMARY AND ANALYSIS

This case represents an example of a change in communications and influence patterns toward increased organization effectiveness. The strategy included:

an identification of the subsystems (field management, human resource development staff, etc.) who had relationship problems;

strengthening their own internal functioning;

bringing up top management (line and staff) representatives from interfacing units together;

bringing full membership of interfacing units into joint problem solving activities;

creating new organization forms (permanent problem solving groups) to meet changing needs.

The consultant roles in this case included:

Diagnosis of relevant subsystems.

Consulting with change managers (top manager [inspector] head of human resource development).

Procedural consultant to intergroup meetings (station-management, human resource development [management systems]).

Consultant to teams in team-development (human resource development; management systems; divisional station group).

Methods consultation on new organization forms (permanent problem solving model).

Trainer of internal resources (training and OD specialists).

Catalyst between field and headquarters managements.

ORGANIZING:

The Art of Hierarchy

And thou shalt teach them ordinances and laws, and shalt show them the way wherein they must walk, and the work that they must do.

Moreover thou shalt provide out of all the people able men, such as fear God, men of truth, hating covetousness; and place such over them, to be rulers of thousands, and rulers of hundreds, rulers of fifties, and rulers of tens:

And let them judge the people at all seasons: and it shall be, that every great matter they shall bring unto thee, but every small matter they shall judge: so shall it be easier for thyself, and they shall bear the burden with thee. . . .

And Moses chose able men out of all Israel, and made them heads over the people, rulers of thousands, rulers of hundreds, rulers of fifties, and rulers of tens.

And they judged the people at all seasons: the hard causes they brought unto Moses, but every small matter they judged themselves.[1]

One can find in this model such traditional concepts as authority commensurate with responsibility, appointment by central authority,

[1] Exod. 18:20–22, 25–26.

selection of personnel based on ability, formation of a hierarchy, delegation, decision making, division of labor, span of control, task specialization, unity of command, and policy determination at the top of the hierarchy. An exhaustive analysis could probably identify other classifiable concepts in the quotation. Even without such an analysis, the great antiquity of most of our traditional ideas about organizational theory and management is vividly illustrated in this remarkable quotation. Traditional organizational patterns, however, are beginning to change, and our experience in local law enforcement reflects some of these changes. Yet the phenomenon known as *organization* is neither understood nor appreciated by most people, even though organizations are among the most important institutions in every part of the world and have a pervasive influence upon almost all human activity. Because of their increasing influence, we find an ever-expanding interest in the whys and wherefores of organizations. It is recognized that organizations are not a modern invention. The pharaohs of Egypt and the emperors of China depended upon organizations for constructing a variety of complex structures, and conscious interest in theories or principles of organization began in ancient Greece.

Organizational theory is "problem" centered, the problem being how to construct human groupings that are as rational as possible and simultaneously to produce a maximum of individual job satisfaction. There is a record of both progress and regression in the search for the best combination of these objectives. Significantly, the police manager can foster these objectives or detract from them in an attempt to do either one or both. He plays a critical role in coordinating human efforts to accomplish organizational goals. This chapter seeks to describe for the police manager the changing aspects of organizational theory and behavior. More specifically, it indicates for the police manager the state-of-the-art and possible future trends in organizing the police structure. Hence, in one sense the chapter is historical, since it deals with the formal side of organization, and in another sense it is contemporary, because much of the historical or classical thinking remains in practice. However, it also reports on a *reaction* and an emerging *synthesis*. The reaction is to those who cannot see beyond the mechanistic doctrine of the traditionalists—it is referred to as the informal side, or human relations in organizational theory. The ultimate synthesis combines these two theoretical concerns— formal and informal—into the much more sophisticated systems theory of organizing. From this vantage point we proffer a learning exercise that synthesizes the thinking to date on "organizing" police "organizations."

ORGANIZATION DEFINED

Organizations are social units (human groupings) deliberately constructed and reconstructed to seek specific goals.[2] Corporations, armies, schools, churches, and police departments are included; ethnic groups, friendship groups, and family groups are excluded. An organization is characterized by (1) goals, (2) a division of labor, authority, power, and communication responsibilities in a rationally planned, rather than a random or traditionally patterned, manner, (3) a set of rules and norms, (4) the presence of one or more authority centers which control the efforts of the organization and direct them toward its goals.

In defining organization, it is helpful to define some other concepts frequently confused with it. First, let us again consider management. *Management* is action intended to achieve rational cooperation in an organization. Second, there is *administration,* which is, quite simply, organization and management. The crux or central idea of administration is to deliberately construct a rational plan of human action for goal accomplishment. Third is the much discussed and "cussed" concept known as *bureaucracy.* For those familiar with Weber's work, bureaucracy implies that the unit is organized according to the principles he specified. But many organizations are not bureaucratic. Since many police departments are to a great extent, if not totally, bureaucratic, this concept is covered in more detail later in the chapter. Bureaucracies (1) are organizations that have numerous *formalized* rules and regulations and (2) are among the most important institutions in the world because they not only provide employment for a very significant fraction of the world's population but also make critical decisions that shape the economic, educational, political, social, moral, and even religious lives of nearly everyone on earth.[3] (Chapter 3 discussed the subject of organizational goals. The importance of goals to an organization lies in the realization that they are the main reason for the very existence of the organization.)

ORGANIZATIONAL THEORY: THE FORMAL APPROACH

By *classical* theory of organization is meant the theory that developed over a number of centuries and finally matured in the thirties. It is exemplified in Luther Gulick's essay "Notes on the Theory

[2]Talcott Parsons, *Structure and Process in Modern Societies* (New York: The Free Press of Glencoe, 1960), p. 17.

[3]Anthony Downs, *Inside Bureaucracy* (Boston: Little, Brown and Company, 1967), p. 1.

of Organization,"[4] in Monney and Reiley's *Principles of Organization*,[5] and in Max Weber's writing on bureaucracy.[6] All these theorists were strongly oriented toward economy, efficiency, and executive control. These values, when combined, create a theory of organization that has four cornerstones—division of labor, hierarchy of authority, structure, and span of control. Of the four, division of labor is the most important; in fact, the other three are dependent on it for their very existence. The hierarchy of authority is the legitimate vertical network for gaining compliance. Essentially, it includes the chain of command, the sharing of authority and responsibility, the unity of command, and the obligation to report. Structure is the logical relationship of positions and functions in an organization, arranged to accomplish the objectives of organization. Classical organization theory usually works with two basic structures, the line and the staff. According to Gulick, both structures can be arranged four ways: purpose, process, people (clientele), and place where services are rendered.[7] The span of control concept deals with the number of subordinates a superior can effectively supervise. It has significance, in part, for the shape of the organization. Wide span yields a flat structure; short span results in a tall structure.

Our approach to classical organization theory is three fold. The first area deals with rationality and its critical role in a bureaucratic structure. The principal theorist in this case is Max Weber. The second area is devoted to maximizing efficiency by making management a true science. In this instance, most of our thinking is derived from Frederick W. Taylor. The third area is best termed *principles*, and here we turn to the works of Gulick, Urwick, Mooney, and Reiley. Keep in mind that the concepts and developments are not mutually exclusive but overlap a great deal.

Weber Rationality

Max Weber was a founder of modern sociology as well as a pioneer in administrative thought. Weber probed bureaucracy, here essentially synonymous with large organization, to uncover the rational relationship of bureaucratic structure to its goals. His analysis led him to conclude that there were three types of organizational

---

[4] Luther Gulick, "Notes on the Theory of Organization," in *Papers on the Science of Administration*, ed. Luther Gulick and Lyndall Urwick (New York: Institute of Public Administration, 1937), pp. 1–45.

[5] James D. Mooney and Alan C. Reiley, *Principles of Organization* (New York: Harper & Row, Publishers, 1939).

[6] The best-known translation of Max Weber's writings on bureaucracy is H. H. Gerth and C. Wright Mills, trans., *From Max Weber: Essays in Sociology* (New York: Oxford University Press, Inc., 1946).

[7] Gulick, "Notes."

power centers: (1) traditional—subjects accept the orders of a supervisor as justified on the grounds that it is the way things have always been done, (2) charismatic—subjects accept a superior's order as justified because of the influence of his personality, and (3) rational-legal—subjects accept a superior's order as justified because it agrees with more abstract rules which are considered legitimate. The type of power employed determines the degree of alienation on the part of the subject. If the subject perceives the power as legitimate, he is more willing to comply. And, if power is considered legitimate, then, according to Weber, it becomes authority. Hence, Weber's three power centers can be translated into authority centers. Of the three types of authority, Weber recommended that rational structural relationships be obtained through the rational-legal form. He felt that the other two forms lacked systematic division of labor, specialization, and stability and had nonrelevant political and administrative relationships.

In each principle of bureaucracy described below, Weber's constant concern about the frailness of a rational-legal bureaucracy is apparent. His primary motive, therefore, was to build into the bureaucratic structure safeguards against external and internal pressures so that the bureaucracy could at all times sustain its autonomy. According to Weber, a bureaucratic structure, to be rational, must contain these elements.[8]

1. *Rulification and routinization.* "A continuous organization of official functions bound by *rules.*" Rational organization is the opposite of temporary, unstable relations, thus the stress on continuity. Rules save effort by eliminating the need for deriving a new solution for every situation. They also facilitate standard and equal treatment of similar situations.

2. *Division of labor.* "A specific sphere of competence. This involves (a) a sphere of obligation to perform functions which have been marked off as part of a systematic division of labor; (b) the provision of the incumbent with the necessary authority to carry out these functions; and (c) that the necessary means of compulsion are clearly defined and their use is subject to definite conditions."

3. *Hierarchy of authority.* "The organization of offices follows the principle of hierarchy; that each lower office under the control and supervision of a higher one."

4. *Expertise.* "The rules which regulate the conduct of an office may be *technical* rules or norms. In both cases, if their application is to be fully rational, specialized training is necessary. It is thus normally true that only a person who has demonstrated an adequate technical training is qualified to be a member of the administrative staff. . . ."

[8]Max Weber, *The Theory of Social and Economic Organization,* ed. Talcott Parsons, trans. A. M. Henderson and Talcott Parsons (New York: Oxford University Press, Inc. 1947), pp. 329–30.

5. *Written rules.* "Administrative acts, decisions, and rules are formulated and recorded in writing . . . ."

6. *Separation of ownership.* "It is a matter of principle that the members of the administrative staff should be completely separated
from ownership of the means of production or administration. . . .
There exists, furthermore, in principle, complete separation of the
property belonging to the organization, which is controlled within
the spheres of the office, and the personal property of the official. . . ."

Weber did not expect any bureaucracy to have all the elements he
listed. The greater the number and intensity of these elements an
organization possessed, however, the more rational and, therefore,
the more efficient would be the organization. His contribution to
organizational theory is becoming more recognized and appreciated.
Our modern police organizations would find it hard to deny that he
has to some degree influenced their structure. Mr. Manager—are
you now working in a bureaucratic organization?

Taylorism: Scientific Management

Frederick W. Taylor, production specialist, business executive,
and consultant, applied the scientific method to the solution of factory problems and from these analyses established principles which
could be substituted for the trial-and-error methods then in use. The
advent of Taylor's thinking opened a new era, that of *scientific management.* Taylor probably did not invent the term or originate the
approach. Taylor's enormous contribution lay, first, in his large-
scale application of the analytical, scientific approach to improving
production methods in the shop.[9] Second, while he did not feel that
management could ever become an exact science in the same sense
as physics and chemistry, he believed strongly that management
could be an organized body of knowledge and that it could be taught
and learned. Third, he originated the term and concept of *functional
supervision.* Taylor felt that the job of supervision was too complicated to be handled effectively by one supervisor and should therefore be delegated to as many as eight specialized foremen. Finally,
Taylor believed that his major contribution lay in a new philosophy
for workers and management.

Now, in its essence, scientific management involves a complete
mental revolution on the part of the workingmen engaged in any particular establishment or industry—a complete mental revolution on
the part of these men as to their duties toward their work, toward
their fellowmen, and toward their fellow employees. And it involves
the equally complete mental revolution on the part of those on the

---

[9] Frederick W. Taylor, *Shop Management* (New York: Harper & Row, Publishers,
1911).

management's side—the foreman, the superintendent, the owner of the business, the board of directors—a complete mental revolution on this part as to their duties toward their fellow workers in the management, toward their workmen, and toward all their daily problems. And without this complete mental revolution on both sides, scientific management does not exist.[10]

Taylor consistently maintained—and successfully demonstrated —that through the use of his techniques it would be possible to obtain appreciable increases in a worker's efficiency. Furthermore, he firmly believed that management, and management alone, should be responsible for putting these techniques into effect. Although it is important to obtain the cooperation of the workers, it must be "enforced cooperation." He emphasizes this point as follows:

> It is only through *enforced* standardization of methods, *enforced* cooperation that this faster work can be assured. And the duty of enforcing the adaptation of standards and of enforcing this cooperation rests with the *management* alone. . . .[11]

Taylor prescribed five methods for "scientifically" managing an organization. First, management must carefully study the worker's body movements to discover the one best method for accomplishing work in the shortest possible time. Second, management must standardize its tools based on the requirements of specific jobs. Third, management must select and train each worker for the job for which he is best suited. Fourth, management must abandon the traditional unity-of-command principle and substitute functional supervision. As already mentioned, Taylor advocated that a worker receive his orders from as many as eight supervisors. Four of these supervisors were to serve on the shop floor (inspector, repair foreman, speed boss, and gang boss) and the other four in the planning room (routing, instruction, time and costs, and discipline). Fifth, management must pay the worker in accordance with his individual output.

Ironically, Taylor's general approach to management is widely accepted today in production-oriented business organizations. Scientific management became a movement, which still has a tremendous

[10] Frederick W. Taylor, "The Principles of Scientific Management," in *Classics in Management*, ed. Harwood F. Merrill (New York: American Management Association, 1960), p. 78. A comprehensive account of Taylor's achievements in this field can be found in three basic documents: "Shop Management," a paper presented to the American Society of Mechanical Engineers in 1903; "The Principles of Scientific Management," which Taylor wrote in 1909, when his work was becoming an object of public attention, but which was not published until 1911; and his 1912 "Testimony before the Special House Committee," which consisted largely of a justification of his views in the light of public attack. These three documents have been published in one volume, *Scientific Management* (New York: Harper & Row, Publishers, 1947).

[11] Frederick W. Taylor, "Principles of Scientific Management," p. 83.

influence on industrial practice. More specifically, it had a major effect on the reform and economy movements in public administration and thus also influenced police administration. Its impact on public organizations is readily apparent at the present time. One can find numerous managers and supervisors (private and public alike) who firmly believe that if material rewards are directly related to work efforts, the worker consistently responds with his maximum performance.

Gulick and Urwick: The Principles

While the followers of Taylor developed more scientific techniques of management and work, others were conceptualizing broad principles for the most effective design of organizational structure. Luther Gulick and Lyndall Urwick were leaders in formulating principles of formal organization. Not only did they develop such principles, but Gulick went even further and defined administration as comprising seven activities.[12] Together these activities spell out the acronym POSDCORB.

> *Planning*: working out in broad outline what needs to be done and the methods for doing it to accomplish the purpose set for the enterprise;
>
> *Organizing*: the establishment of a formal structure of authority through which work subdivisions are arranged, defined, and co-ordinated for the defined objective;
>
> *Staffing*: the whole personnel function of bringing in and training the staff and maintaining favorable conditions of work;
>
> *Directing*: the continuous task of making decisions, embodying them in specific and general orders and instructions, and serving as the leader of the enterprise;
>
> *Coordinating*: the all important duty of interrelating the various parts of the organization;
>
> *Reporting*: keeping those to whom the executive is responsible informed as to what is going on, which includes keeping himself and his subordinates informed through records, research, and inspection;
>
> *Budgeting*: all that does with budgeting in the form of fiscal planning, accounting, and control.[13]

The Gulick-Urwick principles deal primarily with the structure of the formal organization. Underlying all their principles was the

---

[12]Gulick's seven elements of administration are drawn from Henri Fayol's list of five: planning, organization, command, coordination, and control. See Henri Fayol, *General and Industrial Management*, trans. Constance Storrs (London: Sir Isaac Pitman & Sons Ltd., 1949), pp. 43–110.

[13]Gulick, "Notes," p. 13.

need for an organizational *division of labor*. In other words, their approach rests firmly on the assumption that the more a specific function can be divided into its simplest parts, the more specialized and, therefore, the more skilled a worker can become in carrying out his part of the job. According to Gulick, any division of labor should be homogeneous, and homogeneity can be achieved if one or more of four determinants are used to characterize the type of work each individual is performing.

> The major *purpose* he is serving, such as furnishing water, controlling crime, or conducting education;
>
> The *process* he is using, such as engineering, medicine, carpentry, stenography, statistics, or accounting:
>
> The *person* or *things* dealt with or served, such as immigrants, veterans, Indians, forests, mines, parks, orphans, farmers, automobiles, or the poor;
>
> The *place* where he renders his service, such as Hawaii, Boston, Washington, the Dust Bowl, Alabama, or Central High School.[14]

This four-determinant approach is replete with problems. General determinants are difficult to apply to a specific organization because they often overlap, are sometimes incompatible with one another, and are quite vague. For example, when looking at a police organization, it would be difficult not to conclude that the four principles fail to provide a satisfactory guide to division of labor in that organization. Furthermore, it can be seen that these determinants are prescriptive rather than descriptive, that they state how work should be divided rather than how work is actually divided. The planning of the division of labor in a given organization is affected by many considerations not covered by the four principles. The division may be determined by the culture in which the organization is situated, by the environment of the organization, by the availability and type of personnel, and by political factors. Organizations are made up of a combination of various layers which differ in their type of division. The lower layers tend to be organized according to area or clientele, and the higher ones by purpose or process. Even this statement, however, should be viewed only as a probability. In a police organization, all four determinants operate at the same time, and it is their unique mix that makes the department either effective or ineffective.

In addition to Gulick's and Urwick's central principle of division of labor, seven other related principles merit our attention.[15]

[14] *Ibid.*, p. 15.

[15] This list is in part suggested by Gross. See Bertram M. Gross, *The Managing of Organizations* (New York: The Free Press of Glencoe, 1964), pp. 145–48.

1. *Unity of command.* "A man cannot serve two masters."[16] This principle is offered as a balance to the division of labor.

2. *Fitting people to the structure.* People should be assigned to their organizational positions "in a cold-blooded, detached spirit," like the preparation of an engineering design, regardless of the needs of that particular individual or of those individuals who may now be in the organization.[17]

3. *One top executive (manager).* Both Gulick and Urwick strongly supported the principle of one-man administrative responsibility in an organization. Hence they warned against the use of committees or boards.

4. *Staff: general and special.* The classical writers' concern about staff assistance to top management deserves special attention. When management expressed a need for help from larger and larger numbers of experts and specialists, this need immediately raised the question of the relation of these specialists to the regular line supervisors and employees. In this instance, Gulick recommended that the staff specialist obtain results from the line through influence and persuasion and that the staff not be given authority over the line. The next question to be answered was that of coordination. Top management would have more people to supervise, since they would be responsible for not only the line but the special staff as well. The Gulick-Urwick answer to this problem was to provide help through "general staff" as distinguished from "special staff" assistance. Significantly, general staff are not limited to the proffering of advice. They may draw up and transmit orders, check on operations, and iron out difficulties. In so doing, they act not on their own but as representatives of their superior and within the confines of decisions made by him. Thus, they allow him to exercise a broader span of control.

5. *Delegation.* Urwick emphasized that "lack of the courage to delegate properly and of knowledge how to do it is one of the most general causes of failure in organization." In larger organizations, we must delegate even the right to delegate.[18]

6. *Matching responsibility with authority.* In this case, Urwick dealt with both sides of the authority-responsibility relationship. It is wrong to hold people accountable for certain activities if "the necessary authority to discharge that responsibility" is not granted. On the other side, "the responsibilities of all persons exercising authority should be absolute within the defined terms of that authority. They should be personally accountable for all actions taken by subordinates." He set forth the widely quoted principle that "at all levels authority and responsibility should be coterminous and coequal."

7. *Span of control.* Again, Urwick asserted that "no supervisor can supervise directly the work of more than five or at the most, six

[16] Gulick, "Notes," p. 9.

[17] L. Urwick, *Elements of Administration* (New York: Harper & Row, Publishers, 1943), pp. 34–39.

[18] *Ibid.*, pp. 51–52.

subordinates whose work interlocks. When the number of subordinates increases arithmetically, there is a geometrical increase in all the possible combinations of relationship which may demand the attention of the supervisor."[19]

In review, classical organization theory was built on three interlocking cornerstones: rationality of structure, scientific management, and principles of organization. One way of classifying these three concepts is as follows: First, Weber's writing was primarily descriptive; however, it did indicate that a particular form of organizational structure was preferable. Second, the theories of both Taylor and the Gulick-Urwick team were prescriptive; that is, they expressed the one right way to manage and organize. Interestingly, Taylor's notion of a scientific management, while being purely mechanistic at first glance, is at the same time motivational. Taylor viewed man as a rational-economic animal; hence, the way for management to motivate him it through economic incentives that include improved work methods.

The Consequences

Having considered some of the attributes of the classical approach, we turn now to the present results of its teachings. This historical era lives on in the form of many contemporary formal organizational structures. It keeps those that listen to its tenets constantly gazing at the formal hierarchical jobs, positions, and procedures. Hence operations are stressed over people. Classical organization theory has given rise to not one but four formal structures. Since we live with these structures on a daily basis, it seems worthwhile to discuss them further. The four types of structures that have emerged from the literature are (1) job-task, (2) rank, (3) skill, and (4) pay.[20]

The job-task structure focuses on people working at specialized tasks. There is a division of labor, which in the assembly-line tradition is broken down into the smallest repetitive operations. In small organizations these positions develop rather naturally and are not formalized in writing. As organizations grow and become more complex, two developments usually occur: (1) classification of duties and (2) centralization of the authority to establish new positions. Both these developments provide a basis for establishing a system of position classification. Briefly, position classification is the grouping of positions, according to the similarity of duties and responsibilities, into job categories having identical job descriptions.

---

[19] *Ibid.*, pp. 45–46, 125.

[20] The remainder of this section is drawn primarily from the work of John M. Pfiffner and Frank P. Sherwood, *Administrative Organization* (Englewood Cliffs, N.J.: Prentice-Hall, Inc. 1960), pp. 66–71.

The structure of rank involves an officer class, an obvious example being the police. Other examples include the United States Foreign Service and the military. A structure of rank differs from the job hierarchy in that status does not attach to the particular job; a police sergeant is a sergeant whether supervising a patrol unit or conducting an investigation. The job structure emphasizes the duties to be performed, while the concept of rank stresses the personal status, pay, and authority of the incumbents. This is not to say that the latter has no relation to the tasks and level of job responsibility—a police sergeant, for instance, is considered a first-line supervisor; however, some sergeants who spend time in this rank never supervise!

An organization is constructed from a structure of skills. The job descriptions used for personnel administration usually contain a statement of the required training and experience for each position, in addition to the duties to be performed. At or near the top of the organizational structure are the positions demanding the managerial skills of organizing, planning, controlling, and coordinating. In addition to this structure of managerial skills, there is also a hierarchy of professional skills. In any large- or medium-scale police organization we find numerous specialists, such as records analysts, juvenile officers, trainers, researchers, and public information officers. Interestingly, these skills are becoming more concerned with and, in some instances, dependent upon college training. In police organization, the more general positions (patrolman) are frequently broken down into specialized positions (robbery detective, narcotics investigator, juvenile officer, and so forth).

The larger police organizations tend to have a standardized pay structure, often referred to as a compensation plan. Salary and wage administration frequently incorporates some elements of scientific method, using statistical approaches. Consequently, levels of difficulty of positions are established, which helps in the internal comparison of various jobs.

All four of these organizational structures can be found in our police departments.

ORGANIZATIONAL THEORY: THE INFORMAL APPROACH

In the 1920s the classical approach to organization experienced a reaction to its mechanistic prescriptions for managing and organizing. This reaction is commonly referred to as (1) the informal, or human relations, approach or (2) the neoclassical theory of organization. It evolved out of the discovery that within formal organizations man tends to establish informal organizations. This theory emphasized communication, shared decision making, and leadership.

The two major assumptions underlying the human relations approach are that (1) the most satisfying organization (for the worker) is the most efficient and (2) it is necessary to relate work and the organizational structure to the social needs of the employee. The informal approach is not without its shortcomings. The reaction to the reaction is discussed in the next section.

The origins of informal theory are usually associated with the Hawthorne studies and, in particular, the writings of Elton Mayo, John Dewey, Kurt Lewin, and Mary Follett.[21] This theory stressed the affective and the social and was both caused by and a cause of increasing attention of psychology, social psychology, and sociology to contemporary organizations. It "discovered" the small (or face-to-face) group in large organizations and, in broad terms, emphasized the notion that formal organizations also have a large informal, that is, social and emotional, component. An *informal organization* includes both the social relations that develop among the personnel and the organizational operations as they naturally evolve from the formal organization and from the needs of the individual workers. In essence, classical organization theory failed to recognize that formal organizations tend to breed informal organizations within them and that in the informal organization, workers and managers are likely to establish relationships with each other which influence the manner in which they carry out their jobs or fulfill their roles.[22] To clarify this point, we look to a highly significant piece of research—the studies conducted by Mayo, Roethlisberger, and Dickson in the Hawthorne plant of the Western Electric Company in Chicago.

The Hawthorne Studies

The Hawthorne studies were conducted during the late 1920s through the mid-1930s. This series of studies (we review only a part of them) produced some important, unexpected findings.[23]

A group of girls who assembled telephone equipment were selected as subjects for a series of studies designed to determine the

[21] Edgar H. Schein, *Organizational Psychology* (Englewood Cliffs, N.J.: Prentice-Hall, Inc., 1963), p. 27.

[22] Mary Follett's contribution to neoclassical organization theory is beginning to be better understood and certainly more appreciated. In essence, she developed a theory of human interaction based on the "law of the situation," which means the bringing together of various inputs and acting in accord with their syntheses. An excellent overview of her thinking can be found in Elliot M. Fox, "Mary Parker-Follett: The Enduring Contribution," *Public Administration Review*, 28 (November-December 1968), 520–29.

[23] A more comprehensive description of these researches can be found in F. J. Roethlisberger and W. J. Dickson, *Management and the Worker* (Cambridge: Harvard University Press, 1939).

effect of their working conditions, length of the working day, number and length of rest pauses, and other factors relating to the "non-human" environment on their productivity. The girls were located in a special room under close supervision.

As the researchers varied working conditions, they found that each major change was accomplished by a substantial increase in production. When all the conditions to be varied had been tested, they decided to return the girls to their original, poorly lighted work-benches for the usual long working day without rest pauses and other benefits. To the astonishment of the researchers, *output rose again, to an even higher level that it had been under the best of the experimental conditions.* A new hypothesis had to be found. The hypothesis was that motivation to work, productivity, and quality of work were all related to the nature of the social relations among the workers and between the workers and their boss. New groups were created for additional experimentation. The findings of the study can be summarized as follows:

1. The productivity of the individual worker is determined more by his social capacity than his physical capacity.
2. Noneconomic rewards play a prominent part in motivating and satisfying an employee.
3. Maximum specialization is not the most efficient form of division of labor.
4. Employees do not react to management and its norms and rewards as individuals but as members of groups.

The tendency of experimentally chosen groups to show increased productivity and job satisfaction is known as the "Hawthorne effect" and is one of the most widely recognized findings of the social sciences.

In the Hawthorne experiments treatment was the significant factor. The girls selected for the experiment were (1) assigned the best supervisor in the plant, (2) accorded special privileges of genuine importance to them, and (3) *made into a cohesive group* by encouragement of patterns of interaction. Note that the group was created at the beginning of the experiment. Consequently, the group did not hold previously established norms on what its level of production should be. Follow-up studies attempting to achieve similar results failed when the researchers did not create new groups. Essentially, the workers' cohesion around their own norms was too strong to change. Apparently, these researchers forgot the primary lesson contained in the original study—that the level of production is set by social norms (man's social capacity), not by physiological capacities.

Neoclassical Organization Theory after the Hawthorne Studies: The Human Relations Era Continues

In the years since the Hawthorne experiments, a long line of research has added to the evidence that group solidarity and loyalty is associated with productivity, effectiveness, and job satisfaction. Moreover, these experiments have provided a better understanding of organizational leadership, decision making, and communication. In regard to leadership, it has been observed that the leader is able to set and enforce group norms through his particular style of leading a group.[24]

The human relations approach to managing and supervising is still widely accepted in administrative circles. Our fundamental reason for discussing it, however, is that this period in management thinking set the stage for identifying and understanding the informal organization. After man's social capacity was discovered, social scientists began to direct their attention to how such factors as power and expertise operated in a nonformal or informal sense. Thus we see the human relations approach to organization carving out a neoclassical theory, which devoted most of its study to an improved knowledge of the informal organization. John M. Pfiffner and Frank P. Sherwood have most convincingly described not one but five informal organizations that can, and usually do, exist within a formal structure:

The sociometric network
The system of functional contacts
The grid of decision-making centers
The pattern of power
Channels of communications[25]

The recognition of and the intense interest in the informal organization was brought about by the weakness inherent in the formal structure. According to Svenson:

The informal organization is nature's response to management's artificial structuring of an orderly business event. Driven by assumptions about functional division of work, the formal organization splits the natural unity of a business event into segments according to title authority. Informal organization attempts to heal

---

[24]See, for example, R. Lippitt and R. K. White, "An Experimental Study of Leadership and Group Life," in *Readings in Social Psychology*, ed. G. E. Swanson, T. M. Newcomb, and E. L. Hartley (New York: Holt, Rinehart & Winston, Inc., 1952), pp. 340–55.

[25]Pfiffner and Sherwood, *Administrative Organization*, pp. 18–27.

the managerial rupturing by weaving an authority of knowledge about the fracture.[26]

The classical and neoclassical organization theories are in many ways directly opposed to each other. The attributes one theory considers important, the other usually does not mention at all. The two theories do hold one thing in common: An organization's desire for rationality and human happiness could be completely resolved if each theory's particular body of knowledge were utilized. The classical theorists assumed that the most efficient organization would also be the most satisfying one because it would maximize both productivity and the employees' salary. In contrast, the neoclassical theorists assumed that the happier the employees were made through satisfaction of their social needs, the greater would be their cooperation and efficiency. It rejected man as an economic entity and defined him as a social animal.

In summary, both theories said, "Hey, manager and supervisor, follow me and I'll provide you with efficiency and your workers with happiness." Thus they were saying that a perfect balance between organizational goals and employees' needs could be found in their own specific approaches to the problem of organizing and managing. The reason for their different approaches to the utopian dream rests mainly in their view of man—economic versus social.

Before proceeding to the third, or modern, theory, note that there is no sharp discontinuity between the usages of the three theories, that the new is added to and more or less modifies the old rather than displacing it. Classical theory is still very much alive, is widely used, and has its defenders, and while there is now a tendency to regard "human relations" as passé, as associated with certain excesses and naïvetés of the past, there is a massive spillover of concepts, attitudes, and research interests into the modern theory.

ORGANIZATIONAL THEORY: THE SYSTEM (MODERN) APPROACH

> Big fleas have little fleas upon their
> backs to bite 'em;
> Little fleas have lesser fleas
> And so ad infinitum.

The diversity and number of systems is great. The molecule, the cell, the organ, the individual, the group, and the society are all examples of systems. Furthermore, there are communication, informa-

---

[26] Arthur L. Svenson, "Lessons from the Informal Organization," *Systems and Procedures,* 19 (May-June 1968), 14.

tion, computer, and hardware systems. In some respects they are alike; however, they differ in their level of complexity and over a host of other dimensions—living, nonliving, or mixed; material or conceptual; and so forth. This section describes the organization, more specifically a police organization, as an open social system. Increasingly, organizations are being considered through a system perspective.[27] The modern organization is thus dominated by the systems approach which, in turn, is itself a set of theories, analytical methods, and plans.

The police manager operates in a system. *A system is any entity, conceptual or material, that consists of interdependent parts.* Certainly this broad definition encompasses a police organization. The primary difference between an organization and a system is that the former has a goal or goals to accomplish, and the latter may not. While we have referred to the police organization as an open social system, it is in reality a mixed social system, since it contains men, machines, and materials (living and nonliving entities). Moreover, it coordinates (integrates) them in a dynamic manner in order to conduct the work of the system (goal attainment). Consequently, *our idea of an organization is changing from one of structure to one of process.* To foster the view of an organization as a process, or system, this section continues with reasons for the development of a systems approach and its benefits for modern organizational theory. We then consider what is meant by a systems approach. Finally, the characteristics and subsystems of an open social system are described as they relate to a police organization.

Forces toward a Systems Point of View

The reader is perhaps beginning to ask why organizations should be approached as open social systems. The main reasons are (1) the increased complexity and frequency of change in our society, and (2) the limitations of the previously discussed organizational theories, namely, that both the classical and the neoclassical theories viewed an organization as a *closed* structure. Such nearsightedness produces an inability to recognize that the organization is continually dependent upon its environment for the inflow of materials and human energy. Thinking of an organization as a closed structure, moreover, results in a failure to develop a feedback capability for obtaining adequate information about changes in environmental forces and goal accomplishment.

---

[27] Perhaps the most outstanding contribution and convincing argument for viewing an organization as a social system is Daniel Katz and Robert L. Kahn, *The Social Psychology of Organizations* (New York: John Wiley & Sons, Inc., 1966). Another example supporting a systems approach to organizations is Stanley Young, *Management: A Systems Approach* (Glenview, Ill.: Scott, Foresman & Company, 1967).

Beyond the more general reasons are specific and compelling ones which cause a police organization to consider itself an open system. These reasons are in terms of the benefits to be derived from such consideration. First, we are beginning to recognize that police organizations are a component of, and positioned within, a system of relationships. And, these relationships are not exclusively confined to a single organizational environment such as a city government. The police agency can be thought of logically as either a system (a single police department) or a subsystem. In viewing the police organization as a subsystem, it is naturally involved in a complex set of interfaces with other subsystems external to its particular organizational boundary, such as the district attorney, parole agencies, and courts. The systems approach effectively helps us to cross boundaries to identify, establish, and make use of significant interrelationships of various organizations. Police departments now undergoing analyses for either of the computer-based information systems are being made more aware of the requirements for external transactions. Second, many police agencies are becoming increasingly aware of the limitations of simplistic research. Organizations and problems in the sphere of law enforcement, as in other fields of endeavor, are seen to exist within a broader system. While the use of a systems approach is new, as a concept it is a product of the past decade. In essence, it has been and remains an attempt to synthesize the research contributions of relevant fields (operations research, educational psychology, etc.). Third, a systems approach provides us with a new perspective on the internal operations and environmental relationships of police organizations. It compels the involved manager or researcher to view the phenomena in an entirely different manner. The solutions arrived at are not likely to be overt in the data or in the stated objectives; yet they must be consistent with existing data and current objectives. Additionally, the available data and theoretical framework are likely to be incomplete and somewhat ambiguous, so that certainty is out of the question. In essence, those who use the systems approach need imagination, judgment, and courage to generate a new perspective. Fourth, the systems approach relies greatly on empirical (hard facts) data. The data of interest to us generally include facts not only on a particular police department but also on the processes, interactions, goals, and other characteristics of all organizations (public and private) that exert an influence on it. Fifth, an important benefit of the systems approach for those in police work is that it is intended to be action oriented. Data are gathered not merely to inform or to describe a relationship, and ideas are evaluated not merely on their cleverness; these activities are pursued because they are instrumental in fulfilling a set of objectives or in solving a problem.

THE POLICE ORGANIZATION AS AN OPEN PARTICIPATIVE SOCIAL SYSTEM

The police organization as an open participative social system provides the point of departure for our forthcoming discussion. All systems possess the following nine characteristics:[28]

1. *Input.* Open systems input various types of energy from their external environment.
2. *Processing.* Open systems process the energy available with an output.
3. *Output.* Open systems output products or services into the environment.
4. *Cyclic character.* The product or service output furnishes the source of energy for an input and thus the repetition of a cycle.
5. *Arresting of disorganization.* Social systems process and store energy in order to combat the natural trend toward disorganization.
6. *Information: input, processing, output, and feedback.* Information is handled much the same as energy. In fact, information can be considered a form of energy.
7. *The steady state.* Open systems seek to maintain a viable ratio between energy input and service output. This state is not to be confused with the *status quo.* A steady state allows for change by constantly adjusting the input and the output so as to achieve a healthy relationship between the two.
8. *Specialization.* Open systems move in the direction of specialization.
9. *Equifinality.* Open systems can reach the same final state from differing initial considerations and by a variety of paths.

In the addition to these nine characteristics, all modern social systems are comprised of the following five subsystems, which enable the total system to accomplish its goals and to survive: (1) operations subsystems to get the work done, (2) maintenance subsystems to indoctrinate people and service machines, (3) supportive subsystems for procurement and environmental relations, (4) adaptive subsystems concerned with organizational change, and (5) managerial subsystems for the direction, coordination, and control of the other subsystems.[29] Obviously, if we were to reshape the present structure of a police organization according to the five subsystems, the result would appear quite different. It would be even more revolutionary when experienced in terms of its new processes—the *new* way of conducting its business. Table 5–1 contains a more detailed explanation of the purpose, functions, and activities of each subsystem.

[28] These common characteristics are drawn from Katz and Kahn, *Social Psychology,* pp. 19–26.

[29] This typology of subsystems is suggested in *ibid.,* pp. 39–44.

To the concept of the police organization being an "open" system, we now add one other idea—that of the police department becoming an open and participative organizational structure. The latter idea centers on increased community involvement through greater decentralization of services. Robert Wood expresses this need and the challenge as follows:

> Our experience in urban administration suggests that one of the critical components in our new urban programs calls for a historical reversal in American administrative doctrine.
> Specifically the confrontation now posed is between the several versions of citizen participation that have been foundations in the federal government's urban strategy and the century-old effort in public administration to establish coherent executive structures manned by professionally competent managers. The satisfactory resolution in American political thought is the principal precondition for success in our urban programs. It is on this issue—between effective, purposeful, expert action and widespread public participation—that I focus.[30]

TABLE 5-1. **The Subsystems of a Police Organization: Their Purposes, Functions, and Activities**

Subsystem	Purpose	Function	Activity
1. Operations Patrol, traffic, investigation, jail, communications, etc.	Efficiency in field operations	Task accomplishment—processing of inputs within the organization	Division of labor: specialization and job standards
2. Maintenance Training, personnel	Maintenance of subsystems: their functions and activities	Mediating between organizational goals and personal needs, indoctrination, and servicing man-machine activities	Establishing operating procedures, training, and equipment maintenance
3. Supportive Community relations	Environmental support for the organization	Exchange with environment to obtain social support	Building favorable image by contributing to the community and by influencing other social systems

[30] Robert C. Wood, "A Call for Return to the Community," *Public Management*, 51 (July 1969), 3-4.

TABLE 5-1. (Continued)

Subsystem	Purpose	Function	Activity
4. Adaptive Planning and research	Planned organizational change	Intelligence gathering, research and development, and planning	Making recommendations for change and implementing planned change
5. Managerial Chief of police, staff and subsystem commanders	Control and direction	Resolving internal conflict, coordinating and directing subsystems, coordinating external requirements and organizational resources and needs	Use of authority, adjudication of conflict, increasing of efficiency, adjusting to environmental changes, and restructuring the organization

With participation comes a heightened sense representation and reduced apathy and resentment toward an organization.

> *But in that century of building professional bureaucracies and executive capacities for leadership, the need for new modes of representation designed to keep pace with new economic, social, and political developments did not arouse equal concern. Partly for this reason, and partly because the burgeoning of large-scale organizations in every area of life contributes to the sensation of individual helplessness, recent years have witnessed an upsurge of a sense of alienation on the part of many people, to a feeling that they as individuals cannot effectively register their own preferences on the decisions emanating from the organs of government. These people have begun to demand redress of the balance among the three values, with special attention to the deficiencies in representativeness.*[31] (Italics added.)

The movement for representativeness in this generation centers primarily on administrative agencies such as the police. Since administrative agencies have grown dramatically in size, function, and authority—especially in the middle third of this century—this is not surprising. Chief executives, legislatures, and courts make more decisions of *sweeping* effect, but the agencies make a far greater number of decisions affecting individual citizens in *intimate* ways. In them resides the source of much present unrest; in them, consequently, the remedies are sought.

One type of recommendation for making administrative agencies

---

[31] Herbert Kaufman, "Administrative Decentralization and Political Power," *Public Administration Review*, 29 (January-February 1969), 4.

more representative is traditional—situating spokesmen for the interests affected in strategic positions within the organizations. Frequently, this means nothing more than filling vacancies on existing boards and commissions with appointees enjoying the confidence of, or perhaps even chosen by, those interests. In the case of the controversial police review boards, it involves inserting into administrative structures new bodies, dominated by ethnic minority groups or their friends, to survey and constrain antisocial behavior. Structurally, such plans do not require major modifications of existing organizations, and their purposes could probably be met by changes in personnel at high organizational levels.

Unorthodox, but rapidly gaining acceptance, is the concept of a centralized governmental complaint bureau, with legal powers of investigation, to look into citizen complaints against administrative agencies and to correct inequities and abuses—the office of "ombudsman." The most sweeping expression *of the dissatisfaction over lack of representativeness is the growing demand for extreme administrative decentralization, frequently coupled with insistence on local clientele domination of the decentralized organizations.* Present manifestations of this movement have occurred in the antipoverty program and in education.

The issue of citizen participation is a moral issue—the powerless should have a share of power. It is a legal issue—the right of participation is conferred by law in anti-poverty, model cities, and other programs. And it is a practical source—the poor and others of low influence now have enough political power to protect and expand their participatory role.

> In short, *"decentralization of administration" is in the air everywhere.* While it is sometimes defended on grounds of efficiency, *it is more truly justified in terms of effective popular participation in government.* Reformers of earlier generations succeeded in raising the level of expertise and professionalism in the bureaucracies, and to a lesser extent, in improving the capacity of chief executives to control the administrative arms of government. Now, *people are once again directing thier attention to representativeness, and are seeking to elevate it to a more prominent place in the governmental political arena.*[32] (Italics added.)

The police department's response to the problem of participation and decentralization is under way on a major scale. In general, it can be referred to as *team policing.* Admittedly vague in its meaning to date, team policing is a sincere and intensive effort to better relate

---

[32] James L. Sundquist, "Citizen, Participation: A New Kind of Management," *Public Management,* 51 (July 1969), 9.

the police department to the community. Essentially, team policing is a vast structural-functional change in local law enforcement. The impetus for team policing rests on the presently recognized ambiguous and transitory nature of the beat officer's relationship with his clientele. No clearly placed responsibility exists for the adequacy of police service in any particular neighborhood. Final accountability is placed only in the chief of police. This is because of the highly centralized command structure (common to all American police departments today), which is primarily organized around time shifts (e.g., 4:00 P.M. to midnight) and includes considerable rotation of full personnel. The beat officer's responsibility is further diminished by the police organization's considerable emphasis on job specialization. Thus, when the beat officer comes upon a crime, he turns over investigation to a detective. If juveniles are involved, the juvenile specialists handle the case from that point. Traffic control activities, too, are handled by functional specialists.

Community-centered team policing attempts to change this situation. This concept seeks transition from a centralized organization to a decentralized one where the beat officer has more responsibility and the citizen has an improved means for participating. The officer will be involved in all police field functions. These can be categorized into three types: *major crime functions* (including the use of patrol strategies and tactics to prevent serious crimes and disturbances, the collection of information on such activities, and the endeavor to apprehend perpetrators); *traffic functions* (including the control of pedestrian and vehicular movement, the investigation of accidents, and the alleviation of congestion when it arises); and *social service functions* (including the pursuit of order and peace-keeping activities demanding use of police advice and authority—control of minor disturbances, intervention in family crises, etc.—as well as activities where assistance rather than authority is required, e.g., aid to injured and elderly persons, and improvement of relations with the community).

The generalist-officer will have total responsibility for these functions on his beat. Further modifications would be made on the basis of such factors as community wishes, evaluation of functional and cost effectiveness of the police teams with regard to a particular function, and evaluation of functional and cost effectiveness of possible alternative agency (or citizen) discharge of the function. To illustrate, thirty police officers and thirty community service officers, directed by a supervisor and lower-level group leaders, might be the best team for a given geographical area. To assist in the impetus of bureaucratic change, it is expected that team members will have distinctive uniforms, automobiles, and equipment. Members of the teams will be allowed to dress in uniform or out of uniform according to the assignment they expect to be on. One team model would provide that team officers and leaders undergo a four-week training program designed to teach needed skills, including family crisis intervention and investigative methods. Members will then be required to live with a family in their beat neighborhood for a few days to learn the values and norms of the local culture.

In addition to police officers and supervisors, a number of integrative or supportive personnel will work on the team. Community service officers are one such possibility. They will attempt to increase police responsiveness to neighborhood concerns and will thus be responsible for handling many of the social service tasks which now fall to the police and are of great importance to the neighborhood. At the same time, they will also work with individual team members in dealing with special problems where the community service officer's experience would be beneficial. A position of community coordinator is also envisioned. This person will develop within the community an understanding of what the police are doing, interpret policy to the community, and, most importantly, assist the community in representing its concerns and interest to the department. The community coordinator will be a resident of the neighborhood hired to assist the community in developing defensive security tactics, community concern, and community action.

In summary, then, the term *team policing* describes an endeavor to increase decentralization in order to enhance the level of citizen participation and acceptance of the police department. Thus it involves a new organizational form for providing required services. One of many such forms suggested is the Kansas Police Department's "Area Responsibility Giving Unified Service," or ARGUS, which is shown in Figures 5-1–5-4. Another team policing structure has been adopted by the Palo Alto Police Department in California and is shown in Figure 5-5.

Regretfully, space does not permit a more thorough description of the police organization as an open and participative system. Such an attempt would require the writing of another text, in addition to considerable research. For those interested in a start in this direction, see the texts *The Human Organization* and *Organizing Men and Power: Patterns of Behavior and Line-Staff Models*, which suggest new organizational structures for decentralizing the efforts of employees for greater effectiveness.[33] While they differ in several re-

[33]Rensis Likert, *The Human Organization* (New York: McGraw-Hill Book Company, 1967); and Robert T. Golembiewski, *Organizing Men and Power: Patterns of Behavior and Line-Staff Models* (Chicago: Rand McNally & Co., 1967). See also Paul R. Lawrence and Jay W. Lorsch, *Developing Organizations: Diagnosis and Action* (Reading, Mass.: Addison-Wesley Publishing Company, Inc., 1969).

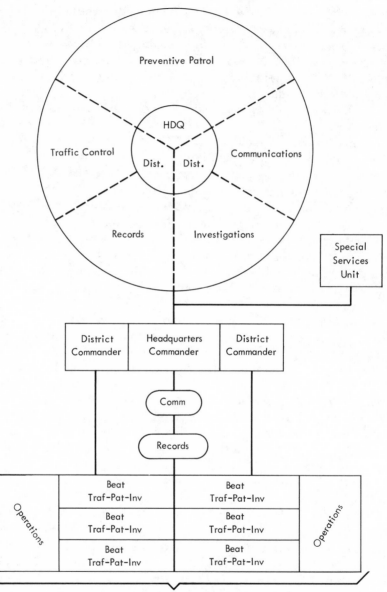

FIGURE 5-1. **Argus Operations Unit Concept: Kansas Police Department**

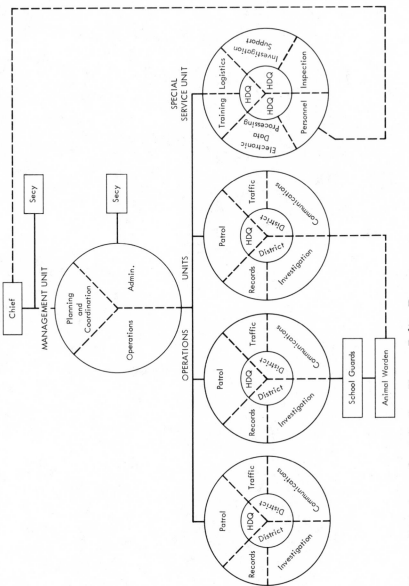

FIGURE 5-2. **Argus Organization: Kansas Police Department**

175

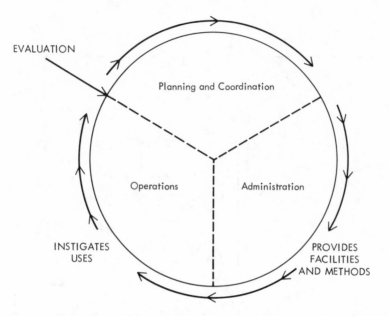

FIGURE 5-3. **Argus Management Process and Areas of Special Concern: Kansas Police Department**

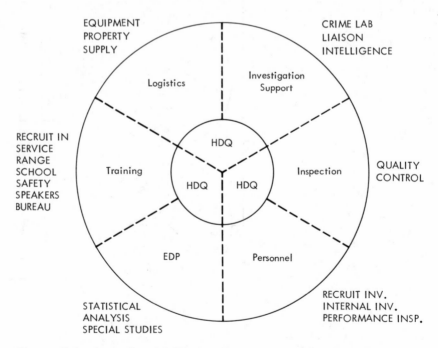

FIGURE 5-4. **Argus Special Services Unit: Kansas Police Department**

Team Policing:

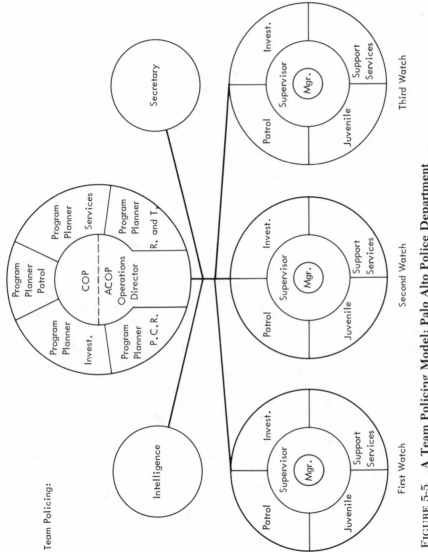

FIGURE 5-5. A Team Policing Model: Palo Alto Police Department

spects, both possess a twofold focus: the organization as an open system of interdependent relationships and various structural forms for improving citizen and employee representation through decentralization and generalization of functions.[34]

LEARNING EXERCISE

The following learning exercise is drawn from a paper presented to the Police Foundation (an independent board created by the Ford Foundation in 1970). Briefly, the paper seeks to assist police officials in identifying various organizational arrangements for reducing crime and for building support by the vast majority of the citizens.

IMPROVEMENT OF POLICE ORGANIZATION

Thomas A. Reppetto

I

A. KEY ISSUES

Reorganization—the very word implies innovation, progress, efficiency.[35] Thus, in this present era of intense controversy over the role of the police, it is not surprising that numerous proposals for restructuring police organization should be heard. Basically, the demands made by various clientele groups boil down to two: (1) that the police be made representative of and accountable to the communities they serve; and (2) that they improve their ability to deal with crime and disorder.

Neither of these demands appears unreasonable in general terms, yet when reduced to specific organizational considerations, such as the locus of ultimate authority, the degree of citizen participation and the type of personnel required, certain strains and "contradictions" manifest themselves. The first demand is usually voiced by minority group members, particularly those residing in ghetto areas. Specifically, they urge that the police force be made to reflect the social composition of the community by hiring minority group members in proportion to their numbers in the population; that citizen groups be allowed a major voice in the formulation of policy and the supervision of operations at the neighborhood precinct level;[36] and that citizen organizations,

[34] The literature is equally vast and vague on this subject. See the President's Commission on Law Enforcement and Administration of Justice, *Task Force Report: Police* (Washington, D.C.: Government Printing Office, 1967); and various papers submitted to the Police Foundation, especially Thomas F. McBride "A Large Grant for Comprehensive Improvement of Police Service in One City" (Washington, D.C.: Police Foundation, 1970).

[35] This paper was presented under contract to the Police Foundation, Washington, D.C., in 1970. It is printed with their permission.

[36] In this paper, precinct may be considered as synonymous with neighborhood. Even though many small- or medium-sized cities do not maintain precinct (division, district) stations, the term is used to convey the meaning of local as opposed to citywide.

such as security patrols, be allowed to supplement, monitor, or, in certain instances, even replace the regular police.

While many minority citizens also endorse the second demand, its chief support comes from white middle-income citizens and from police administrators. The latter argue that to control crime and disorder, higher caliber men must be recruited to the sworn ranks of police departments, that ultimate authority must reside in the office of the chief of police, and that citizen participation must be confined to advisory and auxiliary roles so that authority will not be separated from responsibility and so that unqualified individuals will not be permitted to exercise enforcement powers.

In the concrete, then, how does one organize a police force? Should sworn personnel be recruited from among the college-educated or from ghetto dwellers? Should precinct station captains look to the local community or to the chief of police as the prime source of policy guidance? Should citizens be encouraged or discouraged from taking direct responsibility for enforcing the law?

B. HISTORICAL BACKGROUND

There are two basic types of police organization in the United States. The one commonly found in municipalities is the general purpose force, which is given responsibility for the performance of most police functions within its geographic jurisdiction. Such an organization will routinely handle everything from homicide to stray dogs. The alternate type, the special purpose force, is the one utilized by the Federal and many state governments. This arrangement provides for separate police agencies to undertake each of a variety of missions, e.g., one force to patrol national borders, another to capture counterfeiters, a third to police public parks, etc.

The general purpose type of department dates from 1829, when the London Metropolitan Police came into being as a uniformed patrol force replacing the inefficient and loosely organized local watchmen who had maintained public order in the streets of British and American cities during the seventeenth and eighteenth centuries. Within a decade of its founding, the Metropolitan Police also assumed the criminal investigation (detective) function previously exercised by magistrates and their assistants. Police forces in American cities followed a similar line of development. But unlike the London Police, American police bodies in the nineteenth century did not rise above the level of the local government of the time, which meant that patronage, corruption, and poor performance were the rule. In the twentieth century, however, the municipal reform movement began to demand of the police the qualities it urged in government generally—merit personnel, integrity, technical efficiency, and economy. While most police "reform" efforts were shortlived, certain cities such as Berkeley, Wichita, and, later on, Los Angeles and Cincinnati were able to institutionalize "good government," with the result that their police departments were qualitatively different from most contemporary forces.

C. PRESENT PRACTICES

At present, two styles of general purpose policing characterize the central cities. One might be labelled the traditional, the other the professional.

Based on social scientists' descriptions of actual forces, and ideal type can be sketched for each style.[37]

The traditional force is one which is governed by particular policies that vary according to individual attributes or the nature of the situation. For instance, whether a traffic violator is arrested, given a warning, or ignored depends on who he is, what section of town the incident occurs in, or which officer handles the affair. Personnel are recruited from among local residents of limited educational attainment and are often drawn heavily from certain ethnic or neighboring backgrounds. Their initial training usually stresses department lore and local mores. Such a force is usually decentralized and loosely controlled, and in many instances informal authority relationships are more important than formal structure. Precinct station captains, in particular, are likely to possess considerable autonomy and to feel more beholden to local notables than to the police chief. At the operating level, the patrolman is required to keep his beat orderly, but he is not expected to be overzealous in the enforcement of the law since this only stirs up antagonisms. The public relations image of a traditional force is usually a poor one. Buildings and equipment are often old and in poor repair; individual officers are sometimes unkempt; routine business is conducted in a haphazard fashion; and scandals are frequent. Finally, traditional-style forces are usually unable or unwilling to eliminate organized crime and vice activities.

The professional-style force, in contrast, is one which adheres to general and impersonal rules whose relevance is independent of time, place, and personality. For example, if the police chief's son is caught speeding, he is ticketed. Personnel are recruited on the basis of open competition, without regard to residency or ethnicity, and their training is based on texts written by experts in the field.

The professional style is likely to prevail in cities where middle-class voters predominate, where local government is at least formally nonpartisan, and where accepted practice prescribes that the operation of city services be left to technical experts. The traditional style, on the other hand, is more likely to be found in lower-income, ethnically conscious, highly politicized communities where the personnel practices and operating policies of city agencies are of such vital concern to a variety of interest groups that they form the basis for much of the local political activity.

Although there have not been any completely validated studies comparing the two styles of policing in terms of their effectiveness, certain gen-

[37] See, for example, James Q. Wilson, *Varieties of Police Behavior* (Cambridge: Harvard University Press, 1968); Jerome H. Skolnick, *Justice Without Trial* New York: John Wiley & Sons, Inc., 1966); Joseph D. Lohman and Gordon E. Misner, *The Police and the Community*, Vols. I & II (Washington, D.C.: Government Printing Office, 1967). Skolnick and Wilson (in earlier writings) both used the term professional. Later Wilson substituted "legalistic." The traditional style has also been referred to as "watchman" (Wilson) or "old line" (Skolnick). Many recruits possess college training, and the department makes clear that higher education will play a significant role in individual career progression. The force is usually highly centralized both to prevent corruption and to insure that uniform policies apply throughout. Authority accrues to formal position and discipline is strict. Such departments posit crime control as their prime mission and quantitative measures are used to gauge officers' productivity in effecting arrests and clearing crime. A professional department usually enjoys a favorable public relations image. It is neat and precise in bearing; routine business is efficiently conducted according to detailed procedures; scandal is rare; and vice activity is minimal.

eral observations can be made. Cities with professional-style departments have for the most part been spared police corruption scandals and are usually free of major organized crime and vice activities. Thus, for certain law enforcement tasks, professionalism is clearly superior. But where crime control is concerned, it is difficult to make comparisons between cities, and many observers feel that while the professional style may ensure integrity and economy, it has little actual impact on crime. However, a recent study at Harvard which contrasted similar communities with different police styles found that for the prevention of certain types of crime and the apprehension of some categories of offenders, the professional force had significant advantages over the traditional.

Even the professional style of policing, however, has not departed substantially from traditional patterns of organization which place heavy emphasis on hierarchical authority and the primacy of law enforcement tasks. This means that ambitious officers must seek their career rewards through promotion to supervisory rank or by way of transfer to high status posts such as that of detective. Yet it is the uniformed patrolman who engages in daily interaction with the public, and studies have repeatedly shown that most police activity involves order maintenance tasks, e.g., settling family fights, dispersing youth groups, or rendering services such as the collection of stray animals.

Nor do even the largest departments appear to have fully developed the potential of their staff units. Even when augmented by civilians, staff personnel normally constitute no more than 20% of a police department. Even then, most are engaged in the auxiliary tasks of record keeping, communications, jail duty, and maintenance activities rather than in the management areas of planning, training, personnel, or inspection. It is particularly in these latter areas that virtually all police organizations fall short. For while computer science and other technologies have permitted some important gains to be made in records and communication activities, the management services have *not* witnessed similar progress. Most planning divisions do not plan; personnel divisions have generally not developed career management programs to replace the present patterns of assignment based on seniority, chance, or influence; training divisions often conduct courses so unrelated to reality that the most common advice given to rookie patrolmen on reporting to their first assignment is to forget everything they have been taught; while inspection and internal investigation divisions usually wait for citizen complaints, operating on a case-method system instead of initiating far-reaching inquiries in order to eliminate the underlying causes for misconduct. Most significant of all perhaps are the community relations units which do not relate to the community but are often mere public relations bureaus.

D. CONSTRAINTS UPON CHANGE

The possibility of bringing about change in a given situation depends on the nature of the community and its police style. In cities with a traditional-style department, the first step is usually to try to bring the force up to minimal standards, in effect, to professionalize it. But such changes often upset long-familiar local arrangements and this in turn leads to political protests which frustrate major innovative programs. In recent years one of the chief obstacles to change has been the organized police rank and file led by militant spokesmen.

In professional-style cities or those with at least minimally competent departments, the control of police affairs is often in the hands of technically proficient individuals who are not basically hostile to change but who are limited by the pressure of daily operations and somewhat narrow perspectives.

Perhaps the most formidable obstacle to the improvement of police services in the United States is their seeming inability to establish rapport with minority groups. Apparently, there is not a major city in the United States where police-minority relations are wholly satisfactory. In this respect it does not appear to make any difference whether a community employs the traditional or professional style of policing. Indeed, there is some reason to believe that the aggressive crime-fighting tactics of the professional style may even exacerbate ghetto tensions. Thus, the challenge to police is to develop an organizational system capable of reducing crime and disorder while at the same time maintaining the support of the vast majority of citizens.

II

The 1967 report of the President's Commission on Law Enforcement and Administration of Justice formulated a number of proposals to improve police service. Although many of the recommendations overlapped, those related to police organization might be subsumed under the following headings:

a) Make community-relations activities an integral part of police organization by:
   1) creating community-relations units in all police departments;
   2) establishing citizen advisory committees in minority neighborhoods;
   3) recruiting more minority-group officers;
   4) establishing adequate procedures for processing citizen complaints.
b) Upgrade the caliber of police services by:
   1) providing state assistance for management surveys;
   2) employing legal advisers;
   3) strengthening central staff control;
   4) creating administrative boards composed of key ranking personnel;
   5) establishing strong internal investigation units.

The proposals are in some ways contradictory. How, for example, does one raise standards and simultaneously recruit ghetto dwellers? However, the Commission attempted to solve this by two further recommendations which have major significance for police organization. First, it proposed that police departments adopt a tri-level personnel structure involving three positions—agent, police officer, and community service officer. The first named would be a college-trained individual who would work on the most complex police problems. The second would have duties similar to those of the present regular police officer, while the third, recruited from among youthful individuals, especially minority-group members, would engage in tasks of community service but would not bear arms or have powers of arrest. It was envisioned that this arrangement would lead to the entry of large numbers of minority citizens into the police at the CSO level and that it would upgrade policing by providing for the lateral entry of college men as agents. Once in service, the CSO's would be given special training enabling them to become regular officers or agents.

The second recommendation was that patrol, detective, and community-relations functions be more closely integrated by the creation of teams of agents, police, and CSO personnel which would have the responsibility for the total policing of a small area. It was anticipated that assigning the teams permanently to specific areas would enhance police-community relations.

III

Since the report's publication, there have been many innovations designed to alter traditional police organizational arrangements. A paper of this limited scope can only outline a few representative programs that have been undertaken.

A. NEW PATROL CONCEPTS WHICH EMPHASIZE COMMUNITY RELATIONS

1) Beat Commander—Detroit, Michigan

In this program a team of 21 officers under a sergeant (beat commander) is given 24-hour responsibility for the total policing of a small high-crime area. The commander is also given authority to distribute his men as he sees fit.

2) Team Policing—Dayton, Ohio

A team of 10 to 12 patrolmen together with 5 or 6 community service officers performs duties similar to those described above; in addition, each regular officer must qualify not only as a general police officer but must also develop capability in a specialty such as detective or juvenile work.

3) Crime Control Teams—Syracuse, N.Y.

Three teams, each composed of 8 officers and 1 sergeant, cover a beat on a 24-hour basis, with two teams concentrating on crime and one on community service.

4) Basic Car—Los Angeles, California

Each police division (precinct) is divided into basic beats and each beat requires 9 patrolmen servicing it on a 24-hour basis. One man is designated leading officer and is the coordinator. As nearly as possible, all calls on the beat are referred to the basic car. The team members do not engage in follow-up investigation activity per se; instead, normal specialist units are utilized.

5) Community Service Officers — Chicago, Illinois

Under the auspices of the model cities program, local residents
(both male and female) in each of six areas are appointed to sala-
ried and uniformed (green rather than blue) nonsworn positions
to work on community service problems. Each team of two aides
is supervised by a patrolman and each area by lieutenants and
sergeants. The Chicago program does not replace normal beat
patrol but merely supplements it.

Programs 1 and 3 provide for "job enlargement" by allowing team members to assume total responsibility for police activity in their area, including
follow-up investigations, although they may call on headquarters specialists
for assistance. All these programs attempt to personalize police service by
reviving the tradition of the "cop on the beat." Each program involves extensive meetings and other interaction with neighborhood residents. In
Dayton, for instance, the local community is given veto power over the selection of the team commander and the patrolmen members a similar power
over the selection of sergeants. Dayton even proposes to orient team members
by having them temporarily reside with neighborhood families.
   Since the programs are relatively new, it is difficult to evaluate them in
detail. All except the Chicago program suffer from the disadvantage that "ear-
marking" of personnel reduces flexibility in allocating manpower and poses
problems in dispatching and other procedures. For example, at peak demand
hours, if area teams are tied up, calls emanating from their beat must be
stacked or outside units brought in. Occasionally, overloads in adjacent areas
require team members to be sent off their beats. Stacking causes delay in
rendering police service while cross beat dispatching defeats the purpose of
permanent beats.
   The Chicago aide program is the most costly in terms of manpower inasmuch as the teams do not replace the regular police but merely supplement
them. In addition, the fact that the CSO's are not engaged in actual policing
responsibilities may lessen their credibility in people's eyes because they
are not the ones citizens will have to deal with in a moment of crisis.

B. PROGRAMS DESIGNED TO IMPROVE COMMUNITY RELATIONS BY PERMITTING CITIZEN PARTICIPATION IN POLICING

1) Pilot Precinct — Washington, D.C.

This provides for a 17-member elected citizen board to meet at
regular intervals and be consulted by police concerning the formulation of policy and the conduct of operations within a precinct.
Officers assigned to the program are required to take several hours
of weekly training in company with community residents. Such
training stresses relevant local problems. It has been reported that
the more militant members of the advisory board have been
frustrated by their inability to enlarge their role from one of advice to one of control. This program is now receiving extensive
OEO evaluation.

2) Citizen Police—Various Cities

A number of citizen volunteer units have arisen in recent years under such titles as security patrols, auxiliaries, etc. Generally, these fall into one of two categories: those that see themselves as a supplement to the regular police, and those that act as a check on the police, with the determination usually being based on ideological considerations. Most such organizations patrol unarmed (although the carrying of weapons is not unknown) and maintain radio contact with some central location. Often they monitor police calls and respond to the scene. Police reaction to such organizations has been mixed. Obviously, those patrols set up in opposition to the police are not viewed favorably by the latter. However, even patrols which exist to assist the police are not always approved, because the police feel that the dangers of untrained individuals engaging in police work far outweigh the advantages. A recent study of all types of citizen patrols indicates that they are usually shortlived and ineffectual. A basic problem in this connection is that in order to be effective in dealing with crime and disorder, a unit must take on many of the characteristics of the regular police and this is often difficult for or unappealing to certain organizations. On the other hand, as such units do begin to resemble the regular police, they may lose whatever rapport they once had with the community.

C. PROGRAMS DESIGNED TO IMPROVE PATROL EFFECTIVENESS AGAINST CRIME

1) Split-Force Patrol—Chicago, Illinois

An experiment conducted in Chicago split the patrol division into response and preventive forces. While the former handled citizen calls, the latter was permitted to concentrate on preventive patrol within high-crime areas. The rationale behind this arrangement was that when individual patrol units had to perform both missions, they usually had little time for preventive activity during peak crime hours because they were too busy responding to routine calls. By splitting the forces and initiating a queuing system for the response units, more resources were freed for preventive patrol. This plan is administratively complex, however, and the experiment has not been institutionalized.

2) 24-Hour Patrol Power—Indianapolis, Indiana

This is an arrangement in which the police department allows its personnel to drive their fully marked patrol vehicles home and use them as private automobiles. This is expected to increase the degree of police visibility and the number of units available for emergency response. Preliminary reports indicate an increase in criminal arrests. Potential drawbacks, besides the expense, are the risks attendant upon allowing officers to operate without supervision and the possibility of injury to civilian passengers who might be caught up in an emergency situation.

D. PROGRAMS DESIGNED TO INCREASE THE EFFECTIVENESS OF STAFF SUPPORT FOR LINE OPERATIONS

1) Conflict Disorder Assessment Group — Mass. State Police and Dayton, Ohio

A small staff, including civilian employees and citizen volunteers, attempts to plan for the prevention and control of civil disorder by actual field work in the community. The basic idea is that particular problems can be identified in advance and arrangements for dealing with them made on a prior planning basis rather than ad hoc after a crisis has erupted.

2) Police Legal Aides — Various Cities

A program that is becoming increasingly widespread is one whereby the police hire licensed attorneys to furnish in-house advice on both future planning and immediate operational concerns. While the attorneys may also function as department advocates at trial boards they do not prosecute criminal matters.

3) Operations Research Task Force — Chicago, Illinois

In 1967 the Chicago department obtained a major grant to set up an operations research team which would consider problems of resource allocation and develop methods for improving crime control. The team, composed of civilian specialists and police generalists, engaged in extensive data collection and limited experimentation. The split-force patrol pattern mentioned earlier was sponsored by this unit. The task force has recently been disbanded.

The results of these experiments have been mixed or uncertain. The chief problem stems from communication barriers between civilian specialists and police generalists. Apparently, the more complex his field, the greater the difficulty the specialist has in communicating his expertise to the police administrator. Legal advice has always played a prominent role in police thinking and this usually presents no problem, whereas new disciplines such as operations research have not yet won wide acceptance in the law enforcement field. In this respect, it is hoped that the increase of higher education among police officers, together with the experience gained from some of these experiments, will facilitate greater police utilization of a variety of civilian skills in the future.

E. NEW STRUCTURING OF CAREER PATHS WITHIN A POLICE ORGANIZATION

1) Use of Police Specialists — Cincinnati, Ohio

Men who pass a special department exam are appointed as "specialists" and may then be assigned flexibly to any of a variety of complex police duties, including criminal investigation, uniformed patrol, or staff work. The program attempts to upgrade police performance by offering higher pay and status to those who demonstrate special qualifications. This is analogous to the Presidential Commission's proposal for the creation of agent positions, though the Cincinnati plan does not permit lateral entry.

2) Internal Restructuring — Dayton, Ohio

In conjunction with the concept of team policing an attempt is being made to restructure the internal organization. Basic components will be the *field service division*, envisioned as the sum of all the area teams; the *Services Division*, which will include all support specialists such as detectives and juvenile officers whose relationship to field personnel will be analgous to that of client (field) and consultant (service); and the *coordination and evaluation* field units and evaluate their performance by means of surveys of community attitudes.

3) Use of Police Generalist — Lakewood, Colorado

This police department in a middle-class suburb of Denver recruits college-trained personnel and outfits them in civilian blazers instead of uniforms. The new men are designated as agents and their work is of a generalist nature, along the lines of team policing. The experiment is too recent to be evaluated and its locale is so socially different from the central city areas where most police work is carried on, that questions are raised as to its transferability.

IV

In attempting to synthesize the foregoing discussion of police organization into coherent analytic models, certain assumptions must be made clear. What follows presupposes basic agreement on the following points.

1) Minority groups must play a significant role in policing of their communities. Otherwise, the forces of law and order will be seen as an occupying army.
2) Although crime may stem from elemental social conditions, the police *can* make significant contributions to reducing its volume.

A. THE NEO-PROFESSIONAL MODEL

This model is an extension of the recommendations of the President's Crime Commission. It would solve the problem of securing both minority group representation and college men by use of a tri-level (agent, officer, CSO) personnel pattern and would endeavor to promote better community relations by decentralizing authority to local structures, such as the beat commander program and precinct advisory councils, while leaving ultimate control in the hands of the police chief.

Advantages

Since highly qualified agent personnel would be the directing elite and final authority would continue to be centralized, this model should be most acceptable to professional-type police administrators. However, the provisions for limited decentralization, citizen participation and team policing should promote better community relations through increased attention to the needs of minority-group neighborhoods. With quality personnel, both sworn and civilian, and good community relations, such a force would be in a strong position to develop and employ a variety of crime-control strategies.

Disadvantages

The problem of lateral entry into the force by agents might create resistance among present in-service personnel. In professional-type forces, many members could probably qualify as agents; thus, opposition should be much less severe than in traditional forces where the successful adoption of the model would probably require the wholesale influx of outsiders, with resultant upset to organizational equilibrium.

A more crucial question is the degree to which minority citizens would accept the program. Would an advisory role be sufficient for local leaders, and would enough men be attracted to duty as CSO's, or could a substantial number of CSO's be trained to be policemen and agents? If not, then minorities would likely oppose the whole scheme. On the other hand, if CSO's were, over time, simply blanketed into higher positions, their lack of qualifications would be apparent to their better qualified colleagues and would be a likely source of tension.

Summary

This model would be promising if there were some evidence as to whether young ghetto dwellers were both willing and able to meet its requirements. The reverse dimension of the question is whether nonminority regular police and agents could learn to meet the challenge of policing ghetto areas.

B. THE NEO-TRADITIONAL MODEL

The second model is based on certain urban realities such as:

1) The present rather limited potential of many in-service police personnel.

2) Minority-group demands for appointment as regular police officers without the necessity of qualifying by successful performance on normal civil service tests.[38]

---

[38] In 1968 the Boston City administration proposed that minority-group members be appointed directly from civilian life to all ranks, including captain, and in numbers proportionate to their percentage in the population. Although the City Council disapproved the measure, the federal court has entertained a class suit on this issue brought on behalf of unsuccessful blacks and Puerto Rican police applicants.

3) The power of police unionism to block the implementation of innovative proposals, such as lateral entry.

Therefore, a model must be constructed based on the likelihood that police departments of the future will continue to be composed of average or even substandard personnel.

The neo-traditional model is largely an updating of standard operating procedures used by city police departments at the turn of the century. It would strive for good community relations by assigning large numbers of officers of minority background to ghetto precincts and would accept the fact that the commanding officers of such units would have to reflect the ethnic preferences of the neighborhood. It would suppose a high degree of control of local precincts by neighborhood councils. Such a model would not be expected to develop a strong crime-control capacity. On the other hand, the increased rapport between police and citizens resulting from it could be expected to contribute to lowering the crime rate. Although the model envisions a high degree of precinct autonomy, it does not rule out a supportive role by headquarters personnel.

Advantages

The advantage of such a model is that it gives real power and high visibility to minority citizens.

Disadvantages

The disadvantages that could be expected are those which have commonly developed in classic traditional forces—corruption, favoritism, and a low level of efficiency. In addition, one would expect a good deal of headquarters-precinct conflict.

Summary

This model would be acceptable if the virtues claimed for community control could, in fact, be realized, that is, if it promoted greater peace within the community. Unfortunately, there are no studies yet available relative to this question.

C. THE SPLIT-LEVEL MODEL

A third model might be used in cities where group conflict was so intense that agreement on the formulation of police policy was virtually impossible. In addition, this model would introduce an element of choice into urban policing. In this model, states or metropolitan districts would create professional-style police departments and offer their full or partial services to any community on a contract basis. Coincident with this, city neighborhoods would be authorized to form police departments in the same manner that independent towns now do. Thus, residents of a suburb or city neighborhood could choose to be policed entirely by the professional force or simply to receive overhead support from functional specialists. The professional force would also be available to assist in major emergencies such as riots and would move into communities where local police failed to enforce the law. In essence, the model applies to cities an expanded version of the arrangement which presently exists in rural areas of states with professional-style police departments.

Advantages

Presumably, the locally controlled police would maintain good community relations, while the professional force would concentrate its resources on crime control. The split-level system has an advantage over the neo-traditionalist in that it does not leave the bulk of field work in the hands of limited-skill individuals. Instead the professional force would supplement local policing by highly trained personnel. The notion that a community could, in effect, "fire" its police force and obtain another one should promote greater responsiveness of both forces.

Disadvantages

Such an arrangement might foster notions of separatism or create forbidden zones. It also has the potential for creating serious friction between the professionals and the locals, a situation not unknown in contemporary state police operations.

D. DIVESTMENT OF FUNCTION MODEL

Models A, B, and C assumed the present basis of the function of the police as given. In this model the police are essentially a uniformed patrol force and perform only those functions relating directly to the immediate control of crime and disorder. Other functions are referred to government or private agencies, for example:

1) The follow-up investigation of crime and vice would be conducted by agents of the prosecutor's office.
2) The regulation, investigation and enforcement of traffic matters would be turned over to state or municipal highway or motor vehicle departments.
3) The processing of juvenile offenders would be carried on by youth service bureaus composed of public welfare officials and local citizens.
4) Service tasks, such as ambulance driving or the collection of stray animals, would be turned over to private contractors.

Advantages

Highly trained police officers would be free to concentrate on their prime mission while technical functions would be carried on by specialist personnel with abilities markedly superior to those of the regular enforcement police; e.g., there would be trained lawyers or accountants to conduct criminal investigations, safety specialists to oversee traffic work, and special workers to process youthful offenders. The model institutionalizes at the municipal level the present practices of other levels of government. For example, the United States and certain state attorney generals now maintain detective forces which are separate from uniformed agencies; some states provide highway patrols which perform little or no criminal work; and ambulances and towing services are performed only by private agencies in many communities.

Disadvantages

Objections might be raised that the preliminary (patrol) and follow-up (detective) phases of police must be kept within the same containing unit, and that crime is so bound up with motor vehicles that police control of traffic is essential. It could even be argued that certain service functions help to present the police in a positive image.

E. THE ASSUMPTION OF FUNCTION MODEL

In this model the police would expand their activities beyond the present functions to embrace new areas of law enforcement and public service. For example, special squads would be created, enforce laws relating to housing violations, air pollution, sanitation, consumer frauds and racial or other discrimination. Other units would be concerned with youth employment, family counseling and drug or alcoholic treatment.

Advantages

While many of the above functions are technically within the scope of present police activities, they usually do not command a prominent place. The redefinition of the role of police to reflect present urban concern would place them in the forefront of activities designed to assist ordinary citizens, particularly minority groups. This should serve to enhance the image of the police in the eyes of those who normally see them exclusively as the protectors of landlords, businessmen and other "establishment" types.

Disadvantages

At least three objections might be offered to this model:

1) The extensive use of armed and uniformed officers to enforce the law against those unlikely to offer physical resistance is not desirable.
2) The ability of police to perform social service activities is questionable.
3) The expansion of functions might dilute the capability of police to perform their basic tasks in the areas of crime and disorder.

The first two objections could be met by employing trained civilian personnel, but unless their activities can be closely integrated with regular police work, the purpose of the model would be negated. If the image of the street-level policeman is to benefit from the assumption of new functions, the ordinary citizen must become aware of police activity in these areas.

Cost Factors Present in Each Model

None of the models assumes the necessity of increased manpower, therefore salary costs (90% of the typical police budget) should not be expected to show a significant rise. However the neo-professional model would require extra pay for agents and civilian technicians at a level 50% higher than regular patrolmen. Assuming these personnel constitute 25% of the force this would necessitate a 12½% increase in annual salary costs. The neo-traditionalist model does not anticipate any increased salary levels while the professional component of the split-level model would probably require compensation at a rate approaching the agent level. Assuming that the professional component would constitute no more than one third of the whole, the increased annual salary expenditures would be approximately 10–15%.

It should be noted that where cities which presently employ the professional style of policing to adopt either the neo-traditional or split-level model, it would require the creation of neighborhood traditional forces. Since these forces tend to operate at lower levels of efficiency and economy they normally require higher ratios of police per population. Thus the creation of traditional forces where none presently exist might occasion increases in manpower as great as 50% with resultant reflection in annual budgets.

The divestment of function models would obviously lead to reduction of these budgets but would require increases in the expenditures of other agencies. However, given the rapid escalation of current police salaries, it is likely that certain tasks, such as highway safety, might be performed more cheaply outside the police department. Certainly the removal of service functions to the private sector would result in public savings.

In contrast, the expanded function of an administrative police force would require additional personnel. While this might partially be offset by the transfer of resources from agencies such as the building department, the bulk of expanded activities would probably require new appropriations at an initial level at least 10% higher than current costs.

None of the above models need be seen as mutually exclusive. The neo-professional could be combined with the assumption of function models. Split-level policing could be expanded into a version of the divestment of function model. Indeed, this latter is the normal state of certain European countries where separate agencies exist to perform criminal investigations, inspection, patrol, traffic duty, administrative regulation and riot control.

In attempting to determine which of the above five models would be most effective in controlling crime and maintaining good community relations, an essential question seems to be which type serves best in the inner-city area, a professional or traditional, or combinations of both. It may be that each has different strengths and weaknesses. When this question is answered, the structure of police organization can be approached more confidently.

Indeed, the problem in police organization is to determine what works rather than what sounds attractive. This is a particularly difficult task because so few innovations are followed up by careful evaluation. In this respect what is needed is some objective measure of success or the lack of it, and an analysis of the factors involved.

A paper of this scope cannot begin to explore the many variables present in even the limited sphere of police organization embraced by the experiments in team policing. However, a single illustration may convey some of the complexity. One factor related to the success of team policing is the degree of strain it places on the administrative system due to its tendency to reduce the flexibility of personnel assignments. Thus, team policing might work well in a department of under 500 because the increased administrative burden could be absorbed, but in a force of 5,000 the administrative system might become overburdened to the point of collapse.

In the real world, of course, there is a strong preference for action over research. Thus, should city X suddenly experience a decline in ghetto tension which it attributed to team policing, one could expect many cities to turn their forces upside down in an effort to adopt that system. No matter that the "peace" in city X might have come about for other reasons or that it is only temporary, team policing would be regarded as the magic remedy. Even truly successful programs sometimes lack transferability. The London police of the nineteenth century, for instance, were a brilliant success, their American imitators spectacular failures.

Given the above considerations, the most logical approach in the field of police organization would involve the following:

1) The careful evaluation of promising ongoing programs by disinterested individuals commanding appropriate resources. Such evaluations should include assessments of each program's transferability.

2) In certain instances, the formulation of experiments designed to produce data on important untested questions. One high-priority item would be to determine whether the neo-professional or neo-traditional (or other) style of policing was most effective in inner-city areas. An experiment could be conducted by staffing one ghetto precinct with college graduate rookies recruited on the basis of open competition, and another similar precinct with men appointed from the local neighborhood, without the necessity of passing a written exam. Then, after a suitable period, the performance of each could be evaluated.

3) An attempt to develop connections between the various strands of police organizational theory. For example, studies could be undertaken to determine

    a) By which agency and at what level of government are certain functions most effectively performed? For example, is the task of major criminal investigation best handled by the generalist neighborhood police, by headquarters specialists or by members of the prosecutors' staff?

    b) What functions could be removed from police responsibility? For example, to what extent should the police be involved in traffic activities? Model enforcement is often related to crime control, while parking and intersection regulation is much less so. Another question is whether such service tasks as ambulance driving are valuable for community relations because of the positive image they give to the police.

    c) To what degree does staff support, especially managerial units, facilitate the successful performance of field duties? The military has long known that extensive use of rear echelon personnel can increase the efficiency of line troops enormously. It is possible that a well-staffed planning section could increase patrol apprehension by developing sophisticated crime analysis techniques. In this respect, model police general staffs (management services) might be established on a demonstration basis. It is also possible that such units would not need to be organic to any given police department since military staffs frequently operate on behalf of constantly changing troop components.

d) What patrol tactics are most effective in controlling crime? Most police preventive patrol amounts to little more than random "cruising," while "in progress crime" response and area search are equally unsystematic. Despite the fact that crime clusters by time and area, the President's Commission estimated that the chance of a patrolman actually encountering a robbery in progress was only once in fourteen years. There is good reason to doubt that this appraisal is valid in high-crime areas. Nor does the statement adequately deal with the problem. Police departments such as Cincinnati's have experienced some success in felony apprehension by use of quadrant methods. Others have brought about at least temporary crime reduction by methods of area saturation. It would seem that the development of crime-control tactics for both prevention and apprehension would constitute an essential building block of police organization.

In conclusion, the most productive approach to police organizational problems would seem to lie in action oriented research which stresses experimentation, evaluation, and synthesis into large notions which can themselves be tested. Indeed, the present dynamic state of American police work seems ideally suited to such an endeavor.

6

CONTROLLING:
The Use of Authority, Power,
and Influence

One of the most exciting and complicated products invented by mankind thus far is the magnificent jet airliner, a unique blend of materials and systems brought together for a specific purpose. Perhaps not so exciting, but nonetheless complicated, is the modern police organization, a unique blend of personalities brought together in a most complicated society for a specific purpose. Regardless of the beauty or ability of the wondrous jet aircraft, its continued operation would be impossible without control. Greater control provides for greater reliability in reaching all its stated goals. The same holds true for any organization, but perhaps none more critically so than the modern police organization. Obviously the jet aircraft can operate—for a time at least—with some rather loosely handled controls. But in the end poor control is the harbinger of failure. The same is true of the modern police organization.

Perhaps the greatest difference in the analogy is that aircraft failure is normally consummated in one obvious and final plunge. On the other hand, a police organization without proper control may struggle along for some time, with few outward signs of crises. The inward signs are, of course, more apparent—absenteeism, employee turnover, inefficiency, apathy toward the public served, and perhaps the most damaging of all in terms of the total police service, dishonesty and general corruption.

We are not suggesting that every policing agency should have controls of the same magnitude. Obviously, a two-man police department is not likely to have the same communication problems as will a department of five or five hundred men and women. As police organizations grow in size, it is proportionately less likely that every member will have a clear understanding and acceptance of organizational goals. More controls will undoubtedly be necessary to insure reasonable goal achievement.

The President's Commission on Law Enforcement and Administration of Justice displayed substantial concern for the internal control of police agencies in its 1967 *Task Force Report: The Police*. Its observations and recommendations are especially relevant to this chapter. The report clearly states the critical need for adequate control. It also defines the methods by which controls or their lack prevent the organization from reaching broader expectations and goals. The following section is drawn from this report.

INTERNAL CONTROLS

It is in the nature of an administrative organization that the establishment of policies to guide the exercise of discretion by individuals is not enough. There is need also for the development of methods for assuring compliance. This requires a system of administrative controls to be applied within an agency.

METHODS OF INTERNAL CONTROL

An analysis of patterns of deviations from appropriate policy standards indicates that such deviations usually fall into three general categories: situations in which an officer violates departmental regulations or policies; situations in which an officer's behavior is considered improper, but does not constitute a violation of existing department policy; and situations in which an officer's behavior is clearly illegal or improper, but is consistent with the routine practice of the particular agency and is generally condoned by its administration.

1. There are a limited number of situations today in which police administrators have issued policy statements to control police conduct. These tend to mirror the requirements of appellate cases as, for example, policies to implement the specific interrogation requirements of the *Miranda* case. Field studies conducted by the commission indicate that such policies, promulgated at the top of the agency,

are often disregarded in practice. Occasionally situations may arise in which a failure to adhere to existing policy becomes a source of embarrassment to the top echelons of the police agency, as, for example, if a failure to give the warnings required by the *Miranda* case were to prevent the conviction of a dangerous criminal in a highly publicized case.

The fact that administrative policy for dealing with crime or potential crime situations does not have a very significant impact upon the actions of individual officers appears to be primarily attributable to two factors: the ambivalent attitude which often accompanies the pronouncement of a policy implementing a decision like *Miranda,* and competing influences brought to bear by subordinate command staff who are subject to more immediate pressures from the community they serve.

Top police officials have been quite outspoken in registering their opposition to recent decisions of the U.S. Supreme Court. Personnel within an agency are fully aware of the public pronouncements of their superiors. They recognize that an order which purports to urge compliance with a recent decision is necessitated by the decision and is reluctantly issued by their superior. Without a special effort on the part of the administrator to distinguish between his right to enter into public debate over the wisdom of court decisions and the need for compliance with court decisions, it is likely that departmental policies which simply mirror the requirements of an appellate decision will be largely disregarded.

A somewhat similar situation exists when operating personnel believe that a change in departmental policy reflects a somewhat reluctant effort on the part of the administration to appease some community group that has made a complaint against the department.

In current practice, such departmental policy as exists is but one of a number of competing considerations that influence police actions at the operating level. Tremendous pressures are generated upon the various command levels in a large police agency by community groups—pressures from which such personnel cannot be easily isolated. The desire on the part of a supervisory officer or precinct commander to satisfy a prominent citizen, to meet the demands of a community group on whose support his continued effectiveness and acceptance depend, to obtain favorable publicity, or simply to satisfy his most immediate superior may override any desire he may have to adhere to established policy. Subordinates, in turn, have their eyes upon their superior rather than upon formal pronouncements which come to them in written form. The extent to which they conform with policy formulated at the top levels will be determined, in large measure, by the spirit and tone in which it is communicated to them by their more immediate superiors. Each of the many levels of super-vision in a large agency, therefore, constitutes a point at which poli-cies may be diluted or ignored.

2. An entirely different set of problems is raised when an indi-vidual officer acts in a manner which none of his superiors would con-done, but there is no formulated policy to serve as a basis for discipline or condemnation.

The problems are complicated by the peculiar nature of the police function. Officers are usually spread out about an entire city. They do not have the opportunity for immediate consultation with superior officers when called upon to take action. The danger of mass disorder is always present, and the need for quick decisions often requires that the officer take some form of action before he has the opportunity to acquire all of the facts. It is, therefore, difficult for the police administrator to hold an individual police officer to the same standard one would hold a person who had an opportunity to consult and to think about the matter before acting.

The actions of individual police officers are not easily subject to review. Contacts between police officers and citizens are often con-tentious, tending to evoke an emotional response on the part of both the officer and the citizen. They occur at times and in locations where others are not present. And an informal code among police officers, which bands individual officers together for mutual support when challenged from the outside, silences fellow police officers who may be the only witnesses to an incident. As a consequence the typical complaint will consist of an assertion of wrongdoing on the part of a citizen and a denial by the officer. There usually is no available basis for corroborating either story. The consequence of continually dis-believing the officer would obviously mean a loss of morale. Hence, the tendency in such cases is for the police administrator to accept the officer's version unless there is some reason to believe the officer is being untruthful.

3. The most complicated situations that arise in current practice are those in which the actions of an officer are clearly illegal or im-proper but are consistent with prevailing practices of a department. Such practices are commonly found in the police agencies serving large urban areas, where the practices constitute part of the informal response which the police have developed for dealing with prob-lems of a recurring nature. It is, for example, common for police officers to search the interior of a vehicle without legal grounds in high crime-rate areas. It is similarly common for police to search gamblers or arrest known prostitutes without adequate grounds. Since such actions are generally encouraged by superior officers, it is in-conceivable that the officer would be administratively criticized or

disciplined upon the filing of a complaint. Nevertheless, complaints tend to be processed administratively in the same way as complaints alleging a violation of administrative policy by an officer. As a consequence, the complaint procedure does not serve as a vehicle to challenge and cause a reconsideration of policies which are sanctioned by the department even though not articulated.

PROPOSED IMPROVEMENTS IN METHODS OF INTERNAL CONTROL

Some of the problems of achieving control over the conduct of individual police officers would be simplified if there were a commitment by the police administrator to a systematic policy-formulation process. This would require specific attention to present unarticulated policies which are clearly illegal and as a consequence would create administrative pressure to reject them or develop alternatives rather than assume the indefensible position of formally adopting illegal practices as official departmental policy. The development of adequate policy statements would afford the individual police officers greater guidance with respect to important decisions like the use of force, and the decision to arrest or to search.

But the mere adoption of administrative policies will not alone achieve compliance. This will require "good administration," that is, the use of the whole array of devices commonly employed in public administration to achieve conformity. These include, but are not limited to, the setting of individual responsibility, the establishment of systems of accountability, the designing of procedures for checking and reporting on performance, and the establishment of methods for taking corrective action.

The police administrator currently achieves a high degree of conformity on the part of officers to standards governing such matters as the form of dress, the method of completing reports, and the procedures for processing of citizen complaints. Sleeping on duty, leaving one's place of assignment without authorization, or failing to meet one's financial obligations are all situations against which supervisory personnel currently take effective action.

The success of internal controls as applied to such matters appears to be dependent upon two major factors: (1) the attitude and commitment of the head of the agency to the policies being enforced and (2) the degree to which individual officers and especially supervisory officers have a desire to conform.

The average police administrator, for example, has no ambivalence over accepting responsibility for the physical appearance of his men. He does not wait to act until complaints are received from a third party, He undertakes, instead, by a variety of administrative techniques, to produce a desire in his subordinates to conform. This desire may reflect an agreement by the subordinates with the policy. Or it may reflect respect for their superior, a lack of interest one way or the other, or a fear of punishment or reprisal. Whatever the reason, the officer in a sort of "state of command" does what he is told rather than follow a course of his own choosing.

In sharp contrast, the police administrator is typically ambivalent over the responsibility he has for controlling the activities of his force in the exercise of discretionary power in dealing with crime or potential crime situations. While he views the physical appearance of his men as his concern, he often sees the methods by which the law in enforced as involving matters which are the primary responsibility of others outside the police establishment. This deference may, in part, be attributable to the sharing of responsibilities with other agencies—particularly the courts. Unlike internal matters over which the police administrator has complete control, much of what the police do relating to crime and criminals is dependent for approval upon the decisions of nonpolice agencies.

Strengthening of administrative control requires the creation of the same sense of personal responsibility on the part of the police administrator for the implementation of proper law enforcement policies as he presently has for implementing policies relating to internal matters.

This will require that the administrator be given the education, training, and resources necessary to fulfill the role. It requires also a change in what is expected of police administrators by the public and by those occupying key positions in other agencies in the criminal justice system. Police officials cannot be expected to develop a sense of responsibility, if they are treated like ministerial officers, and excluded from important policy-making decisions, such as those regarding the revision of substantive and procedural laws.

Also required is the development of a professional identification which can serve police officers as a frame of reference within which they can see the importance of their conforming to appropriate law enforcement policies. Blind obedience to orders, such as is currently elicited for some aspects of police operations, is limited in both its values and desirability to purely administrative functions. Personnel called upon to deal with complex problems of human behavior and expected to make decisions on the basis of professionally developed criteria must, themselves, have some form of professional identification as a common basis from which to function.

Professional identification has, for example, been a major element in the rapid development of what are now some of our more highly regarded correctional systems. With training and education in social casework as a prerequisite to employment, operating personnel function from a framework for decision-making which is consistent with and supportive of departmental policies. The whole administrative process is facilitated because both administrators and field personnel are on the same "wave length," talking the same language and supporting the same values.

A somewhat similar development is essential in the police field. Individual police officers must be provided with the training and education which will give them a professional identification consistent with the police role in a free society. Such training and education will equip them to understand the policies of their superiors; make them receptive to efforts to make law enforcement both fair and effective; and enable the officer to take appropriate action in the unpredictable situations not dealt with by even the best efforts at policy formulation.[1]

Private Organizations

Private business organizations have consistently moved ahead of government in recognizing the need and in searching for greater efficiency—control. This is not to say that government and, more specifically, policing organizations have not exercised controls, for they have. But apparently there has been and continues to be a primary reliance, almost a preoccupation by many, upon hierarchical authority. We are not suggesting that traditional concepts of authority, responsibility, and accountability be scrapped or bypassed. We are suggesting that the state of the managerial art has progressed to the point that it offers other options and complementing additions.

In recognizing the necessity for more effective controls, private organizations have had at least one built-in motivating factor not shared by government—profit. Private organizations simply cannot continue to exist without profit. On the other hand, we believe that police organizations in the future will be asked to operate at a profit; that is, profit in terms of greater, more efficient services for the people served. Traditionally, police organizations have grown proportionately with the general population. As police goals and expectations have expanded, the growth has become somewhat disproportional. Our belief is that police organizations will not be able to solve tomorrow's problems by simply adding new personnel, nor will there be the dollars to do so. Perhaps, then, it is reasonable to look to business for some of the answers. Granted, there are vast differences between government and private business; however, one theme that

---

[1] The President's Commission on Law Enforcement and Administration of Justice, *Task Force Report: The Police* (Washington, D.C.: Government Printing Office, 1967), pp. 28–30.

we trust will emerge in the following chapters is that the similarities are greater than these differences. If we, the writers and the reader, can agree with this idea, then perhaps we can also agree that many managerial concepts and rules held to be truths by business managers and contemporary writers in that field are applicable to the modern police organization.

George D. Eastman, professor and director of the Institute of Government Research and Services at Kent State University, as editor of *Municipal Police Administration* gave some recognition to this same proposition in his discussion of the principles of organization:

> Students of public and police administration, sooner or later in the course of their studies, are presented with "principles of organization." The principles often are offered as organization dogma and their acceptance taken for granted. Thoughtful people in business, industry, and government, however, have long since questioned their validity. General merit of the so-called principles is not basically at issue; rather, there is a challenge to their universality of application. It would seem appropriate, at this time, to simply identify them as a set of concepts or propositions believed by many to be a basis for sound organization.
>
> Confusion exists in their presentation because some relate to structure and some to process; in the sense of process some could be considered more meaningfully as matters of administrative action. Nonetheless, an organization structure should assure reasonably that there is provision for:
>
> 1. Sound and clear-cut allocation of responsibilities.
> 2. Equitable distribution of work loads among elements and individuals.
> 3. Clear and unequivocal lines of authority.
> 4. Authority adequate to discharge assigned responsibilities.
> 5. Reasonable spans of control for administrative, command, and supervisory officers.
> 6. Unity of command.
> 7. Coordination of effort.
> 8. Administrative control.
>
> Significantly the organization can only "make provision for" but cannot guarantee anything. It has no life or vitality of its own; it is simply a vehicle for management. As Urwick says, "It is the men and not the organization chart that do the work."[2]

FORMALIZATION AND AUTHORITY

As in police organizations, private organizations tend to formalize their hierarchical structure in the pyramidal shape. Pyramids are convenient in that they clearly signify differences in rank; the

---

[2]George D. Eastman and Esther M. Eastman, *Municipal Police Administration* (Washington, D.C.: International City Management Association, 1969), pp. 20–21.

higher one's position in the pyramid, the greater one's responsibility and authority. Perhaps private organizations have fewer levels of responsibility within the pyramid, nonetheless there exists the theory of increasing responsibility and authority while conversely the span of control is diminished. The pyramid permits a centralized control over the organization and places the final responsibility and authority in the hands of a single individual.

AUTHORITY

It becomes clear, then, that authority resides in the position. Superiors in any organization tend to rely on their rank authority to resolve organizational conflict, to change behavior—the superior being identified as the changer, the subordinate the changee. The use of authority to bring about change in behavior is expeditious, to say the least. Unfortunately, authority does not necessarily guarantee the degree or permanence of change.

Organizational heads are commonly held responsible for the formalization of policy that will assist the organization toward its stated goals. In police organizations, authority to bring about desired change is commonly exhibited in the form of general orders and departmental manuals. The following example is extracted from the *Manual of the Los Angeles Police Department:*

> **4/292. Disposing of rewards and gratuities.** When an employee receives a reward or contribution, he shall transmit it to the Commander, Personnel and Training Bureau, for deposit in the Fire and Police Pension Fund.
>
> If an employee is given a check or money order coming within the meaning of this Section, he shall endorse it "Pay to the Order of the City of Los Angeles," followed by his signature as it appears on the face. In addition, he shall complete two copies of the Employee's Report, Form 15.7, which shall be transmitted with the reward or contribution to the Personnel and Training Bureau and shall include the following information:
>
> * Name and address of person giving the reward or contribution.
> * Reason for giving reward or contribution.
> * Amount of the reward or contribution.[3]

Responsibility with commensurate authority to insure that the regulation is carried out is delegated to subordinates down to the appropriate level. In our opinion, however, it is pure fallacy to assume that the implied authority of the written order has any greater degree of success than that of the spoken word.

[3]*Manual of the Los Angeles Police Department* (Los Angeles, Calif.: Los Angeles Police Department, 1970), IV, Chap. 2, Sec. 292.

Harold J. Leavitt, in his book *Managerial Psychology*, has depicted interesting pros and cons of the use of authority:

> From the manager's viewpoint the advantages of authority, especially restrictively used authority, are huge. We have already cited one of them, the control and coordination advantage. There are many others, too.
>
> For one thing, one doesn't have to know much about any particular Joe Doaks to be fairly certain that firing him or cutting his pay or demoting him will strike at some important needs and thereby keep him in line. But one might have to know a good deal about the same employee to find out how to make work more fun for him.
>
> A corollary advantage, then, is simplicity. Authority as a restrictive tool does not require much subtlety or much understanding of people's motives. How simple it is to spank a child when he misbehaves, and how difficult and complicated to distract him or provide substitute satisfactions or to "explain" the situation. Given a hundred children, how much easier it is to keep them in line by punishing a few recalcitrants than to teach them all to feel "responsible." . . .
>
> Restrictive authority has another kind of advantage: speed. A do-it-or-else order eliminates the time consuming dillydallying of feedback. . . .
>
> Employees who expect to be censured whenever they are caught loafing may learn to *act* busy (and *when* to act busy) and also that the boss is an enemy. They are thereby provided with a challenging game to play against the boss: who can think up the best ways of loafing without getting caught; a game in which they can feel that justice is on their side and a game they can usually win. . . .
>
> The tenuousness and the self-defeating weakness of reliance on restrictive authority becomes apparent right here. When his authority has been "undermined" by the "sabotage" of subordinates, the superior who has depended on authority is likely immediately to assume that what he needs is *more authority*, because authority is the only tool he knows how to use.[4]

POWER

Although some of Leavitt's examples may appear rather simplistic or basic, his message that authority is an important element of organizational control, of change, is quite clear. On the other hand, Leavitt is just as resolute that reliance upon pure authority leaves the superior with very little reason for security.[5]

In discussing the concept of authority, social scientists Pfiffner and Sherwood observe that authority implies the *right* to command

---

[4] Harold J. Leavitt, *Managerial Psychology*, 2nd ed. (Chicago: University of Chicago Press, 1958), pp. 171–73, 175.

[5] *Ibid.*, p. 180.

another person, and the subordinate person has the *duty* to obey the command. They make specific note, however, that "the *right* to command does not necessarily connote the *capacity* to command."[6]

Since most law enforcement agencies are developed around the military model, authority in this case does afford a superior the ability to exercise, to a lesser or greater extent depending upon his hierarchical level, control over the subordinate's continued employment, salary increases (merit principle), work hours, assignments, promotions, and infinite other rewards and punishments. The superior does not, however, own the subordinate, nor can he hope for much more than a rather limited control. It is the subordinate, in the end, who makes the decision of whether or not it is worth it; in fact, whether or not he should report for work at all. Authority in a police organization, then, has its limitations.

Power, on the other hand, resides in the person, not necessarily in the position. It may or may not coincide with the official structure of authority. Power in itself is not institutionalized in the sense that one can look to the organizational manual and find out where it resides.[7] Conversely, almost every organization or organizational unit has the "person to see." Typical of such persons is the boss's secretary, the boss's assistant, the boss's wife. Other people, of course, may hold this same power potential, though remaining less obvious. It is not unusual for persons to be totally unaware of their own power potential. This normally occurs where the power is deferred. This is to say that the influencing party may be operating at several levels removed from the point of action. Power, simply stated, is the ability to influence behavior.

While we have taken care to emphasize that true power does not necessarily follow hierarchical lines or authoritative positions, the advantage to authoritative figures who also possess concomitant power should be obvious.

The term *power*, perhaps because of its own ominous sound, sometimes connotes being deceitful, or even illegitimate. The reader should bear in mind, however, that the expert, the consultant, exhibits power; that the person whose opinion is respected exhibits power; and that often a person who is simply "liked," who for one reason or another is an attractive person, exhibits power.

Bennis more clearly describes power as falling into five components:

1. *Coercive power,* or the ability of A to reward and/or punish B.

6 John M. Pfiffner and Frank P. Sherwood, *Administrative Organization* (Englewood Cliffs, N.J.: Prentice-Hall, Inc., 1960), p. 75.
7 *Ibid.,* p. 25.

2. *Referent, or identification power,* or the influence which accrues to A because he (or the group) is attractive, a person whom B wants to like and be liked by—in short, a role model.

3. *Expert power,* or the power that we associate with science and "truth."

4. *Legitimate* or *traditional* power, or power which stems from institutional norms and practices and from historical-legal traditions.

5. *Value power,* or influence which is gained on the basis of attraction to the values of A.[8]

Pfiffner and Sherwood have defined power as the politics of how things get done.[9] Though not particularly profound, it is important to recognize that in the real political arena, authoritative heads, while occupying a position of relative importance, must rely a great deal upon their knowledge of where the power-politics lies; otherwise they cannot hope to carry out long-range programs and goals. They can, of course, heroically buck the power, but heroics cannot be relied upon to "get things done." Internal power-politics is a part of every organization and police departments are no exception; to deny its existence and to neglect its utilization is foolhardy.

Pfiffner and Sherwood's definition has special meaning when viewing *power* as a component of organization control. Obviously, if the *power* is held by persons other than those in authority, it becomes a matter of political necessity for the authority figures to have access to that power. This becomes especially sticky for the "old guard" type of police manager who simply is not accustomed to "dealing" with subordinates. When an administrator fails to recognize the realities of present-day organizational politics, the result is often a friction-building impasse that causes organizational dysfunction. As we stated earlier, authoritative failure usually results in a drive for more authority which, of course, further complicates the problem.

Practitioners in the field can no doubt conjure up their own nightmarish recollection of examples in which the administrator got himself so far out on a limb that it was finally chopped off. Administrative heads of government tend to back their police managers when the first internal conflicts arise, but history has shown that sooner or later their support wanes.

At this late point the police manager should recognize the political facts of life and change his style, utilizing the organizational power-politics to its best advantage. In many cases where the unswerving managerial style prevails, however, the manager is eventually

---

[8] Warren G. Bennis, *Changing Organizations* (New York: McGraw-Hill Book Company, 1966), p. 168.

[9] Pfiffner and Sherwood, *Administrative Organization,* pp. 310–11.

demoted, retired, fired, or elevated to a state of limbo where he no longer has any influence. There are, of course, those few who have acquired considerable personal power through outside-of-the-organization politics. They seem to remain almost indefinitely, surrounded by a kind of bureaucratic moat, blindly impeding the organization and its individual elements from reaching optimum goals.

We are in general agreement with contemporaries in the field that authority is an essential component of power, while power itself is not necessarily synonymous with authority. Power and authority are, however, legitimately a part of control.

INFLUENCE

In the following paragraphs we will be using the term *influence* in the most positive sense. Influence in our context then, as an element of control, means giving recognition and support to the hypotheses that people are more likely to do what is desired of them with minimum formal control—supervision—if they are *self-motivated*. To establish continuity with other contemporary writers in the field, the term *self-actualization* will be used synonymously with *self-motivation* throughout the discussion.

Influence, at least effective influence in modern organizations, is not limited to a "top-down" system. Effective managers in the private sector have for some time realized that influence should flow in all directions, at all levels. Contemporary behavioral scientists generally agree that organizations in which subordinates as well as superiors feel a personal sense of influence are most likely to be highly productive. We believe this to be true of modern police organizations as well.

The police manager who has developed modern leadership skills, who has learned to consider the personal needs of his subordinates and has given them a feeling of self-importance, of worth, is likely to have a high-producing unit. *Feedback* is certainly not new to the police manager, but the kind of feedback in which the subordinate's opinion is respected, even solicited, and has direct influence on the organizational operations may well be. This type of subordinate influence, which at times may manifest itself in the form of criticism or at least appears to question the superior's judgment, can be quite threatening, especially if the manager has not gained a proper level of leadership sophistication. Actually, a substantial degree of personal security must always be present for all who participate in the use of influence for organizational effectiveness. This kind of security, together with satifactory relationships between the manager and the managed, is the cohesiveness that builds effective organizations.

Through research, Rensis Likert in *New Patterns of Management* has verified that high-producing managers build better management systems than do low-producing managers. Likert discovered that a better management system, "while giving the men more influence, also gives the higher producing manager more influence."[10]

Likert's study did not reveal that all high-producing managers use the "influence" concept. Our own experience in police organizations offers some confirmation of this. Highly structured, highly authoritarian, highly bureaucratic, highly goal centered police management systems can also be high producers. High production is used in this case to denote impressive statistics in the solution of crimes, the repression of traffic accidents, and all the other bench marks traditional with police agencies.

These data, however, do not reveal other important factors, such as employee attitudes, which present themselves in less-measurable ways—excessive absenteeism, employee turnover, negative discipline, and the like. High production, then, is not necessarily a barometer of organizational health and does not insure the internalization of organizational goals by the employee.

One can expect that subordinates in such a system will operate "by the book." They will tend not to extend themselves beyond what is considered to be their responsibility. Blau and Scott, in their study of formal organizations, were concerned with the results of routinized jobs of certain workers. They discovered that "the contractual bond of nonsupervisory white collar employees to formal organizations normally obligates them to fulfill role prescriptions only in accordance with minimum standards."[11]

To relate this to the police officer, he may be producing at a level acceptable to his supervisor, but if Blau and Scott's finding is applicable, he is normally only producing at an acceptable minimum; he has the capacity to do more with proper control—in this case motivation, self-actualization.

While statistics, or whatever measurement used to determine organizational effectiveness, may appear encouraging, a careful examination must be made of the more vital signs of organizational health, such as employee morale, tardiness, absenteeism, turnover, and the growing necessity for negative disciplinary measures. If statistics is the game being played, subordinates soon learn to play the game, not unlike an earlier example of learning to "look busy" when the boss is around. True organizational health is more difficult to observe.

[10] Rensis Likert, *New Patterns of Management* (New York: McGraw-Hill Book Company, 1961), p. 58. (For a more complete discussion of *influence* and *performance*, see pp. 44–60.)

[11] Peter M. Blau and Richard W. Scott, *Formal Organizations* (San Francisco: Chandler Publishing Company, 1962), p. 140.

At the beginning of our discussion of *influence,* we incorporated the terms *self-motivation* and *self-actualization.* Our hypothesis is that subordinates are more likely to work harder to achieve organizational goals, in the most desirable manner, if they are a part of the decision-making process. Self-motivation is fairly simple; if one has a personal stake in reaching organizational goals, he will require less supervision, will be more likely to operate in an acceptable manner, and will sense a deeper feeling of achievement in reaching those goals. Self-motivation can occur from a variety of stimuli. Self-actualization is somewhat different in that it deals with an inner self. Abraham Maslow describes *self-actualization* as referring "to the desire for self fulfillment, namely, to the tendency for one to become actualized in what one is potentially."[12] Self-actualized, self-motivated people, then, are more likely to be influenced to do what is desired of them because of a personal commitment rather than because of a concern for authority or power.

Since World War II greater emphasis has been placed on attracting high-caliber young men into the police services. In 1967 the President's Commission on Law Enforcement and Administration of Justice focused attention on the need for formally educated police officers. "The ultimate aim of all police departments should be that all personnel with general enforcement powers have baccalaureate degrees."[13] High-ranking officers' objectives should be advanced degrees.

We concur with the commission's recommendations but foresee some administrative problems for those organizations that continue to operate with the traditional authoritarian model.

Maslow's theory takes on new and special meaning for police organizations. It appears likely that a better-educated young man will be more critical of the organization and of himself and less likely that he will be content to simply "carry out orders." There is a danger that police organizations, police managers, may not recognize the new type of recruit and may not use his *self-actualizing* needs properly. If this occurs, it can be anticipated that retention rate of our brightest resource will sharply decline and today's problems will continue to be tomorrow's.

Reliance upon strict authoritarian controls may continue to insure respectable crime statistics, but as previously mentioned, these may not be a reliable barometer of organizational effectiveness.

[12] Abraham H. Maslow, *Motivation and Personality* (New York: Harper & Row, Publishers, 1954), pp. 91–92. (Maslow's *hierarchy of needs* will be more thoroughly discussed in Chapter 7, "Leading: Leadership Styles.")

[13] The President's Commission on Law Enforcement and Administration of Justice, *The Challenge of Crime in a Free Society,* (Washington, D.C.: Government Printing Office, 1967), p. 110.

CHAPTER SUMMARY

In the preceding pages we have tried to show that organizations whose managers exercise poor control, or whose control is inconsistent at different levels, tend to have limited organizational effectiveness and, conversely, that organizations whose managers exercise proper control at every level tend to have a higher degree of organizational effectiveness. We have also explored three concepts of control: the use of authority, power, and influence, and we hope that all three emerged as legitimate and as having a direct and supportive relationship with each other. It should be obvious that we have leaned strongly toward the integration of the man and the organization. It is our belief that true high level police organizational effectiveness can be achieved only when each able human component of the organization is encouraged to make use of his personal influences.[14]

LEARNING EXERCISE

DEPENDENCY-INTIMACY PERCEPTIONS: A STRUCTURED EXPERIENCE

GOALS

    I.   To focus on participants' relations to authority figures.
    II. To focus on participants' relations to each other.
    III. To study how these personal dimensions affect group process.
    IV. To provide instrumented feedback to members on how they are being perceived in the group.

MATERIALS UTILIZED

    I.   Dependency-Intimacy Rating Forms. (It is advisable to write in group members' names on the forms in the same order before the session.)
    II. Dependency-Intimacy Tally Forms.
    III. Pencils.

PROCESS

    I.   Facilitator gives lecturette on the relationship between group participants' personalities and group development, stressing the centrality of the dimensions of dependency (group participants' orientations to authority, toward the distribution and handling of

[14] The learning exercise is taken from J. William Pfeiffer and John E. Jones, *A Handbook of Structured Experiences for Human Relations Training* (Iowa City, Iowa: University City Associates Press, 1969), pp. 86–88.

power, to structure), and intimacy (orientations toward each other, closeness, personalness).

II. Participants complete the Dependency-Intimacy Rating Form anonymously.

III. The facilitator collects the completed forms and distributes tally forms.

IV. The facilitator reads the ratings aloud, and each participant tallies the ratings which he receives. The facilitator redistributes the rating forms randomly.

V. Participants react to their ratings—how they feel about them, how accurate they feel they are—and are encouraged to solicit feedback on what aspects of their behavior may have elicited the ratings.

VI. The group discusses its development in terms of roles that various "types" of participants have played.

Dependency-Intimacy Rating Form

Below are scales on which you are to rate yourself and all of the other participants of your group on two traits, dependency and intimacy. Go through the following steps:

1. Read the descriptions of the two personality traits.

2. In front of the names of the participants, listed below, write the number corresponding to where you would place them on the dependency scale.

3. Then record your rating of each participant on the intimacy scale.

DEPENDENCY

1	2	3	4	5	6
Dependent Relies on structure, leader, group, agenda		Independent		Counterdependent Rebels against almost all forms of structure	

INTIMACY

1	2	3	4	5	6
Overpersonal Need to establish close personal relations with everyone, to keep the group on a personal level		Personal		Counterpersonal Need to keep relations with others formal and impersonal and to keep group interaction for- mal and impersonal	

DEP	INT	Group Member	DEP	INT	Group Member
——	—	_____	——	—	_____
——	—	_____	——	—	_____
——	—	_____	——	—	_____
——	—	_____	——	—	_____
——	—	_____	——	—	_____
——	—	_____	——	—	_____
——	—	_____	——	—	_____
——	—	_____	——	—	_____

Dependency-Intimacy Tally Form

_____

Name

Dependency and intimacy are not seen as linear dimensions; that is, the extremes of dependency and counterdependency are dynamically close together, as are overpersonalness and counterpersonalness. The person who is conflicted on either dependency or intimacy may display behaviors on both ends of the continuum. He may alternately be dependent and counter-dependent in a stressful situation, even in the same group meeting. The circles below graphically demonstrate the relationship between the extremes of these two dimensions. Tally the ratings which you receive from your fellow group members by marking X's on the circles.

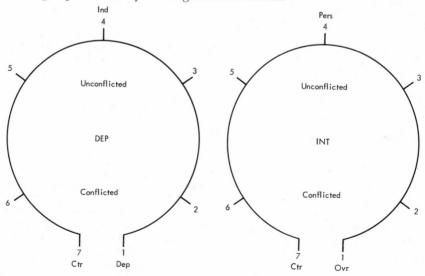

LEADING:
Leadership Styles

The quality of an organization is often judged by the perceived quality of the leadership.[1]

In the preceding chapter we discussed the hierarchy and the use of authority, power, and influence in relationship to controlling the organization. Because authority, formalized and legitimized by hierarchical designation, is also part of leading, the concepts discussed there bear a direct relationship to our position on leadership. Although organizations are influenced by both formal and informal leaders, we are directing our present attention to the formally designated leaders—to those persons charged with the responsibility of moving the organization and reaching the stated goals. The "definition of leadership includes many routine acts of supervision; the essence of leadership, however, has to do with that *influential increment* which goes beyond routine and taps bases of power beyond those which are organizationally decreed."[2]

The police, like other modern organizations, have an ever-

[1] Jack R. Gibb, "Dynamics of Leadership," *Behavioral Science and the Manager's Role* (Washington, D.C.: NTL Institute for Applied Behavioral Science, 1969), p. 123.

[2] Daniel Katz and Robert L. Kahn, *The Social Psychology of Organizations* (New York: John Wiley & Sons, Inc., 1966), p. 334.

growing need for effective, creative leaders at every level. Hierarchical levels are traditionally depicted on organizational charts, which are of course helpful in formalizing areas of leadership responsibility. Charts, however, and their accompanying role descriptions do not necessarily portray the kind of leader who will fill a given position or tell how effective he will be.

Obviously, those persons who fill the leader positions are of vital importance, far beyond their immediate scope of influence, for it is they who set the tone for the present and future health of the organization. Organizational health means the difference between success and failure in the private sectors. In government, the organization can often continue to exist, though unhealthy, in the sense that it is not operating in a most efficient manner. This kind of operation does reflect its inadequacy in other ways, however, such as being unable to approach the attainment of desirable or acceptable standards of service.

Granted, many variables can influence the health of organizations, but none are more critical than those of leadership.

While leadership is a variable of organizational health, it, too, is comprised of multiple subvariables, some of which will be discussed later in the chapter. Transplanting or superimposing a proven successful leader over an ailing organization in no way insures success. There is a concomitant need to choose the right leader for the particular job.

Pfiffner and Sherwood support this belief with a rather poignant example:

> We have all observed occasions where a change in the leadership has had a pronounced effect on the organization. There is, as one illustration, General Omar Bradley's story of the problem of command in the 90th Infantry Division during World War II. The 90th was brought to Europe by a new division commander who had had no chance to train with it. It was thrown into the Normandy bridgehead and performed miserably. After four days, the division commander was relieved. But a new general and a thorough shakeup of the staff made little difference. The division was floundering so badly that Bradley's subordinates wanted to break it up, sending the men to other units.
>
> However, Bradley rejected the idea. His refusal was at least in part based on his own philosophy of command in the military: "... man for man one division is just as good as another—they vary only in the skill and leadership of their commanders." Thus the answer to the 90th's problem was not to destroy the division but to find the right man for command. Bradley's next choice turned out to be such a person. The new commander made exactly 16 changes in the 16,000 man organization. When he left the division a few months later to assume command of a corps, "his successor inherited one of the finest divisions in combat on the allied front."

> Bradley's strong conviction that the men at the top make the difference—and his vindication by the performance of the 90th —is rather dramatic testimony that leadership can be an important modifier of organizational behavior.[3]

Obviously, a great deal of information is acquired on career men in the military service. Both predecessors of the successful Ninetieth Division commander had undoubtedly demonstrated successful leadership before their appointment or they would never have been given such a critical assignment, and yet they failed.

This phenomenon is not particularly unusual, for we have all observed successful leaders from the private sector or from other areas of government who have been appointed to positions at the presidential cabinet level and have failed. Leadership in itself is not enough—they must be the right leaders.

In addition to a discussion of the leader we will explore the emerging leadership posture we feel most appropriate for modern law enforcement organizations. This chapter will also cover the various styles of leadership and their applications; the need for supportive relationships; the need for self-actualization; and the selection of future leaders.

LEADERSHIP

At this point it seems appropriate to examine the rather elusive term *leadership*, which in itself "is the art of coordinating and motivating individuals and groups to achieve desired ends."[4] As a rule, "leadership" is used to generalize a myriad of qualities, some learned, some inherent, that are brought together in the right combination for the right job. Typically, as small boys imitate their fathers, organizational members with leadership aspirations often strive to "be like" the leaders they admire. While it is possible to learn some aspects of leadership, and to at least partially emulate certain leadership styles, it is our belief that the truly successful leader is a man who *has found himself*, not a man who continues to "be like" another. Research on the subject of leadership has apparently been unable to isolate any significant number of qualities or traits common to all our successful leaders; no one seems to have discovered an all-encompassing, "sure-fire" formula for guaranteed successful leadership. We do know, however, as mentioned in the introduction, that weak organizations have grown healthy with dynamic leadership and that healthy organizations have crumbled for lack of it. In a further extension applica-

[3] John M. Pfiffner and Frank P. Sherwood, *Administrative Organization* (Englewood Cliffs, N.J.: Prentice-Hall, Inc., 1960), pp. 348–49.

[4] John M. Pfiffner and Robert V. Presthus, *Public Administration* (New York: The Ronald Press Company, 1960), p. 92.

tion, a number of our more singularly academically oriented colleagues believe that a successful professional leader can, without regard for his field, be effectively superimposed on any organization. We do not subscribe to this theory.

Although it may be true, to some degree, that a good manager may be able to move about and direct different kinds of organizations, we do not believe this is wholly true in government. Laws that control our operations in government are substantially different from those in private enterprise. The nongovernment management sector has a great deal more latitude, more discretion, fewer regulations to contend with, and most often, greater flexibility. Governmental agencies at all levels are highly complex, but in our opinion none is more so than law enforcement. We doubt the validity of the thought espoused by some learned persons that we could actually bring on board a highly successful lawyer or a good chamber of commerce manager, for example, and have either of them run a police department adequately. We believe that the complexities of modern law enforcement are such that successful police leaders must be reared in the police service.

Different kinds of organizations, even different kinds of policing organizations, call for different kinds of leaders. As authors, we could perhaps carry it even a step further and say that different kinds of communities might require different kinds of leadership. This does not imply that one leader would be strong and another weak, but rather, that one kind of community might, for example, require a leader who, in addition to other prerequisite skills, was endowed with particular attributes that permitted him to accomplish some goals on a social plane, while another community might have no such need. There are exceptionally affluent communities within our society where a police chief would be expected to have deep social commitments or involvements. On the other hand, there are industrialized areas where a police chief would probably have little or no social involvement. Hence, the personality need of these leaders would tend to be different. In leadership, then, personality does appear to play a vital role not only from within the organization but from without as well.

The needs of an organization, the needs of the people themselves, and the product involved all play vital roles in the type of leadership required. Yet "typing" a leader is almost, if not, impossible.

We must again emphasize that few common attributes, save perhaps self-confidence and personal commitment to specific goals, can be identified as being held by all great leaders, and this is more fully realized when one considers the unique individualities of men like Gandhi and Churchill. It takes many different attributes to make a leader. For example, the late Martin Luther King had certain qualities that made him a successful leader. Yet, when one attempts to equate him with a man like the late General George Patton, there is a total spectrum of difference even though the two men undoubtedly had some traits in common.

We have acknowledged the inability to isolate any significant number of traits common to successful leaders. Davis, however, in discussing successful managers, did list ten traits he viewed as *essential* for success:

1. Intelligence
2. Experience
3. Originality
4. Receptiveness
5. Teaching ability
6. Personality
7. Knowledge of human behavior
8. Courage
9. Tenacity
10. A sense of justice and fair play[5]

While Davis was looking at industrial organizations, we believe that his observations are equally applicable to police leaders.

Actually, Davis identified fifty-six managerial characteristics and traits but doubted that all would be possessed by any single individual.

He did not include *creativity* in his ten basic traits. Perhaps at the time of his study creativity was not a popular term. We believe, however, in light of the complexity of police organizations and the criticalness of the time, that creativity is an essential managerial element. "The creative person is able to be flexible; he can change course as the situation changes (which it always does); he can give up his plans, he can continuously and flexibly adapt to the law of the changing situation and to the changing authority of the facts, to the demand character of the shifting problem."[6]

A CHANGING ART

It is not our desire to develop a treatise on the evolution of management or leadership concepts. Since we are speaking of leadership in a modern police organization, we will confine our remarks to applicable contemporary thought except to acknowledge that an evolution-

---

[5]Ralph Currier Davis, *Industrial Organization and Management* (New York: Harper & Brothers, 1940), p. 32.

[6]Abraham H. Maslow, *Eupsychian Management* (Homewood, Ill.: Richard D. Irwin, Inc., and The Dorsey Press, 1965), p. 192.

ary process has been taking place since the recorded history of man. In modern times, however, we have not observed the police leadership process evolving at the same rate as the private sector—nonetheless, it is changing.

In law enforcement, as in business, we have tended to be goal oriented. There has been, to oversimplify, a shift from goal to employee orientation, with a blend of both in the private sector. In our opinion, however, the police for the most part have remained singly oriented toward the organizational goals. We are not implying that law enforcement goals are passé. We are suggesting that a more effective leadership posture for modern law enforcement is to be equally concerned with the personal needs of the employee as well as those of the organization.

Schein, with Maslow and other social scientists, has "come to the conclusion that organizational life has removed meaning from work."[7] They were primarily concerned with industry, but we feel that the same problem is occurring in police departments as they become compartmentalized into highly specialized units. "This loss of meaning is not related so much to man's *social* needs, however, as to man's inherent need to use his capabilities and skills in a mature productive way."[8] Few police officers are assigned to a given area and simply made responsible for certain law enforcement goals there, or are permitted wide latitude as to how those goals are approached. Instead, like those in the factory, policemen's responsibilities tend to be carefully set forth in operation-procedure manuals, breaking the total responsibility into small, measurable segments. We, like the social scientists, are concerned that jobs have become so specialized or fragmented that they neither permit the policeman "to use his capabilities nor enable him to see the relationship between what he is doing and the total organizational mission."[9] An example is the policeman who writes traffic citations "to keep the sergeant off his back" and is unaware of the total traffic safety mission and of how his inputs at the proper time and place could be a significant contribution to the reduction of traffic accidents.

SELF-ACTUALIZED MAN

Schein brings the concept of self-actualization into better focus for us in a discussion of man and his relationship to Maslow's *hier-*

---

[7] Edgar H. Schein, *Organizational Psychology* (Englewood Cliffs, N.J.: Prentice-Hall, Inc., 1965), p. 56.

[8] *Ibid.*

[9] *Ibid.*

archy of needs. "The kinds of assumptions which are implied about the nature of man can be stated as follows:

> a. Man's motives fall into classes which are arranged in a hierarchy: (1) simple needs for survival, safety and security; (2) social and affiliative needs; (3) ego-satisfaction and self-esteem needs; (4) needs for autonomy and independence; and (5) self-actualization needs in the sense of maximum use of all his resources. As the lower-level needs are satisfied, they release some of the higher-level motives. Even the lowliest untalented man seeks self-actualization, a sense of meaning and accomplishment in his work, if his other needs are more or less fulfilled.
>
> b. Man seeks to be mature on the job and is capable of being so. This means the exercise of a certain amount of autonomy and independence, the adoption of a long-range time perspective, the development of special capacities and skills, and greater flexibility in adapting to circumstances.
>
> c. Man is primarily self-motivated and self-controlled; externally imposed incentives and controls are likely to threaten the person and reduce him to a less mature adjustment.
>
> d. There is no inherent conflict between self-actualization and more effective organizational performance. If given a chance, man will voluntarily integrate his own goals with those of the organization.[10]

Most of the young people being recruited into the police service today have been born since World War II and know little about life in a major depression; their fathers have always been employed, as they themselves; they have been raised in a social affiliative era and have belonged to such organizations since entering elementary school; they are accustomed to being patted on the back for a job well done; and finally, they have enjoyed a greater degree of independence than have the young people of any previous generation. By the time they are recruited into the police service, their basic needs have been met and accepted as a way of life and they have been conditioned to expect a great deal of independence.

We believe that police organizations and police leadership will need to be modified to accommodate the emerging generation of police. We are convinced that some autonomy can be built in at every level and that, with this, an emphasis on self-actualization can be a most responsible approach to leadership in modern police organizations.

In leaving this area, we should point out that assisting others in self-actualization is much easier when the leader himself is self-actualized, when he is making the best use of his own potential, and when his job has meaning and importance.

[10] *Ibid.*, pp. 56–57.

LEADERSHIP STYLES

In suggesting that leaders in modern police organizations should be equally concerned with both the organizational goals and the employees' needs, we refrained from referring to this posture or philosophy as a "style." It appears that there are a number of leadership styles, any one of which can be used in conjunction with a particular managerial philosphy. "Consideration of the situation, the followers, and the personality of the leader would determine which approach would be most successful."[11]

Pfiffner and Sherwood, Argyris, Bennis, Etzioni, Schein, and others have recognized and discussed leadership styles in varying degrees. Applewhite lists five main styles which are generally representative: authoritarian, democratic, laissez-faire, bureaucratic, and charismatic.[12]

In a more contemporary manner, University of Southern California Professor Terry Polin has suggested seven appropriate styles of leadership, four of which were originally identified by Tannenbaum and Schmidt in their study of boss-centered versus employee-centered leadership.[13] Polin's seven styles are "tells, sells, tests, consults, joins, abdicates, and blocks."[14] Examples of each of these follow.

For the first leadership style, "tells," imagine a large metropolitan police station. The sergeant reports to the station commander that he has just discovered a bomb in the lobby and that it may go off at any moment. The commander quickly calls his staff together and says, "Men, we have a little bomb problem here and I wondered if we could have a discussion to decide what we should do about it." Obviously, no one in an emergency situation such as this expects to have a discussion type of communication. What is wanted is a dictator. At this time the commander had better become an autocrat and say, "Evacuate the area, notify the bomb detail," and so forth.

In the second leadership style, "sells," the sergeant approaches the station commander and inquires, "Do you want the men to wear helmets or their soft hats for the fourth of July parade duty?" There is normally a morale problem when officers are required to wear helmets on hot days. On the other hand, the commander has information that a radical activist group may take advantage of the large crowd to

[11] Philip B. Applewhite, *Organizational Behavior* (Englewood Cliffs, N.J.: Prentice-Hall, Inc., 1965), p. 131.

[12] *Ibid.*

[13] R. Tannenbaum and W. H. Schmidt, "How to Choose a Leadership Pattern," *Harvard Business Review*, March-April 1958, p. 36 (*The Journal of Applied Behavioral Science* [Montpelier, Vt.: Capital City Press, 1970], Vol. 6, No. 1, 7).

[14] Terry Polin, a lecture delivered at the University of California School of Business Administration, 1967.

cause a disturbance. The commander should say, "We will wear helmets," and he should explain why.

In the third leadership style, "tests," the sergeant approaches the commander and says, "We have a vacation problem. Six men with equal seniority have applied for vacation leave at the same time. Normally this wouldn't have created a problem, but this year all personnel have been granted an extra week, and we only have coverage for twelve man-weeks." The commander has two immediate alternatives—he can grant each of the six their normal two weeks, saving one week for a later time in the year, or he can try to get two of them to take vacations in a different time period. In this case he should say to the six, "All of you are entitled to three weeks' vacation this year and all of you have requested the same vacation period. The problem is that we can't cover all of your positions for more than twelve work-weeks. Are there two of you who would just as soon take your three weeks' vacation at a different time?" What he is saying is, "What do you think of the idea?" If they react against it, he is not in the position where he must back down. If the men say that they do not like the idea at all, he can go back to the original two-week plan, scheduling the odd weeks at a later time.

In the fourth leadership style, "consults," there is some selling and some testing; a kind of manipulating. The object is to get the person to buy without telling him to do so. In this situation, the sergeant comes to the commander and says, "On July first we shifted into summer uniforms. I noticed in this morning's paper that the expected high today is going to be an unusually low sixty degrees. What should we do?" In this case the commander should say to the men, "The newspaper indicates that we will probably have sixty degree weather today. We have two choices: one, to remain in the summer uniform in hope that the weather will warm up; or two, to shift into the winter uniform for this one day. If you would like to remain in the summer uniform, raise your hand." The men are then instructed to wear the uniform that received the most popular vote. This is a sort of, "You tell me what you want."

In the fifth leadership style, "joins," the sergeant comes to the station commander and says, "There is a child vomiting in the lobby. What do you want me to do?" The commander replies, "You handle this yourself." What he is saying is, "I'm no different than any other person in the building. I'm not going to tell you how to clean up vomit. You must handle it yourself. I'm part of the group. I'm joining the group."

In the sixth leadership style, "abdicates," the station commander sees the sergeant coming and he turns quickly and locks the door. What he is saying is, "I do not want to become involved with you."

In the seventh leadership style, "blocks," the station commander may decide that the best way to handle this sergeant is to keep him busy. He gives him so many projects to do that he cannot think of problems for the commander to resolve.

Our position is that no *one* leadership style is sufficient unto itself and that all seven styles are appropriate for law enforcement leaders when utilized at appropriate times.

Telling is most appropriate in those situations requiring immediate action; when any delay is likely to result in negative consequences for the organization and where the leader doing the telling is in the best position, and has the best information, to do so. For maximum effectiveness his subordinates must also be perceptive of the above elements.

Selling is simply recognizing that most people are in a better position to, and are more likely to, support the boss if they understand *why*.

Testing provides the leader with some indication of a decision's likely success *before* he makes it and, at the same time, allows an alternative course of action should the reaction be negative.

Consulting should in reality be separated into several parts, which can be generalized as follows: The first involves situations in which there are two or more appropriate solutions to choose from, any of which is acceptable to the leader. He furnishes the list of solutions and takes a vote, selecting the most popular. An arbitrary decision has been avoided and a high degree of compliance is likely. The second involves the leader's sharing a problem with qualified subordinates; qualified in the sense that the background of each is appropriate to the problem. Each is expected to make contributions to the solution, and when all possible alternatives have been explored, each is polled for his opinion of the best solution, which is finally selected by majority vote. The third and last involves the leader's sharing a problem, in which he has discrete information, with subordinates. He makes it known that he needs their inputs to add to his own information and that using the total data he personally will make the necessary decision.

Consulting has many important facets. It includes a sharing of responsibility, participative management, team building, personal commitment, and developing future leaders. It also assists present leaders in that it broadens their base of influence, provides better solutions, relieves part of the burden of command, and develops future support.

Joining, in a sense, is acknowledging that the boss does not have all of the answers and that in some instances his opinion has no more value than that of any other person in the group. In another way it provides the vehicle, the climate, for decisions to be made at the appropriate level. In law enforcement, as in the military, there is often a tendency to expect decisions to be made, or at least cleared, by the highest-ranking officer present. In these instances, it is important to place the responsibility back down where it belongs.

Abdicating will undoubtedly cause concern for those who believe that they must be available at all times. But an important factor in the development of future leaders, of leaders who are capable of assuming greater levels of responsibility, is the learning of decision-making skills. Every police officer is faced with critical decisions when there is no superior to turn to. Indecisive police officers are a luxury that law enforcement cannot afford. People who learn to make appropriate decisions under nonstress situations are more likely to be effective when emergencies do occur.

Obviously, effective leaders would not abdicate in critical situations where a bad decision might have far-reaching implications. On the other hand, if it is true that people learn by doing, it must also be true that intelligent people learn from their mistakes. We believe it absolutely vital that neophyte decision makers, in addition to being forced to make decisions, be permitted to experience the consequences of inappropriate decisions—in noncritical areas, of course.

Blocking may be perceived as the least acceptable of the seven leadership styles. Nevertheless, at times some subordinates appear to view each new situation as a crisis to share. Verbally telling a subordinate that he was "being bothersome or distracting" could solve the immediate problem more directly. It could also serve to confuse the subordinate in his interpersonal relationship with the leader. Equally important, the subordinate might be diverted at a later time when he legitimately should have sought advice.

As we stated earlier, these seven techniques, while somewhat simplified, are legitimate styles of leadership. The problem, however, as we view it is that many law enforcement leaders continue to rely on a single style, perhaps in the erroneous belief that it is necessary to be consistent.

In our enthusiasm for the use of various leadership styles, we would offer the caution that styles are in a sense games. *It is essential that people be told which game is being played,* for they will not continue to play unless they understand all the rules, or if the rules are violated.

To illustrate, let us assume that a leader has told his group that he wants their opinion on a certain matter and their decision will be his decision. He takes a vote, only to discover that the group has not voted as he had hoped they would. Since the leader is already committed elsewhere, he sets aside their vote and goes in his own direction. It can be anticipated that the next time he calls his group together, genuinely wanting their help, he will discover they are unwilling to play the game, for they "know" that in all probability he has already arranged things in his own way. Subordinates are quick to perceive when their leader is "conning" them, that he is seeking only their support, not their ideas, and that he will not hesitate to go around them if their decision is not to his liking.

There are times, of course, when a leader will ask his group for their opinions, not for a decision. Under these conditions, the leader should make it very clear that he will take all the information, filter it through his own filtering process, equate it with the information he already possesses, and make the final decision himself. In this way, leadership becomes an important aspect of decision making. Things must get done; decisions help get things done, and leaders must make proper decisions. It is equally important that people in the organization know exactly where they stand in regard to the decision-making process of their leader.

The point here is that people must understand the game that is being played. If confusion tends to develop from time to time over leadership styles, the group will simply not participate, and the manager will not have the kind of supportive subordinate relationships that are an absolute necessity for the dynamic organizations of the present and the future.

It was noted earlier that a successful leader is usually a person who has discovered himself; he is not someone who is content to imitate another. We have avoided referring to this development of self as a "style," although it might legitimately be considered such. Our view is that one can develop, or exhibit, a particular profile and and yet freely use a number of different leadership styles, depending upon the circumstances involved. Some contemporary writers refer to this same concept as adaptive, or changing leadership, behavior. Our belief is that adaptive leaders are more likely to be successful than are those who remain inflexible in times of great social change.

Being flexible enough to move within the various leadership styles creates a complete type rather than a one-kind leader. Flexibility connotes a *dynamic leadership* quality that includes sharing, and it removes the individual from the bureaucratic category where leaders tend to make even the most minute decisions.

SUPPORTIVE RELATIONS

In our discussion of the leader we have attempted to build a case for the concept that his very being is predicated upon those who are led. Since leadership is dependent upon followership, some thought must be given to the relationship that exists between the two.

In a strict authoritarian setting, the relationship can be described as one of dominance and submission. A model of this relationship can be observed in those police academies adhering to the "stress-training" concept. The authoritarian tends to be impersonal in his relations with subordinates.

On the other hand, the enlightened leader is concerned with the entire spectrum of interpersonal relations between himself and his subordinates, between the subordinates themselves, and between his group and other affiliative groups as well.

The principle of supportive relationships can be briefly stated as follows:

> The leadership and other processes of the organization must be such as to ensure a maximum probability that in all interactions and all relationships with the organization each member will, in the light of his background, values, and expectations, view the experience as supportive and one which builds and maintains his sense of personal worth and importance.[15]

Studies indicate that leaders who are perceived by subordinates to be supportive are likely to have high-producing units, that "supervisors with the best records of performance focus their primary attention on the human aspects of their subordinates' problems and on endeavoring to build effective work groups with high performance goals."[16]

To fully appreciate the importance of supportive leadership, we must return to the theory of self-actualized man. Man has certain personal needs: safety-security, social and affiliative, ego-satisfaction and self-esteem, and autonomy and independence, as well as self-actualization. He must feel that his job is important, and he must have a sense of accomplishment.[17]

In summary, the enlightened leader is aware of the necessity to support his subordinates in their drive for self-actualization. He is supportive of their needs for autonomy and is especially supportive in assisting them in reaching both their personal goals and the goals of the organization.

SELECTING FUTURE LEADERS

As our twentieth century grows more complex, there is a concurrent growth of complexity in our policing organizations as they attempt to deal effectively with the increasing ambiguities of their ever-ex-

[15] Rensis Likert, *New Patterns of Management* (New York: McGraw-Hill Book Company, 1961), p. 103.

[16] *Ibid.*, p. 7.

[17] Schein, *Organizational Psychology*, pp. 56–57.

panding roles. While, obviously, the more suburban-rural communities have not yet felt the same crush for improved increased police services as have their central-city cousins, even they are not immune. More effective managers will be needed to provide the necessary leadership for better-equipped, better-prepared, better-informed police officers. As observers of this phenomenon called "progress," we are concerned that current traditional methods of identifying, selecting, and preparing future leaders may no longer be optimal. Perhaps in light of the methodology employed by major private business organizations, consideration might be given to a less-bureaucratic approach in selecting the twentieth-century leaders in law enforcement.

Typically, police organizations have had rigidly formalized promotional criteria. Usually a basic prerequisite to applying for any promotional examination is certain experience-tenure in the job immediately preceding the one sought. More recently, with the publication of *The Challenge of Crime in a Free Society*, some agencies have added requirements such as specific educational achievements commensurate with the desired position: "The ultimate aim of all police departments should be that all personnel with general enforcement powers have baccalaureate degrees . . . The long range objective for high ranking officers should be advanced degrees."[18]

With the necessary criteria met, candidates are usually required to complete some formalized examination process. When this has been accomplished, the candidates' names appear on a promotional list in a rank ordering of their examination scores.

This procedure may appear all too logical for those who have been reared with the process. We feel, however, that the process creates inherent problems that are fourfold:

1. The process may not necessarily reveal the most promising leaders available.
2. Promotions are typically made before any specific training for the new level of responsibility.
3. Personnel to be promoted are not identified early enough to be afforded the opportunity of prepromotional advanced level experience.
4. At some point in the process, seniority often becomes a final or tie-breaking criterion.

V. A. Leonard, professor emeritus of Police Science and Administration at Washington State University, expressed his concern as follows:

> Too frequently, it is assumed that the man who has the longest

[18] The President's Commission on Law Enforcement and Administration of Justice, *The Challenge of Crime in a Free Society* (Washington, D.C.: Government Printing Office, 1967), pp. 109–10.

service or if several are approximately equal on this point, then the man with the best record as a policeman may confidently be expected to be successful in the management of the department as its chief. The fallacy of this procedure is demonstrated by it failure in many American cities. The administration of a police department is a technical undertaking, requiring not only successful experience as a policeman, but also special talent and a number of peculiar skills that are not acquired in the course of ordinary police training and experience.[19]

In our associations with police administrators, we have not found unanimity in the belief that currently available written examinations are valid except, perhaps, as a method of reducing the number of candidates for the job. As for the interview process, it seems even less dependable. Consideration must be given to the myriad of possible leadership qualities and traits that may be possessed by a candidate in an almost infinite number of combinations. It seems unlikely that even the most perceptive police administrator is capable of making a valid, in-depth evaluation during the brief time frame allowed in the typical "oral."

Choosing leaders on the basis of performance in lesser jobs, popularity, seniority, and written and oral examinations primarily concerned with technical skills is simply not efficient in today's people-oriented world. We are not suggesting that the system be abandoned, but rather that an overhaul is in order.

Certain practices currently employed by private organizations and the military in the search for leaders seem applicable to the selection of law enforcement leaders. We believe they should be explored. While we subscribe to the theory that law enforcement administrators must have a backgroud of "police experience," we do not mean to be limited to the traditional process of beginning everyone in the same way—at the bottom. The thought may hinge on heresy; however, we firmly believe it is possible, even desirable, to initially recruit some police management types by circumventing the normal process. In private business, recruiters canvas universities and colleges for potential management personnel trainees. The selected recruits are then provided special training programs. Beyond simple orientation, they spend little time in routine jobs. Instead, they are exposed to the business of management. As interns and aides, they are thrust, almost immediately, into a world of personnel, budgets, and accumulation and interpretation of decision-making data. Normally, the trainees do not assume any line authority. Rather, they are expected to provide staff service while developing management sense.

Few generals spent their formative years learning how to be a

---

[19] V. A. Leonard, *Police Organization and Management* (Brooklyn: The Foundation Press, Inc., 1964), p. 46.

rifleman; the president of General Motors did not work his way up from the assembly line.

It may seem ludicrous to equate the United States Army or a gigantic corporation with a police department, but the point is that law enforcement is simply not that unique.

Another method, one that might be somewhat more acceptable to the traditional thinker, evolves from the concept that every manager, at every level, is, among other things, a *trainer*. One facet of such a function is to train other leaders. We are suggesting that police leaders should assume the responsibility for identifying those men who appear promotable, for placing them in experience-gaining situations, and for literally grooming them for eventual promotion.

Concurrently, the promotional system appears to elevate a man first and *then* determine whether or not he is capable of handling the job. Traditionally he is trained for his new level *after* he has been placed there. Today, in the middle management of law enforcement, the approach appears to have developed, at least in some organizations, a number of frustrated individuals known as the "old guard" who have tended, through no fault of their own, to become sedentary in positions beyond their capabilities. To remain stable and retain their *status quo*, they simply do nothing that will rock the boat. As a result, they frustrate people below and above them. They force managers to devise ways to work around them, and the overall situation becomes most difficult. We believe that management has the responsibility for developing men and *then* for promoting them on the basis that they are prepared to do the job to which they are being promoted rather than on the basis of competency in their current assignment.

Laurence Peter in a rather humorous approach to the business of promotions developed what is commonly known as the "Peter Principle."[20] His simple hypothesis is that "In a Hierarchy Every Employee Tends to Rise to His Level of Incompetence."[21] And even more simply, that "the cream rises until it sours."[22]

Peter supports his theory with a number of cases, of which the following is representative:

Military File, Case No. 8. Consider the case of the late renowned General A. Goodwin. His hearty, informal manner, his racy style of speech, his scorn for petty regulations and his undoubted personal bravery made him the idol of his men. He led them to many well-deserved victories.

When Goodwin was promoted to field marshal he had to deal,

[20] Laurence J. Peter and Raymond Hull, *The Peter Principle* (New York: William Morrow & Co., Inc., 1969).

[21] *Ibid.*, p. 26.

[22] *Ibid.*, p. 36.

not with ordinary soldiers, but with politicians and allied general-
issimos.

He would not conform to the necessary protocol. He could not
turn his tongue to the conventional courtesies and flatteries. He
quarreled with all the dignitaries and took to lying for days at a
time, drunk and sulking, in his trailer. The conduct of the war
slipped out of his hands into those of his subordinates. He had
been promoted to a position that he was incompetent to fill.[23]

Given that many organizations are guilty of contributing support
to the Peter Principle, what normal action is taken when the problem
is discovered? Peter has an answer for that, too, in what he entitles
"The Lateral Arabesque":

> The lateral arabesque is another pseudo-promotion. Without be-
> ing raised in rank—sometimes without even a pay raise—the in-
> competent employee is given a *new and longer title* and is moved
> to an office in a remote part of the building.
>
> R. Filewood proved incompetent as office manager of Carley
> Stationery Inc. After a lateral arabesque he found himself, at the
> same salary, working as co-ordinator of inter-departmental com-
> munications, supervising the filing of second copies of inter-
> office memos.[24]

While the preceding quotations were undoubtedly written as a
spoof, they are entirely accurate in all too many instances. Law enforcement, too, has had its share of taking competent personnel and
promoting them to their level of incompetency. And when the in-
competencies are discovered, these employees are seldom returned
to the proper level. Instead, as in Peter's example, they tend to be
laterally transferred to less-sensitive areas, where they often continue
to be incompetent.

What we are suggesting is that the dynamic, flexible, coping
police organization necessary to meet the needs of a rapidly changing
society can no longer afford the luxury of the Peter Principle. There
appear, on the basis of existing business models, to be several ways in
which our leadership selection process could and should be improved.

CHAPTER SUMMARY

Leading in modern police organizations requires, in addition to
specific prerequisite skills and experience, a knowledge of modern
management theory. Traditionally, law enforcement, like many government agencies, has followed the bureaucratic model with impersonality of interpersonal relations, heavy reliance upon written rules

[23] *Ibid.*, p. 24.
[24] *Ibid.*, p. 40.

and regulations, and promotions based upon technical competence. In this chapter we have attempted to build a case for taking leave of the bureaucratic model. The leader in his optimum role has become sensitized not only to the organizational needs but to the needs of his subordinates as well. He is aware that subordinates must perceive their work as important and that they must be afforded a measure of autonomy if they are to be self-actualized.

The leader in our model has the ability to move flexibly among seven different leadership styles, making certain that subordinates are aware of the particular style being used.

We have also suggested that there is support for the theory that current leadership selection methods are in need of modification; that leaders should be competent in the position sought, before promotion; and that provisions should be made to move qualified persons around the system as opposed to the traditional concept that each man must start at the bottom.

The leader is not just the purveyor of routine orders, but the one who is capable of bringing order to confusion—in the face of emergency.[25]

LEARNING EXERCISE

DEVELOPING GROUP COMMITMENT: A STRUCTURED EXPERIENCE

GOALS

   I.   To aid the group and/or organization in studying the degree to which members agree on certain values.

  II.   To focus on the decision-making norms of the group.

 III.   To discover the "natural leadership" which is functioning in the group.

TIME REQUIRED

Approximately one hour.

MATERIALS UTILIZED

Functions of police unions (associations).

---

[25] The learning exercise is taken from J. William Pfeiffer and John E. Jones, *A Handbook of Structured Experiences for Human Relations Training* (Iowa City, Iowa: University City Associates Press, 1969), pp. 33–39.

PROCESS

The facilitator announced that the group will engage in an activity to accomplish the goals spelled out above and distributes the ranking forms. The facilitator functions as a timekeeper according to the schedule on the form. One member may function as process observer. After the allotted time, the group discusses the process in which it engaged.

The form is easily revised to fit groups other than police unions. The content may be the goals of the organization or group, characteristics of an ideal leader, desirable characteristics of teachers (principals, ministers, counselors, supervisers, employers, etc.), or any other relevant list. One suggestion might be to conduct a problem census of the organization or group and to use that list as the items to be rank ordered.

When several groups in the same organization (class, institution, etc.) engage in this experience simultaneously, it is sometimes helpful to summarize the rank orders for the several groups on a chalkboard and to have discussion of the agreements and disagreements among the groups.

Functions of Police Unions

Instructions: Rank the following functions of police unions according to the importance you attach to them. Place a "1" in front of the most agreement, a "2" before the second most agreement, etc. You have seven minutes for this task.

After the members of your group have finished working individually, arrive at a rank ordering *as a group*. The group has 25 minutes for the task. Do *not* choose a formal leader.

_____ 1. Police unions have a cohesive or unifying affect on the police department.

_____ 2. Police unions should militate for improved working conditions.

_____ 3. A police union is where you develop professional and social relationships that tend to improve the efficiency of the organization.

_____ 4. Police unions provide a sense of belongingness to the department.

_____ 5. The police union seeks to protect its memberships in the face of authoritarian management.

_____ 6. The union is an organization within an organization where one is stimulated to personal growth.

_____ 7. Participation in union activities is similar to training for leadership within the police organization.

_____ 8. Supervisors should not belong to police unions.

_____ 9. Binding arbitration should be fostered between unions and police management.

_____ 10. Where they exist, management should in good faith maintain constant communication with the union on matters of mutual interest.

DECISION MAKING

All Police Administrators are constantly called upon to make decisions: the wisdom of these decisions will depend, in large measure, upon the information and advice available to them. If decisions are made without proper analysis of facts, or without regard for standard practices developed as the result of research, the chances are that they will be mediocre decisions—and it is the accumulation of mediocre decisions that produces mediocrity in police administration.[1]

"Decision making is that thinking which results in the choice among alternative courses of action."[2] As we have stated in earlier chapters, it is a primary function of management. Decisions are made at all levels of endeavor, of course, but the administrative decision-making process is set apart, for it provides the basis upon which all other rational organizational decisions are made. The late Los Angeles Chief of Police William H. Parker, as demonstrated above, was concerned about the quality of police decision making. He was especially

---

[1] William H. Parker, "Practical Aspects of Police Planning" (Paper delivered at the 61st Annual Conference, International Association of Chiefs of Police, New Orleans, September 27, 1954), p. 7.

[2] Donald W. Taylor, "Decision Making and Problem Solving," in *Handbook of Organizations,* ed. James G. March (Chicago: Rand McNally & Co., 1965), p. 48.

cognizant of the relationship between sound information and sound decisions, or as he put it, "the accumulation of mediocre decisions . . . produces mediocrity in police administration."[3]

In the more contemporary manner of the computer, cyberneticists have a saying: "Garbage in—garbage out." Decisions made on the basis of low quality decisions: Garbage in—garbage out.

In the preceding chapters on planning, communications, and leadership, we developed a concept of interdependence that included the process of decision making; that these several concepts are interwoven.

In this chapter we will focus on an array of decision-making facets, including the rationale of decision making. Again, for reference and validation, we must turn to the literature of business and the social scientists, for modern law enforcement writers have provided little in this area save to acknowledge that it is a process of management. This void is particularly interesting, since it appears that every decision will affect, to some degree, the success or failure, the growth and development, the health, welfare, and prosperity of individuals and organizations. We can think of no other field in which decisions are so open for introspection, so vulnerable to the Monday-morning quarterbacking of politicians and pressure groups and average citizens alike.

SEQUENTIAL STEPS TO EFFECTIVE DECISIONS

Effective decisions are not the result of happenstance but rather are the product of a logical process. Peter Drucker, a leading management thinker, refers to this process as a series of elements which he systematically arranges into six sequential steps:

1. *The classification of the problem.* Is it generic? Is it exceptional and unique? Or is it the first manifestation of a new genus for which a rule has yet to be developed?
2. *The definition of the problem.* What are we dealing with?
3. *The specifications which the answer to the problem must satisfy.* What are the "boundary conditions"?
4. *The decision as to what is "right," rather than what is acceptable, in order to meet the boundary conditions.* What will fully satisfy the specifications *before* attention is given to the compromises, adaptations, and concessions needed to make the decision acceptable?
5. *The building into the decision of the action to carry it out.* What does the action commitment have to be? Who has to know about it?
6. *The feedback which tests the validity and effectiveness of the decision against the actual course of events.* How is the decision

---

[3] Parker, "Practical Aspects of Police Planning," p. 7.

being carried out? Are the assumptions on which it is based appropriate or obsolete?[4]

These sequential steps are applicable throughout the chapter
and are considered as basic to the process regardless of the model or
style used.

DECISION-MAKING MODELS

For the purpose of this chapter we have divided the decision-
making process into three models: *rational,* the most formalized and
perhaps the most difficult to fully achieve; *bounded rationality,*
which takes man's limitations, his frame of reference, into account;
and *heuristic,* which introduces the human element. All three are
viable and are relevant to the business of effective decisions by law
enforcement managers.

Rational Decisions

Decision making in law enforcement, as in other organizations,
is the selection of a course of action from two or more alternatives.
Sound decisions are more likely to occur (1) when all the variables
are clearly understood and when the decision maker (or makers) is
privy to all the available related information, and (2) when all possible alternatives have been thoroughly explored and narrowed down
by a rational elimination process.

Herbert Simon explains that "rational decision-making always
requires the comparison of alternative means in terms of the respective ends to which they will lead." He cautions us that "the ends to
be attained by the choice of a particular behavior alternative are often
incompletely or incorrectly stated through failure to consider the alternative ends that could be reached by selection of another behavior."[5]

One example would be the selection of a crowd control plan.
Following Simon's view, it would not be sufficient to select a plan of
action on the mere probability that it would satisfactorily meet desired goals. Rational behavior would require that all possible alternatives be explored in terms of the respective ends to which they will
lead. "This means that 'efficiency'—that attainment of maximum values with limited means—must be a guiding criterion in administrative decision."[6] The *rational* selection must therefore be made on the

---

[4]Peter F. Drucker, "The Effective Decision," reprinted from *Harvard Business
Review,* January-February 1967, and derived from his book, *The Effective Executive*
(New York: Harper & Row, Publishers, 1966).

[5]Herbert A. Simon, *Administrative Behavior,* 2nd ed., (New York: The Macmil-
lan Company, 1961), p. 65.

[6]*Ibid.*

basis of which of the available alternatives was the most *efficient/ economical* combination. To be efficient without being economical or vice versa would not be considered a rational decision.

Feldman and Kanter refer to a similar though somewhat more complicated model as "comprehensive decision-making," wherein they point out certain inherent limitations. They observe that it is possible to identify and examine all possible alternatives in only the most simple problems. "For even moderately complex problems, however, the entire decision tree cannot be generated."[7] Time, economics, and other constraints prevent the projection of every possible alternative to its ultimate end.

Bounded Rationality

Simon, too, discussed the limitations of rational decision making, not so much in terms of the multiplicity of possible alternatives as in terms of rational man himself. Simon observed that decision-making man was bounded by a triangle of limitations. "On one side, the individual is limited by those skills, habits, and reflexes which are no longer in the realm of the conscious." These take into consideration the physical and mental process developed in one's lifetime. "On a second side, the individual is limited by his values and those conceptions of purpose which influence him in making his decisions." These include his conception of self-worth and his relationship to the total organization. "On a third side, the individual is limited by the extent of his knowledge of things relevant to his job"[8]—not just knowing his job, but what he knows about those other elements of the organization.

In the preceding chapter we discussed the need for man to understand the importance of his job to the total organizational mission. This concept is again reinforced by Simon in his view that man's ability to make rational decisions is bounded by the limitation of his knowledge of the total organization.[9]

The point is that a group of experts, given exactly the same information, considering the rational process, would theoretically reach identical conclusions. In reality, however, as we view Simon's theory, the inherent limitations by which each individual is bounded varies to some degree. The result is that each expert's conclusion may very well be rational in terms of his own perception—but there is a reasonable possibility that all will not have reached identical conclusions.

---

[7] Julian Feldman and Herschel E. Kanter, "Organizational Decision Making," in *Handbook of Organizations*, ed. James G. March, pp. 614–15.

[8] Simon, *Administrative Behavior*, p. 40.

[9] *Ibid.*

We have observed, especially in the more authoritarian hierarchical setting such as the police, that failure to make what the "boss" views as a rational decision may result in a withdrawal of support when it is most needed. It is essential that managers have an appreciation of the uniqueness of personal boundaries when viewing the decisions of subordinates.

Heuristic Decisions

In addition to the processes of rational decision making and those of bounded rationality, William Gore identifies what we view as a most potent third process, the "heuristic model."[10] The heuristic model is especially appropriate to the modern police administrator in that it legitimizes a process we sometimes hear referred to as a "gut level decision" and at the same time affords a latitude not recognized in the rational models. Rational systems tend to presume that all the elements of truth are built into the prescribed process—they are codifications of truths in cause-and-effect relationships. These systems enjoy acceptance because they have always worked. But truth and knowledge are transitory things, and if man adheres to his rational systems alone and is mindless of their changing elements of truth and data; then he deludes himself.

The rational process can be seen as one that includes isolating the problem and the almost impossible task of logically identifying all possible alternative solutions from which the best is selected and implemented. Conversely, Gore views the heuristic process as "a groping toward agreements seldom arrived at through logic. The very essence of the heuristic process is that the factors validating a decision are internal to the personality of the individual instead of external to it."[11]

A rational process ultimately involves concrete, here-and-now arrangements that pertain to collective action. Conversely, the heuristic process is an almost verbal process, reaching backward into the memory and forward into the future, touching any number of personalities and people. In addition to using the rational system of cause and effect, the heuristic process takes advantage of the unseen emotional motivations that energize the organizational system.

The heuristic model for administrative decision making, in a way, formalizes the processes used by many. It adds the human dimension. For example, we can put reams of data into a computer and it will respond to certain inquiries with mechanical outputs. The

[10]William J. Gore, *Administrative Decision-Making: A Heuristic Model* (New York: John Wiley & Sons, Inc., 1964).
    [11]*Ibid.*, p. 12.

more data supplied, the more accurate the output. Unfortunately, the computer cannot supply the human element, the stuff that one develops in a lifetime of experiences. In the heuristic model, the administrator may also bounce his problem and the gathered data off other management team members (or others) and gain responses based on their conglomerate experiences. Thus armed, the administrator is free to disregard the rational model and make a decision outside the mechanical logic.

We sense that Gore sees heuristic applications as adjuncts to rational models or as alternatives to rational models, depending upon the circumstances. It is simply a case of granting credence to man's proclivity and talent for subjectivity as a viable element in the act of decision making or problem solving.

The heuristic model makes room for effective as well as cognitive input. Thus, what a man *is* becomes a force that conditions the decisions he makes.

AUTONOMY IN DECISION MAKING

The age of modern organizations and enlightened management has brought about the broader sharing of authority and responsibility. There is more autonomy at every level and greater expectations from above and below.

The degree of autonomy accorded is directly related to a number of factors, not the least of which is the relationship between the various levels in the hierarchy. While it is possible and most often efficient for various levels or subunits to enjoy a measure of autonomy in the decision-making process, the danger of introspection is present. It is absolutely vital that there exist an appreciation for the total organizational goals and policies and for those of the supporting subunits. Decisions made in one unit are likely to have an effect on other units. If units or a collection of units were to become so introspective as to adversely affect other units, the autonomy would by necessity be drastically reduced.

In his study of private organizations, Rensis Likert observed that decisions that might affect subordinates whose interests were not represented in the decision-making process were not likely to be accepted wholeheartedly.[12] He suggests that this is less likely to occur in what he calls "the overlapping group form of organization." (See Figure 8-1.) In the traditional organization, Likert is concerned about the narrowness of influence relationships which are normally

---

[12] Rensis Likert, *New Patterns of Management* (New York: McGraw-Hill Book Company, 1961), p. 107.

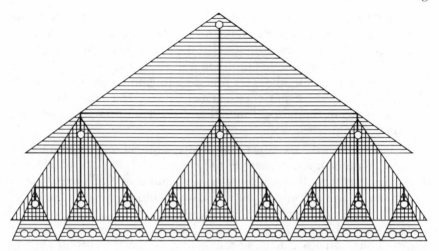

Work groups vary in size as circumstances require, although shown here as consisting of four persons. As illustrated in Rensis Likert, *New Patterns of Management* (New York: McGraw-Hill Book Company, 1961), p. 105.

FIGURE 8-1. **The Overlapping Group Form of Organization.**

one to one, or "man to man."[13] This concept can be more readily understood if the reader will review his own organizational chart or one of any typical police agency, for it will also convey the lines of communication and influence — one person reports directly to one person.

Likert's diagram of overlapping groups shows that in each group one member holds dual membership in another group and so on; no one individual or group of individuals is mutually exclusive. As one moves up Likert's organizational chart, the superior in one group becomes a subordinate in the next group and has relationships with all others in each group.[14] Likert views this as a "linking pin" concept, which *insures that each group* is able to influence the total organization. (See Figure 8-2.) For example, the field sergeant and his subordinates form a group. The sergeant also holds membership in a second group, made up of other sergeants and one lieutenant. The lieutenant also holds membership in a group of lieutenants headed up by a captain, and so on.

In our view the group overlay and linking pin effects would also reduce the incidence of decisions in any one group being made in a vacuum, without regard for other groups within the organization.

[13] *Ibid.*, p. 106.
[14] *Ibid.*, p. 105.

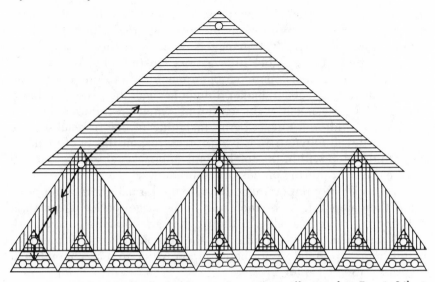

The arrows indicate the linking pin function. As illustrated in Rensis Likert, *New Patterns of Management* (New York: McGraw-Hill Book Company, 1961), p. 113.

FIGURE 8-2. **The Linking Pin.**

INFORMATION SYSTEMS

In all three of our decision-making models, two primary factors were present—the identification of the need to bring about some change and the acquisition of enough information upon which to base the selection of a proper decision. Both of these factors are predicated to a great extent upon the flow of information through channels to the point of action.

Formal Channels

In Chapter 4 we discussed the multiple channels of communication. These same channels are in fact concurrently information-gathering channels upon which there is absolute dependency by the decision maker. As we stated earlier, the formal channels comply with the recognized official structure of the organization. A great deal of information, both that which has been requested and that which has been discovered independently, travels up these channels. Much of this information is routine, such as monthly reports, logs, and computer printouts, upon which deployment and other operating decisions are made. The degree to which all levels of the hierarchy are sensitized to the nonroutine information that might have value to the next higher level or levels is a limiting factor as to what independently discovered information is likely to be transmitted up the formal channel. Another common problem is the filtering process through which information must travel. Top managers do not have the time to assimilate each piece of available information. On the other hand, many seemingly sound decisions have been made only to prove unsound later because the decision maker did not have all the necessary information. This is especially disheartening when the information was available but filtered out as being insignificant before reaching the necessary level. Obviously, it is a primary responsibility of management to develop within the total organization a set of values that will reduce this overfiltering process to a minimum.

An especially important addition to the formal information process is the computer. A common unit in the larger police agencies, it is becoming more available to the smaller jurisdictions on a shared-time basis. A major contribution of the computer is that it provides better, more up-to-date information upon which to make operational decisions. (See Chapter 11.)

Even the computer, however, with its awesome memory and logic, coupled with the other formal communication links, is not all-seeing, all-knowing. Because of the previously mentioned filtering process and the inflexibility, cumbersomeness, and other limitations of formality, there are serious gaps in the information-gathering process, and these gaps are a factor in Parker's observation of mediocre decisions.

Informal Channels

Since information needs are directly related to decision making, "plugging" the communication gap is in reality plugging the information gap that obviously appears in formal channels.

It is interesting to note that many police administrators appear uncomfortable with the concept of encouraging informal channels of communication—information transmission. This is to say that they have been steeped in the tradition of "unity of command," the proper channels concept. We have observed this philosophy carried to the point where some administrators actually block these types of communication links. In our view, informal communication links are not in any measure a violation of the unity-of-command doctrine. Our belief is that they should be opened up broadly, in a natural manner. The "boss" should at times be available, not in his own forbidding office, but in a place where the lower-level employees are likely to gather informally. This kind of information gathering cannot be ordered; it must occur naturally, for we are not suggesting a running-to-the-boss type situation. In many instances it is not even necessary to acknowledge that information has been received.

If there is acknowledgment, there need not—should not—be any open evaluation of the information at that point. Any single source of information, especially that which is received in this manner, is in need of independent validation. A second admonition regarding informal information sources is that the receiver must be sensitive to the message being delivered, not simply to the words being spoken. This is especially true in the identification of organizational problems. Dissatisfaction with such things as working hours, salary, and supervisors may very well have nothing whatsoever to do with those issues. It has been our observation, especially in the lower hierarchical levels, that many people have difficulty in saying what they mean, especially if the issues are serious, and especially if they have already been ignored by an immediate supervisor. Instead, their frustrations are voiced in a manner they perceive to be acceptable and noncommitting—"I can't get into trouble for saying it that way." The real message may be that things are not running as smoothly as the boss has been led to believe and he had better begin by initiating the proper action to properly identify the problem.

The point to be made is that the use of informal communication links or channels is legitimate. They are especially important in that they bypass the natural restrictions within the system and provide administration with practical information without requiring commitment or action at that juncture.

In Chapter 5 we discussed certain organizational concepts, including authority, hierarchy, and unity of command. We are not now suggesting a disregard for those concepts and principles, for they are an integral part of the decision-making process. It is simply that we do not view the reception of information or even the informal fraternization between the various levels as necessarily leading to a violation of those concepts.

Our belief is that the problems police administrators are most likely to consider will be so critical in terms of the health and operational success of the organization that they must have the best available information upon which to base decisions.

Extraorganizational Communication Links

Information with which to identify problems and upon which to develop alternative solutions is being generated outside as well as inside the organization. Earlier we discussed Likert's theory of linking pins and overlapping groups. Application can be readily seen in the membership of the top law enforcement executive in a group composed of city department heads—fire, public works, and the like. Some city managers have gone so far as to design new city halls in which all the various department heads have offices clustered together. There may be any number of motivating factors, but at the top of the list most assuredly is the communication/decision-making process.

In Chapter 7 we observed that in some jurisdictions police leaders will find a need for additional community involvement; we were pointing at a more social aspect. In a purely problem-identification-and-solution sense, we believe that extradepartmental-community communication links are absolutely essential in every jurisdiction. We do not view these links as exclusively important to management, but rather as a total department function. This concept will be explored more fully in Chapter 12, "Police Community Relations."

Alert patrolmen and detectives have long pursued the development of informal communication links; for the most part, however, these have been with the world of informers. Their object, as ours, is gathering information with which to identify problems ("Who stole the merchandise?") and the development of alternative solutions ("The best way to catch the thief"). Every seasoned policeman knows that the bulk of solved crimes is cleared in this manner. It logically follows that if the "working cop" is able to develop and use extradepartmental communication links in terms of his assigned departmental goals, police managers should be able to do the same in terms of the broader goals of total organization.

SOME ELEMENTS OF INFLUENCE

Decisions by intelligent leaders are not normally made in a vacuum. In addition to those influences identified by Simon as boundaries, there are others, some of which lend themselves to this discussion. We have chosen to view these influences as elements and have observed that they primarily serve two purposes, which seem on the surface at least to be dichotomous. First, they serve to enlighten the decision maker, providing him with a broader base from which to make rational decisions. Second, and conversely, they tend to restrict the decision-making base by erecting certain parameters or describing the arena in which the decision maker must function.

Legal Elements

For example, legal elements that are often present in the decision-making process of the police administrator are not a concern for his counterpart in the private sector. In the hiring or the discharging of employees, the private sector administrator has much more latitude. His decision can more closely coincide with his perception of the right man for the job. The police administrator, on the other hand, must concern himself with the best individuals from those names appearing on an eligibility list. This type of element is usually covered in ordinances or laws covering personnel practices.

Information Elements

We have been discussing communication links and channels as information-gathering devices. The reason for gathering information is to facilitate the making of sound decisions. The information itself becomes an element of influence. In our experience over the years we have met a number of police administrators who have shunned informal communication links for the very reason that they did not *want* to be influenced. For some, at least, there has been some sinister connotation in the concept of influence. Our view is that the successful administrator must be privy to all forms of information—influence. The weighting he gives it is quite another thing. We are not giving space to the I've-got-influence-at-city-hall huckster, for his lack of validity is obvious. It is simply not feasible, however, to operate a law enforcement organization in a vacuum.

Community Elements

What the police department does affects the total organization (e.g., city government) and ultimately the total community. Community goals, therefore, exert an important influence. (Police departments cannot exist without the community, and vice versa.) The jurisdiction may, for example, be a resort community dependent upon visitors for its economy. Within legalistic latitudes, the police department would undoubtedly need to examine its priorities in terms of encouraging rather than discouraging tourist traffic.

An excellent case in point concerns the semiresort city of Newport Beach, California, a favorite vaction community for half a century. Over the years, however, the younger generation began to take more and more latitude. The younger generation visitors are obviously important, as are their older counterparts, for they, too, contribute to the economy by occupying hundreds of the rental units and purchasing services, food, and other commodities. On the other hand, a certain lawlessness was present which had been tolerated for some time. In 1961 Captain James Glavis retired from the Los Angeles Police Department to become the Newport Beach police chief. Chief Glavis was well aware that at least a part of the community looked upon the young people as "good business," and he was also conscious of the need for the establishment and maintenance of good order, not only for the harmony between generations but for general community welfare as well. During the three years following his appointment, Chief Glavis pursued a course of action that was to bring the youthful visitors into line without discouraging their visits. He was able to satisfy the goals of the business community, the residential community, the adult vacationing community, and the police department, and those of the young people as well, through a course of action decided upon, not in a vacuum, but with information inputs from all sectors.

It is not our intent to discuss methodology. Rather, we are reinforcing our hypothesis that political awareness, sensitivity to total community goals in viewing the identification of problems and solutions, need not be a prostitution of the police mission. In our Chapter 2 learning experience we used a classic case study that is pertinent to the discussion at hand and is almost the opposite of Glavis's approach to Newport Beach's problems. In the case study, the chief's tenure was short lived; conversely, Chief Glavis became an institution in Newport Beach.

Family Elements

When one considers all possible influencing elements, their numbers become infinite. For that reason the development of such a list will be left to the reader. We find it impossible, however, to leave this section without some recognition of the most personal of all exterior influences—the family.

Decision makers at every level report for work each day with fluctuating attitudes that seem to be reflected in their total conduct. A suddenly ill child, unexpected out-of-town guests, financial crises, a wife's wrecking the car are all examples of behavior influences. A test of this is to review a decision made on a previous day, especially one leading to negative action. Our guess is that without the updating of any information, a different course of action may appear more appropriate, especially if home conditions have changed in any way. Grandma may not have been a social scientist, but her admonition to sleep on a decision because "things may look different in the morning" was not based on folklore—they often do.

Our point is that when an employee is hired, the organization is also subject to the influence of his total family unit, a fact that deserves recognition.

Priorities and Timing

Priorities and timing are closely related influence elements. Both include the identification of problems and solutions, and both involve an element of risk. When more than one course of action is called for at the same time, involving the same personnel, priorities must be set. Timing involves the *when* of a course of action and is not necessarily predicated on resources. Every police manager is frequently faced with the problem of appropriately deploying limited personnel in light of conflicting demands for service (e.g., "If you don't slow down the traffic in this area, the blood of our children will be on your hands!" concurrently with, "Daylight burglars are carrying the town away!").

> A decision therefore has to be made as to which tasks deserve priority and which are of less importance. The only question is which will make the decision—the executive or the pressures . . . If the pressures rather than the executive are allowed to make the decision, the important tasks will predictably be sacrificed.[15]

As for timing, it may be prudent to arrest a person running for public office the day after the election instead of the day before, especially if the charges are made by the opposition. Undoubtedly, a few will criticize the delay as having been made for political reasons. On the other hand, the police, rather than the arrestee, will become the focus of general attack if the action is taken the day before. *Everyone* will suspect political overtones.

Sensitivity to the value of proper timing and priorities is a vital component of the decision-making process. Priorities connote a rational compromise between needs and resources. Conversely, timing is not a compromise but rather the maximizing of necessary or desired action while minimizing conflict.

STRATEGIES

In pulling together all the decision-making factors, a suitable strategy must be considered for the particular problem at hand. In some isolated incidents it will be appropriate for a manager to make a decision by himself, as we stated in Chapter 7. Autocratic leadership is most appropriate in a crisis situation when an *immediate* decision is necessary for the welfare/survival of the organization. There will be times when the very sensitive nature of the problem will make the decision a lonely one. This is not to say that such decisions are made in a vacuum without considering alternatives. If we subscribe to Simon's theory of bounded rationality, however, it can be seen that the boundaries of a single person are likely to be more restricted than will be the collective boundaries of a group. Therefore, it is our view that the utilization of available human resources in one way or another is likely to produce more effective, higher quality decisions for organizational implementation. How these human resources are used becomes an application of administrative strategy.

[15] Drucker, *The Effective Executive*, p. 109.

Conflict

"I don't want any yes-men working for me" is a frequently heard cliché. In reality many decision makers, even those who use the group process, prefer to avoid conflict. Conflict is undoubtedly viewed by some as time-consuming and dysfunctional. Others simply prefer to "run things" themselves, a sort of chairman of the board, in a most negative sense.

Peter Drucker observes that "the effective decision does not . . . flow from a consensus on the facts. The understanding that underlies the right decision grows out of the clash and conflict of divergent opinions and out of the serious consideration of competing alternatives."[16]

Drucker suggests that subordinates and experts do not express facts but rather opinions when first viewing a problem. He views this as proper, since "people experienced in an area should be expected to have an opinion . . . People inevitably start out with an opinion; to ask them to search for the facts first is even undesirable."[17] It is from these opinions that facts and alternatives will flow.

> Unless one has considered alternatives, one has a closed mind.
> This, above all, explains why effective decision-makers deliberately disregard the second major command of the textbooks on decision-making and create dissension and disagreement, rather than consensus.
>
> Decisions of the kind the executive has to make are not made well by acclamation. They are made well only if based on the clash of conflicting views, the dialogue between different judgments. The first rule in decision-making is that one does not make a decision unless there is disagreement.
>
> Alfred P. Sloan[18] is reported to have said at a meeting of one of his top committees: "Gentlemen, I take it we are all in complete agreement on the decision here." Everyone around the table nodded assent. "Then," continued Mr. Sloan, "I propose we postpone further discussion of this matter until our next meeting to give ourselves time to develop disagreement and perhaps gain some understanding of what the decision is all about."
>
> Sloan was anything but an "intuitive" decision-maker. He always emphasized the need to test opinions against facts and the need to make absolutely sure that one did not start out with the conclusion and then look for the facts that would support it. But he knew that the right decision demands adequate disagreement.
>
> Every one of the effective Presidents in American history had

[16] *Ibid.*, p. 143.

[17] *Ibid.*, p. 144.

[18] Alfred P. Sloan, Jr., president, General Motors Corporation, 1923 to 1937; chairman of the board, 1937 to 1956.

his own method of producing the disagreement he needed in order to make an effective decision. Lincoln, Theodore Roosevelt, Franklin D. Roosevelt, Harry Truman—each had his own ways. But each created the disagreement he needed for "some understanding of what the decision is all about." Washington, we know, hated conflicts and quarrels and wanted a united Cabinet. Yet he made quite sure of the necessary differences of opinion on important matters by asking both Hamilton and Jefferson for their opinions.[19]

Conflict as a strategy, as can be seen by Drucker's reference to our nation's presidents, is not new. It may, however, be new to many police managers who continue to believe that agreement and harmony are the foundations upon which strength and control are built.

Brainstorming

One of the most constraining factors to effective decision making is the limitation of alternative courses of action. In the process of developing alternatives, there is a tendency to be hypercritical at the wrong point—the inception. This applies to both individual and group decision makers but is more likely to occur in the group process. There appears to be an inherent tendency to "shoot down" ideas that do not follow what is considered to be a normal course. Many potentially good ideas fall by the wayside because they are too quickly rejected, not preserved for later consideration. One method of rejection is the verbal "shooting down." Another, equally effective, is no response at all. Without some kind of second, ideas tend to fall flat. Silence in itself is not always rejection. Other group members may be momentarily absorbed in their own thoughts, but the effect is just the same. An idea without support dies.

Dan Pursuit, a professor at the University of Southern California, has for over twenty years been peddling a most effective solution to these problems—brainstorming. In essence, brainstorming is exactly what it sounds like. It is the forcing of ideas off the top of the participants' heads with a complete disregard for validity. None are rejected; all are recorded in writing on a chalkboard or on an easel-held, large newsprint tablet. (We favor the newsprint for all decision-making exercises in that the sheets may be displayed around the room, then preserved for later contemplation.)

When the group has run dry, the ideas are gathered together and are grouped under similar headings. One by one they are examined and commented upon without regard for the author. Gradually they

---

[19] Drucker, *The Effective Executive*, pp. 148–49.

are refined until only a workable number remain. Interestingly enough, ideas considered "far out" often become *not* so far out as they are manipulated and built upon.

Another facet of brainstorming is that it permits the nonexpert to become involved, and in the end it might be he who, for the very reason that he *was not* close to the problem, made the important contribution.

Perhaps the phenomenon is not restricted to police organizations, but over the years we have observed that newcomers to the field are not normally encouraged to voice their opinions, especially in group settings. Since decisions are made at all levels, and group decisions are equally valid at both ends of the hierarchy, we view this as a waste of potential power in the decision-making process.

This is especially true today as we see young men whose formal education represents a wide variety of fields entering law enforcement. The engineering student is likely to approach a problem in a manner completely different from that of the sociology major, and both may be at odds with the criminologist. Knowledge is power—using the knowledge of others is the harnessing of power.

Risk Technique

In many decision-making sessions, a concept or a course of action is already on the floor. The boss believes he would like to undertake a major deviation from the *status quo* in one manner or another. His staff is called together to examine his "baby." As in Drucker's conflict model, the last thing the boss needs is consensus. What he needs, first of all, is to know the risks involved. An excellent course of action is to impose the risk technique, which amounts to negative brainstorming; no one is permitted to make a positive statement. As in brainstorming, all ideas are recorded without comment and participants are encouraged to go as far out as possible. As each page from the newsprint tablet is filled, it is taped (masking, not cellophane, tape) on the wall to stimulate new ideas and avoid redundancy. Once the group has been drained of negatives, members are free to explore the positive aspects, which, too, are listed and posted. If in the end the negatives are outweighed by the positives in such a manner as to indicate that implementation of the decision should be made, a third set of pages is developed under the heading of "Thing to Do for Implementation."

A side value in preserving these lists is that they can be shared with other subordinate or superior groups. Other groups can be invited to add to each list as it is displayed in sequence. This not only provides broader involvements and utilization of greater resources but also lets others know what other ideas were developed and rejected. A great deal of wheel spinning is avoided in that the implementers are spared the normal reaction of wondering why some other solution was not considered.

All three strategies require the investment of valuable time by a relatively small group, the staff. The payoff comes in the saving of valuable time by a relatively small group, the operating personnel.

IMPLEMENTATION

The most crucial point of every decision is that of implementation. Many excellent decisions fall unproductively by the wayside for lack of decisive action. Decisive action involves risk, commitment, and often some unpleasantness. As Drucker observes, "There is no inherent reason why medicines should taste horrible—but effective ones usually do. Similarly, there is no inherent reason why decisions should be distasteful—but most effective ones are."[20] As we stated earlier, timing is important in effective decisions. However, one cannot wait forever.

Examples of "good decision—no action" include a metropolitan police department comprised of a large administrative division in the center of the city, with a number of outlying divisions strategically located geographically to serve the outlying areas. These outlying divisions primarily furnish the patrol function, with most backup functions controlled by the centrally located administrative division. The various divisions operate in areas substantially different from one another in terms of population, industry, economic level, ethnic makeup, and the like. While having some commonality, their problems and needs are for the most part quite different.

The police chief and his staff officers felt that centrally controlling backup functions was not the most efficient use of personnel or the most appropriate answer to regional or area needs. An extensive study was conducted, and at its conclusion, several possible compromise solutions were considered and rejected. The final decision was to decentralize; to create in effect satellite police departments, each complete with all normal services and each responsible to a single regional head—its chief. The plan was to give a great deal of latitude-autonomy to the regional chiefs so that they in turn could be more sensitive to local needs and could react more quickly. They would continue to work within the philosophical framework of the total organization.

All the gathered data, the best judgment of the staff members, and everything in the process apparently indicated the decision for

[20] *Ibid.*, p. 157.

regionalization to be rational in the purest sense of the term. In this, however, as in many plans, the final decision rested with an external body whose members exercised control over the police department, and they were reluctant to move. Perhaps the reasons were political, or perhaps the risk appeared too great. After all, the old program was effective—to some degree.

The best decision in the world is *no decision* if it is not implemented. Wars have been lost and businesses have become bankrupt when the decisions that would have meant survival were at hand but remained for one reason or another unimplemented.

It should be reemphasized that decisions are more effectively implemented when those who must implement them are involved. Typically, implementation is thought of at the physical doing level, but it can be seen by our example that there is merit for involvement of those at the ultimate approval level as well.

FEEDBACK

Implementation is the action element of decision making, while *feedback* is the validating or correcting element. Feedback is necessary to determine whether or not the change is being properly carried out, whether or not it is achieving desired results, and what, if any, are the unanticipated side effects. Decisions, or at least changes brought about by decisions, do not always spring forth in full-blown success; often some modification or adjustment may be necessary. With the utilization of prompt feedback, these problems can often be identified and rectified quickly.

Feedback is available in various forms, but Drucker asserts that the most reliable is one's personal observation. "One needs organized information for the feedback. One needs reports and figures. But unless one builds one's feedback around direct exposure to reality—unless one disciplines oneself to go out and look—one condemns oneself to a sterile dogmatism and with it to ineffectiveness."[21]

Few decisions are indefinitely adequate, for organizations are not static. Even implemented decisions that do what they are supposed to do have need for periodic reexamination to be kept current. Feedback is an ongoing process.

SUMMARY

Effective managers make effective decisions—or they are not effective managers. Such decisions are not the by-products of charisma but are carefully developed within a logical process which begins with identification of the problem. Following through the process there is the selection of a proper decision and its implementation.

[21] *Ibid.*, p. 142.

Decision without implementation is no decision at all. The final state of the process is feedback, an evaluation of the implementation. The decision maker must know whether or not the action did in fact solve the problem, if it created other problems, or if it needed modification.

Three different decision-making models were discussed: *rational decisions*, *bounded rationality*, and *heuristic decisions*. Essentially, *rational decisions* are possible when one has access to *all* pertinent information, can trace *every* possible solution to its end, and make a selection from all alternatives based upon the most efficient/economical combination. *Bounded rationality* acknowledges that man's ability to make rational decisions is bounded by certain limitations which include his experiences, his values, and the amount of information to which he has access. *Heuristic decisions* involve elements of both the other models, adding a most powerful third dimension, the *human* element. The heuristic decision maker is free to internalize all the available data and possible solutions, reflecting this information against his personal experiences, his values, and his perception of what has been and what is likely to be. He then chooses the decision that he "feels" is the right one.

The chapter moved to the information-gathering process, which involved formal and informal communication links as well as extra-organizational links, those things going on outside the organization. In addition, consideration was given to the kinds of influence that are likely to affect the decision maker.

The point of the chapter is that effective decision makers do not operate in a vacuum. They are subject to all the elements of organizational, community, and personal life. Decisions made within organization or subunit settings are likely to have impact beyond their parameters—the effects of which must be considered before implementation. Implementation is the action part of the decision-making process. It must be monitored through feedback, and modified if need be, to serve identified objectives.[22]

LEARNING EXERCISE

PROBLEM-SOLVING: A STRUCTURED EXPERIENCE

GOALS

    I.   To study the sharing of information in task-oriented groups.

    II.   To focus on cooperation in group problem-solving.

    III.   To observe the emergence of leadership behavior in group problem-solving.

[22] J. William Pfeiffer and John E. Jones, *A Handbook of Structured Experiences for Human Relations Training* (Iowa City, Iowa: University City Associates Press, 1969), pp. 26–30.

GROUP SIZE

From six to twelve participants. Several groups may be directed simultaneously in the same room.

TIME REQUIRED

Approximately forty-five minutes.

MATERIALS UTILIZED

    I.   Problem-Solving Task Instructions.
   II.   Information for Individual Group Members (26 cards).
  III.   Problem-Solving Task Reactions Forms.
  IV.   Pencils.

PHYSICAL SETTING

Group members are seated in a circle.

PROCESS

    I.   Problem-solving task instruction sheets are distributed to the group members.
   II.   After members have had sufficient time to read the instructions sheet, the facilitator distributes the information cards randomly among the members of the group. He announces that the timing begins.
  III.   After twenty minutes (or less, if the group finishes early), the facilitator interrupts and distributes the Problem-Solving Task Reaction Forms, to be completed *independently*.
  IV.   The facilitator leads a discussion of the problem-solving activity, on information-processing and the sharing of leadership in task situations. Group members are encouraged to share data from their reaction forms. (The solution to the problem, by the way, is 23/30 wors.)

Problem-Solving Task Instructions

Pretend that lutts and mipps represent a new way of measuring distance, and that dars, wors, and mirs represent a new way of measuring time. A man drives from Town A through Town B and Town C, to Town D. The task of your group is to determine how many wors the entire trip took. You have twenty minutes for this task. Do not choose a formal leader.

You will be given cards containing information related to the task of the group. You may share this information orally, but you must keep the cards in your hands throughout.

Information for Individual Group Members

Each of the following questions and answers is typed on a 3 x 5 index card (26 cards). Those are distributed randomly among group members.

How far is it from A to B?
It is 4 lutts from A to B.
How far is it from B to C?
It is 8 lutts from B to C.
How far is it from C to D?
It is 10 lutts from C to D.
What is a lutt?
A lutt is 10 mipps.
What is a mipp?
A mipp is a way of measuring distance.
How many mipps are there in a mile?
There are 2 mipps in a mile.
What is a dar?
A dar is 10 wors.
What is a wor?
A wor is 5 mirs.
What is a mir?
A mir is a way of measuring time.
How many mirs are there in an hour?
There are two mirs in an hour.
How fast does the man drive from A to B?
The man drives from A to B at the rate of 24 lutts per wor.
How fast does the man drive from B to C?
The man drives from B to C at the rate of 30 lutts per wor.
How fast does the man drive from C to D?
The man drives from C to D at the rate of 30 lutts per wor.

Problem-Solving Task Reactions Form

1. Whose participation was most helpful in the group's accomplishment of the task? _____
What did he/she do that was helpful?

2. Whose participation seemed to hinder the group's accomplishment of the task? _____
    What did he/she do that seemed to hinder?

3. What feeling reactions did you experience during the problem-solving exercise? If possible, what behavior evoked a feeling response on your part?

4. What role(s) did you play in the group as it worked on the task?

COORDINATING:
The Integration
of Specialized Units

Viewing police departments as administrative systems seems to offer us the best approach to making them more effective and their workers more satisfied. It is undoubtedly more complex, however, to view them as systems as opposed to static pyramids. For example, it is far simpler to view police departments in terms of the universal prescriptions developed by early management theorists who have been labeled the *classicists*, such as Taylor, Fayol, Mooney, and Urwick. If one follows their prescriptions to the letter, there is only "one best way" to organize. It is not necessary to understand the requirements of different tasks or the complex issues raised by the varying needs of different sets of organization members. All one has to do is understand these principles and apply them.

The literature on organizations is filled with criticism of the classical approach. More recent evidence questions the creditability of this criticism. Some are now arguing that if we truly believe there is no one best way to organize, then how can we arbitrarily dismiss the older ways in favor of accepting the newer ways of organizing? According to three leading organizational theorists—Argyris, Lawrence, and Lorsch—we cannot. Argyris writes that

> We may conclude that *organizations (of the future) will tend to vary the structures that they use according to the kinds of de-*

cisions that must be made. If one asks the individual in the organization of the future to see the company organizational chart, he will be asked, "For what type of decision?"[1]

While according to Lawrence and Lorsch:

> The temptation to follow this simpler approach is obviously great; and we must admit that even our own evidence suggests that for organizations faced with stable and uniform environments this approach makes a great deal of sense.[2]

Therefore, we find: *First, there is no one best way for a police department to organize; second, the organizational structure should be directly dependent on the types of decisions that the police personnel must make and on the demands of their environment.*

Who would doubt that most police personnel are daily confronted with monumentally complex decisions? And who would doubt that many police organizations are faced with dynamic and uncertain environments where the classical principles of management do not work at all well? Significantly, we qualified the above statements with "most" and "many." The reason is that not all police departments require the same type of organizational structure. In those situations where a department is not confronted by difficult decisions or by a highly diverse environment, the classical approach may be the most effective of all possible approaches, although it is apparently seldom used today.

What does coordination and specialization have to do with the above discussion? Moreover, what does the manager have to do with specialization and coordination? Each question is now furnished with an answer. One brief but vital point of clarification. The terms *specialization* and *differentiation* and, similarly, *coordination* and *integration* will be used synonymously. It is felt that the term *differentiation* is more descriptive of the change created in organizations through specialization. Furthermore, the term *integration* best suggests the interdependency of work units mentioned earlier.

DIFFERENTIATION AND INTEGRATION

The structure of an organization is based on (1) the division of work into small, single task units, and (2) the coordination of work into a cohesive whole so as to propel it toward its stated goals. A

[1]Chris Argyris, *Integrating the Individual and the Organization* (New York: John Wiley & Sons, Inc., 1964), pp. 211–12.

[2]Paul R. Lawrence and Jay W. Lorsch, *Developing Organizations: Diagnosis and Action* (Reading, Mass.: Addison-Wesley Publishing Company, Inc., 1969), p. 91.

quick glance at the *Municipal Police Administration* provides us with a fairly good notion of how the police service has in many instances "broken up" its organizational structure.[3] In addition to *horizontal differentiation* (work specialization), police organizations are also broken up on a vertical basis (levels of authority): line, supervisor, middle manager, manager, and administrator. Clearly, differentiation is of major degree in most medium- to large-scale police departments. Why? Because the environment and the types of decisions to be made demand it! Hence we are stuck with the need for differentiation. At the same time we become victims of its harmful effects. Stahl alleges:

> In my judgment, the most serious fault in organization life is not the much overworked "interference by staff with the line" but the curse of specialization. I submit that the preoccupation of any specialist, whether line or staff, with the trivia of his profession and his tendency to relate all that goes on about him to the particular orbit of his work assignment, causes more trouble than anything else.[4]

Recent research findings show that specialized (differentiated) groups within an organization (1) exhibit less risk-taking behavior ("Don't make any waves!"), (2) are less efficient, and (3) are less productive than nondifferentiated groups.[5] And:

> Surprisingly, the emphasis upon integration has received little notice. The principle of specialization has had the lion's share of attention.[6]

Thus far we have seen that differentiation in a police department is on the one hand a necessity and on the other hand—a problem. We need a differentiated structure in order to respond effectively to called-for police services; although, at the same time, differentiation causes the organization to become fragmented, which results in reduced effectiveness. At first sight we appear to have an irresolvable dilemma. Our vehicle for either reducing or eliminating the injurious effects while sustaining the advantages of differentiation is through integrative measures and devices. It is well recognized that high levels of differentiation and integration are naturally antagonistic states. But, even though antagonistic to each other, both can be

---

[3] George D. Eastman and Esther M. Eastman, eds., *Municipal Police Administration*, 6th ed. (Washington, D.C.: International City Management Association, 1969).

[4] O. Glenn Stahl, "More on the Network of Authority," *Public Administration Review*, 20 (Winter 1960), 36.

[5] For details, see Edwin M. Bridges, Wayne F. Doyle, and David F. Mahan, "Effects of Hierarchical Differentiation on Group Productivity, Efficiency, and Risk Taking," *Administrative Science Quarterly*, 13 (September 1968), 305–21.

[6] Robert T. Golembiewski, *Organizing Men and Power: Patterns of Behavior and Line-Staff Models* (Chicago: Rand McNally & Co., 1967), p. 261.

achieved and to a high degree! In due recognition of the fact, Lawrence and Lorsch write:

> But this finding still leaves us with a curious contradiction. If, as we have found, differentiation and integration work at cross purposes within each organization, how can two organizations achieve high degrees of both? The best approach to explaining this apparent paradox becomes evident if we consider how organizations might go about achieving both of these states. If organizations have groups of highly differentiated managers who are able to work together effectively, these managers must have strong capacities to deal with interdepartmental conflicts. A high degree of differentiation implies that managers will view problems differently and that conflicts will inevitably arise about how best to proceed. Effective integration, however, means that these conflicts must be resolved to the approximate satisfaction of all parties and to the general good of the enterprise. This provides an important clue to how two of these organizations met the environmental requirements for high differentiation and high integration. These two organizations differed from the others in the procedures and practices used to reach interdepartmental decisions and to resolve conflict.[7]

An off-setting degree of integration is critical for organizational health and effectiveness. Appropriate levels of integration are advantageous for two reasons. First, intraorganizational conflict is decreased which, in turn, improves the quality of internal communications, group and individual task functions, group and individual problem solving, leadership, intergroup cooperation, and overall efficiency.[8] The following section describes some of the more useful procedures and practices for conflict resolution. Second, under twentieth-century conditions of constant change there has been an emergence of human sciences and a deeper understanding of man's complexity. Today, integration encompasses the entire range of issues concerned with incentives, rewards, and motivations of the individual and the way the organization succeeds or fails in adjusting to these issues. Thus, an integrated organizational structure facilitates the merging of individual needs and administrative goals.

MANAGING DIFFERENTIATION AND INTEGRATION

Within the role of a police manager is the often neglected responsibility for integrating the various parts of the organization with one another, and the individual with his organization. The fundamen-

---

[7] Paul R. Lawrence and Jay W. Lorsch, *Organization and Management: Managing Differentiation and Integration* (Boston: Harvard University Press, 1967), p. 53.

[8] Considerable research evidence shows that structural features that inhibit integration and cooperation produce conflict. For example, see Richard E. Walton, John M. Dutton, and Thomas P. Cofferty, "Organizational Context and Interdepartmental Conflict," *Administrative Science Quarterly*, 14 (December 1969), 522–43.

tal process establishing and maintaining integration is referred to as *conflict resolution*. The various mechanisms and techniques for resolving organizational conflict must be tailored to the unique conditions existing within the structure. The conditions are, in turn, a product of the organization's environment. Therefore, the police manager must first understand the demands of the environment before he is able to decide how much differentiation and integration is required in his department. Based on this understanding he is in a position to select those conflict resolvers that will furnish the proper balance between differentiation and integration.

The police manager starts by first looking at how much differentiation should exist among the various groups. As already suggested, this depends upon what internal characteristics each group must develop to carry out planned transactions with its assigned part of the environment. More specifically, it depends primarily upon the extent to which the certainty of information within the various parts of the environment is similar or different. If these parts of the environment (e.g., the community, criminal events, traffic safety, noncriminal services) are fairly predictable in their degree of certainty, the work units will need to be fairly similar in formal organizational practices and members' orientations. If these parts of the environment have quite different or unpredictable degrees of certainty, the units will need to be more differentiated, for example, the information required by the traffic officer is more certain as compared with that needed by the detective.

Next, the police manager focuses his attention on two aspects of the integration issue: (1) Which units are required to work together? and (2) How tight is the requirement for interdependence among them? But there is a strong inverse relationship between differentiation and integration. As we have indicated, when units (because of their particular tasks) are highly differentiated, it is more difficult to achieve integration among them than when the individuals in the units have similar ways of thinking and behaving. As a result, when groups in a police organization need to he highly differentiated (as is the case in most medium to large metropolitan law enforcement agencies), but also require tight integration, it is necessary for the organization to develop more complicated integrating mechanisms. The principal organizational mechanism for achieving integration is, of course, the management hierarchy. Downs attests to this fact in his law of hierarchy:

Coordination of large-scale activities without markets requires
a hierarchical authority structure. This Law results directly from

> *the limited capacity of each individual, plus the existence of*
> *ineradicable sources of conflict among individuals.*[9]

Let us repeat our central proposition—how well the police organization will succeed in achieving integration, therefore, depends to a great extent upon how the individual personnel resolve their conflicts.[10] The means of conflict resolution can be divided into *structural* and *behavioral* (in operation they are not mutually exclusive but highly interrelated).

The former is exclusively determined by the environment—a variable. The latter is determined in part by the environment, and in part is constant for all administrative systems—variable/constant. Both means of handling conflict are critical to those police organizations faced with the requirement for both a high degree of differentiation and tight integration. The structural integrating devices are (1) individual coodinators, (2) cross-unit teams, and (3) whole bureaus of individuals whose basic contribution is achieving integration among other groups. An example of the first device is a single police inspector functioning as a linkage between specialized units such as patrol and traffic. The latter two devices can sometimes be seen in such units as planning and research, and police community relations.

As mentioned above, the pattern of behavior that leads to effective conflict resolution varies in certain respects depending upon environmental demands, and in other respects is the same *regardless* of variations in environmental demands. The conflict management factor that varies with *environmental demands* is essentially power within and among groups. The power within and among groups means the organizational level *at which power resides* to make decisions leading to the resolution of conflict. If conflict is to be managed effectively, this power must be concentrated at the point in and between the various group hierarchies where the *knowledge* to reach such decisions also exists. Obviously, this will vary depending upon the certainty of information in various parts of a particular environment. The factors that lead to effective conflict resolution under all *environmental conditions* are (1) the mode of conflict resolution and (2) the basis from which influence is derived. In police organizations existing in quite different environments we have found that effective police management occurs when the police personnel deal openly with conflict and work the problem until they reach a resolution that is best

---

[9]Anthony Downs, *Inside Bureaucracy* (Boston: Little, Brown and Company, 1967), p. 52.

[10]For an interesting survey research study, see Everett G. Dillman, "A Source of Personal Conflict in Police Organizations," *Public Personnel Review*, 28 (October 1967), 222–27.

in terms of total departmental goals. In essence, effective police organizations confront internal conflicts rather than smooth them over or exercise raw power to force one unit or person to accept a solution.

In police departments dealing effectively with conflict, one also finds that the police personnel primarily involved in achieving integration, whether they be superiors or persons in coordinating roles, need to have influence based largely upon their perceived *knowledge and competence.* In other words, they are followed not just because they have formal positional influence but because they are seen as knowledgeable about the issues that have to be resolved. Before leaving the subject of conflict, we want the reader to realize that organizational conflict is inevitable and not necessarily always harmful. Conflict becomes injurious to the police department when it is at too high a level, ineffectively handled, and not tolerated at all. An organization that does not have a certain amount of internal conflict is not doing anything! To summarize:

> Conflict can have both dysfunctional and functional consequences, as Coser (1956) has pointed out. It can lead to heightened morale within a subsystem and it can lead to solutions which move more in an integrative than a compromise direction. Organizations generally develop mechanisms to handle internal struggles and devices to dull the sharp edges of conflict. As we have already noted in large complex organizations one of the main functions of top management is the adjudication of competing claims and conflicting demands.[11]

LEARNING EXERCISES

Two case studies have been selected as learning exercises in regard to differentiation and integration within the police organization and in the public safety sector. On the surface, the first case appears to be nothing more than a reorganization. Upon analysis, however, we observe an attempt to reduce differentiation while simultaneously increasing the degree of integration within the department. The reader should begin by asking the question *why.* Why did the Los Angeles Police Department make the described change in its structure? Clearly, the answer involves the values of management and field personnel alike and includes such issues as power and prestige within the department. Who gains and who loses? Moreover, does the change stand to benefit the internal "tightness" of units or not? Finally, the reader should examine the change in light of furthering integration so as to decrease conflict. What was done, if anything,

[11] Daniel Katz and Robert L. Kahn, *The Social Psychology of Organizations* (New York: John Wiley & Sons, Inc., 1966), p. 108.

both structurally and behaviorally to keep intergroup conflict within
due bounds?

The second case is replete with vested interests, intergroup
tensions, and potential battlegrounds. Many of the issues cited above
are also present here. The authors state that the creation of a single
public safety department can eliminate interdepartmental competition. Granted, but cannot the former conflicts be transferred to the
new framework? Cannot the intergroup pressures be heightened
through such a merger? What does the *environment* have to do with
determining the success or the failure of such a change? Finally, what
was done structurally and behaviorally to enhance the chances that
a Department of Public Safety would be effective in Glencoe?

LOS ANGELES POLICE DEPARTMENT EXPERIMENTS
WITH INVESTIGATOR UNIFICATION

Robert A. Houghton

Los Angeles Police Department, under the leadership of Chief Thomas
Reddin, has endeavored to be responsive to the needs of the community
through the development of new and more effective methods of controlling
crime.[12]

New and successful recruitment methods have been devised, training
programs have been revised, use of automated data processing has been
broadened, community relations activities intensified, and application of
scientific technology increased. In an attempt to improve the quality of our
efforts in crime and juvenile investigation, the Department's delinquency
control program has been expanded and measures have been taken to increase
the involvement of other segments of the Department.

Before September, 1966, the detective and juvenile investigation functions of the Department were performed under separate organizational
structures. Detective policy and procedures were established by the Detective Bureau, while Juvenile Division personnel operated under the direction
of the Patrol Bureau. The Detective Bureau has general responsibility for the
investigation of adult arrestees and of crime reports that did not identify a
juvenile as the perpetrator or victim. Juvenile officers had limited responsibility for crime investigation, but general responsibility for investigating juvenile arrests.

Each police station had two separate investigative units, one for juvenile investigation and the other for detective investigation. Normal surges
in the workload of one unit could not be absorbed by the other. Disputes
concerning responsibilities occasionally occurred at the operating level.
A coordinated investigative effort for crime control was difficult to achieve.
When the detective investigation of a crime revealed the offender to be a

[12]Reprinted with the permission of the *Journal of California Law Enforcement*,
3 (April 1969), 209–12.

juvenile, the case was turned over to a juvenile investigator, often resulting in duplication of work effort.

Workload was increasing. For example, during the most recent five-year period, reports of Part I offenses in Los Angeles had increased 38.3%.

Court decisions, particularly *In Re Gault and Miranda*, created considerable change in Juvenile Court proceedings. California state legislation expanded the requirements of those decisions. The previously informal atmosphere of the Juvenile Court gave way to more formal requirements. The Juvenile Court proceedings became adversary in nature, not unlike criminal court cases involving adults. This required investigators' case preparation in juvenile cases to meet the same standards as adult cases. Those of us who regretted the changes find slight comfort in the comment of a California Supreme Court Justice who said at the California Bar Convention that, although the Gault decision goes against the whole trend of the Juvenile Court movement, courts are bound by it. We in police agencies recognized that the Gault decision also binds us.

Despite a continuing increase in workload, manpower limitations precluded any significant increase in investigative strength. The Department was faced with a choice between reducing the level of service or finding methods of improving investigative effectiveness.

A decision was made that the Patrol Bureau's Juvenile Units should be realigned organizationally to a position closer to Detective Bureau components. In September, 1966, then Chief of Detectives Thomas Reddin and then Chief of Police Thad Brown received authorization from the Police Commission to assign the Juvenile Division and the fifteen decentralized Juvenile Units from the Patrol Bureau to the Detective Bureau.

Each Juvenile Unit was placed under command of the divisional detective commander, providing unification at the operating level to facilitate increased communication and to simplify coordination and control. Instead of a fragmentation of responsibility and effort, there was a more effective pooling of personnel, equipment, information and investigative effort.

The Commander of the centrally located Juvenile Division, with his headquarters personnel responsible for liaison, training, supervision, record keeping, advice and the overall coordination of juvenile matters, retained his important responsibilities in those fields as an essential staff service to the Chief of Detectives and Chief of Police.

The night watch plain clothes patrol units which had previously been assigned to the Juvenile Units were retained, but their specialized juvenile patrol responsibility was altered to include more follow-up investigation functions, providing assistance to both the Juvenile and Detective investigators. This caused a return to Patrol Bureau field units of the major responsibility for night watch patrol of juvenile problem areas. The positive response to this change may be noted in a 20% increase in juvenile arrests by Patrol Bureau units during the next year.

Uniform School Patrol Units operated by the Patrol Bureau were retained in that Bureau and continued to provide special patrol attention to school problems where need existed.

During this step in unification, the Juvenile Units retained their individual unit identities and personnel, although they had become "Detectives" and were under Detective Bureau command. The unified command did improve investigative coordination and communication. However, the basic division of Juvenile and Detective investigative responsibilities remained.

Detective commanders were encouraged to institute regular cross-training of investigators between the two assignments, further improving communication and coordination.

One detective commander, who had considerable prior experience as a supervisor of juvenile officers, sought and received authorization to form a special unified detail as a regular component of his division. This consisted of one juvenile investigator and two detective investigators who were responsible for all theft or burglary from motor vehicles, regardless of the age of the perpetrator. The division was one of the city's major problem areas for that crime. The coordinated emphasis resulted in an increase of two-thirds in that crime's clearance rate during a period of six months.

The success of that experiment led the detective command to form similar unified investigative details for auto theft, then burglary.

In February, 1968, two detective divisions were authorized to begin experimental programs with maximum unification of investigator assignments. This meant a combining of juvenile and detective investigators into crime-area details responsible for burglary and theft from motor vehicle, auto theft, burglary, assaults and homicide, and robbery. Each detail was responsible for investigation and disposition of all crimes and arrests in its functional specialty.

Additionally, one special juvenile detail, with a male and a female investigator, was formed in each division to process such juvenile cases as dependent children or missing juveniles, and to conduct follow-up on arrests such as curfew or Alcoholic Beverage Control violations which did not involve a separate crime.

The "Assault and Homicide" team which handled cases of rape and child molestation in each division included a policewoman sergeant investigator.

Supervision of the various details in each division was evenly divided between the lieutenant previously assigned as detective watch commander, and the supervisory sergeant previously assigned as Officer-in-Charge of the Juvenile Unit. Budgetary allotment has since provided an additional lieutenant's position to replace the supervisory sergeant.

Liaison with other youth-serving agencies, in addition to that routine to investigation, was maintained by the supervisors and the special juvenile detail. The experimental program was explained in detail at Coordinating Council meetings and at meetings with school administrators. The detective commanders participated actively in these liaison activities.

Coincident with this program, an attempt was being made to find if time could be saved in reporting of investigations. The Juvenile Court Judge and the Probation Department approved submission of simplified reports which eliminated duplication of reporting effort. It was found that the time spent in completing juvenile disposition reports was reduced 70%, while the same information as in the past was provided to Juvenile Court, Probation Department and other concerned agencies.

Continuous review of the pilot unification program in the two detective divisions over a four-month period included the evaluation of statistical data, sampling subjective opinions of involved personnel, and close supervision of reports and other work products. Indications pointed toward the unification program's success as a method for more effectively utilizing investigative manpower.

Close review of juvenile arrest dispositions was continued, and it was found that normal high standards were maintained. The Probation Department personnel concerned were queried, and reported satisfaction with the work products. The proportion of juvenile arrests which resulted in petition requests remained constant. Some school personnel and community agencies had expressed concern that juvenile investigations might not receive as much attention as previously accorded, but they soon found that juvenile police problems were actually receiving attention from more than twice as many investigators.

Nearly 50% of the detectives had worked in juvenile investigation assignments prior to their assignment to the Detective Bureau. They experienced no difficulties in juvenile investigation, juvenile and parental counselling, or in making appropriate dispositions and referrals of juveniles. Other detectives who had not acquired those skills during prior assignment, became knowledgeable through cross-training and through routine experience and supervision. Juvenile officers found little difficulty in assimilating detective investigative skills.

A great deal of the unification training resulted from personal interaction of investigators. The former juvenile officers guided detectives through the unfamiliarities of juvenile law and procedure, while detectives provided a reciprocal of information on their functional specialties. The transition was facilitated by the fact that juvenile and detective investigators are a preselected, experienced, high caliber group of police officers.

While resistance to unification was noted in individual cases, it represented the traditional human resistance to change, not lack of ability to adapt to the change. As experience in the new program developed, individual resistance to the change declined.

In July, 1968, we extended the unification experiment to the remaining thirteen geographic Detective Divisions. The organization of investigative assignments in each of those divisions is now patterned after the two divisions previously described. Unification was also applied to centralized investigative units such as Forgery, Arson and Traffic Follow-up.

So that the Department's activities in the juvenile field will continue to emphasize not only delinquency control, but also a concern for the welfare of juveniles who become victims or violators, we have retained and strengthened the organizational components, procedures and policies which will help to insure that result.

The Juvenile Division, commanded by the same Captain as before unification, retains Division status and exercised broadened staff responsibilities in evaluating, supervising and directing juvenile activities. Juvenile Division prepared and distributed to each detective division twenty-one training bulletins on juvenile policies, procedures and laws. Detectives received the training as lectures, discussion and written material.

A lieutenant and a sergeant from Juvenile Division conducted additional training for detectives and patrol supervisors on the unification program and the report simplification program. Juvenile Division is responsible for maintaining current this Department's "Juvenile Manual," which describes juvenile procedure in detail. This manual is being revised to reflect current operations.

Juvenile Division operates a Liaison-Report Audit Unit to audit police reports concerning juveniles for conformity to Department policy, and to maintain liaison with the Juvenile Court and Probation Department in the filing of applications for petitions.

A Coordination and Training Unit is being further developed at Juvenile Division, to insure uniformity of policies regarding the investigation of juvenile matters, and to maintain a high level of performance through the training of detective personnel in approved juvenile investigative procedures. A lieutenant, who is highly experienced in juvenile control activities, is assigned full time to examine the unification program. As he discovers problems and training needs, appropriate action is instituted.

We consider our new "detective-juvenile officer" as being still in the training phase of this program. The initial results have been encouraging. We are providing the community with a new detective, who is qualified in both fields, highly skilled in investigative techniques and well qualified in the processing of arrestees of any age. As detectives become more proficient in the dual role, contacts with other youth-serving agencies increase, as does the exchange of information. Any difficulties we have encountered during the initial training phase should be offset two-fold by the increased number of thoroughly rounded investigators. We are continuing to evaluate and improve our experimental program. As further changes appear necessary, we will make them.

THE EFFECTIVE DE-SPECIALIZATION OF JOBS: A CASE STUDY

Bernard H. Baum and Robert H. Goodin

The theory of formal organization focuses much attention on division of labor.[13] Refined job specialization is a by-word of efficient management. A perennial management question is, "How can human resources be used more effectively?" This is both a theoretical and practical problem. In practice managers focus on reconciling number of employees and peak periods of work.

There is an old Army gag about digging up stones, painting them white, burying them, etc., that exemplifies the problem of keeping men busy when there is nothing particularly constructive to be done. This article reports on an experiment in improving functional use of manpower.

In 1954 the Village of Glencoe, Illinois, began training its firemen in police duties and its policemen in fire duties to give residents a higher level of public safety service.

Glencoe was the first community in Illinois to cross-train its police and fire officers. Now other Illinois communities with some cross-training include Champaign, Elgin, Evanston, Lake Forest, Park Forest, and Waukegan.

THE COMMUNITY

Glencoe is a totally residential suburb 20 miles north of Chicago on the Lake Michigan shore. It has a high social and economic standing; the median annual family income exceeds $25,000 and median education of adults exceeds 14 years.

Glencoe has stable government. It was the first council-manager village in Illinois and the eleventh in the nation. Its first manager began serving the community in 1914 and it has had only three managers in the 53 years since.

[13]Reprinted with the permission of the *Public Personnel Review*, 29 (October 1968), 222-26.

Residents elect a Village Board in a nonpartisan election. The Village Board appoints a Village Manager who in turn appoints his staff. Three department heads administer the municipal functions: Director of Finance, Director of Public Works, and Director of Public Safety. Parks, schools, and the library are administered under other elected boards.

Separate police and fire departments followed traditional roles in Glencoe until 1954. The police department functioned to maintain law and order. Most contacts of residents with police officers involved law violations in which the officer gave a warning, issued a ticket, or made an arrest—usually "negative" contacts.

Fire department personnel were defensive because they were idle much of the time. This is consistent with our observation that men hired to respond to crises are typically defensive about their jobs between the crises. Competition and jealousies had developed between police and fire personnel. It was not too alarming—it probably happens between all police and fire departments.

CROSS-TRAINING

Alarming or not, could the built-in personnel problems of police officers (enforcement image) and firemen (defensiveness) be solved? The proposed solution on an organizational level was to consolidate the two activities. On a personnel level this meant the "de-specialization" of jobs. This solution contradicts the now classical Weberian dictum that organizational effectiveness varies directly with the degree of specialization of the task.

Between 1950 and 1953, 90 per cent of all calls answered by the fire department were handled by minor equipment carried on the fire apparatus—hand fire extinguishers, ropes and brooms—or by manpower for turning switches off, pulling plugs, or raising windows. In only 10 per cent of the calls was it necessary to use volume pumps, booster hoses, or ladders.

During that period, fire apparatus was out of the fire station answering fire or emergency alarms on an average of only 12 minutes in a 24-hour day—four minutes in an eight-hour shift!

Policemen would not be overburdened by spending four minutes each eight-hour shift in fire duties. Also, firemen would not be overburdened by performing police station duties during periods when they were not making fire prevention inspections or responding to emergency fire service alarms.

In February, 1954, the Chief of Police and Village Manager first discussed the feasibility of such a combination of the thirteen-man police department and eight-man fire department. The idea was not new. Oakwood, Ohio, a residential suburb of Dayton, had operated successfully under a combined police-fire program since 1928. Oak Park, Michigan, had just combined its police and fire services.

The Manager, Police Chief, and police and fire supervisory personnel studied the operation in other towns and thought it would work in Glencoe. To make it worthwhile to the men, an incentive pay plan was developed to provide each voluntary participant with a $600 annual increase at the completion of two and one-half years of intensive police and fire cross-training.

When the combination was made all men were kept on. It is difficult to imagine selling a personnel change such as this with the threat of discharge of even one man. The future saving on manpower was an administrative consideration in 1954 that is today a reality.

Training police and fire officers to perform the duties of their counterparts was the most important prerequisite for successfully combining Glencoe's police and fire departments. It was intensive, comprehensive, continuous, and voluntarily participated in by every police and fire officer. Officers could have stayed if they had not volunteered for cross-training, but the $600 pay increase (a 15 percent pay boost based on an average annual salary of $4,320) was persuasive.

Classroom training in police subjects for firemen included criminal law, interrogation, patrol techniques, rules of evidence, methods of arrest, accident investigation, report writing, and other police techniques.

Policemen studied fire pump operation, care of apparatus, fire defense, hydraulics, water measurement, use of equipment, and fire prevention and inspection techniques. Policemen during the training period spent a 40-hour work shift as full-time firemen while firemen spent a 40-hour work shift as full-time policemen.

Since 1954, recruit training has been intentionally worked out as a slow (two and one-half year) and thorough program stressing the importance of providing top-grade life and property protection to the residents, and in providing policemen and firemen with defenses against hazards they have always faced in their separate duties.

THE COMBINED DEPARTMENT

There are still policemen and firemen in Glencoe, and there is still a Police Chief and Fire Chief. However, the Police Chief is now the Director of Public Safety and the Fire Chief was appointed Assistant Director of Public Safety.

Supervisory officers include two Police Captains, one Fire Captain, three Police Lieutenants, and three Fire Lieutenants. Regular station duty is under command of the ranking officer.

Police and fire services are housed jointly. Firemen trained in police work perform police duties that can be done in the station: record work, communications work (that can be left when a fire alarm comes in), fingerprinting, photographic work, counting parking meter receipts, repairing parking meters, and dog and bicycle registration. Firemen wash police patrol cars as well as wash and maintain fire apparatus.

Police officers operate four police-fire station wagon patrol squad cars equipped with 35 different fire-rescue items, including fire extinguishers, inhalators, stretchers, fire clothing, and other tools. The station wagons double as ambulances.

When a fire call comes in, fire apparatus and police-fire patrol station wagons respond at the same time. In almost every case, one of the station wagons arrives at the scene of the fire before the fire apparatus. (Ordinarily two or three cars are on patrol, they are faster, and they are called instantly by radio.)

In the event of simultaneous police and fire alarms, men perform their traditional police and fire duties. In the event of double fire emergencies, immediate response of well-trained firefighters to both scenes is possible because more trained men are on duty at one time. In addition, there is still a force of some 20 paid-on-call firemen which existed prior to the reorganization.

Under the combined operation it is possible to send all available fire and police officers to any fire because all of these men are well-trained and experienced firefighters. Previously only eight men could have been dispatched.

In 1966, there were 623 major offenses in Glencoe, 5,950 minor offenses (by FBI categories), and 5,570 arrests made. During that year, 340 alarms for fire apparatus were made and "call firemen" were called out on 90 occasions.

Combining police and fire duties increased the number of trained policemen, increased the number of trained firemen, and added fewer men to the force to perform combined duties. It reduced the work week from 48 hours prior to 1954 to 40 hours in 1967 for police officers, and from 78 hours prior to 1954 to 56 hours in 1967 for fire officers. It increased salaries from an average salary for nonsupervisory policemen and firemen prior to 1954 of $360 per month to a top pay now of $725 per month.

PROFESSIONAL PERFORMANCE

What changes in behavior can be expected when duties of two traditionally separate professions are performed by individuals in one department?

Behavior of operating members has changed. Blau and Scott define professions as having six characteristics: neutrality with clients, professional status achieved by performance, decisionmaking not based on self-interest, a specific area of expertise, decisions and actions based on universal standards, and control structure by the profession. (Peter M. Blau and W. Richard Scott, *Formal Organizations*, San Francisco, Chandler Publishing Co., 1962, pp. 60–62.)

The first three were not changed by the combined police-fire service, but the area of expertise increased, new decisions and actions were based on more encompassing universal standards, and the profession versus hierarchy controlled structure was altered.

The professional in a bureaucracy finds tensions in satisfying both organizational and professional demands. This is a much discussed problem of administrators. Blau and Scott suggest that if an organization limits professional opportunities, men will find a higher commitment to the profession. However, in Glencoe, increased professional opportunities for police and fire officers resulted in higher commitment to the organization (greater loyalty). The fact that no one left the organization because of the change in duties gives some evidence to support our position.

Morale is high. A most significant factor is that policemen are not only seen as performing enforcement functions but are also engaged in many life-saving operations. A patrol car usually arrives at the scene of a fire or rescue call before the fire apparatus. Frequently fire-trained policemen have the fire or other incident under control before fire apparatus arrives. An officer who arrested a man today for a speeding violation is the same officer who put out the man's house fire last week!

Firemen have substantially less idle time and are less on the defensive. They no longer have to answer the question: "Why do you sit all day at the fire station?"

Undoubtedly a "Hawthorne effect" also affected the police-fire personnel—all 21 men were working on a unique program. This, however, was probably not as strong as the effect of changing the roles of police and fire officers to reduce the police "enforcement image" and firemen's defensiveness.

Police and fire officers in neighboring towns have enjoyed "razzing" Glencoe's officers because of their dual duties. However, the pay of Glencoe officers exceeds the pay of officers in neighboring villages, which reduces razzing when salaries are compared.

At professional training schools, Glencoe's new recruits have consistently been either the highest, or nearly highest, ranked students. One man was the class leader in each of eight weeks of training, had the highest grades ever given, and was the graduating class president. This is one result of recruiting more capable men, which Glencoe is doing because of the greater professional opportunities and the higher salary.

The creation of a single department has eliminated interdepartmental competition. Blau and Scott report that performance in competitive groups has been found to be inferior to that in cooperative groups. During riots in some towns, firemen were frequently "out of service" when they could not reach a fire because of sniper problems. Firemen had to wait until policemen made the area safe. In Glencoe, policemen and firemen have all received riot training.

Behavior of line supervisors has changed. There is now only one command in the public safety service. There is no conflict on routine or emergency functions. For example, formerly there was a question of jurisdiction on vehicle traffic control and firefighting are under the supervision of the ranking officer at the fire.

Coordination of all routine and emergency functions and intradepartmental communications are vastly simplified. Further, recruiting and selection consists of one advertising, one testing, and one selection of recruits for the service.

RESULTS

The innovation provides improved service. The response from the prime beneficiary, the public, to the Village Board and staff has been enthusiastic. Village Board members have never had a police or fire subject as an issue in an election.

A resident does not care whether the equipment that extinguishes the fire in his home, or saves a life, comes on the fire truck or in a patrol car. Formerly, the public was critical of police officers who arrested them and fire officers who sat in front of the fire station. Now the Village Manager receives at least one complimentary letter per week concerning actions by police and fire officers.

The combined service works well. There have been no added personnel problems in cross-training. There is no substitute for a well run organization, and this innovation has helped make the police and fire functions run more effectively.

There is economical use of personnel. Unfortunately in the public service, there is nothing comparable to the profit and loss statement of private industry. However, by comparison, one of Glencoe's neighboring residential villages with the same amount of area and only 15 per cent greater population has twice the police and fire manpower.

Men in the organization are satisfied. They are well-paid compared with other villages. Increased duties warrant such pay and actually make it economical. Because of the flexible use of men, they actually work shorter hours.

There is an extremely low turnover in the organization. Of 21 men in both police and fire departments in 1954, 13 are still in the service. Of the eight men no longer with the Village, five retired, one is on health disability, one died, and one resigned for personal reasons.

Of the 29 men now in the Public Safety Department, which has expanded to meet greater demands since 1954, nine have five years or less of service, six from six to ten years, four from 11 to 15 years, nine from 16 to 20 years, and one man (the Director of Public Safety) has 31 years of service.

The Glencoe case illustrates the value of taking a broad look at an organization's overall function and as a result of analysis developing new approaches. We submit that this example of management technique is more generally applicable than is currently the case.

10

CONFLICT RESOLUTION:
Smoothing Troubled Waters

Conflict is a fact of life.[1]

The reader will be quick to note that the subject matter in this chapter is biased, or directed toward internal (within the organization) conflicts as compared to external (outside the organization) conflicts.[2] The former basically involves interpersonal or group disagreement, while the latter is centered around such extraorganizational conflicts as collective violence and press relationships. To put it another and more overt way, the police manager, like his counterparts in other public and private organizations, spends a large part of his time either avoiding or resolving interpersonal difficulties.

[1] André L. Delbecq, and L. L. Cummings, *Organizational Decision Making* (New York: McGraw-Hill Book Company, 1970), p. 229.

[2] In the course of conducting or attending numerous police management programs, we have invariably asked the participants, "Are most of your daily conflicts inside or outside the department?" The response has overwhelmingly been, "Inside!" In other words, we are convinced that the majority of the police manager's problem-solving activities are limited to the confines of his agency. We are also well aware, however, that there is a rapidly growing problem with police unionization. The "blue flu" work slowdown and even strikes are not uncommon as of this moment. Hence, a part of this chapter is devoted to the subject of conflict resolution à la employer-employee relations.

We will, in most instances, view the police manager as "the third party" in a dispute. While possessing sufficient raw authority to dominate the interpersonal or group argument, we choose to envision the police manager in his emerging role of "problem resolver" rather than "problem suppressor." For it has been shown that in nearly every instance, if well handled, the direct confrontation between participants can result in resolution or better control of the conflict and, in turn, a healthier organizational setting for all—managers and line personnel alike.

This chapter also includes a discussion of a semi-internal problem situation referred to as employer-employee relations, or *unionism*. In this case the manager is not a third party but is often placed in the role of one of the disputants. The common theme remains, however, the resolution of conflict. The techniques for solving internal interpersonal and semi-internal disagreements can be used in either one of the two situations.

CONFLICT: IT IS EVERYWHERE

"The world would seemingly have known conflict since the formation of human groups—including the family."[3] Numerous early social philosophers, in writing about the evolution of man, stressed the competitive necessity for endurance.[4] Today we see conflict generated by survival needs and amplified through the economic system, with its impact mediated through the bureaucratic structure. Focusing on the latter point for a moment, we observe that the organizational member has opportunity to exercise private choice and that his behavior may therefore be in conflict with collective purpose. Now we want to set forth propositions on structural sources of conflict, those forces internal to the functioning organization; that is, we want to examine bases of conflict created by the formal process of organizing.

---

[3] Shull, Delbecq, and Cummings, *Organizational Decision Making*, p. 228.

[4] Malthus's works (especially, *An Essay on the Principle of Population*, 1798), Darwin proposed the notion that struggle and conflict were essential to the process of survival. In summary, his thesis (*Origin of Species*, 1859) contends that there is competition among species and members of the same species for use of the earth's limited resources. In the competition some organisms will survive, others will not. Further, Hobbes (especially, *Leviathan*, 1651) conceived of man as innately competitive and believed that man, in the pursuance of his desires, would be in constant warfare with his fellowman. Realizing the conflictual nature of his demands, Hobbes argued that man would contract with the "state" to resolve conflicts among men. In contrast, government intervention was to Adam Smith (*Wealth of Nations*, 1776) an anathema against the "invisible hand" of the economic system. In effect, Smith proposed an amplification, but direction, of the natural-struggle hypothesis through an artifact—the economic system.

As mentioned earlier, the latter part of this chapter deals with forces that are semi-internal. Keep in mind, regardless of the conflict, that the organization and in particular the manager is constantly struggling to develop cooperation and reduce useless tension. Clearly, the identification with the department's goals and the cooperation among members do not occur at random. Note the use of the phrase *useless tension*. Not all conflict is harmful. Argyris expresses this proposition as follows:

> Thus it can be seen that mental health is based on a certain degree of tension, the tension between what one has already achieved and what he still ought to accomplish, or the gap between what he is and what he should become. Such a tension is inherent in the human being and therefore is indispensable to mental well-being. We should not, then, be hesitant about challenging man with meaning potentialities for him to actualize, thus evoking his will to meaning out of its latency. I consider it a dangerous misconception of mental hygiene to assume that what man needs in the first place, is equilibrium or, as it is called in biology, "homeostasis," i.e., a tension-less state. What man actually needs is not a tension-less state but rather the striving and struggling for some goal worthy of him. What he needs is not the discharge of tension at any cost, but the call of a potential meaning waiting to be fulfilled by him.[5]

More pointedly, Townsend asserts that conflict is:

> . . . a sign of a healthy organization—up to a point. A good manager doesn't try to eliminate conflict; he tries to keep it from wasting the energies of his people. . . .
>
> Conviction is a flame that must burn itself out—in trying an idea or fighting for a chance to try it. If bottled up inside, it will eat a man's heart away.
>
> If you're the boss and your people fight you openly when they think you're wrong—that's healthy. If your men fight each other openly in your presence for what they believe—that's healthy. But keep all conflict eyeball to eyeball. . . .[6]

THE BASIS FOR CONFLICT

Conflict is encountered within an organizational setting for a number of reasons, which can be categorized as follows: specialization, compartmentalization, and role conflict.

[5] Chris Argyris, *Integrating the Individual and the Organization* (New York: John Wiley & Sons, Inc., 1964), p. 6.

[6] Robert Townsend, *Up the Organization* (Alfred A. Knopf, Inc., 1970), p. 39.

Specialization

The modern complex organization is fractionated. As a police department grows in size and scope, each of the original functional areas tends to become subdivided into several more highly *specialized* task units. Hence, the police manager must assign responsibility, and the organization is coordinated through the progressive devolution of authority to successive tiers of subordinate managers.

Tiers or layers of performing units, more and more distant from the overall objective, are created. As these units evolve, measures of their performance must be devised. Where, for example, crime repression may be the police department's goal, it is too general and is no longer appropriate to some of the individually operating units contained therein (e.g., saturation patrol versus police community relations). More operational standards of performance must be developed in relation to the ends of the next higher containing unit. The "levels" concept of organizations implies seriality of decision making. Authority for decision making may be delegated and decisions reviewed, or tentative decisions may originate at lower levels and then pass upward in the hierarchy. The hierarchical structure of an organization, then, can be conceived of as a means-end chain with trade-offs between operating units (as between vice units and narcotic units), or as a decision tree. The manager, therefore, seeks to replace wasteful conflict with productive tension and efficient coordination.

Compartmentalization

When the growth of the police department generates complexity beyond the manipulative ability of a single executive, the result is some type of segmentation, typically in the form of bureaus or divisions. Thus, a horizontal pattern of relationships develops. The top police manager delegates responsibility for routine and detailed tasks to a group of subordinates and thereby creates formalized subunits in the organization. To fix accountability, a middle manager is assigned to direct these subsections. Then a management team evolves, which knits together these bureau heads. But the police manager is a member, or representative, of a work unit as well as of this management, or command, unit. Since his primary responsibility is measured in terms of his work unit, his decisions may be dictated by the needs of his department. Since his performance is largely judged by the contribution of his work unit, he may value this far more than

cooperation with other units. Regretfully, loyalties may result in in-
capacitating almost any unit head for the task of balancing the objectives of his unit against the objectives of other units. If each unit is
judged by different standards, divergent and conflicting value premises will exist among units, resulting in differing considerations and
evaluations. Intraorganizational conflict is, therefore, partially explained by the complexity of the typical organization and a subordinate manager's inability to *perceive it in its entirety and define his
relationship to it.* Unless the police manager can attain a vision of the
whole, he is forced to try to obtain the optimum for a partial area regardless of the effect on the whole. In summary, the major characteristic of modern management organization is its diversity rather than
its universality. Therefore, we can anticipate disagreement among the
organizational segments (e.g., Is not the following stimulus for conflict: "The goals of my unit are more important to success of our police
department than the goals of your unit"?).

Role Conflict

Differing expectations about job performance or the work-ex-
pected behavior of a person in an assigned position do give rise to
conflict within the organization. Various perceptions of personal
attributes, specialties, and values among incumbents can also pro-
voke conflict. The incumbent of any one organization may maintain
multiple sociological attachments, both within and outside that environment. Those groups with which an individual identifies are his
"reference groups." Because of formal departmentalizing and specialization of tasks, reference groups tend to develop that have the usual
characteristics of primary groups. Each reference or work group has
a peculiar and identifiable psychological environment, quite apart
from that of the formal organization. The nature of these formal or
informal groups determines the directional affinity of the member.
Relevant phenomena reflecting the informal aspects of an organization include decisions that are partially based upon the sentiments and
values of a work group or upon information transmitted by the grape-
vine and decision making that is allocated to, or assumed by, "un-
authorized" individuals.

Based on a number of group attachments (church, family, social
clubs, work, etc.), people experience conflicting demands. The
Judeo-Christian ethic tells us to turn the other cheek after being struck
the first time. The police department clearly does not want its members being slapped around. Furthermore, our hierarchy of needs
causes us to seek friendly relations, yet most often we find ourselves

in a competitive situation. Although referring to a business organization, the following holds true for police departments:

> The business executive also operates within a system of mobility in which others are trying to get ahead. Even if they are really not trying to get ahead, they have to maintain the myth of getting ahead since this is an integral element of our kind of society. The colleagues of the business executive and his trusted subordinates are not only his friends, the people with whom he works and co-operates in getting the job done, but they are friendly enemies; everybody smiles and carries on as if nothing really were happening, but everybody is in competition.
> In some companies, this competition is greater than in others. Some companies are made up of highly mobile, very aggressive fellows who push each other all over the place. If they're all bulls, they don't really mind this, but if there's a milquetoast among them, he is annihilated. But regardless of the degree of competition, executives in any company are in the strange situation of having to cooperate and compete at the same time.[7]

Studies also suggest that role conflict is so prevalent in large, complex organizations that it is virtually impossible to design all jobs so that it is eliminated entirely. Moreover, these studies show that although role conflict tends to produce dissatisfaction and emotional strain, the extent of these undesirable effects varies widely, depending on awareness of role conflict, acceptance of conflicting job pressures, ability to tolerate stress, and general personality makeup. A variety of adjustment mechanisms and psychological defenses are used to reduce role conflict. Where a choice can be made from conflicting role pressures, the experimental literature reports that two variables influencing the choice are perception of the legitimacy of directions received (who has the best right to issue orders) and perception of the sanctions (rewards or punishments) attached to conflicting claims.[8] Attempts to adjust to role conflict depend not only on personal values and personality characteristics but also on yet unanalyzed situational variables. Perception of the legitimacy of directions, or the relative sanctions offered by conflicting claims, depends not only on subjective factors but also on the situation itself as regarded from past experience. Hence, the police manager should constantly strive for *accuracy in his communication, clarity in what is expected of each role incumbent, and a well-understood pattern of authoritative relationships.*

[7]Robert Golembiewski, *Managerial Behavior and Organizational Demands* (New York: Rand McNally & Co., 1968), p. 332.

[8]Robert J. House, "Role Conflict and Multiple Authority in Complex Organizations," *California Management Review*, 12 (Summer, 1970), p. 59.

INTERVENTION

Thus far we have learned that (1) conflict is pervasive, (2) not all conflict is harmful, and (3) within an organizational framework it is most frequently caused by specialization, compartmentalization, and role conflict. While conflict cannot be completely eliminated, it can be reduced to an acceptable level and, most importantly, directed to productive channels. The literature is replete with studies on organizational conflict, most of which deal with interpersonal or intergroup role disputes.[9] We now turn to a discussion of replacing "conflict" with "collaboration." The police manager will be viewed as an intervener, or a third party, in a role conflict (interpersonal and intergroup).

When to intervene in a dispute, if at all, is the most fundamental choice to be made by the manager. Even before that choice must come the realization that he cannot wait for others to request that he intervene in a dispute. Moreover, he cannot allow himself to become a placid and silent observer of "people" problems. The manager—that is, the effective manager—must be alert to organizational arguments and, once detected, must rapidly attempt to resolve them. He must, in a single word, *intervene!*

Once the police manager has decided to intervene, follow-up decisions immediately become paramount:

> Should the place of conflict resolution be entirely neutral to all parties (the disputants and himself), or should it be geared to assist one or the other? For example, if the manager decided to hold the meeting in his office, the location would tend to reflect the aura of his office. Or, if he chose to resolve the participants' problems at a social meeting, positional authority would be manifested.
>
> Should the place of conflict resolution be formal or informal? To illustrate, if the manager insists on job titles being used during group interaction, then considerable formality occurs. But, if the situation permits the use of first names, enhanced informality will result. (We propose that it is just as easy and, by far, more effective to state, "Joe,—you're wrong!" as compared to "Officer Cline, the depart-

---

[9] For example, see Robert Kahn *et al.*, *Organizational Stress: Studies in Role Conflict and Ambiguity* (New York: John Wiley & Sons, Inc., 1964). A valuable and comprehensive text that includes cases and recommended solutions derived from research findings on conflict resolution is Paul R. Lawrence and John A. Seiler, *Organizational Behavior and Administration* (Homewood, Ill.: Richard D. Irwin, The Dorsey Press, 1965). For articles and book reviews on the subject, see *The Journal of Conflict Resolution*, published quarterly by the Center for Research on Conflict Resolution, University of Michigan.

ment is hereby and herein reprimanding you for inappropriate activities.")

Should the time period within which the conflict resolution occurs be short or long? By this we mean, "You two have a problem—please think it through and, when decided, report back to me" or "You two are constantly arguing—resolve your difficulties before the day is over!"

Should the manager include himself or others in the argumentative dialogue, or is it best limited to the disputants? This is to say, "It's just the two of you—closet yourselves and please come forth with a reasonable solution to your problems."

Because of the above decisions, certain additional activities on the part of the police manager become necessary:

Refereeing the discussion (often heated) between employees

Recommending a format that should be followed during the dialogue

Providing clarification of information important to one another

Assisting in the discussion by offering feedback

Seeking to identify the issues that caused the conflict

Suggesting a means of communication that would promote discussion

Indicating the problems in interpersonal communications

Constant counseling relative to the primary goals and standards of the department as they impact on the conflict

THE ATTRIBUTES OF THE MANAGER IN A THIRD-PARTY ROLE

Certain attributes of the manager and of his relations with the disputants influence his ability to perform the functions and implement the interventions described above. The following attributes are required of the third party: professional expertise, personal power, neutrality, and self-reality (candor). A section is devoted to each of these subject areas.[10]

Professional Expertise

The professional qualities attributed to the third party which give the principals confidence in entering an open confrontation and which facilitate confrontation processes include (1) diagnostic skill, (2) behavioral skills in breaking impasses and interrupting repetitive interchange, (3) attitudes of acceptance, and (4) personal capacity to provide emotional support and reassurance to all involved.

[10]Most of the thinking expressed in this section is drawn from Richard E. Walton, *Interpersonal Peacemaking: Confrontations and Third-Party Consultations* (Reading, Mass.: Addison-Wesley Publishing Company, Inc., 1969).

Personal Power

The real or perceived power of the third party and his general knowledge of the principals, issues, and background factors are important attributes. Interestingly, it is an advantage for the third party to exert little or no power over the future of the principals. This type of third-party power decreases participants' sense of risk in confronting issues candidly or is likely to induce them to behave in ways that are calculated to elicit the approval of the third party. Furthermore, at least moderate knowledge of the principals, issues, and historical factors usually is an advantage. It not only enhances the manager's credibility with the principals but also increases the likelihood that his intervention will be on target. The prior knowledge also reduces the amount of time that the principals spend talking to the third party rather than each other (this admittedly is not always an advantage). One argument against a third party's being highly knowledgeable about the issues and the persons involved is that it is difficult for the principals to believe he does not have his own opinions, about either the issues or the persons' views, which disqualify him as a disinterested party.

Neutrality

Naturally, differences in the third party's relationships to the two principals can influence his effectiveness. Three different types of third-party justice and balance are critical: Is the manager neutral with respect to outcome? Is the manager an equal distance from the parties in a personal sense? Does the manager eliminate rules for handling differences that would inadvertently create an advantage for one and a disavantage for the other?

Self-Reality

"To thine own self be true" is the crux of the message contained in this subsection. It *is not* important that the manager's personal style or the way he comes across to others be taken into account if one fully understands his power. Moreover, it *is* critical for the general theory and practice of conflict resolution to know that such personal attributes and styles do condition the role and the behavior of the person. Those involved in the process have to believe that the manager is attempting to "redress the balance" between the differing parties impartially and accurately.

Large police departments are increasingly seeking organizational consulting as a service supplied by the personnel unit or a private consulting firm. How well do internal organizational consultants usually match the above-mentioned role attributes? They are frequently seen as possessing sufficient professional expertise, although not as much as that attributed to the private consultant. This edge in expertise possessed by the external consultant may be offset by the advantage of the internal consultant's more continuous availability. "Internals" are more likely than are the "externals" to be regarded as having an optimum amount of background knowledge. They can usually acquire sufficient control over the setting and process. The internals, however, encounter more difficulty than externals in demonstrating power over the future of the principals and in achieving neutrality.

THE MANAGER AS A THIRD-PARTY INTERVENER IN INTERNAL CONFLICT

The objective of conflict management is threefold: to interrupt the conflict, to achieve a de-escalation of the conflict, and, finally, to initiate a benevolent cycling of the conflict. Significantly, if all goes well, *confrontations not only allow for the exchange of essential information but also increase the authenticity of the relationship and the personal integrity experienced in the relationship.* If they are not well managed, confrontations can further polarize the individuals, enlarge the costs of the conflict, or discourage the disputants from making additional efforts to resolve the conflict. The main task of conflict management is to maximize the potential gains from a confrontation and to minimize the risks for the participants. The results of the confrontation hinge upon many factors, with respect to which third-party intervention can perform key functions. We propose that the following are strategic.

First, by his position, the manager can often assess whether the motivation to reduce the conflict is mutual. If there is insufficient immediate desire on both sides to ensure a give-and-take, the police manager can move to avoid or delay the confrontation. If there is some positive interest on both sides, but one person has unusually high motivation, then the person with the greater motivation can be influenced to moderate the level of opinion that he inculcates and adjust his expectations accordingly. Thus, the third party works to achieve balance in the motivational forces that are activated in the interpersonal or the intergroup confrontation.

Second, imbalance in power will affect the course of the confrontation by undermining trust or inhibiting dialogue between the participants. The manager can attempt to achieve as much balance as possible; for example, by offsetting an organizational power advantage of one, by involving more allies for the other. The third party can regulate the interaction process in a way that favors a person with lesser verbal or fighting skills. Thus, again we propose, as have others, that the third party attempt to achieve *symmetry*—this time in terms of the power of the two principals.

Third, the manager can ensure that one person's initiative to confront is integrated with the other person's readiness for the dialogue. Poorly timed confrontations risk heightened feelings of rejection and are marked by an increased frequency of misinterpreted acts; for example, a conciliatory gesture may be interpreted as a sign of weakness, or a positive expression by one may be seen by the other as an attempt to perpetuate the conflict rather than as a gesture of trust.

Fourth, a related function is to ensure either that the argumentative phase of the dialogue is worked out fully before moving on to the solution phase or, at least, that a sufficient amount of difference has occurred to provide a basis for the amount of resolution hoped for at the time. The underlying principle governing the manager's actions is that the potential for salutary relationships is no greater than the extent of the adjustments already achieved during a confrontation.

Fifth, the manager can assess the extent to which various factors contribute to openness in a confrontation—organizational standards pertaining to expression of differences, emotional backing available to participants, and skills at hand for improving dialogue.

Sixth, the third party can add to the reliability of the interpersonal or intergroup communications by translating the messages until the sender and the receiver agree on the meaning; by procedural devices that require one to show that he understands what the other has said; and by assisting in the development of a common language with respect to conceptual issues, emotional issues, and the communication process itself.

EMPLOYER-EMPLOYEE RELATIONS: OMNIPRESENT CONFLICT

Employer-employee conflicts (grievances) cost money! In many instances, a lot of money. Sometimes a grievance can be settled in a five-minute discussion between a police supervisor and the police officer. Sometimes a grievance may take months or even years, involve many people in numerous meetings, and end up in arbitration or even in court. An example of a labor-management plan can be seen at the Lockheed-California Company.[11] Their strategy is reported as follows:

Step 1. When a complaint is not settled on an informal basis, a written grievance may be filed with the department head. Within five days, unless an extension is mutually agreed upon, the department head and the union steward meet to discuss the grievance. The plant personnel representative is there in an advisory capacity. If the grievance is not settled there, it goes to

Step 2. A full-time union business representative discusses the grievance with a full-time labor relations representative. They may meet together or may arrange meetings of various sizes with different levels of management, depending upon the grievance and the problem involved. If the grievance is not settled at Step 2 it goes to

Step 3. This is a Labor-Management Committee which meets as necessary with a predetermined agenda. This committee of sixteen has seven elected union representatives plus the president of the union and the business representative who presents the case for the union. The company has five management representatives plus the labor relations manager and the labor relations representative who presents the case for the company. If the grievance is not settled by this committee, it goes to

Step 4. This is arbitration. We have "guestimated" that Step 1 grievance costs an average of $50.00, Step 2 $175.00, Step 3 $525.00, and if the case goes to arbitration, it costs $1,500.00 or more. This includes the time of employees, supervision, management and company labor relations personnel. It also includes one-half the time of the seven elected representatives of the union who are also full-time employees during the time the Labor-Management Committee meets. In addition, the cost of the grievance settlements themselves—such as lump-sum payments and back pay—is involved. None of this takes into account the expense to the union.[12]

Management participation and attitude is perhaps *the* most important determinant of departmental-association (union) relationship effectiveness. The philosophy, attitude, and cooperation of police management can determine whether the relationship is relatively harmonious, a state of continuous warfare, or anywhere in between these two extremes. Unfortunately, today most police managers

[11] For details, see J. C. Pettefer, "Effective Grievance Administration," *California Management Review*, 13 (Winter 1970), 12–18.
[12] *Ibid.*, pp. 12–13.

lack knowledge of and experience in the subject of arbitration. Their skills in interpersonal and intergroup problemsolving, however, are readily adaptable to resolving grievances.

A few proven and simple rules are proposed at this time. First, both in negotiations and in day-to-day grievance administration, an attempt must be made to determine the underlying cause and reach a resolution of the problem rather than just consider the words on the face sheet of the union proposal or grievance. Second, *do not* approach grievances from the standpoint of who wins or who loses. The "box score" aspect should be de-emphasized; concentration is best placed on what causes a problem and how it can best be solved. Third, the resolution should occur at the point of contention. Hence supervision and middle management must be involved. All this does not mean or should it mean that either the department or the union is "weak" in dealing with the other. A union should be expected to be adamant about maintaining, protecting, and upholding the rights of the police employees it represents. The department should similarly be expected to be most zealous in protecting and preserving management rights; however, nothing is to be gained and much is to be lost by an antagonistic or the-department-is-always-right approach.

The following material is taken from an article by two police managers who have gained considerable insight and practical experience in interacting with police unions.[13]

Although it has been popular in police administrative circles to denounce the movement toward unionization among police officers, such protests are becoming pointless. With increasing rapidity, executive orders, legal opinions, and legislation are rejecting the classical administrative arguments against police unionization and legitimizing the right of officers to belong to unions and engage in collective negotiations with their employers. At least thirteen states require local governments to bargain in good faith with their police employees, while only seven states have statutes that specifically deny police officers the right to join unions. Therefore, police executives are faced with the necessity of realistically dealing with police unions and other employee organizations that use union tactics.

When one surveys the collective bargaining arena, it is found to be an ill-defined, ambiguous area where the exercise of political knowledge and power is essential. Problems for which classical organizational concepts are inadequate become obvious. This means

[13]Robert M. Ingleburger and John E. Argell, "Dealing With Police Unions," *The Police Chief*, 38 (May 1971), 50–55.

that when faced with the task of dealing with a police union or similar employee group, a chief of police must adopt a flexible managerial philosophy and develop new skills so that he can protect his own authority and power and maintain his effectiveness.

Philosophical Approach

After accepting collective bargaining as a new administrative problem that demands action, most chiefs modify their views regarding the roles and authority of employees. The classical autocratic administrative theory, restricting lower-level employees to following orders of superiors or resigning, does not provide an adequate base for dealing with modern police unions.

Parson's approach conceptualizes an organization as composed of a cluster of interacting positions and roles. Roles are defined by reciprocal behavioral expectations among the actors of the system who are significant because of their position in the cluster. Although this explanation is an oversimplification, it can be used to determine the effectiveness of a social system (i.e., an organization), by assessing the amount of role consensus or conflict that exists within it. A lack of consensus would indicate an ineffective organization.

Using this theory, a police administrator views his own position as only one of several interlocked and related positions in an organizational system. Since the positions are seen as closely linked, changes in one position would affect the others. To maintain an effective organization, the administrator must adopt flexible attitudes and attempt to cultivate role consensus among the various significant actors. Specifically, in dealing with a police union the astute administrator realizes that recognition of the union creates new problems which he has never before faced. Any dealings the chief of police has with the union will affect his relationship with others in significant roles—the city manager, police board members, middle managers, and others who are not members of the union. Therefore, before becoming involved in union negotiations, he should attempt to determine the perceptions and expectations of the other significant actors. If these actors generally agree on the various roles in the system, the administrator can deal with the union in a manner consistent with their attitudes. Where role perceptions conflict, however, he would be wise to attempt to move the participants toward a consensus before unilaterally dealing with the union.

An administrator can facilitate role consensus among his supervisors, his middle managers, and his officers' union by playing an intermediary role. He can furnish all parties with literature and information related to their roles, he can insure that they have opportunities to communicate directly with each other, and he can frequently act as an interpreter and impartial consultant for those involved.

During such a process, he may have to modify and redefine his own perceptions, expectations, philosophy, and role. Throughout the process, however, he should attempt to define formally the areas of agreement on the roles of the various parties. When agreements on the various role definitions are reached, they should be set down in writing for use as the basic guidelines by the actors in the system.

This philosophical approach is more realistic than that suggested by classical organizational theory. Since it does not provide normative solutions on which the administrator can rely, the specific strategies and methods that should be used will vary from police department to police department. This approach forces the police administrator to play an ambiguous role in an often undefined, unstable system. He must be concerned about the welfare of his subordinates and assist in ensuring conditions under which they can achieve their professional objectives. He must assist and be loyal to his supervisors and provide them with good information, service, and advice. He should aid his managers and consider their problems because they will bear the major portion of the responsibility for administering contracts. Most importantly, as a professional administrator, the chief of police should have an allegiance to the citizens that supersedes all other loyalties. Obviously, if he is to maintain a viable and effective organization, his managerial philosophy should enable him to operate in an environment of diverse demands and alternatives.

Under ideal circumstances, the chief quietly advises the city manager and the council. He also represents his managers, the union, and otherwise unrepresented citizens to them. Thus, to the union he negotiates for his managers, the legislature, and the unrepresented. Given such difficult responsibilities, he must design methods and formulate strategies which will ensure him of at least a position of equality with his employees' negotiating agency.

Strategies

Although many of the specifics concerning how a chief of police should deal with a police union will be situationally determined, he can use several specific techniques to increase his effectiveness.

Policy Development

Although policy development was mentioned previously as an administrator's responsibility, it is important enough to merit reemphasizing. Police administrators who have not previously encountered labor problems seldom recognize that relationships between the legislature, themselves, and their employees' union should be defined by policies acceptable to all parties. Only by doing this will the chief know how far the city council will permit him to go in making agreements, the expectations of union leaders, and the role the city administration will play in negotiations.

Formal written policies, which clearly state agreed-upon relationships, will often prevent delays during times of conflict. Periods of trust and respect facilitate agreement on policies and procedures. During such climate, objective evaluations and considered judgments can be made. Once these policies are agreed upon and recorded, they can be used to settle disputes and educate the people involved at later dates. For example, legislators, union officials, or administrators may change. New administrators need information about the existing relationships, new legislators may not understand their role in relation to the union, or new union officials may need to know what commitments previous officials made. If policies and procedures are defined before these changes, misunderstanding and tensions may be avoided.

Staff Development

The job of a chief of police is a complex and time-consuming endeavor. In most cases, while he needs to be extremely close to the negotiation process, he will not have the time or the inclination to be personally involved at the negotiation table. Therefore, with the assistance of his superior he should develop a team of knowledgeable, sophisticated aides who will be able to carry out this responsibility for him. This team should be appointed long before negotiations are to start and should be given adequate support and training to develop their knowledge and skill in the area of collective bargaining.

The team should consist of a chief negotiator and three or four others, including representatives of the city and police department personnel sections, the business office, and the middle managers of the police department. They should have sufficient time and support for research, particularly during the periods of contract negotiation.

Representatives of middle management and the business office are particularly important to a negotiation team. Middle managers will be expected to enforce any contract made; therefore, they will be able to provide particular insight about the supervisory problems that may be created by agreeing to an unwise contract provision. A city business representative is needed to assist with financial problems. Such a person is particularly important to early negotiations with police unions, since the heavy emphasis will undoubtedly be on economic matters.

The chief negotiator should be trained to serve as spokesman for the team during negotiations. Other team members should provide support in their areas of expertise. All members should be given as much training, experience, and information in the area of negotiations as the department can support. Information can be obtained through training programs, university courses, sessions with other negotiators, and consultation with labor lawyers.

A properly balanced and well-prepared negotiation staff is an essential negotiation tool for a police administrator. It improves his ability to maintain effective relationships with the union, his superiors, and the city council.

Establish Information System

It is said that a good military commander is one who knows his opponent. Although to characterize the police administrator-union relationship as strictly an adversary situation similar to war certainly would be wrong, in some ways this portrayal is an appropriate one for the police chief. An administrator needs accurate information about the union and his superiors if he is to be adequately prepared to win when dealing with a police union. In addition to reading and attending conferences, a chief of police can and should establish a storage and retrieval system for information that can be used to keep him and his negotiation team up to date.

Since the information gathered should be public and readily available, it can be obtained entirely by the administrator personally, by a member of his clerical staff, or by the staff of the negotiation team. Information about police unions, negotiations, and police grievances, opinions of union officials and legislators, and information from community groups and other interested parties should be obtained and reviewed. Speeches and papers concerned with police department–union-employee relations should be reviewed. Police managers and supervisors should be expected to send information about grievances, difficulties, and attitudes to the administrator or the negotiation team for processing. Previous local contracts from other police departments should be collected. All such information should be filed and used by the administrator and his assistants to determine the current union issues, positions, and activities; the positions of various influential citizens and groups regarding the issues; the problems that may in the future become negotiable items, and so forth.

By adequately utilizing such materials, the police chief and his negotiating team will have a more accurate picture of the groups and individuals who may oppose them on various issues; therefore, they can better assess the power situation. Armed with such information they will be able to develop sound positions, avoid failures, and maintain effective relationships with the union and other publics. In other words, their negotiation ability will be improved.

Involvement for Solving Issues Quickly

The chief should be reality centered in performing his role. Too many administrators fail to recognize that both the city legislators and the union officials are political figures. They are elected, and, to maintain their positions, they must satisfy their constituents; therefore, the chief must be sensitive to their needs and wherever possible allow them to receive credit for protecting their publics. In addition, when contemplating actions that affect employees or involve change, the chief may be wise to consult with the union and the city council early in the process.

One of the most effective methods of involving the union in problem solving is through a grievance system. In the industrial grievance system model, the union representatives initially receive all job-related complaints from employees. If the lowest-level union offical cannot settle the grievance, he sends it to the union official at the next highest level. This procedure continues until the grievance is either settled or becomes an item for negotiation. This process enables the union to claim a contribution to the welfare of employees, and it assists the administration by weeding out certain kinds of employee complaints. In addition, it provides management with early warnings of employee dissatisfaction, thereby facilitating the early solution of problems before they cause damage to the department. The speedy solution of minor problems is usually easier than trying to solve major consequences of these problems. Other methods for the early detection and solution of employee problems should be devised so that union-management legislative frictions can be reduced and the collective negotiation process can be reserved for major issues. This helps to prevent having an impossibly crowded agenda during negotiations.

Approaching Negotiations

When approaching a collective bargaining situation, the chief of police and his negotiating team have an obligation to be familiar with the law and practices concerning police negotiations, bargaining, and contracts. It is inexcusable for any police administrator, who has the responsibility for enforcing the law, to be ignorant of its provisions in this important area.

Before the collective bargaining sessions begin, the chief of police should have an understanding with the city council and his supervisors concerning the extent of his authority in negotiations. If he is to maintain an effective organization, he must have sufficient authority to bargain. In the past, largely because police administrators assumed that police unions were illegitimate, the activity carried on by union and city management usually involved very little bargaining and negotiating. The chief of police and his aides seldom participated in the process, and the negotiations often consisted of the union's making demands that the city representatives claimed they could not meet because of insufficient funds.

Two outcomes of such a situation are predictable. First, the city representatives may bargain away administrative rights that will severely damage the chief's ability to manage his department. For example, one city recently negotiated a contract that required the chief to assign an equal number of men to each of three shifts on the basis of seniority. Although the chief was not involved in the negotiations that resulted in this agreement, he must now abide by it.

Second, if a city agrees with the merits of a union's demand and the dispute goes to arbitration, the arbitrator will usually award the union its demand. For example, one city was recently involved in negotiations with the union over a two-thousand-dollar pay demand. The city acknowledged that the police officers "deserve all the money they can get," but claimed that the city was not able to finance the demands. The issue went to arbitration, and the arbitrator awarded the union their salary demands.

The realistic chief will get deeply involved in the bargaining process. He will encourage his negotiating team to develop trade-offs and obtain agreement on the conditions and techniques he needs to improve his ability to manage the department. To initiate negotiations and avoid misunderstandings, the chief through his negotiating team will insist that the union present its demands in writing at the outset of the negotiations. After the union's demands are understood, the chief is in a position to respond to their demands and make counterdemands. Counteroffers should be carefully prepared and presented by the chief's negotiator. Several alternatives should be prepared so that the management negotiators will have a variety of items with which to bargain. It may be unwise, however, for management to offer benefits that the police officers have not requested because the union may then demand additional benefits it might never have otherwise sought. The temptation to offer a wide variety of benefits that the union has not requested, or to make unnecessarily generous counteroffers, should be carefully evaluated for their potential impact. Generally such temptations should be resisted.

Negotiations

In the actual negotiation sessions, the negotiation team should have sufficient guidelines from the city council, the city administrator, and the chief of police to enable them to negotiate. Only one person should speak for the team. Others should concentrate on providing the spokesman with sufficient information to carry out his responsibilities. This information might include salary statistics, material related to labor turnover, cost-of-living indexes, material related to previous contracts, reports about the way employees are currently performing, and so forth.

Bargaining should begin with the union proposals, not proposals made by the chief's team. The number of issues involved should be handled first, while others are held in abeyance. An active mediator and the utilization of study committees may be useful in solving impasses.

In making counteroffers the chief and his team should attempt to establish starting points that will accommodate compromise. Since unions are political organizations, management should be prepared to allow unions to win, but it is a good strategy to ensure that they do not win too easily. Therefore, some flexibility is needed to insure that hard-to-win gains can be given the union. Obviously, then, the administration team may at times negotiate for positions and issues that are really not administratively important.

To maintain flexibility an administrator (and his team representatives) must also avoid making categorical assertions concerning his or the city's position on issues. Usually there is more than one acceptable position in any situation; therefore, the chief and his team should collect facts and listen to the ideas, requests, and information from all sources before committing themselves to a position. Even when taking a stance they should attempt to avoid a position that they cannot abandon gracefully.

Both sides in collective bargaining need records of their meetings; however, literal transcriptions stifle communications and should not be made. As an alternative whenever possible, meetings should be summarized by a recorder who is acceptable to both parties. This procedure facilitates more open communication and yet provides a record of the discussions that ensures some control over future behavior. In other words, it helps prevent memory lapses and can be used to avoid misunderstandings.

Settlement

When an agreement is reached on all issues, the wise negotiators usually get a memorandum of understanding signed by both sides before leaving the meeting. This memorandum should contain the essence of all agreements made. It will serve to prevent changes of opinions and omissions from the final contract. The final master agreement should be based on the memorandum but will contain considerably more detail. It should contain the date when it becomes effective and the date it will terminate. It is also wise to include the date when new negotiations are to commence. This date should be at least three months before the time when the budget is to be accepted.

Implementation of the Contract

After the contract has been accepted, the chief administrator has the responsibility for insuring that his subordinates understand and abide by it. He should use the negotiating team members to distribute the document and explain it to other managers and supervisors. In some instances union officials may be useful in explaining the contract. Questions raised should be answered as precisely and accurately as possible.

Even after the initial introduction of the contract, assistance should be available to supervisors who do not understand its provisions. Supervisors may misinterpret the contract and thus establish a precedent that would not be in the best interest of management; avoiding such an occurrence is particularly important.

Conclusion

Police administrators have traditionally taken rigid normative stances against police unions. Their position has been strikingly similar to that taken by industrial managers during the early part of the twentieth century. Currently, however, society is accepting the legitimacy of such unions, and increasingly police administrators are finding that they have no choice but to deal with them. This means that they must adopt new philosophies and learn new techniques if they are to maintain their power and effectiveness.

In dealing with the union, the administrator must insure his employees and their union fair treatment and due process, but he must also be concerned about protecting the interests of citizens, legislators, his supervisors, and his managers. To adequately fulfill these obligations, the chief must view himself as an intermediary between these various significant groups and individuals who are concerned with the outcome of the collective bargaining process. A prerequisite to the competent fulfillment of this position is a realistic approach to collective negotiations through the use of rational techniques and strategies. The approaches recommended are designed to provide structure, information, and support for developing an effective police management-union relationship.

IMPLICATION FOR THE POLICE MANAGER

Since most positions usually entail some role conflict, what can the police manager do in the face of the inevitable?[14] If he is wise, he will be alert to the demands imposed on his subordinates and will offer them the support of not only his authority and position but also his knowledge and experience in resolving conflict. He must also review conflicting demands frequently, for they will not remain static over time. As the organization and its members adjust to changes in technology, personnel practices, and duties, recruited positions within the organization also change, and the expectations of those who impose demands will change as well. Therefore, detection of role conflict and dissatisfaction requires periodic analysis and definition of position content.

Frequent consultation with subordinates, open communication between organizational levels, joint problem-solving meetings, and management by objectives are all means to detect the existence of role conflict. Once the nature of recurring conflicts is understood, it is possible to collect information useful in resolving them. Thus the planned information system in an organization should maintain and make available information of this type.

Conflict can be prevented by providing policies to guide those who find themselves in a potential conflict situation. For example, if a police officer receives orders from multiple sources, the extent to which he experiences conflict will depend on the extent to which the demands are incompatible. If he has a policy to guide him in setting priorities for various demands—and this policy has been communicated not only to him but to those who make the demands—the possibility of conflict arising out of multiple command is significantly reduced. Conflict can also be prevented by temporal or spatial sep-

---

[14] For an excellent series of articles on role conflicts specific to the police officer, see Arthur Niederhoffer and Abraham S. Blumberg, eds., *The Ambivalent Force: Perspectives on the Police* (Waltham, Mass.: Ginn and Company, 1970).

aration. For example, a secretary working for two detectives may find herself in a crossfire of conflicting demands. This conflict can be reduced by assigning her to a secretarial pool so that she has only one supervisor and all her work is channeled through that supervisor. Another means of protecting against the potential effect of conflicting demands is to ensure freedom from reprisal: placing internal affairs inspectors outside the jurisdiction of the line departments, for example.

Finally, the police manager can hold frequent communication and review meetings with those whose positions are likely to expose them to role conflict. To this end, the manager should build his skills in problem solving. It has been shown that training in group problem solving does increase the ability of the police manager to bring about successful resolutions to the problem area and thus obtain interpersonal or intergroup collaboration.

LEARNING EXERCISE

When all is said that can be said, the resolution of conflicts depends on the police manager's skill, more so on his ability to empathize, and most of all on his "moral courage." That these qualities can be felt better than they can be defined sharply indicates the limited value of intellectualizing about them. At the same time, however, one must draw attention to these qualities. The case of "General Patton and the Sicilian Slapping Incidents" is presented in these limited terms.[15] It provides a diverse richness that different individuals may internalize in various ways. Slapping may not be the usual vehicle for resolving conflict in stress situations, for words can do the job just as well or better.

Experiential learning opportunities in the case that follows include deciding upon a strategy for dealing with General Patton, for example, after his attempt to apologize for and to explain his actions. What range of concerns should have been considered by General Eisenhower, for example, in reacting to Patton's efforts? And such strategies also imply role-playing situations in which such a hypothetical decision by General Eisenhower would have been made known to Patton and to other interested publics. Other useful role plays could be staged. One such role play, for example, would involve decisions about overall strategy, specific tactics, and an arena for General Patton's apology to the men he slapped. Or careful attention might be given to how subordinates could have helped keep (conflict avoidance) General Patton from the second slapping. For the sub-

---

[15]From the book *Deadline Delayed* by members of the Overseas Press Club. Reprinted by permission of the author.

ordinates also must learn to manage themselves in ways that make it easier for their supervisor to manage himself, them, and others.

GENERAL PATTON AND THE SICILIAN SLAPPING INCIDENTS: A CASE STUDY

Henry J. Taylor

Headquarters Seventh Army
APO #758, U.S. Army
29th August, 1943

My dear General Eisenhower:

Replying to your letter of August 17, 1943, I want to commence by thanking you for this additional illustration of your fairness and generous consideration in making the communication personal.

I am at a loss to find words with which to express my chagrin and grief at having given you, a man to whom I owe everything and for whom I would gladly lay down my life, cause for displeasure with me.

I assure you that I had no intention of being either harsh or cruel in my treatment of the two soldiers in question. My sole purpose was to try and restore in them a just appreciation of their obligation as men and soldiers.

In World War I, I had a dear friend and former schoolmate who lost his nerve in an exactly analogous manner, and who after years of mental anguish, committed suicide.

Both my friend and the medical men with whom I discussed his case assured me that had he been roundly checked at the time of his first misbehavior, he would have been restored to a normal state.

Naturally, this memory actuated me when I inaptly tried to apply the remedies suggested. After each incident I stated to officers with me that I felt I had probably saved an immortal soul . . .

Very respectfully,

(Signed) G.S. Patton, Jr.
Lieut. General, U.S. Army

General D.D. Eisenhower
Headquarters AFHQ
APO #512–U.S. Army

When General Patton gave me a copy of this letter he lay back on the bed in his field-trailer and said, "What does that sound like to you?"

"It sounds to me like only half of the story," I said.

So, first, let's see what actually happened.

Private Charles H. Kuhl (in civilian life a carpet layer from South Bend, Indiana), ASN 35536908, L Company, 26th Infantry, 1st Division was admitted to the 3rd Battalion, 26th Infantry aid station in Sicily on August 2, 1943, at 2:10 p.m.

He had been in the Army eight months and with the 1st Division about thirty days.

A diagnosis of "Exhaustion" was made at the station by Lieutenant H.L. Sanger, Medical Corps, and Kuhl was evacuated to C Company, 1st Medical Battalion, well to the rear of the fighting.

There a note was made of his medical tag stating that he had been admitted to this place three times during the Sicilian campaign.

He was evacuated to the clearing company by Captain J.D. Broom, M.C., put in "quarters" and given sodium amytal, one capsule night and morning, on the prescription of Captain N.S. Nedell, M.C.

On August 3rd the following remark appears on Kuhl's Emergency Medical Tag: "Psychoneuroses anxiety state—moderately severe. Soldier has been twice before in hospital within ten days. He can't take it at front evidently. He is repeatedly returned." (signed) Captain T.P. Covington, Medical Corps.

By this route and in this way Private Kuhl arrived in the receiving tent of the 15th Evacuation Hospital, where the blow was struck that was heard round the world.

"I came into the tent," explains General Patton, "with the commanding officer of the outfit and other medical officers.

"I spoke to the various patients, especially commending the wounded men. I just get sick inside myself when I see a fellow torn apart, and some of the wounded were in terrible, ghastly shape. Then I came to this man and asked him what was the matter."

The soldier replied, "I guess I can't take it."

"Looking at the others in the tent, so many of them badly beaten up, I simply flew off the handle."

Patton squared off in front of the soldier.

He called the man every kind of a loathsome coward and then slapped him across the face with his gloves.

The soldier fell back. Patton grabbed him by the scruff of the neck and kicked him out of the tent.

Kuhl was immediately picked up by corpsmen and taken to a ward.[16]

Returning to his headquarters Patton issued the following memorandum to Corps, Division and Separate Brigade Commanders two days later:

Headquarters Seventh Army
APO #758 U.S. Army
5 August, 1943

It has come to my attention that a very small number of soldiers are going to the hospital on the pretext that they are nervously incapable of combat.

---

[16]There Kuhl was found to have a temperature of 102.2 degrees F., gave a history of chronic diarrhea for the past month, and was shown by a blood test to have malaria.

Such men are cowards, and bring discredit on the Army and disgrace to their comrades whom they heartlessly leave to endure the danger of a battle while they themselves use the hospital as a means of escaping.

You will take measures to see that such cases are not sent to the hospital, but are dealt with in their units.

Those who are not willing to fight will be tried by Court-Martial for cowardice in the face of the enemy.

(Signed) G.S. Patton, Jr.
Lieut. General, U.S. Army
Commanding

Five days later General Patton, not a medical man, again took matters into his own hands.

He slapped another soldier.

Private Paul G. Bennett, ASN 70000001, C Battery, Field Artillery, was admitted to the 93rd Evacuation Hospital on August 10th at 2:20 p.m.

Bennett, still only twenty-one, had served four years in the Regular Army. He had an excellent record. His unit had been attached to the II Corps since March and he had never had any difficulties until four days earlier when his best friend in the outfit, fighting nearby, was wounded in action.

Bennett could not sleep that night and felt nervous. The shells going over "bothered" him. "I keep thinking they're going to land right on me," he said. The next day he became increasingly nervous about the firing and about his buddy's recovery.

A battery aid man sent him to the rear echelon, where a medical officer gave him some medicine which made him sleep. But he was still nervous, badly disturbed.

On August 10th the medical officer ordered him to the 93rd Evacuation Hospital, although Bennett begged not to be evacuated because he did not want to leave his unit.

General Patton arrived at the hospital that day.

Bennett was sitting in the receiving tent, huddled up and shivering.

Patton spoke to all the injured men. He was solicitous, kind, and inspiring. But when he and Major Charles B. Etter, the receiving officer in charge, reached Bennett and Patton asked the soldier what his trouble was, the soldier replied, "It's my nerves," and began to sob.

Patton turned on him like a tiger, screaming at him:

"What did you say?"

"It's my nerves," sobbed Bennett. "I can't take the shelling any more."

In this moment Patton lost control of himself entirely. Without any investigation of the man's case whatever, he rushed close to Bennett and shouted: "Your nerves, hell. You are just a— — —coward, you yellow b— —."

Then he slapped the soldier hard across the face.

"Shut up that— — —crying," he yelled. "I won't have these brave men here who have been shot seeing a yellow b— — sitting here crying."

Patton struck at the man again. He knocked his helmet liner off his head into the next tent. Then he turned to Major Etter and yelled, "Don't admit this yellow b— —, there's nothing the matter with him. I won't have the hospitals cluttered up with these SOB's who haven't got the guts to fight."

Patton himself began to sob. He wheeled around to Colonel Donald E. Currier, the 93rd's commanding Medical Officer. "I can't help it," he said. "It makes me break down to see brave boys and to think of a yellow b— — being babied."

But this was not all. In his blind fury, Patton turned on Bennett again. The soldier now was managing to sit at attention, although shaking all over.

"You're going back to the front lines," Patton shouted. "You may get shot and killed, but you're going to fight. If you don't, I'll stand you up against a wall and have a firing squad kill you on purpose.

"In fact," he said, reaching for his revolver, "I ought to shoot you myself, you — — — whimpering coward."

As he left the tent Patton was still yelling back at the receiving officer to "send the yellow SOB back to the front line."

Nurses and patients, attracted by the shouting and cursing, came from the adjoining tent and witnessed this disturbance.

Patton made no initial report of these affairs to his superior, General Eisenhower, who was then in his Headquarters at Tunis on the North African mainland.

"I felt ashamed of myself," General Patton told me, "and I hoped the whole thing would die out."

But an official report by Lieut. Colonel Perrin H. Long, Medical Corps consulting physician, was already on the way to Allied Headquarters through Medical Corps channels.

"The deleterious effects of such incidents upon the well-being of patients, upon the professional morale of hospital staffs and upon the relationship of patient to physician are incalculable," reported Lieut. Colonel Long. "It is imperative that immediate steps be taken to prevent a recurrence of such incidents."

General Eisenhower received this report on August 17th. His communication to General Patton was sent off that night.

In his message, which Patton showed me, the Commanding General told Patton of the allegations, told him that he could not describe in official language his revulsion, informed Patton that he must make, on his own initiative, proper amends to the soldiers involved and take steps to make amends before his whole army.

"This all happened practically on the eve of a new attack in which I had been written in for a large part of the plans, already issued," Patton explained, "and General Eisenhower stated therefore that he would temporarily reserve decision regarding my relief of command until he could determine the effect of my own corrective measures.

Then Eisenhower did four things: He sent Maj. General John Porter Lucas to Sicily to make an investigation of charges, sent the Theatre's Inspector General to investigate command relationships in my entire army, sent another general officer to interview the two soldiers and made a trip to Sicily himself to determine how much resentment against me existed in the army.

"Eisenhower's problem was whether what I had done was sufficiently damaging to compel my relief on the· eve of attack, thus losing what he described as my unquestioned military value, or whether less drastic measures would be appropriate.

"I went to see both Kuhl and Bennett," Patton continued, "explained my motives and apologized for my actions.

"In each case I stated that I should like to shake hands with them; that I was sincerely sorry. In each case they accepted my offer.

"I called together all the doctors, nurses and enlisted men who were present when the slappings occurred. I apologized and expressed my humiliation over my impulsive actions.

"Finally, I addressed all divisions of the 7th Army in a series of assemblies, the last of which was an address before the 3rd Division on August 30th.

"I praised them as soldiers, expressed regret for any occasions when I harshly treated individuals and offered my apologies as their Commanding General for doing anything unfair or un-American.

"Beyond that, except to leave the Army and get out of the war, I do not know what I could have done."

11

MANAGEMENT AND MACHINES:
The Capabilities
and Challenges of the Computer

> One of the most obvious facts about our present situation
> is the official commitment to using technology in solving almost
> all of our currently recognized social and political problems.
> This seems apparent whether the problems have to do with
> the present or in our feeble attempts to invent the future. There
> is almost no end of topics enjoying the notice of technology as
> problem solver. . . .[1]

Today police management is confronted by the explosive development of police and criminal justice information systems with resultant prolific and complex problems; but these systems promise an era of unparalleled progress in management efficiency, in operational effectiveness, in overall organizational control, and—as an end result—in improved police services to the community.

To survive and thrive in this complicated society, police management must master and make full use of the new information technology. By *full* use we mean the marriage of computer systems to communications systems—and all the various techniques of information control, storage, retrieval, and transmission which are evolving from that wedlock. Even now this relatively young science

---

[1]Todd R. LaPorte, "The Context of Technology Assessment: A Changing Perspective for Public Organization," *Public Administration Review*, 31 (January-February, 1971), 64.

is having a profound effect on our life and times, due to the development and use of these systems in police departments, urban government, and criminal justice agencies.

This chapter is not designed to provide the reader with specific and technical information or the electronic attributes of the computer or, as it is also referred to, electronic data processing (EDP). To put it another way, your reading of the following pages will not make you an expert on the hardware, software, and peopleware that constitute an EDP system. As a police manager you should be more concerned with the promises and perspectives that are contained within the power of the computer.

It is to this purpose that we now turn. The following discussion will include (1) the critical need for computer-based police information systems, (2) a brief consideration of the involved technology, (3) a quick look at the state-of-the-art, (4) design approach—vertical or horizontal dimensions, (5) management information systems, (6) the changing of obstacles into opportunities, and (7) the learning exercise.

THE CRITICAL NEED FOR COMPUTER-BASED POLICE INFORMATION SYSTEMS

When analyzing the developments of the last few years in local law enforcement *information processing,* we can quickly observe the growing need for assistance from computer-based systems. Acquisition and use of large-scale digital computer and communications systems to cope with these rapidly growing information requirements have been made by some local and state jurisdictions (see the appropriate figure). By examining existing and potential applications of these new information-processing techniques and equipment, we can see that the police agencies have considered two major categories of information processing pertinent to local law enforcement activities.

The first category is termed real-time, on-line information processing and retrieval. This approach is important for providing want, record, identification, or vehicle data to field police officers on a fast basis in order to support them in their operational environment. *Real-time, on-line* means basically that the information system is capable of processing individual inquiries simultaneously with field operational needs. *The second category is termed batch information processing and retrieval.* Batch processing signifies that the processing of information does not occur on demand. Rather, all informational requests or needs are processed within some reasonable time convenient to both the computer facility's capability and the needs of the police. This type of processing includes statistical analysis of "called-for services" for management review and decision making, the retrieval of specific documents or information for the purpose of investigation, analysis of crime patterns, and other processes of analysis deemed important to police management or investigation. The criticality of computer-based information systems being applied to the processing of police information requirements is emphasized as follows:

> Information is the life blood of any law enforcement agency. Name and address files, fingerprint records, location indicators, and intelligence and investigation reports are all examples of data to be found in the files of most local police agencies. Added to these, and of equal use, are the files of prosecutors, probation and parole agencies, and state and federal investigative agencies. In other words, we find that the informational needs of the police department are both interrelated and dependent upon other systems within the administration of criminal justice.[2]

COMPUTERS: A GENERAL-PURPOSE TOOL

The first general-purpose automatic digital computer was developed in 1944, and the years from 1944 to 1951 were years of research and development by universities, government, and business. In 1951 the computer age was born with the delivery of the first large-scale computer to the U.S. Bureau of the Census, and it marked the beginning of the application of mass production techniques to the building of computers. From the delivery of this one computer in 1951, the industry moved to the production of 10,000 to 12,000 computers in 1962. This amounted to about $1.3 billion in sales in 1962. It is estimated that during the 1970s annual shipments will reach the $7 billion to $10 billion range.

Basically, the computer is a general-purpose tool that will process any information that can be coded for it. When the computer is first assembled, it is useless until one ingredient is added to it—the computer program or, as it is called to distinguish it from the computer hardware itself, the computer software. The computer can perform only about fifty to one hundred unique kinds of operations; its great advantage is the speed with which it performs these operations. In addition, a program can link together many operations in a series so that the computer will perform a complex set of computations with great speed. Software development is vitally important to computer users. Investment costs in the development of software have now surpassed the total cost of computer hardware itself.

[2]Paul M. Whisenand and Tug T. Tamaru, *Automated Police Information Systems* (New York: John Wiley & Sons, Inc., 1970), 1.

All EDP systems, regardless of size, type, or basic use, have common fundamental concepts and operational principles. In our discussion of these concepts and principles as background information on computers, the subject matter has been generalized and therefore does not refer to any particular machine. Specific operating systems are mentioned only to illustrate a general principle, not to compare one system with another. Although a variety of material is covered, technical detail is intentionally kept to a minimum.

Five phases, as seen in Figure 11-1, comprise all information processing systems: input, output, storage, communications, and processing. A subphase, inquiry, is a combination of all five major phases interacting in order to generate a response to a given query. When associating each of the phases to a computer-based information system, we encounter complex and highly specialized equipment for handling information. Consequently, all such equipment can be similarly divided into five types of functional units. All devices and units serve to increase the capability of each phase.

Input

The units that function as input devices often double as output equipment, for their basic structures are usually the same. Since the objectives of these phases differ, however, as does the hardware, they will be handled as separate functions within the system. The input phase and equipment are planned to collect and insert data into the system. The punched card is a well-known input medium, primarily because it is an inexpensive and a multifaceted means of storing information. Considering the tremendously fast speed at which a computer can operate, however, card input is a slow and costly means for placing data into the system. Therefore few computers use direct card input; most transform the information from cards to paper tape or magnetic tape, since these two mediums can be processed at higher speeds. Paper tape has two benefits that a punched-card system does not have: First, it is a faster input medium; second, the coding can be done during the regular typing process. Related to the punched cards and punched paper tape equipment, a magnetic tape unit can operate as both an input and an output device. Magnetic tapes also store data for future use. A magnetic read-write head reads or records the information. The principal advantages of magnetic tape input are the speed with which data can be placed into the computer and the large quantities of information that can be stored on tape; furthermore, it is much easier to manipulate this material and to update it. Unlike cards and paper tape, magnetic tape is reusable.

Magnetic ink and optical scanning devices are more recent

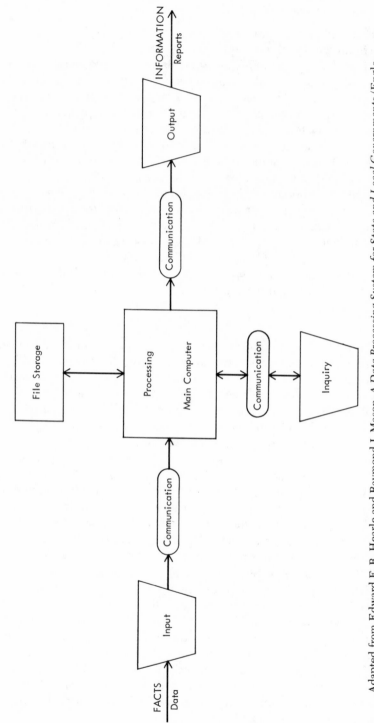

Adapted from Edward F. R. Hearle and Raymond J. Mason, *A Data Processing System for State and Local Governments* (Englewood Cliffs, N.J.: Prentice-Hall, Inc., 1963), p. 4.

FIGURE 11–1. **A Data Processing System**

developments. Both innovations produced a great advance in data processing technology, for they involve writing that is understandable to both men and machines. Source documents containing print in magnetic ink may be entered directly into the system, for example, bills and checks on which information has been preprinted in magnetic ink. Data may also be read directly into a computer by optical character (optical scanning) recognition equipment which can interpret printed copy and handwritten numbers. Today optical reading devices provide the greatest potential for better input operations. Optical scanning devices, now in operation in some companies, will eventually enable computers to "gobble up" all kinds of information visually. The machines will then be able to memorize and store whole libraries, in effect producing matchless classical and scientific records by capturing all the knowledge to which man is heir.

Output

The output of the processing that has taken place within the computer may be recorded on magnetic tape, cathode-ray tube (CRT), punched paper tape, or punched cards; or it may be recorded by direct connection between the processing unit and a printing device. The most prevalent means of receiving data from the system is by printed output. Printed data output equipment is continually being improved for greater speed and flexibility. Considerable interest has been aroused by CRT or visual display output devices.

At this point it seems logical to discuss the inquiry subphase, which is a combination of input and output devices. Inquiry is a way of requesting and receiving required information from a central processing unit (CPU) or storage location. The already described input-output (I/O) devices are methods for generating an inquiry. Although at this time most input is by keyboard and most output is mechanically printed, optical scanning and CRTs can handle inquiries and are expected to be the preferred equipment in the future.

Storage

A storage device might be described as an electronic filing cabinet, completely indexed and capable of being instantaneously accessible to the computer. Information is read into storage by an input device and is then available for internal processing. Locations, positions, or sections of storage are numbered so that the stored data can be readily found by the computer as needed. The computer may rearrange data in storage by sorting or aggregating different types of information received from a number of input units. The computer may also take the original data from storage, generate new information, and return the result to storage. The size or capacity of the storage device determines the amount of information that can be held within the system at any one time. In some computer-based systems, storage capacity is accessed in millions of digits or characters, providing space to retain entire files of information. In other systems storage capacity is smaller, and data are held only while being processed. Therefore, the capacity and the design of the storage device determine the method in which data are processed by the system.

Communications

Improvements in communications equipment are extraordinary. In fact, one of the most significant advances in the computer era has been the introduction of data communications equipment. The need for high-speed data transmission over land lines or microwave facilities is threefold. First, quite obviously it is imperative that data move from one point in the system to another. Second, and of equal if not greater significance, a modern communications system permits the data processing equipment to operate in a real-time, on-line mode rather than in a batch-processing mode. A real-time system is a combined data processing and communications system which involves the direct transmission of transaction data between remote locations and a central computer. Such a system allows data to be processed while the immediate need is being met or the transaction is actually taking place. Real-time, on-line processing is the underpinning for the California Highway Patrol's (CHP) statewide law enforcement Auto Statis system and the regional want and warrant Police Information Network (PIN). The Automated Want and Warrant System (AWWS) of the county of Los Angeles is an example of a real-time, on-line data communications system using rapid access mass storage devices, CRT input/output devices, and special communications-oriented computers. The FBI's National Crime Information Center (NCIC) is also predicated on a real-time, on-line processing capability. Real-time, on-line information systems may therefore be considered as communications-oriented, computer-based data processing systems.

The sharing of data within an information system is highly dependent on an adequate system for creating files, updating them, and retrieving data—in other words, an automatic and extremely reliable communications network. The concept of data sharing, with many agencies contributing on a continuous basis to a single (integrated) computer-oriented file of information, has been successfully demonstrated. The statewide Criminal Justice Information System (CJIS) for California's Department of Justice and the New York State Identification and Intelligence System (NYSIS) are based on the recognized value and viability of the sharing of data among police agencies.

Central Processing Unit

To explain the central processing unit (CPU) in the simplest terms possible, it is an electronic machine that can do arithmetic and retrieve information with unbelievable speed. The CPU is the controlling center of the computer processing system and can be divided into three parts: (*a*) the arithmetic-logic unit, (*b*) the control section, and (*c*) the central storage (memory) section.

The arithmetic-logic unit performs such operations as addition, subtraction, multiplication, division, shifting, transferring, comparing, and storing. It also has logical ability; it can examine various conditions presented during processing and take the action called for by the evaluation. The control section directs and coordinates the entire computer system as a single multipurpose machine. Its functions include controlling the input-output units, the arithmetic-logic operation of the central processing unit, and moving data to and from storage within given, predetermined limits. The control section directs the system according to the plan originated by its *human* (that's us) designers. The central storage section stores the computer programs that operate upon the data placed into storage, as well as any tables necessary in the processing.

STATE-OF-THE-ART: A FOLLOW ON

The purpose of the survey-research information reported below is to further convince you of the pervasiveness and intensity of EDP developments in criminal justice agencies, and more specifically in police departments. Remember that criminal justice *per se* is comprised of a group of organizations which *should* function as a system (one critic recently referred to the criminal justice system as a "system out of service").[3] As you will recall, the component organizations consist of police, prosecution, probation, courts, corrections, and parole. The creation of a single automated information system to serve all these users is a tremendous challenge to the bravest of system designers and builders. Operational and value

---

[3]Gary V. Dublin, "A System Out of Service" (1970), a paper which will form one of the chapters in Mr. Dublin's forthcoming text entitled, *New Frontiers in Criminal Justice Research.*

conflicts are but a few (the technological problems rate low in a list of "barriers to overcome") of the problems encountered when interrelating their various information processing requirements and data base needs. For our purposes, we can view an automated criminal justice information system (CJIS) or automated police information system as consisting of people, computer equipment and related programs, a dynamic data base, and institutional procedures interacting in a prescribed systems pattern. Logically, it is designed to collect, store, update, and facilitate the automated use of data on a continuing basis. Such data and their processing and analysis are related to both the internal affairs of the criminal justice system or component organizations and the external environment. The multifaceted purposes of such an information system are (1) to meet operational requirements, (2) to provide various summarizing or analytical techniques relevant to the definition of community problems, (3) to assist in the search for program goals, (4) to generate cybernetic data flows for evaluation and control, and (5) to permit the exchange of information among governmental units (other criminal justice agencies and noncriminal justice government organizations) and with the public.

A sampling of earlier research findings indicates the following: (1) Of the police departments responding to the questionnaire (252 of 592—43 percent), a group of 110, or 44 percent, reported that they were using automatic data processing. (2) By 1971 this group was expected to increase to 159, or 63 percent of the departments responding. (3) A vast majority of the ADP equipment being used were computer systems (84 percent) as compared with electronic accounting machines (16 percent). (4) Automatic data processing, while not new to law enforcement (21 percent of the departments with ADP were using it before 1960), was relatively new to most municipal police departments, as 60 percent of the responding agencies with ADP did not start using it until 1964. (5) Within three years some 46 percent (or 51 of the 110 respondees using ADP) expected to upgrade their information system with more sophisticated equipment. Surprisingly, the above findings and predictions now appear to be underestimated. In other words, a lot of ground has been covered by criminal justice organizations in developing CJISs within a fairly short time period.[4]

Let us look at Table 11-1, which depicts a number of automated criminal justice information and communications systems either

---

[4]Paul M. Whisenand and John D. Hodges, Jr., "Automated Police Information Systems: A Survey," *Datamation*, 15 (May 1969), 91–96.

shared by or within the state of California.[5] Significantly, this listing is incomplete and thus only suggests what exists in total. The entire inventory (thirty-five information systems) is given in the pamphlet entitled *Automated Criminal Justice Information and Communications Systems.*[6] The question may be asked, Why Table 11-1? The answer, simply put, is, To provide an awareness of the magnitude, complexity, and types of design relative to CJIS configurations. Not included, however, is an implication or an inference concerning future efforts within California. Consequently, let us now focus our attention on Figures 11-2—11-8 to comprehend what the future may hold for those in the business of designing, developing, and operating CJISs.[7] The data reported in these seven figures were acquired through questionnaires sent to 371 police departments (185 responses), 167 sheriff agencies (37 responses), 48 state police units (27 responses), 48 state correction agencies (30 responses), 50 attorney general units (19 responses), and 7 federal agencies (4 responses). While not covering the full spectrum of a criminal justice system (regretfully, the survey did not encompass local prosecutors, probation departments, parole units, and the courts), it did succeed in eliciting a wealth of information about the largest number—in frequency, scope, and size—of organizations in the criminal justice system.

Figure 11-2 shows that the response rates for the agencies polled were Police—33 percent, Sheriff—18 percent, State Police—36 percent, State Corrections—58 percent, Attorney General—28 percent, and Federal Agency—37 percent. Of those responding, 60 percent were currently using some form of ADP, while 40 percent were not. Furthermore, Figure 11-3 shows that of the 40 percent not currently using ADP, 39.2 percent planned to implement such a program by 1972; however, 60.8 percent neither had plans nor a definite time set for implementation. Figure 11-4 reports that at the time the initial survey was administered, the percentage of the type of ADP equipment used by all agencies combined was as follows: Electronic Data Processing (EDP), 35 percent; Electronic Accounting Machines (EAM), 6.5 percent; and both EDP and EAM,

---

[5] Most of this is taken from Paul M. Whisenand, "Criminal Justice Information Systems: Research Results and Current Perspectives," *Datamation,* 17 (June 1971), 30–36.

[6] *Automated Criminal Justice Information and Communications Systems* (Sacramento, Calif.: California Crime Technological Research Foundation, 1970).

[7] An excellent conceptual and functional examination of related information systems can be found in Edward F. R. Hearle, "Information Systems in State and Local Governments," *Annual Review of Information Science and Technology* (Chicago: Encyclopedia Britannica, Inc., 1970), V, 325–49.

TABLE 11–1. Automated Criminal Justice Information and Communications Systems: A Partial Listing of California Related Systems

Jurisdiction	Project System Name (CCCJ No.)	Funded By	Agencies Involved	Type of Files Information	General Description
Multi-State System					
Law Enforcement Assistance Administration	System for Electronic Analysis and Retrieval of Criminal Histories (SEARCH)	LEAA	Arizona California Connecticut Florida Maryland Michigan Minnesota New York Texas Washington	1. Criminal History 2. Statistics	Development of a prototype criminal Justice information system which will: 1. Demonstrate the feasibility of an on-line inter-state exchange of offender history files 2. Design and demonstrate a computerized, transaction-based statistics system
National	Law Enforcement Teletype System (LETS)		All states except Hawaii and Alaska	Sending Receiving and Switching of All Points Bulletins, Area Bulletins, Directed (point to point) messages	A national law enforcement communications system enabling the exchange of information regarding criminal activities between states and between states and federal agencies. California is included in one of eight national regions, the Western Area Network Teletype System (WANTS). See below.
Statewide Systems					
Department of Justice	California Law Enforcement Telecommunications System (CLETS)	State	All City, County and State Law Enforcement Agencies	Sending Receiving and Switching of All Points Bulletins, Area Bulletins, Directed (point to point) messages	CLETS is a modern telecommunications system which replaces the current, outmoded State teletype system installed in 1931. Computers are used as message switchers with four time-sharing computers (two in Sacramento and two in Los Angeles). In each switching center, one computer is constantly "On-line" with the second computer serving as a backup in case of failure. The second computer continually monitors the status of the switching computer, keeps message logs, prepares message traffic statistical reports, and permits immediate recovery in event of failure of the primary computer.

Duration of Project (Date Op)	Est. Yearly Operational Budget (Developmental Cost)	Similarities to Other Systems Project	Interfaces With	How Accessed
(18 months) June 30, 1969 to Dec. 31, 1970	2.520 K (Developmental)	No similar system exists	Ten Project States (7 states on-line computer to computer interface) In California, system will probably interface with CJIS	In California probably on-line through CLETS Teletype
(1956)	1.953 K		NCIC (FBT) SEARCH CJIS Auto-statis AMIS	Teletype

TABLE 11–1. (Continued)

Jurisdic-tion	Project System Name (CCCJ No.)	Funded By	Agencies Involved	Type of Files Information	General Description
Department of Justice	Criminal Justice Information System (CJIS)	State	All State Regional and Local Criminal Justice Agencies	1. Criminal History Record 2. Wanted Persons File 3. Juvenile Records 4. Other Files Firearms, Stolen Property, and Drug Control	CJIS will develop a fully integrated, statewide criminal information system based on user need. The various files can be accessed by remote terminals through the California Law Enforcement Teletype System (CLETS).
Department of Motor Vehicles	Automated Management Information System (AMIS)	State	Police, Courts & Other State Agencies	1. Motor Vehicle Registration 2. Driver License	The Automated Management Information System is one of the largest Inquiry and people Identification Systems ever developed. The System creates, maintains and revises more than 30 million randomly accessed records.
Highway Patrol	Automatic Statewide Auto-theft Inquiry System (Auto-Statis)	State	Police	Stolen Vehicle Information	Automated system which provides for the centralized storage of information on vehicles stolen or wanted anywhere in California, neighboring states and thefts handled by the National Auto Theft Bureau. Also provides message switching involving Dept. of Justice and National Crime Information Center.
Multi-County Systems					
Alameda County	Police Information Network (PIN)	Alameda County	Alameda County Sheriff and all Bay Area Law Enforcement Agencies	Want Warrant files	PIN provides for input, retrieval, update and deletion of warrant data, coupled with message switching. On-line inquiry can be made by all 93 law enforcement agencies in the Bay Area. Files are

Duration of Project (Date Op)	Est. Yearly Operational Budget (Developmental Cost)	Similarities to Other Systems Project	Interfaces With	How Accessed
(July 1972)	1.600 K (Developmental)	CJIS includes some elements common to most state and local Criminal Justice Information Systems	NCIC AMIS Auto-Statis	On-line random access through California Law Enforcement Telecommunication System (CLETS)
(1971)	Not Available	AMIS may have initally duplicated some county and metropolitan information system files. It is believed that local agencies no longer maintain similar files in that all large agencies have on-line access to the files.	NCIC Auto-Statis CJIS	CLETS
(April, 1965)	1.035 K	Central repository for all auto-theft information may duplicate or be similar to some local files.	NCIC AMIS	On-line access through CLETS
(1964)	350 K	Similar to the Riverside County Rapid Warrant System, Los Angeles Police Department, San Diego and Ventura County Want Warrant Systems.	NCIC CJIS Auto-Statis AMIS	On-line from remote terminals

TABLE 11–1. (Continued)

Jurisdiction	Project System Name (CCCJ No.)	Funded By	Agencies Involved	Type of Files Information	General Description
					keyed to license number and name. PIN also disseminates stolen and wanted vehicle information through a tie-in with Auto-Statis.
County Systems					
Los Angeles Sheriff's Office	Optimum Records Automation for Courts and Law Enforcement (ORACLE)	Los Angeles County	Sheriff's Office. Eventually will involve entire county justice system and City Police Dept.	Mass Storage & Retrieval of Documents, Photos, Graphics, Support Documentation, Arrestee Identification Dossier System Mugs, Rap Sheets, Investigator Reviews, Jail Documents, Master Fingerprint File	A "videofile information system" which can be accessed from remote video-terminals and provides hard copy or visual displays of any file. A digital computer locates and searches file of video tapes and transmits materials to holding equipment for viewing.
County Systems					
Los Angeles Sheriff's Office	Regional Justice Information System (RJIS) (068)	Los Angeles County & CCCJ	Entire county Justice System, will eventually include all Police Departments in county	Will include 3 main county criminal justice information systems: ORACLE Justice Data System, Automated Want Warrant (see Los Angeles Police Dept.)	A Systems Analysis of the information needs of Los Angeles County which will establish a county-wide Automated, Integrated Justice Information System including Want Warrants, case following and document storage. Files will be established by an original entry into the System and will be accessed by all local Law Enforcement Agencies.
Los Angeles Sheriff's Office	Justice Data System	Los Angeles County	Sheriff's office will eventually include all County Justice and Law Enforcement Agencies	Case Following System 1. Arrest-Booking Jail Information 2. Management Info. 3. Statistics 4. Court	County-wide, automated, integrated Justice Information System with an original case entry establishing a file. The case following system will eventually include input from all Law Enforcement Agencies in Los Angeles County.

314

Duration of Project (Date Op)	Est. Yearly Operational Budget (Developmental Cost)	Similarities to Other Systems Project	Interfaces With	How Accessed
Start March 1969 Operational Phase I April 1971 Phase II Sept. 1971 Totally Operational 1972	960 K Total cost approximately 10 million (Developmental)	Unique to California. Two Federal Agencies and the Royal Canadian Mounted Police have ordered similar Systems.		On-line from remote terminals
(18 Months) Start May 1970	727 K (Developmental)	The Regional Justice Information System, when completed, will probably have some similarity to other Criminal Justice Information Systems such as the proposed Santa Clara County System (CJIC), San Francisco Law Enforcement Information System, the Long Beach Public Safety System and CJIS.	NCIC Auto-Statis AMIS	On-line from remote terminals and teletype
Start July 1970	2000 K (Operational and Developmental)	Similar to CJIS, the Santa Clara CJIC Project and other case following systems.	Auto-Statis CJIS NCIC SEARCH	On-line from remote terminals and teletype

TABLE 11–1. (Continued)

Jurisdic-tion	Project System Name (CCCJ No.)	Funded By	Agencies Involved	Type of Files Information	General Description
			and Police Depts.	Calendars 5. Traffic Offender 6. Misc. Files	
Orange County	Municipal Court Automated Procedures Project (0122)	CCCJ (pending)	Police Courts	1. Traffic Citations 2. Failure to Appear Warrants	Project would computerize traffic citations processing for all 5 Orange Co. judicial districts. Would also provide for "on-line" access to citation and warrant data.
Santa Clara County	Criminal Justice Information Control (CJIC) (0151)	CCCJ (Pending)	Police Probation Courts District Attorney Public Defender	Person-case Information at all stages of county criminal justice system	CJIC is an integrated regional criminal justice information system concentrating mainly on case following information and interagency operation. All criminal Justice Agencies in the County, are actively participating in the design and development of the system.

County Systems

County of San Diego	Prior Traffic Violations	San Diego County	Municipal Court and All Police Departments and Sheriff's Office	Traffic Warrants and Traffic Violations	All traffic citations are processed for all Municipal courts in the city. System provides for accounting for citations and the automatic creation of warrants for delinquent citations.

Multi-City

Consortium of the following cities in the San Gabriel Valley: Arcadia Claremont Covina	San Gabriel Valley Municipal Data System	Participating cities and Carnegie Foundation	All City Police Departments in Consortium	Police Statistics	13 Cities in the San Gabriel Valley have joined together to establish a cooperative, interurban computerized information system. The system is primarily a management information system encompassing general accounting, utility accounting,

Duration of Project (Date Op)	Est. Yearly Operational Budget (Developmental Cost)	Similarities to Other Systems Project	Interfaces With	How Accessed
24 Months	276 K (Developmental)	Some conceptual similarities to CJIS, PIN and other systems. Close similarity to citation component in Santa Clara and probably similar to other county systems for processing traffic citations.		On-line from remote terminals
48 Months	1.331 K (Developmental)	Similar to CJIS, SEARCH, NCIC in format for personal descripters. Has been revised to make project compatible to 079—San Francisco, and 150—Walnut Creek. Portions of System will be similar to Los Angeles County Regis, Orange County Juvenile index—122 Orange County and Municipal Court Procedures Project and the San Diego County System, if made operational.	SEARCH NCIC CJIS CDIP Auto-Statis PIN AMIS	On-line from remote terminals
Start 1967	400 K 150 K (Developmental)	Probably similar to the Orange County Automated procedures project and other automated citation processing systems		Batch Input
27 months Start Oct. 1968 (Operational by January 1971)	558 K (Developmental)	Cooperative effort for a comprehensive system is unique although similar cooperation is involved in the Bay area PIN system. Application of computerized, statistical reports to predict required police deployment is similar to LEMERAS		On-line from remote terminals

TABLE 11–1.   (Continued)

Jurisdiction	Project System Name (CCCJ No.)	Funded By	Agencies Involved	Type of Files Information	General Description
Glendora La Puente Monrovia Montclair Monterey Park Ontario Pomona San Dimas Sierra Madre Westminster					police statistics and accounting. Police statistics are primarily concerned with statistical reports and deployment information, based on the incidents occurring during a previous day. An effort was made to avoid duplication of state and Regional systems.
City Systems					
Long Beach	Public Safety System	HUD and 8 Federal Agencies (Dept. of Justice) City of Long Beach	Police Fire Civil Defense	To be determined but will probably contain traffic resource allocation, offense, arrest, want warrant, Geo-Coding	Prototypical operational data base oriented management information system to serve all public safety functions in a model municipality. Design must insure a high degree of transferability.
San Francisco Police Department	San Francisco Law Enforcement Information System (079)	City CCCJ	Police	1. Warrants and Retrieval of Crime Report Information 2. Accident Data 3. Case History 4. Management Data	Project would develop a 4 module police information system consisting of Field Support, Management Analysis, Personnel Management and Command and Control Modules. Project has been revised to make it compatible with Regional Planning. Project is currently being reviewed by proponent and may be revised.
Los Angeles Police Department	Traffic Information System (TIS)	City and Department of Transportation	City Traffic and Police	1. Accident Reports 2. Traffic Volume flow 3. Citations 4. Traffic arrests	Traffic Information System (TIS) involves conversion of an existing electric accounting statistical system to the City's computer system and a detailed analysis of the Police Department's information needs in the area of traffic enforcement.

Duration of Project (Date Op)	Est. Yearly Operational Budget (Developmental Cost)	Similarities to Other Systems Project	Interfaces With	How Accessed
24 months start April 1970	1,000.000 (Developmental)	Transferability to other centers is unique: will probably contain some files similar to Los Angeles Regional Justice Information System, Santa Clara County Criminal Justice Information Control. San Francisco Law Enforcement Information System.	AMIS NCIC Auto-Statis	On-line with remote terminals
	973 K (Developmental)	Originally duplicated the Santa Clara Co. CJIC but was revised at the request of the Region to make the systems compatible and to avoid duplication. Will have similar components with the Los Angeles Co. RJIS & other systems in Los Angeles Co.; also to the San Diego Co. Information System Project.	Auto-Statis PIN NCIC CJIS AMIS	On-line from remote terminals
Start Sept. 1968 Totally Operational May 1971	198 K	Some similarity to the San Diego traffic Enforcement System and the Management Analysis module of the San Francisco Law Enforcement Information System.		Batch Processing

TABLE 11-1. (Continued)

Jurisdiction	Project System Name (CCCJ No.)	Funded By	Agencies Involved	Type of Files Information	General Description
City Systems					The System will provide comprehensive traffic accident information which will enable the Department to deploy officers at high accident locations at the specific times the hazards are anticipated to occur and will also forecast the probable accident reduction resulting from such enforcement activity and indicate potentially hazardous locations based upon predicted traffic volume and building construction increases.
Los Angeles Police Department	Automated Want Warrant System (AWW)	City of Los Angeles (to County Jan. 1, 1972)	Los Angeles Police Department Los Angeles Sheriff's Office and All County and City Law Enforcement Agencies	Want Warrant File	Automated Want Warrant System is a county-wide system providing for input retrieval and update of legal warrant and booking abstracts. Warrant abstracts can be obtained via on-line remote terminals and can be used as legal basis for arrest and booking. Warrants are automatically cleared when served. AWW will be transferred to the county on January 1, 1972.
Los Angeles Police Department	Law Enforcement Computerized System for Tactical Information Correlation and Retrieval (PATRIC-003)	CCCJ and City	Police	1. Crime Report 2. M.O. File 3. Filed Interview Data 4. Pawned Articles Data	A computerized information system which will be used to provide assistance in crime investigation and patrol deployment. Will include 1. retrieval of information from crime reports 2. Automatic correlation of crime data to indicate patterns of criminal behavior 3. Recognition of crime patterns for deployment of patrol 4. Provide managers with decision making support thru frequent counts of events 5.

Duration of Project (Date Op)	Est. Yearly Operational Budget (Developmental Cost)	Similarities to Other Systems Project	Interfaces With	How Accessed
(September 1969)	825 K	Similar to Police Information Network and Riverside, San Diego and Ventura County Warrant Systems.	NCIC Auto-Statis	On-line from remote terminals
12 months (pending)	714 K (Developmental)	Similar to the Management Analysis Module in the San Francisco Law Enforcement Information System and the San Diego Crime Case System.	Will Interface with the automated Want Warrant and Automated Field Interview Systems.	On-line access from remote terminals

TABLE 11–1. (Continued)

Jurisdic-tion	Project System Name (CCJ No.)	Funded By	Agencies Involved	Type of Files Information	General Description
County Systems					Provide appropriate training for personnel
San Diego Police Department	Criminal Records and Wanted Persons (0270)	City and CCCJ (Pending)	Police	1. Criminal Histories 2. Want Warrants 3. Statistical reports 4. Fingerprint Classification File	Files would include criminal records and wants from any source which would be incorporated into the San Diego Municipal Command and Control System.
San Diego Police Department	Wanted Property	City of San Diego	Police	Stolen and Pawned Property	System provides information on stolen and pawned property by serial number or case number and name of person pawning property or reporting it stolen. Includes all stolen property reported to the San Diego Police Department and Stolen property in Southern Calif. reported via teletype.
Walnut Creek Police Department	Consolidation and Centralization of records (0150)	City and CCCJ	Police	1. Incident Reports 2. Location Index 3. Traffic accidents and Citations 4. Stolen Propoerty 5. Central Juvenile Index 6. Probation File 7. Modus Operandi 8. Field Interrogation File 9. Misc. File	Project would conduct a feasibility study and design a criminal justice information system for several independent police agencies in a closely related geographical region. The system will standardize record keeping and data reporting among the agencies as a prerequisite to share in the use of file and system.

Prepared by the California Crime Technological Research Foundation, 1970.

Duration of Project (Date Op)	Est. Yearly Operational Budget (Developmental Cost)	Similarities to Other Systems Project	Interfaces With	How Accessed
Design completed February 1969 (Pending 0270)	3.700 K (Developmental)	Similar to most city and county criminal information systems and Want Warrants: use and final design of system will await completion of criminal and control design.		On-line from remote terminals
(March 1969)	54 K	Similar to the Department of Justice property file.		On-line from remote terminals
14 Months	124 K (Developmental)	There is no presently operational system with all the characteristics of this project. Several of the files may duplicate existing or planned statewide files and other files, such as the MO and traffic accident files have been implemented in other localities.		On-line from remote terminals

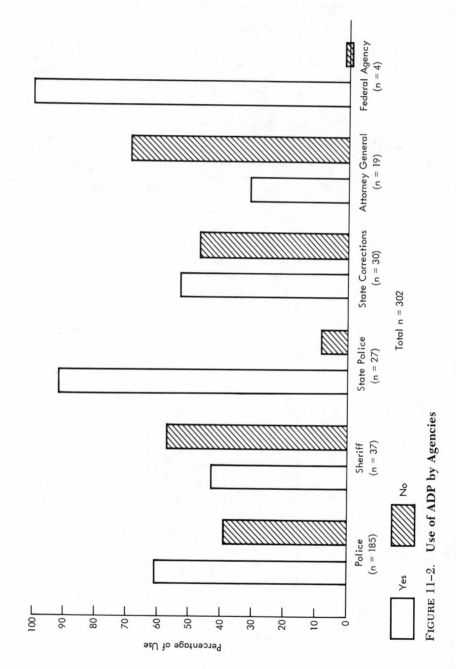

FIGURE 11-2. Use of ADP by Agencies

324

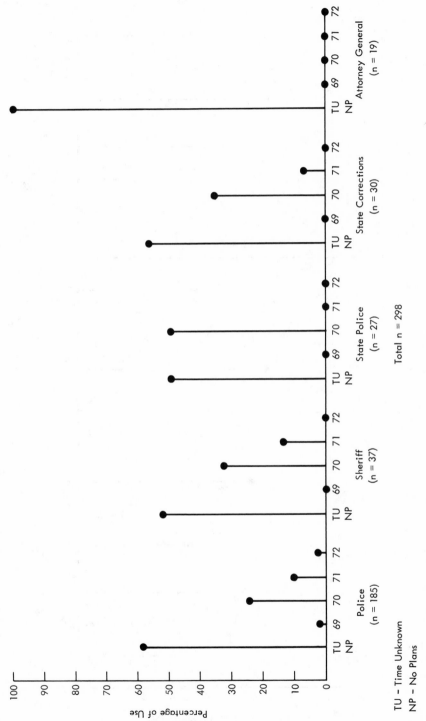

TU – Time Unknown
NP – No Plans

Total n = 298

FIGURE 11-3. Planned-for Use of ADP

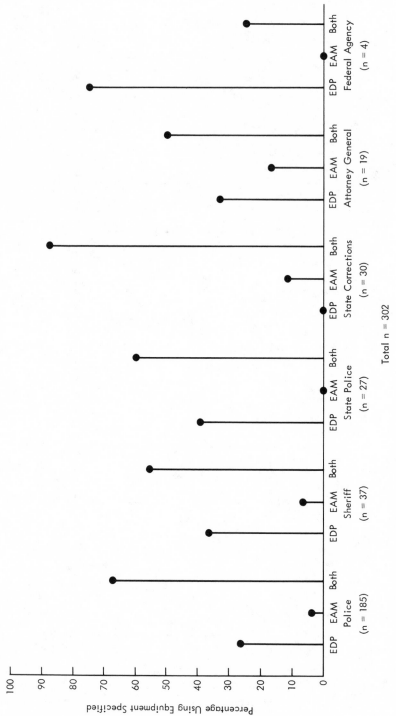

FIGURE 11-4. By-Agency Use of Specific ADP Equipment

326

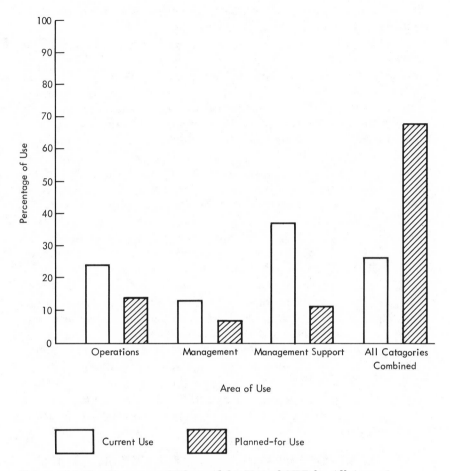

FIGURE 11–5. **Current and Planned-for Use of ADP by All Agencies**

57.3 percent. When analyzing each agency separately on this basis, State Corrections appears to be the least advanced in terms of using the more powerful equipment. This assumption (erroneous or not) is based on the fact that at the time the survey was administered none (0 percent) were using just EDP. Related to these findings are the data contained in Figure 11-5 on current and planned-for ADP use. Current use of ADP in the class categories of Operations, Management, and Management Support is higher than in the same categories for projected, or planned-for, use; however, the planned-for use of ADP for all categories combined is 68 percent, or 42.2 percent higher than the current use of all categories combined with a 25.8 percent. This may be interpreted to mean that the future will see a more integrated approach, through total-system development in the utilization of ADP by all agencies.

Figure 11-6 is somewhat misleading in that 63 percent of the responding agencies (185 + 37 + 27 + 30 + 19 + 4 = 302 total respondents) did not have an on-line capability. With this in mind, it is not surprising to learn that 94.3 percent of the agencies' equipment perform off-line or batch-processing operations, and only 5.7 percent are exclusively on-line systems. Figure 11-7 is self-explanatory. Note that the most diversified, in terms of type of computer operation, is the police department with 46 percent in-house, 32 percent shared time, 8 percent public service bureau, 12 percent private service bureau (commercial corporations), and 2 percent other. Finally, Figure 11-8 indicates the estimated average per agency annual budget allocation for ADP for all agencies between fiscal years 1969 and 1972—8.4 percent anticipated no revenue; 32.4 percent, less than $50K; 13.5 percent, $50K–$100K; 9.3 percent, $100K–$250K; 22.2 percent, $250K–$500K; and 14.2 percent, more than $500K. By analyzing each agency category, one is able to observe that the police are highest in the "Less than $50K" range, with 38 percent; sheriffs are highest in the "None" category, with 44 percent; state police are third in the "Less than $50K" range with 34 percent; state corrections are fourth in the "Less than $50K" range with 23 percent; attorney general agencies are spread over a number of categories; and federal agencies are highest in the "$50K–$100K" range, with 31 percent. (Regretfully, the FBI did not respond to the survey, hence the National Crime and Information Center figures are missing.)

THE DESIGN OF INTEGRATED AUTOMATED LAW ENFORCEMENT SYSTEMS: VERITABLE TOWERS OF VERTICALNESS, OR WHERE IS THE HORIZONTALNESS?

This section is based on three premises: (1) that all of us who are either in or associated with law enforcement are enamored with the potentialities of computer-based systems; (2) that the vast majority of the systems design and implementation efforts to date focus on vertical intergovernmental law enforcement relationships—note that this means most are only partially integrated (in a vertical sense); and (3) that most would concur that it is often difficult to exchange information quickly and effectively among governments. We are, however, progressing quite well with the building of automated law enforcement information systems, and acronyms such as LEADS, PIN, ALERT, LEMRAS, NYSIIS, CJIS, and NCIC undoubtedly have meaning to some of you. Note that the term *integrated* does not precede the term *automated*—although several systems exist or are being rapidly developed, the important linkages

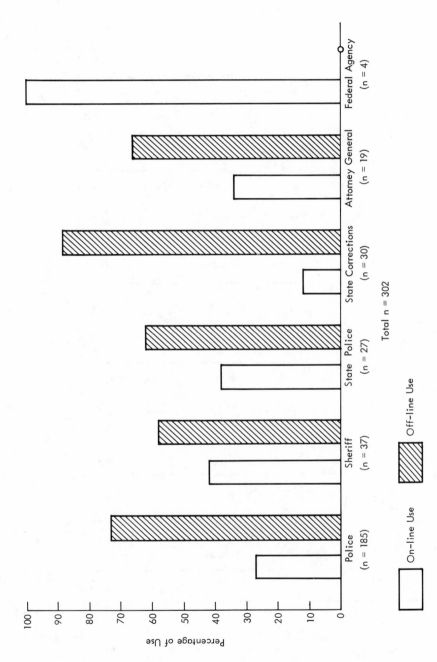

FIGURE 11-6. **On-Line and Off-Line Use by All Agencies**

329

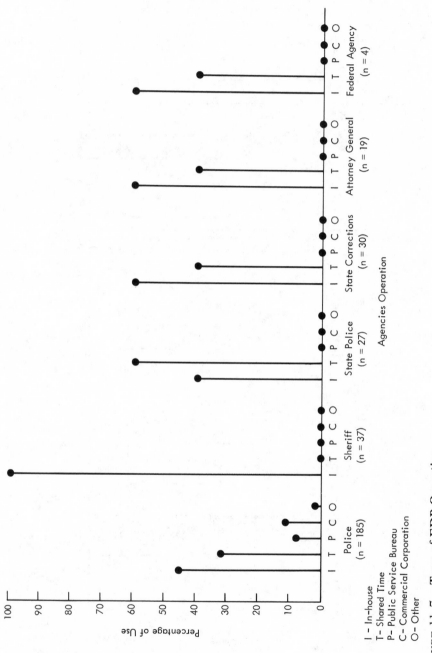

I - In-house
T - Shared Time
P - Public Service Bureau
C - Commercial Corporation
O - Other

FIGURE 11-7. Type of EDP Operation

330

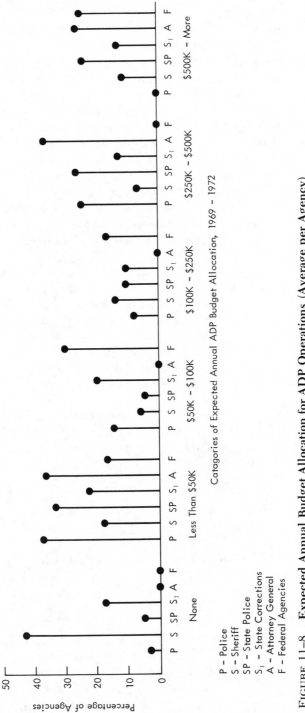

FIGURE 11–8. **Expected Annual Budget Allocation for ADP Operations (Average per Agency)**

331

for an integrated criminal justice or law enforcement information system have not been created. The experiments over the last decade have demonstrated that the technical subsystems can be devised to produce at least the results intended by their designers. But the storage and retrieval, managerial problem-solving, and process-control capabilities of the computer have yet to be put together into a single operating CJIS or police information system (though such unified systems do exist in the industrial world). Consequently, our "veritable towers of verticalness" are being forged with weak linkages, both internally and externally. Moreover, we find that there are horizontal connections. Internally, on the one hand, we find that the various computer-based law enforcement information systems have not been effectively integrated. On the other hand, we can see that the development of external linkages is progressing quite favorably.

Obviously we are not the only ones to discern the described hang-up—witness Project Search, which is an attempt (and a highly important one) to improve needed linkages within law enforcement and between other criminal justice organizations. Briefly, Project Search (System for Electronic Analysis and Retrieval of Criminal Justice) is a research and demonstration study of the value and feasibility of (1) the instant retrieval of criminal history data by criminal justice agencies on a national basis and (2) a national statistics service.

Let us examine in more detail the two primary goals of Project Search. *The first goal is the development of a system for the interstate exchange of criminal history data.* It will revolve around a central index, which will be directly accessible by each of the participating states and will supply the name of the state holding the required record. Information can then be directly accessed from the holding state by the requesting state. *The second goal is the development of a criminal justice statistical system.* It will consist of a set of summary statistical data files on a computer, enabling immediate analysis and comparison of the summary data submitted by the states.

To sum up the vertical dimension in systems design we have seen that information linkages are admittedly somewhat weak but growing in number and have been forged among police agencies from the local through the state to the federal level of law enforcement. We have only begun to look outside our borders for significant linkages between law enforcement and other criminal justice components. Even less attention has been given to the advantages of linkage—the sharing of certain types of information with other government departments such as fire, disaster planning, licensing, personnel, and finance. Project Search plus other efforts on the part of a growing number of state governments will assist in the development of information systems that encompass and interrelate all the criminal justice components.

Let us now concentrate on the horizontal dimension in systems design. The Federal Urban Information Systems Inter-Agency Committee (USAC) is a mechanism for coordinating the interest in urban information systems. USAC's goal is to build urban information systems and subsystems—now and well into the future. Its byword is horizontal and vertical *integration,* and it has the following four goals:

1. To improve the information and decision-making capabilities of municipalities.
2. To provide a broader approach in the research and development of municipal information systems, specifically the following:
   a. To encourage the standardization of data and inventories of data, both *vertically* through successive levels of government and *horizontally* at each level.
   b. To develop economic solutions to the problems of data acquisition, data managements, and data use.
   c. To develop solutions to the problems generated by sensitivity of information, e.g., the protection of confidentiality.
   d. To develop solutions to the problems of subsystems and systems linking, both vertically and horizontally, e.g., the technique of facilitating systems compatibility or interfacing.
3. To learn more about the impact of the implementation of municipal information systems, e.g., their implications for administrative organization and behavior.
4. To provide for expansion and interfaces with other public or private systems, and for *interfaces* with existing municipality-related planning agencies, e.g., in urban transportation and comprehensive area planning.

USAC is firmly dedicated to the proposition that the fundamental building block for urban and other governmental information systems is the municipality. This is to say, most governmental information systems, whether jurisdictionally (a single government area) oriented or functionally (several jurisdictions on various levels of government) oriented, depend upon municipal information systems (see Figure 11-9). The urban information system is conceptualized as having a number of subsystems, one of which is public safety. This subsystem is depicted in Figure 11-10. Each subsystem will be integrated within itself and designed for eventual integration with other subsystems, thus forming a totally integrated municipal information system.

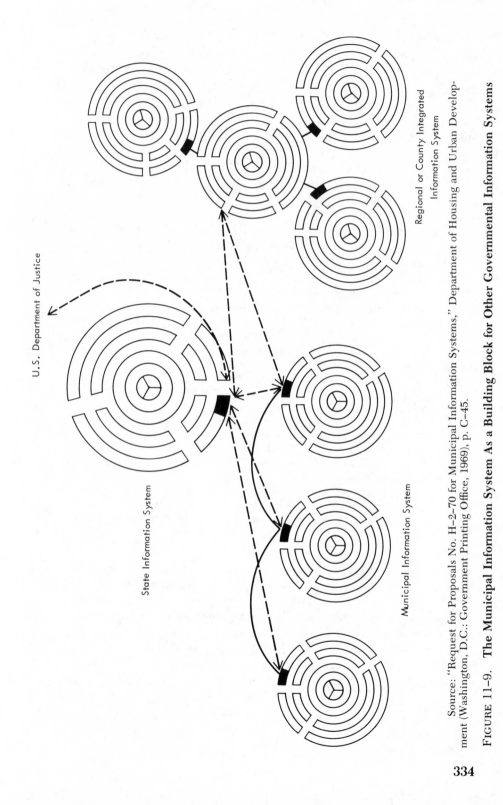

U.S. Department of Justice

State Information System

Municipal Information System

Regional or County Integrated Information System

Source: "Request for Proposals No. H–2–70 for Municipal Information Systems," Department of Housing and Urban Development (Washington, D.C.: Government Printing Office, 1969), p. C–45.

FIGURE 11–9. **The Municipal Information System As a Building Block for Other Governmental Information Systems**

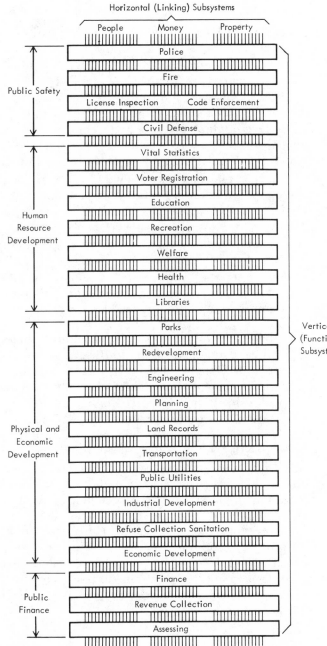

Horizontal (Linking) Subsystems

People   Money   Property

Public Safety
- Police
- Fire
- License Inspection   Code Enforcement
- Civil Defense

Human Resource Development
- Vital Statistics
- Voter Registration
- Education
- Recreation
- Welfare
- Health
- Libraries

Physical and Economic Development
- Parks
- Redevelopment
- Engineering
- Planning
- Land Records
- Transportation
- Public Utilities
- Industrial Development
- Refuse Collection Sanitation
- Economic Development

Public Finance
- Finance
- Revenue Collection
- Assessing

Vertical (Functional) Subsystem

Source: "Request for Proposals No. H–2–70 for Municipal Information Systems," Department of Housing and Urban Development (Washington, D.C.: Government Printing Office, 1969), p. C–58.

FIGURE 11-10. **Horizontal and Vertical Subsystems**

Since USAC defines local law enforcement as a part of a public safety subsystem (police, fire, civil defense, and portions of licensing), let us enlarge upon their concept of both systems and subsystems. Essentially, USAC defines municipal government as a *system.* Groupings of related municipal governmental functions are defined as *subsystems.* Thus, functional groupings such as public safety, human resources development, physical and economic development, and public finance can be thought of as subsystems where the municipal government is defined as the system. These functional groupings, however, may or may not correspond to organizational units within the municipality. Therefore, at this point an important distinction must be made between organizational units to which functions are assigned and information subsystems of a municipality. *The latter are independent of any organizational structure.* To put it another way, an information subsystem can be identified in terms of information input, storage, processing, transmittal, and output. Thus, except with respect to size, municipal information subsystems are defined exactly the same as the integrated municipal system.

USAC also believes that subsystems have three dimensions: vertical, horizontal, and sophistication. Vertical subsystems are a grouping of components that are reasonably related to common goals and activities and are arranged in a hierarchical manner to constitute a functional subsystem. Vertical subsystems are, therefore, functional systems. Illustrative of functional subsystems are police, fire, planning, building, recreation, finance, and public works. Such functional subsystems and components are shown graphically in Figure 11-10. *Horizontal* subsystems are mechanisms that support automated linking of data within and among vertical functional subsystems. A variety of classifications are available. One frequently used divides the horizontal system into three subsystems, each identified by the kind of information that flows in it, that is, information about people, property, and money. The critical problem in the design of horizontal subsystems is organizing the data in such a way that any current or future requirements for a combination of data, for example, from more than one horizontal subsystem, can be made readily available.

Sophistication subsystems facilitate the conceptualization of incremental development of the information system capabilities. At the least sophisticated level, according the USAC are automatic data processing techniques employed in the administrative affairs of the municipality. These include personnel, finance, and property accounting, billing and disbursing, registering and licensing, and other routine tasks. The next level of sophistication is the support of operational control in a municipality. This includes scheduling, dispatching, allocation, and monitoring, for example, traffic control, and command and central emergency vehicle dispatching. Emphasis here is on a rapid response capability, and therefore the on-line, real-time mode is more generally appropriate. A third level of sophistication is in terms of the hardware, software, and files required for planning support. Here, both batch processing and on-line, real-time modes are important. Generalized software required includes PERT or CPM for planning and scheduling, simulation, and statistical analysis programs. The ultimate level of sophistication is at the policy-making and management level. Here the requirement is at its fullest development: planning reports, time- and event-triggered report generation, and controlling administrative processes.

MANAGEMENT INFORMATION SYSTEMS

In a day when words are used with very little attempt to define them, it should not be surprising that some people are puzzled by the term *management information system*. For one thing, people tend to confuse a management information system with a computer system. Are they the same? If so, are all computers management information systems? If not, can you have a management information system (MIS) without a computer? In answer to these questions: An MIS is not identical with a computer system; however, most formalized, complex MISs are computer based. And, the mere presence of an EDP system does *not* mean you have an MIS.

Another series of questions surrounds the concept of the so-called total system. To what extent can all the managerial and decision-making processes of a police organization be systematized? How necessary is it that all systems of the department be combined into one "total system"? In short, does an MIS have to be a total system? Finally, whether or not this is so, can an MIS help you in planning and controlling your police department? In answer to these questions: Only a few of the departmental processes can be "programmed" or systematized. An MIS does *not* have to be total to be useful.

Now, what is an MIS? It is an information system (usually computer based) that selects, processes, stores, and furnishes data of interest to management for two purposes and usually in three modes. The purposes: *control* (internal) and *planning* (external).[8] The modes: time-triggered reports, event-triggered reports, and on-demand. The latter two modes require on-line, real-time inquiry-response capabilities.

[8] For a number of pertinent articles on this subject, see Peter P. Schoderbek, ed., *Management Systems: A Book of Readings* (New York: John Wiley & Sons, Inc., 1967).

While timely, the degree of MIS importance is uncertain. The view of the MIS proponent is typified by Widoner, who predicts that

> The formal desk will disappear as paper is replaced by display systems. Conference. . . tables will "get in the way" and will be traded in for comfortable, tilt-back swivel chairs that permit easier interaction between people and the displayed data. The atmosphere will be one of confident control, rather than the hectic, somewhat erratic pace we maintain today . . . [The management information facility] will be on line to the computer through report interrogation consoles and large-screen displays. Management will be able to "hold conversations" with business systems, ask questions and get answers in seconds, probe problem areas in minutes, review actual trends and trend projections against plans.[9]

Drucker raises some reservations about computers and MISs when he writes:

> The computer is a logic machine, and that is its strength—but also its limitation. The important events on the outside cannot be reported in the kind of form a computer (or any other logic system) could possibly handle. Man, however, while not particularly logical is perceptive—and that is his strength.
> The danger is that executives will become contemptuous of information and stimulus that cannot be reduced to computer logic and computer language. Executives may become blind to everything that is perception (i.e., event) rather than fact (i.e., after the event). The tremendous amount of computer information may thus shut out access to reality.
> Eventually the computer—potentially by far the most useful management tool—should make executives aware of their insulation and free them for more time on the outside. In the short run, however, there is danger of acute "computeritis." It is a serious affliction.[10]

The reader will observe one suggested form of an MIS in the learning exercise at the end of this chapter (referred to as the *administrative component*). Hence, the remainder of this section will deal with the considerations in designing an MIS.[11] All interested

---

[9]W. Robert Widoner, "New Concepts of Running a Business," *Business Automation*, 16 (April 1966), 33.

[10]Peter F. Drucker, *The Effective Executive* (New York: Harper & Row, Publishers, 1966), p. 17.

[11]Not included at this time is a discussion of command and control systems. For information on this rapidly growing management application, see Peter J. Pitchess, "New Computer-Based Dispatching System Acts to Increase Response Time," *Police Chief*, 38 (February 1971), 858–59; and S. Arthur Yefsky and John D. Hodges, "Field Communications for Command and Control," *Police Chief*, 37 (July 1970), 34–42.

in operational (the data needed by the line officer) components should also refer to the learning exercise. To begin, let us think of the police organization as having a *data base*. It should not be viewed in terms of separate or discrete applications but instead of as consisting of *elements* of information as shown in Table 1 of the learning exercise. To accomplish anything useful with these elements, it is necessary to give the data base an organization and a structure. Structuring requires that at least three things be done: (1) The *information requirements* of management have to be identified. We need to know which of the elements potentially available are actually required. (2) We need to define them by providing a *data description*, in technical terms, of the data elements: how large they are, what their meaning is, where they are stored, how one can get at them. (3) It is important that *data relationships* among the data base elements be identified. An employee skill number might, for example, be a data element. This data element would be referenced in payroll compilation and in maintaining personnel records. Thus the same data element could be related to many different files or, putting it another way, to many different management usages of information. The same steps are to be taken when designing an operations base. In fact, ideally, an operations and a management data base are one and the same. The user determines which information he needs, and that in itself, decides if it is operations (e.g., a person is wanted) or management (e.g., Are their statistics predicting a change in the types of called-for services within the next three months?).

Not only is the organization of information changing significantly from what it has been in the past, but the utilization of this information is also changing. Police departments engaged in developing MISs are going beyond the use of computers simply to maintain records; they are exploring much more imaginative and ambitious applications. A few of these new uses are identified in Figure 1 of the learning exercise. They include graphics capability to display the elements retrieved from the data base, as well as modeling and simulation. They extend to linking the information system to other systems dedicated to on-line process control, and they involve the application of specialized retrieval techniques to pull information from the data base. Most of these innovations in information systems encourage, and in some instances require, close interaction of the manager, the systems designer, and the machine.

A fundamental question confronting the systems designer when he begins to think about the data base aspect of MISs is, How many levels of data base are there going to be in the organization? There exists, of course, a management hierarchy with different information needs at its various levels, and so the question arises whether the information system can serve all these levels in an organization with but a single data base.

The bottom section of Figure 2 of the learning exercise reflects the omnipresent need to maintain the details of each called-for service having to do with individual citizens. All these details of services still have to be maintained much as they have been in the past, and information about them will typically constitute a fundamental part of the data base. Operating or middle management obviously does not need all this detail, but it does need some portion or subset of it. And, top management needs yet another subset of the overall data base. So the question must be answered, Can these varying needs be served by a single data base, or will the systems designer be forced to structure three different data bases? If he has to fragment the information system by level, then there is necessarily going to be some redundancy in the data elements maintained. Consider an example. In a police department it is necessary for the line officer to have access to the details of warrants and other wanted persons. But it is really not of interest at the operating or middle management levels (lieutenants and captains) The latter level is interested in cumulations statistics about the number of warrants served and wanted persons located. At the top management level the information needs are even broader, dealing with the costs attached to this type of police activity. Thus the designer is confronted with structuring the data base to accommodate these different levels of information seekers.

A similar problem, but "vertical" rather than "horizontal," also occurs in systems design. For not only does the systems designer have to structure horizontally, he also has to determine whether different functional portions of the department can share a common data base, that is, whether he must chop the data base into vertical as well as horizontal segments. Can the patrol bureau use the same data base as the investigative or traffic personnel, or is each intent on having one of its own? There seems to be some tendency in the latter direction, as there exist today systems dedicated, for example, to patrol information and serving the patrol part of the organization only. A major challenge to the information systems designer lies in trying to integrate the departmental data base so that it can be useful to all major organizational levels and components.

Another difficulty confronting the systems designer concerns management's "information threshold." This has to do with the level to which a given executive may want to descend into the data base for information. Executive A may not want to be confronted with the degree of detail envisaged in such a systems design. For example, when General Eisenhower was president, he was said to prefer having all problems brought to him summarized succinctly. He therefore represented the kind of chief executive who does not want to delve very far down into the data base, but instead desires summary presentations of information.

But if the system is developed to accommodate such an executive's information threshold, the systems designer must determine what should be done when his police chief or other managers are succeeded by other executives who have an entirely different information threshold. Consider police executive B who frequently wishes to examine information that has to do with day-to-day control of the department, that is, operating data. Now, the systems analyst does not want to have to restructure, and more importantly, reimplement, the system each time there is a transition from one manager to another. He wishes instead to have, as a design objective, a system that is sufficiently adaptable to accommodate the information needs of different types of executives. This is certainly another of the challenges in information systems design.

An additional aspect of this information threshold problem, or perhaps another way of looking at it, becomes apparent when executive A has, let us say, a traffic background, so that when traffic activities are involved he wants to go all the way down to the bottom of the data base. Such an executive may call for all the details of a particular traffic accident and ask, "What was the amount of the damage?" Management experts may assert that this executive is violating sound organization principles by doing so, but the systems man must realize that in actual situations this is the way executives do operate and, consequently, he must design systems to accommodate these needs. Otherwise, management simply will not make use of the system.

And, of course, police information systems can be tailored in this manner. The designer can allow hypothetical police executive A to satisfy his personal need to know, but it must be remembered that this executive is not going to be in charge forever and may be succeeded by someone from, say, the engineering sector. This could turn out to be executive B who in general wishes much more detail but will want to go down to the very lowest level in the data base only when R & D problems are involved. It is essential to design a system that does not have to be reworked completely when such changes in management information thresholds occur.

These are some of the problems that systems people and, more importantly, police management must carefully address and solve!

OBSTACLES INTO OPPORTUNITIES

As with nearly all technological and scientific innovations, CJIS developments have not been, are not being, nor will they be achieved in the future without seizing on every opportunity to twist barriers into results.[12] Of the many barriers or challenges to existing and prospective CJISs, data *standardization, privacy* and *confidentiality,* and *system security* loom very large at present. While discussed separately, you will be quick to detect that they are inextricably connected with each other.

The importance of data standardization, whether it be in the form of statistics or of data elements, is recognized by designers and analysts alike. For without the capability of "moving" data between CJIS components or data from one CJIS to another, we experience serious system limitations. National, state, regional, and local CJISs would be highly ineffective unless they were able to automatically transmit or make file inquiry of their counterparts. Figure 1 of the learning exercise depicts the critical nature of CJIS interaction. Therefore, data must be standardized to present the opportunity for system interaction or integration. To this end, three highly pertinent documents have been generated by Project Search: (1) *Standardized Data Elements for Criminal History Files* (Technical Report No. 1, January 1970), (2) *Designing Statewide Criminal Justice Statistics Systems—The Demonstration Prototype* (Technical Report No. 3, November 1970), and (3) *Name Search Techniques* (Special Report No. 1, December 1970).[13]

Bluntly, the confidentiality and privacy issues attached to large-scale people-oriented information systems are, by far, too complex and lengthy to discuss within the confines of the space allocated to this chapter. The issues range on a continuum from individual freedom to the need for information on a person's present status and past history in the criminal justice system. In essence, we are dealing with a trade-off relationship of encompassing the "need to know" on the one hand with the "right to know" on the other. CJIS users are perhaps as concerned as anyone else, if not more so, with this issue. They are intensely pursuing the building

---

[12] In this regard, the reader will find of immeasurable interest (in fact, we consider it to be one of the most outstanding contributions to the literature in 1970), Charles P. Smith, "Coordination and Control of Computer Technology in State Government: Constraints and Strategies" (Doctoral dissertation, School of Public Administration, University of Southern California, 1970).

[13] These reports can be obtained from Project Search, California Crime Technology Research Foundation, 1108 Fourteenth Street, Sacramento, Calif. 95814. For those interested in statewide standards and procedures, see the *Long-Range Master Plan for the Utilization of Electronic Data Processing in the State of California* (Sacramento: Office of Management Services, State of California, 1970).

of CJIS locks and keys to preclude errors, misuse of data, and intentional data change. One need not dwell for long on the possibilities of horizontally linking CJISs with welfare, IRS, and other people-data bases before he feels either trapped or threatened, or both. Yet, it appears more clearly than ever before, that certain vertical systems ought to be linked. Where to start and stop remains *the* paramount and unresolved decision. This is also discussed in *Security and Privacy Consideration in Criminal History Information Systems* (Technical Report No. 2, July 1970).[14]

Finally, those who seek to destroy or disrupt our society have discovered that when attacking its formal organizations the visceral area is not only more sensitive but more vulnerable to attack. The area referred to is, of course, the data processing center. The reaction to this situation, to date, on the part of dp managers, has varied from zero to rapid hardening of the potential target site. Apparently the "glass showcase" days for dp centers are over. We find the older dp facilities being mortared in or moved to a more secure location.[15] Further, we see many of the new facilities being buried below the ground, with major physical and personnel security methods being included in their design and operations.[16] Banks, colleges, cities, critical industries, and the like are more anxious than ever before about protecting the physical "life" of their dp centers.

With due regard for the above "opportunities," let us now look at some of the requirements currently being placed on the police manager where automated information systems are concerned. First, there is the always present requirement for police administrators to improve their *intellectual* accessibility to computers so that it matches their growing *physical* accessibility.[17] This rapidly growing use calls for a certain dedication and investment of time that goes beyond the occasional reading of a journal or taking of a course. The computer (if it has not already) will become a potent force in police organizations. It is up to every police manager to

[14] This report can also be acquired from Project Search, *ibid.* Another document of significant import is Annette Harrison, *The Problem of Privacy in the Computer Age: An Annotated Bibliography* (Santa Monica, Calif.: The Rand Corporation, 1967).

[15] For an example of one such endeavor, see Paul M. Whisenand, James L. Cline, and John C. Whisenand, *A Facility Security Analysis of the Data Services Bureau, City of Los Angeles* (Long Beach, Calif.: Department of Criminology, California State College, 1970).

[16] A strong case and recommendation for dp security can be seen in *Physical Security of Data Processing Facilities* (Long Beach, Calif.: Department of Criminology, California State College, 1971).

[17] This expression, as well as the thinking behind this particular challenge, is drawn from Herbert H. Issacs, "Computer Systems Technology: Programs, Projections, Problems," *Public Administration Review*, 28 (November-December 1968), 488–94.

acquire the significant level of understanding necessary to harness this source of intellectual energy. Now the question, When and how?

Second, in conjunction with our efforts to develop vertically oriented police and criminal justice information systems, How can we do so faster and with greater effectiveness? A part of the answer lies with such projects as Search, NCIC, NYSIIS, CJIS, and LEADS. But the question remains,—What can we do to accelerate the development of the necessary data bases at the local level of government? Also, what can we do to assure ourselves that they will be integrated with one another? Herein lie the major barriers to the creation of effective vertical police and criminal justice information systems.

Third, in the absence of any commitment to establish horizontal (linking) subsystems at the local level of government, How can we instill an interest in at least exploring the potentialities and advantages of such subsystems? (USAC is only a partial answer to this challenge.) While progress in the use of computers in police work has been acceptable to a large degree, the gap between the computer's technical capability and its practical application is growing wider. The effective use of computers requires a change in police management strategy, in management's attentiveness to their *full* exploitation, and ultimately to the automated linking of information within and among the vertical subsystems that constitute the urban government information system.[18]

Fourth, simply stated, Where are our police "management information systems"? Police management is largely a process of handling information: selecting it, comparing it, and acting upon it.[19] From people, from paper, from personal observation, the police manager is deluged with data. *Selecting* which data to give his attention to is the manager's first, though often only implicit, information-handling task. *Comparing* data is an even more subtle and complex task, for here the police manager must relate the new data he selects to the old he already possesses. This comparison function is the crux of decision making—it touches setting goals (where we want to be, compared with where we are), establishing programs (which of several programs offers the best comparative advantage), evalua-

[18] Perhaps the strongest and certainly the most thoroughly documented argument in favor of horizontal linkages can be found in Municipal Systems Research, *The Municipal Information and Decision System Research Project: Phase One Final Report* (Los Angeles: Municipal Systems Research, School of Public Administration, University of Southern California, 1968).

[19] For a more detailed discussion of the manager's relationship to computers, see Edward F. R. Hearle, "A Symposium: Computers in Public Administration," *Public Administration Review*, 28 (November-December 1968), 487–88.

ting progress (how we are doing in comparison with our plans). Acting upon these comparisons is that personal step of human will that no machine can ever undertake. But information-handling machines—computers—are increasingly able to perform the managerial tasks of information selection and comparison. It is distressing that despite the tremendous amount of attention that has been afforded the development of computer-based police MISs, those that exist are not used in making policy decisions of any consequence.[20]

Fifth, at some time in the future, police organizations will undoubtedly be structured in accordance with the flow of information and the points of decision. Admittedly, today they are still highly compartmentalized by functional areas that are of our doing. Without the full knowledge of information availability and flow, however, major organizational revisions of police departments based on information requirements will remain in limbo. How do we avoid inaction? What should be the design of our new organizational structures? Pointedly is there any biblical reference or inviolable rule concerning the way we should structure our formal organizations to fulfill their assigned goals? Definitely not! Consequently, let us permit the flow of information and the decision centers to assist us in determining how we should organize our working relationships.

LEARNING EXERCISE

In the following learning exercise, the reader will encounter a theoretical computer-based police information system.[21] In this case, however, the theory is being partially translated into reality. By the time this text is in print (maybe before it is available), parts of the conceptual design will probably be developed and operational. If so, they can be observed in Charlotte, North Carolina; Long Beach, California; and Wichita Falls, Texas. Naturally, the concept as expressed within these pages will have to be modified based on the user needs of the department—and rightly so. Because if system designer and departmental practitioner did not hammer out a design to serve the specific user in mind, all that has been stated above has been compromised in favor of serving the machines and not the manager.

[20] Some of the solutions to this challenge are suggested in "Second Annual Management Meet Examines the Milieu of MIS," *Datamation*, 15 (February 1969), 106–7.

[21] Permission to use this material granted by Paul M. Whisenand and Tug T. Tamaru, *Automated Police Information Systems* (New York: John Wiley & Sons, 1970).

AN AUTOMATED INFORMATION SYSTEM
FOR MUNICIPAL POLICE ADMINISTRATION

The reader will find in this chapter a proposed course of future action. Naturally the proposal is based on findings from the preceding systems analysis. The proposed Automated Police Information System (APIS) is designed for the specific purpose of automatically processing police-related information. We use the term "automated data processing" in a delimiting sense, namely—it refers only to that information which is generated, converted, stored, or retrieved through mechanical or electronic means. *Information omitted in the system should not be regarded as an indication of its lack of importance or utility.* In most cases such an omission on the part of the author is rather due to the information currently displaying relatively little machine-processing amenability. (Note: any references hereafter referring to the author mean the author of this article, not the author of the book.)

Before describing the APIS let us look at its specific benefits.[22] Broadly, the APIS is developed in concept and specification to deal with both the informational and the reporting needs of *medium-sized municipal police agencies.* Further, it is also related to those needs of the pertinent *state and federal agencies* concerned primarily with the administration of criminal justice and to a lesser degree with related supportive organizations. In addition to the vertical relationships, we find that the APIS is also interfaced with other *information subsystems which constitute the city's total informational flow and decisional system.* When subjected to a more detailed evaluation, we observe that the APIS is specifically planned to provide, in addition to the general benefits of an automated information system, the following advantages for a medium-sized local police agency.

1. *Improved Quality of Decisions.* The APIS provides an improved basis for the support of both police operation and police management decisions. This so-called "benefit" is very difficult to gauge since it underlies a concern for the best possible administration of the police organization and its services. (This benefit rectifies Problems 1, 5, 6, 7, and 10.)

2. *Horizontal Interface Relationships.* The APIS participates, through a sharing of data, in the horizontally oriented information subsystems that serve as integrators for a total municipal government information system. (This benefit rectifies Problems 5 and 9.)

3. *Vertical Interface Relationships.* The APIS serves as a vertical oriented data base for both an intergovernmental law enforcement information system and a criminal justice information system. (This benefit rectifies Problem 9.)

4. *Cost/Benefit Savings.* The APIS possesses a modular capability

---

[22] For purposes of a brief review, the general benefits of ADP for a police department are (*a*) new organizational capabilities, (*b*) improvement in existing capabilities, (*c*) elimination of duplication, and (*d*) increased sharing of information.

which facilitates the application of less than the described total system. Therefore, the APIS can be modified to comply with either socioeconomic or technological changes, as they arise to influence its operational characteristics. (This benefit rectifies Problem 9.)

5. *Computer Technology.* The APIS is so constructed as to permit maximum use and benefit of computer technology which appears economically feasible for the medium-sized city. (This benefit rectifies Problems 2, 4, and 8.)

6. *Cybernetics (Feedback).* The APIS includes a cybernetic open-sequence control capability.[23] Oper-sequence control means that the basic responsibility for control in a man-machine system rests in the human rather than mechanical component. Consequently, the APIS provides for limited general and flexible feedback capacity. This capacity is predicated on a police department's ability to circulate information representing its accomplishments. (This benefit rectifies Problems 2 and 3.)

In concluding this analysis of benefits to be gained through the APIS, we note that Problem 10 (Traditionalism) is affected by all of the listed benefits. More importantly, we are able to see that *the APIS meets both present and future police information requirements.* It is stressed, however, that the proposed APIS is fundamentally a computer-based data processing, storage, analyzing, and rapid retrieval system designed to *optimize police-oriented problem-solving capabilities.* Figure 1 depicts requisite vertical and horizontal interfaces of the APIS. Figure 2 illustrates the means for integrating the vertical subsystem in local government. Table 1 presents some of the data elements that possess commonality with other city information systems.

The APIS is based on five integrated files grouped into two major information components. These two components are administrative and operations. The administrative information component (AIC) is comprised of four major interrelated files: supportive, personnel, environmental, and management. The operations information component (OIC) includes a single major file containing operationally oriented data. This file in turn embraces a series of subordinate subfiles. Figure 3 provides for us a schematic overview of the APIS.

The files and subfiles we now describe are those that are computer processed (the traditional, centrally located, Hard-Copy File contains those reports that are retained in hard-copy form). To begin, the data elements required by the APIS are forwarded to the conversion station for input processing. The APIS's files, subfiles, and processing procedures are connected into an integrated whole in which each component supports the other. This set of interdependent files serves as a foundation for the total MSPD information system. Essentially, these integrated files facilitate a reduction in the duplication of information-processing activi-

[23] The literature on organizational feedback is sufficiently extensive that there is no difficulty in locating it. For an interesting and useful discussion of organizational obstacles to two related types of feedback—survival and social—see Robert A. Rosenthal and Robert S. Wiess, "Problems of Organizational Feedback Processes," in Raymond A. Bauer, ed., *Social Indicators* (Cambridge, Mass.: M.I.T. Press, 1966), pp. 302–40.

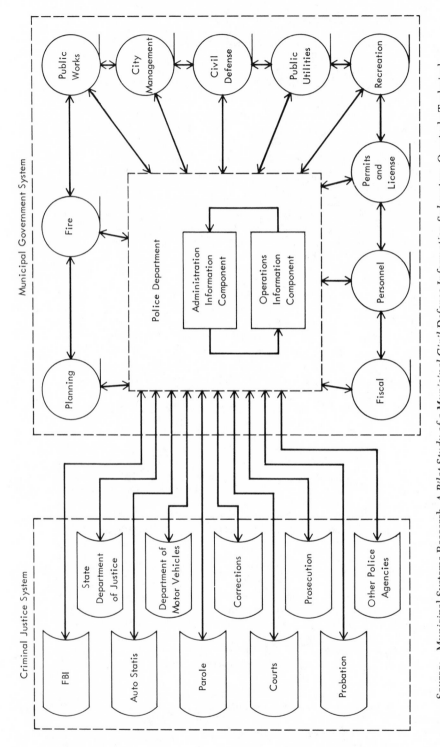

Source: Municipal Systems Research, *A Pilot Study of a Municipal Civil Defense Information Subsystem*, Quarterly Technical Report Number 3 to the Office of Civil Defense, Department of the Army, Washington, October 1967. This figure was prepared by Paul M. Whisenand, Research Associate, Municipal Systems Research, School of Public Administration, University of Southern California (Los Angeles: Municipal Systems Research, 1967), Vol. 3, Sec. 8, p. 34:

FIGURE 1. **An Automated Police Information Subsystem: Vertical Relationships**

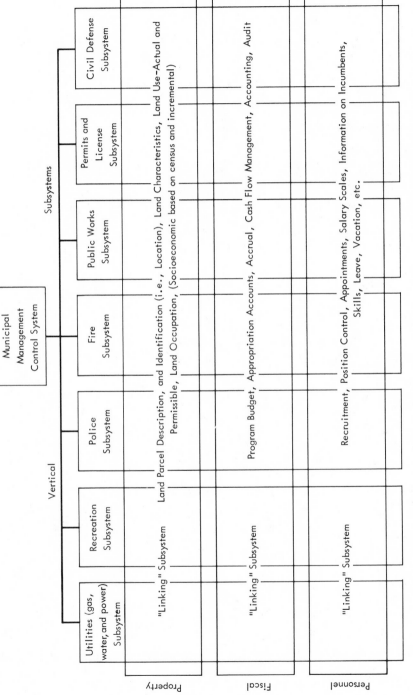

FIGURE 2. **Municipal Horizontal Linking Subsystems**

Source: Municipal Systems Research, *A Pilot Study of a Municipal Civil Defense Information Subsystem*, Quarterly Technical Report Number 3 to the Office of Civil Defense, Department of the Army, Washington, October 1967. Prepared by Municipal Systems Research, School of Public Administration, University of Southern California (Los Angeles: Municipal Systems Research, 1967), Vol. 3, Sec. 8, p. 35.

349

TABLE 1. Information Required for Municipal Operations and Planning: A Selected Listing to Illustrate Data Commonality

Data Elements	Civil Defense	Fire	Human Factors	Planning and Building	Police	Public Works and Traffic	Utilities
Demographic information:							
Population by age and sex	x		x	x	x		
Geographic distribution	x		x	x	x	x	x
Familial status		x					
Dependent persons		x					
Birth and mortality incidence		x					
Demographic projections	x	x	x	x	x	x	x
Economic information:							
Employment							
By occupation	x		x	x			
By industry	x		x	x		x	x
Income							
By household			x	x			
Per capita			x	x			
Income projections			x	x			
Environmental information							
Air							
Quality	x						
Pollution emission	x		x		x	x	
Radiation	x						
Water							
Surface and reservoirs	x		x	x		x	x
Public water system	x	x		x		x	x
Private water system	x	x				x	
Storage	x	x		x		x	
Drainage canals	x	x		x		x	
Quality	x					x	
Use	x					x	
Structures							
Location	x	x	x	x	x	x	x
Use	x	x	x	x	x	x	x
Condition	x	x	x	x	x	x	
Demolitions	x	x		x	x	x	x
Construction	x	x	x	x	x	x	x
Shelter capability	x	x		x			
Capacity	x	x		x	x		
Occupancy		x	x	x			
Sewerage							
System and capacity	x			x		x	
Treatment						x	
Refuse disposal	x			x		x	

Data Elements	Civil Defense	Fire	Human Factors	Planning and Building	Police	Public Works and Traffic	Utilities
Subsystem							

Data Elements	Civil Defense	Fire	Human Factors	Planning and Building	Police	Public Works and Traffic	Utilities
Health and medical facilities							
Drug locations	x				x		
Medical supplies locations	x			x			
Medical personnel	x		x				
Hospitals, nursing homes							
Medical offices, clinics, and treatment and diagnostic centers by							
Location	x	x	x	x	x		x
Condition	x	x	x	x			
Capacity	x	x		x			
Type	x			x			
Ownership	x	x		x		x	x
Human factors information by transaction (land parcel coded)							
Health and restaurant permits	x			x			
Disease incidence			x				
Sanitarian visits			x				
Nursing visits			x				
Rescue calls	x	x			x		
Public assistance			x				
Sex offenses			x		x		
Public health hazards	x		x		x	x	

Source: Municipal Systems Research, *A Pilot Study of a Municipal Civil Defense Information Subsystem*, Quarterly Technical Report Number 3 to the Office of Civil Defense, Department of the Army, Washington, October 1967. Prepared by Municipal Systems Research, School of Public Administration, University of Southern California (Los Angeles: Municipal Systems Research, 1967), Vol. 3, Sec. 8, pp. 38–40.

ties, and increase the accessibility and usefulness of the data. We can see that an output of one component or file process becomes an input for other components, which in turn generate additional subsystem input, thereby creating a circular transmission of information. Significantly, the arrangement of the information components, their files, and their processes are derived from the previously discussed types of decisions made in a police organization.

OPERATIONS INFORMATION COMPONENT (OIC)

The OIC is designed to generate, process, retrieve, and analyze both aggregated (quantitative—for example statistics) and uniquely descriptive (qualitative—for example an individual's characteristics) police information.

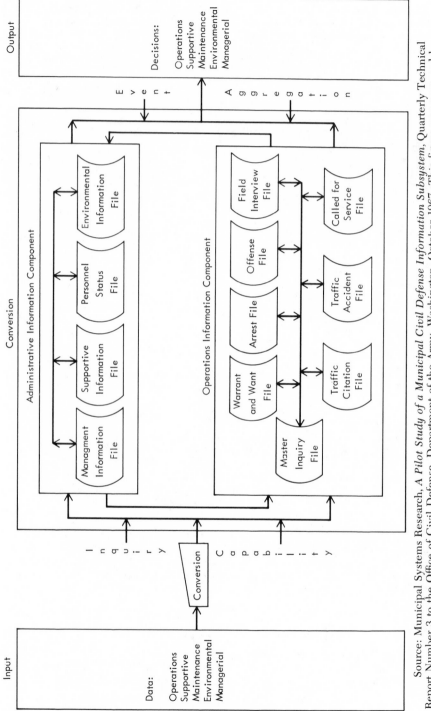

Source: Municipal Systems Research, *A Pilot Study of a Municipal Civil Defense Information Subsystem*, Quarterly Technical Report Number 3 to the Office of Civil Defense, Department of the Army, Washington, October 1967. This figure was prepared by Paul M. Whisenand, Research Associate, Municipal Systems Research, School of Public Administration, University of Southern California (Los Angeles: Municipal Systems Research, 1967), Vol. 3, Sec. 8, p. 41.

FIGURE 3. **An Automated Police Information Subsystem: File Organization.**

Importantly, the collected data also provide a major input into the AIC for administrative decision making. The police administrative level depends on this quantified information to evaluate bureau activities and to perform long-range planning and budgeting. Also, it uses this information for a number of accounting functions having to do with personnel and material inventories. Administrative information therefore contains data with predominantly internal management characteristics ("endogenous" is the systems term for such data). Descriptive information is required by police officers handling called-for services. In these cases the relevant information is used for the purposes of identifying people, personal field interviews, traffic control, and miscellaneous community services. This information, as contrasted to administrative decision making, is used in police operations and thus possesses facts which can reflect the characteristics of an individual ("exogenous data" in systems terms).

The OIC consists of the following subfiles (for purposes of clarity we hereafter refer to the subfiles as files): master inquiry, warrant and want,[24] arrest, offense, field interview, traffic citation, traffic accident, and called-for police service.[25] See Figure 4 for a description of the OIC and its eight files. Note that *the first five files contain operations-oriented data which have rapid response implications.* The type of information contained in these files is typically considered by police administrators to require either real-time on-line machine processing, or rapid retrieval of individual event files as required. These files are used primarily as part of the automated procedures that store and retrieve information used for purposes of identifying people. Significantly, the last three files are part of the automated procedures required to process and analyze aggregated data which usually do not require an immediate response to inquiry.

The type of information contained in these three files is effectively processed and reported through batch machine processing on a time-triggered basis.

The reader should note that the eight files also differ according to another important dimension. In essence, the files are conspicuously either vertical or horizontal in nature. While we frequently think of police information as having a solely vertical dimension, in operation, it also includes a number of horizontal characteristics.

> During the course of our research, it became apparent that the city's administrative and decisional processes can be ordered and handled better if a distinction is made between the two basically different types of subsystems which we have designated "vertical" and "horizontal." The fiscal subsystem, for example, is mainly horizontal. Police, in contrast, is mainly vertical. By viewing the informational flows from this perspective, the computer systems design is facilitated.[26]

[24] As discussed in previous chapters, in the case of warrant and want information there are presently regional and national automated systems which provide this type of data on a real-time and on-line basis.

[25] During the conceptualization of the various information files to comprise the APIS there was considerable doubt as to the proper location of the traffic-oriented and called-for service subfiles. However, in line with dynamic storage theory, it was decided to place these subfiles within the OIC.

[26] William H. Mitchel, "Tooling Computers to the Medium-Sized City," *Public Management*, 49, 69 (March, 1967).

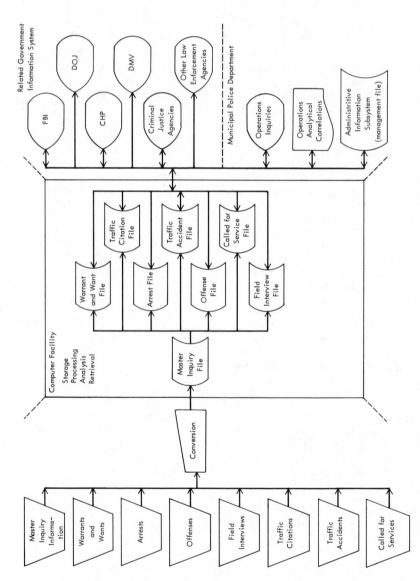

Source: Municipal Systems Research, *A Pilot Study of a Municipal Civil Defense Information Subsystem*, Quarterly Technical Report Number 3 to the Office of Civil Defense, Department of the Army, Washington, October 1967. This figure was prepared by Paul M. Whisenand, Research Associate, Municipal Systems Research, School of Public Administration, University of Southern California (Los Angeles: Municipal Systems Research, 1967), Vol. 3, Sec. 8, p. 44.

FIGURE 4. **Flow Chart of the Operations Information Component: Police Subsystem**

354

The maximum benefits of automatic data processing can be obtained only when the vertical subsystems are integrated through a linking arrangement provided by horizontal subsystems. In summary, we can observe that the eight files vary on the basis of three interrelated dimensions: (a) the character of the data used, namely, operational or analytical, (b) the type of processing required,[27] and (c) the nature of the information flow.

At this point we have included each one of the eight files in an abstract sense and with general interface possibilities. In terms of actual application, however, one must provide for specific and detailed interaction of the APIS with other city, county, state and federal computer-based information systems which are in operation at the time of the implementation of the MSPD APIS. This is especially relevant for all of the files contained in the OIC except the "called-for service" file. To repeat, at the present time, the number of such relevant information systems that have been automated are small. Nevertheless we can see that there are many applicable computer-based systems in the course of being designed. We find it necessary, therefore, to include during the development of the APIS, a continuing awareness of the agencies with which the MSPD will be interacting at the time of implementation. The majority of the external agencies that must be considered while establishing interface requirements are shown in previous flow charts. As computerized systems become operational in other areas of criminal justice the need for local OIC files will, in all probability, diminish. In due regard for this future occurrence, the author recommends that police agencies sharing in the use of a regional or statewide information system be quick to assist in its finanacial support (this can be accomplished, for example, through payment based on the number of records it has on file and/or the number of requests it makes for information).

To continue, inputs for the files comprising the OIC are derived from recorded data submitted on called-for MSPD police services. This embraces arrest, field interview, offense, traffic warrant and want, and community service data.[28] Further, the files are updated as information regarding these events is received by the computer facility. The OIC files process these data as they are generated, and maintain them on a ready status in line with "dynamic storage theory." We mean by dynamic storage theory "that inputs are captured on a continuous basis and at the point and time of generation. The data sources are the routine procedures required for the conduct of city business."[29] Importantly, the OIC files are structured in accordance with this theory. The reader will find the OIC data elements contained in Table 2.

---

[27] All of the OIC subfiles are designed to maximize either the capabilities of real-time, on-line, or batch processing devices. The most current verified multilists and/or linking techniques are employed in constructing the subfiles and in the search-retrieval functions of the appropriate programs. Equipment and economics permitting, consideration should be given to consolidating the eight files into a single file. However, only actual implementation studies can resolve the actual file organization which is most desirable.

[28] One significant restriction is stressed at this point, namely, the OIC does not contain information representing the complete criminal history on any individual. Indications are that this capability will be provided for by state and federal automatic data processing operations.

[29] Mitchel, *op. cit.*, p. 71.

TABLE 2. **Operations Information Component:**
Data Elements and Input Documents

OIC File and Input Documents

Data Elements	Master Inquiry (master inquiry card)	Warrant and Want (warrant and want forms)	Arrest (arrest report)	Offense* (offense report)	Field Interview (field interview card)	Traffic Citation† (traffic citation form)	Traffic Accident (traffic accident report)	Called-for Service‡ (dispatch record card)
Name of individual	1	2	2	2	1	3	3	
Involvement of individual (criminal suspect, victim, witness, or driver)	1	2	2	2	1	3	3	
Resident address of individual	1	2	2	2		3	3	
Date of birth	1	2	2	2	1	3	3	
Type of event and subfile§	1	2	2	2	1	3		3
Reporting district	1		2	2	1	3	3	3
Address of event(s)	1	2	2	2				3
Date and time of event(s)	1		2	2	1	3	3	3
Department record no.	1	2	2	2		3	3	
Place of birth		2	2	2				
Sex	1	2	2	2	1	3	3	
Descent (race)		2	2	2	1	3		
Height		2	2	2	1	3		
Weight		2	2	2	1	3		
Hair		2	2	2	1	3		
Eyes		2	2	2	1	3		
Social security number		2	2	2				
Year and make of vehicle		2	2	2	1		3	
Body type		2	2	2	1			
Color(s) of vehicle		2	2	2	1			
License number		2	2	2	1			
Disposition: arrested, bail, fine dismissed, warrant recalled, date cleared		2	2	2				3
Police agency handling: primary responsibility and assigned responsibility		2						
Issuing authority warrant		2						
Warrant and/or want file number		2						
Date warrant issued		2						
Bail amount		2						
Type of warrant and/or want		2						
Booking number			2					
Date and time of offense			2	2				

356

Data Elements	Master Inquiry (master inquiry card)	Warrant and Want (warrant and want forms)	Arrest (arrest report)	Offense (offense report)	Field Interview (field interview card)	Traffic Citation† (traffic citation form)	Traffic Accident (traffic accident report)	Called-for Service† (dispatch record card)
Type of premises			2	2				
Aliases			2	2	1			
Marks, scars, tattoos			2	2	1			
Clothing worn			2	2	1			
Driver's license number			2	2	1			
Personal property			2					
Reporting officer (number)			2	2	1	3	3	
Date of release			2					
Stolen property description			2	2				
Value of stolen property			2	2				
Driver, passenger, pedestrian					1			
Day						3	3	
Weather						3	3	
Traffic volume						3	3	
Violation or accident occurred and street						3	3	
Violation or accident occurred at or near intersection						3	3	
Direction of travel						3	3	
Type of motor vehicle							3	
Total killed							3	
Status of fatalities							3	
Fatality – date of birth							3	
Fatality – sex							3	
Total injured							3	
Status of injured							3	
Injured – date of birth							3	
Injured – sex							3	
Pedestrian – residence							3	
Pedestrian – date of birth							3	
Pedestrian – sex							3	
Lighting							3	
Type of locality							3	
Road surface condition							3	

TABLE 2.   (Continued)

	OIC File and Input Documents							
Data Elements	Master Inquiry (master inquiry card)	Warrant and Want (warrant and want forms)	Arrest (arrest report)	Offense° (offense report)	Field Interview (field interview card)	Traffic Citation† (traffic citation form)	Traffic Accident (traffic accident report)	Called-for Service‡ (dispatch record card)
Street class							3	
Contributing circumstances							3	
Watch							3	
Beat								3
Dispatch or observed								3
Officer(s) assigned								3
Assigned unit(s)								3
Date and time of unit(s) dispatched								3
Date and time unit(s) arrival								3
Date and time of completion								3
Requests for other emergency unit(s)								3
Climatological data								3

Source: Municipal Systems Research, *A Pilot Study of a Municipal Civil Defense Information Subsystem*, Quarterly Technical Report Number 3 to the Office of Civil Defense, Department of the Army, Washington, October 1967. The above table was prepared by Paul M. Whisenand, Research Associate, Municipal Systems Research, School of Public Administration, University of Southern California (Los Angeles: Municipal Systems Research, 1967), Vol. 3, Sec. 8, pp. 47–51. Code: 1 = real-time, on-line, and event-triggered data for police department use only. 2 = real-time, on-line, and event-triggered data for police department and criminal justice use only. (Note: the data listed are more advantageously stored at some other jurisdictional level.) 3 = batch-processed and time-triggered data for police department use only.

°Based on high offense frequency or a uniquely successful pattern of criminal operation, the offense subfile is automatically triggered to furnish this information by situs address for subsequent mailing to concerned citizens. This mailing can be separate or coordinated with other city mailings such as the water bill. Also, it can be designated as city wide or limited to a specific neighborhood.

†A traffic citation is either a misdemeanor or felony violation. Technically, such violations should be included in the arrest subfile. However, there is an inextricable relationship between the number and type of traffic accidents and the number and type of traffic violations. Therefore, both are located in the same subfile. It is noted that information regarding stolen and recovered vehicles is contained in the offense subfile. The connective relationship between accidents and citations does not appear to include stolen vehicles.

Conversion

The transcription personnel in the Computer Facility receive hard-copy documents regarding arrests, field interviews, offenses, warrants, traffic events, wants, and called-for services. The information contained in these reports is designed so that it can be easily converted to machine language for entry into the OIC.

Outputs

The eight files in the OIC are designed for immediate retrieval of information based on inquires concerning the community events that necessitated MSPD police services. Therefore, we will refer to the eight files as being *event triggered*. Event-triggered data are generated through the occurrence of an event in the community that is of significance to the local government. The master inquiry, warrant and want, arrest, offense, and field interview files are designed to process, analyze, and retrieve descriptive information in regard to a specific event. The warrant and want, arrest, and offense files possess an additional capability in that they transmit new and updated descriptive data elements into the related criminal justice information subsystems. All of the files that we mentioned above plus the traffic citation, traffic accident, and called-for service files offer a means for analyzing events and establishing trend lines. The MSPD requirements for individual event-triggered data normally call for fast response to inquiry; consequently, a real-time, on-line processing capacity is necessary. See Figure 5 which provides a general overview of OIC information processing.

ADMINISTRATIVE INFORMATION COMPONENT (AIC)

The next group of files for us to examine are those that constitute the administrative information component (AIC). The four files in the component are (a) supportive, (b) personnel, (c) environmental, and (d) management.

The data elements contained in the AIC are taken from the OIC files or generated by one of its own sources of input. The data drawn from the files in the AIC are analytical, rather than descriptive in nature. There-

---

‡ The called-for service subfile contains some of the information located in other or subfiles. It is emphasized that the called-for service subfile includes the reported police service need as originally received without subsequent modification based on new information derived from the investigation of the called-for service. This subfile is thus designed to provide police mangement with still another index of the responses made by their department to perceived rather than actual community needs for police services. The need for such a file is based on the article by Phillip H. Ennis, "Crimes, Victims, and the Police," in *Transaction*, 4, 35, 44 (June 1967).

§The type of event varies according to the particular requirements of each subfile. As an example, if the event is a traffic citation, the following information is included: 1. Kind of violation (California Vehicle Code or city traffic code). 2. Type of violation (parking meter, radar, involved in traffic accident, other). Further, if the event is a traffic accident then hit and run (misdemeanor or felony) and type of accident (fatal, nonfatal injury, property damage).

fore, it is quite natural that the information stored in the AIC be selected on the basis of needs as determined by administrative personnel in the MSPD. Thus we find that the AIC data can be processed in terms of both optimizing the probabilities of selecting the correct alternative for administrative problem solving, as well as facilitating routine reporting requirements. Figure 6 provides the reader with a system flow chart of the AIC.

Supportive Information File

The supportive information file (SIF) stores data that are subjected to processing routines for use in maintaining and improving procurement of input resources, and assisting in the processing of called-for police service outputs. Therefore we observe that the SIF provides a dual capability in that it is structured to better relate the department to its surrounding environment, and increase the quality of called-for services. The supportive data are collected through a supportive activity report completed by all police and civilian personnel involved in activities that are related to building environmental support for the MSPD. Some of the activities we place under this heading are, for example, involvement in academic programs, community organizations, crime prevention programs, and professional association membership.

Personnel Status File

The personnel status file (PSF) contains data relating to the present status of all MSPD employees. Briefly, it is designed to present MSPD management, especially those responsible for determining staff needs, information regarding all human resources currently operational in the department.[30] The PSF file is operated on in order to immediately furnish data describing an officer's or civilian employee's present assignment and off-duty location. Relatedly, we can see that MSPD assignment and watch

---

[30] Additional information concerning an individual's career development pattern and personal skills inventory is contained in the personnel information subsystem. The data elements of interest to the police in this related subsystem are as follows: previous divisional assignments, place of birth, date of birth, sex, descent, height, weight, hair, eyes, marital status, number of children, religion, military service record, military service status, blood type, means of recruitment, pre-entry examination grades, date of appointment, position appointed to, post-entry promotional examination grades, date of promotion(s), position(s) promoted to, date of evaluation, evaluation scores, leave of absence record, tenure, date of termination, reason for termination, date(s) of degree or certificate, degree or certificate in, date(s) courses studied, courses studied, date(s) of other training, other training, administrative skills, clerical commercial skills, construction skills, communication skills, criminalistics skills, recreational skills, organization(s) membership (role and degree of involvement), equipment operated, journalistic skills, photography skills, teaching skills, language(s) (degree of competency), and other talents and skills.

The equipment or billing date elements of interest to the police contained in other city information subsystems are as follows: division assigned, object, description, inventory serial number, date purchased or acquired, date of expected obsolescence, cost or value, manufacturers serial number, manufacturers name, model number, year of make, condition at time of purchase, present condition of equipment, time period in use, frequency of use during time period, frequency of maintenance, cost of maintenance, purpose or function, evaluation of object, and estimated replacement cost.

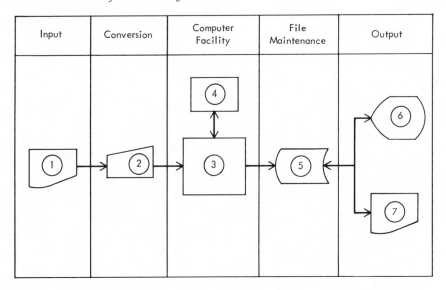

Input	Conversion	Computer Facility	File Maintenance	Output

1. Action-triggered input based on receipt of master inquiry, warrant and want, arrest, offense, field interview, traffic citation, traffic accident, and called-for service data. 2. Data converted to machine sensible language for entry into processor. 3. Computer facility programs. 4. Master file update. 5. System files: master inquiry, warrant and want, arrest, offense, field interview, traffic citation, traffic accident, and called-for service. 6. Information retrieved immediately in response to an inquiry for information concerning a specific event or person. 7. Information retrieved immediately in response to an inquiry for information concerning a series of events or a number of characteristics describing more than one individual.

Source: Municipal Systems Research, *A Pilot Study of a Municipal Civil Defense Information Subsystem*, Quarterly Technical Report Number 3 to the Office of Civil Defense, Department of the Army, Washington, October 1967. This figure was prepared by Paul M. Whisenand, Research Associate, Municipal Systems Research, School of Public Administration, University of Southern California (Los Angeles: Municipal Systems Research, 1967), Vol. 3. Sec. 8, p. 55.

FIGURE 5. **Operations Information Component: Processing**

plan information has rapid access and change potentialities that argue in favor of its being processed in a real-time, on-line mode.

Environmental Information File

The environmental information file (EIF) is operated on by processing routines that supply data designed to assist the MSPD in sensing significant changes in the community's social patterns. The EIF has been designed to handle questions about social, economic, and political changes so that related police practices and policies can be included in departmental planning. However, we should note the environmental information file contains only a small portion of that information deemed useful for identifying changing community needs. In other words, the vast majority of requisite information is located in related city information subsystems, and a host

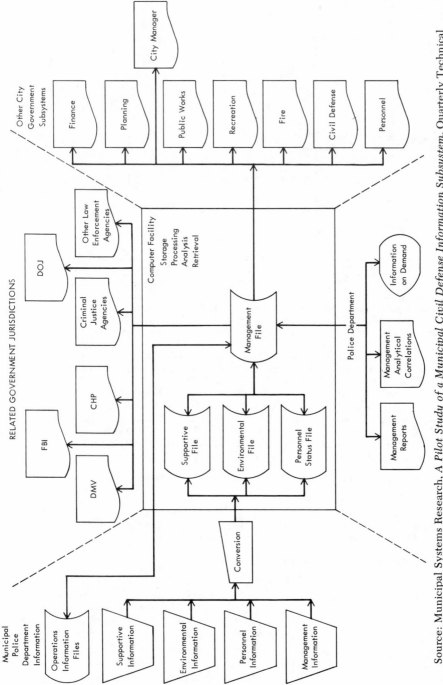

Source: Municipal Systems Research, *A Pilot Study of a Municipal Civil Defense Information Subsystem*, Quarterly Technical Report Number 3 to the Office of Civil Defense, Department of the Army, Washington, October 1967. This figure was prepared by Paul M. Whisenand, Research Associate, Municipal Systems Research, School of Public Administration, University of Southern California (Los Angeles: Municipal Systems Research, 1967), Vol. 3, Sec. 8, p. 56.

FIGURE 6. **Flow Chart of the Administrative Information Component: Police Subsystem**

of exogenous information systems. When integrated or interfaced, we can see that these systems and subsystems provide a series of indicators pertaining to individuals, equality, democratic processes, education, arts and sciences, free-enterprise economy, economic growth, technological change, agriculture, living conditions, and health and welfare.[31]

Consequently, the quantified data provided by this file can be used to indicate significant existing and emergent community problems, and broader socioeconomic issues (sometimes referred to as "social indicators") with law enforcement implications. Furthermore, social indicators are more meaningful when evaluated by the MSPD in relation to pertinent environmental values and departmental objectives.[32]

Management Information File[33]

The management information file (MIF) is subjected to computer facility programs which analyze, and retrieve data required for MSPD management decision making and routine reporting.[34] The MIF both facilitates and *supports effective police management decisioning* through time and event-triggered report generation, monitoring and direction for programs performance (targeting toward organizational objectives), and the sharing of pertinent information of general value for all subsystems comprising municipal government and criminal justice.[35] The reader should especially note the phrase "supports effective police management decisioning." It is employed deliberately to avoid the implication that the computer itself is a decision maker in any important respect. While we find it true that many lower-order decisions have been programmed for the computer, the computer's primary role in a police information system is to furnish data adequate to aid the decision-making function.

Inputs

Concentrating on file inputs, we find that the inputs for the SIF are provided by a hard-copy report containing data about supportive transactions.

[31] This list of indicators is suggested by A. D. Biderman, "Social Indicators and Goals," in Raymond A. Bauer, ed., *Social Indicators* (Cambridge, Mass.: M.I.T. Press, 1966), pp. 147–52.

[32] "Attempts to use social indicators to direct social change will greatly profit by our subjecting social statistics to the same kinds of detached sociological scrutiny that we give other institutional products." *Ibid.*, p. 70.

[33] An extremely worthwhile discussion of management information systems occurs in a series of articles in *Datamation*, 13 (May 1967), and by J. M. Allderige, "Off-Line Management," in *Datamation*, 14, 43 (June 1968). Also, see Martin Landau, ed., *Management Information Technology—Recent Advances and Implications for Public Administration* (Pittsburgh: Fels Institute of Local and State Government, University of Pennsylvania, 1965).

[34] It is to be remembered that not all of the functionally required management information is located within the APIS. This is especially valid when management decisions are analyzed, since a sizeable portion of the useful data remains unprogrammable. Therefore, a significant amount of nonautomated data is either collected by some other means or, in part, disregarded by police management.

[35] The vast majority of information exchanged within the system of criminal justice continues to be of a descriptive or operations nature. See the operations information subsystem.

1. Type of involvement
2. Date(s) of involvement
3. Total time(s) involved
4. Degree of involvement
5. Reporting district
6. Location of involvement
7. Name of organization or association
8. Role of participant
9. Personnel involved
10. Objective(s) of personnel involved
11. Disposition
12. Value of supportive service performed
13. Value of supportive service received
14. Recommendations for future action

The inputs for the PSF are acquired through the MSPD assignment and beat plan form, comprised of the following:

1. Name
2. Serial number (social security number)
3. Date and time period of current duty status
4. Current beat assignment
5. Current divisional assignment
6. Residence address
7. Residence telephone
8. Off-duty status

The inputs for the EIF vary with changing social needs and departmental demands. The EIF is predominantly heuristic in nature thus accommodating frequent changes in required data inputs. Departmental community relations and planning and research units primarily determine and initiate source input documents that contain environmentally oriented data elements:[36]

1. Type of environmental need/problem
2. Time of observance
3. Date of observance
4. Degree of significance to department
5. Type of significance to department
6. Departmental units with major responsibility

---

[36] Since environmental data elements are not constant but highly changeable due to their futuristic characteristics, this list is neither complete nor unchanging. Moreover, the majority of specialized information required by the planning and research unit usually possesses short-term value only. Therefore, environmental information is most often singular in purpose and soon obsolete. Special projects and police research efforts are examples of such environment-oriented programs.

7. Reporting districts involved
8. Source of need
9. Location of need
10. Organizations involved
11. Individuals involved
12. Role of observer
13. Name of observer
14. News media involved
15. Disposition at time of observance
16. Recommended remedial action
17. Recommended departmental changes
18. Final resolution

Inputs to the MIF are as follows:

1. Department performance goals
2. Department performance objectives
3. Department performance standards
4. Department structural goals
5. Department structural objectives
6. Department structural standards
7. Bureau of Uniform Services performance objectives
8. Bureau of Uniform Services performance standards
9. Bureau of Uniform Services structural objectives
10. Bureau of Uniform Services structural standards
11. Bureau of Investigation Services performance objectives
12. Bureau of Investigation Services performance standards
13. Bureau of Investigation Services structural objectives
14. Bureau of Investigation Services structural standards
15. Bureau of Administrative Services performance objectives
16. Bureau of Administrative Services performance standards
17. Bureau of Administrative Services structural objectives
18. Bureau of Administrative Services structural standards

These data elements provide a form of targeting, in terms of goals, objectives, and standards, for the MSPD as a whole, the subunits, and the staff. The relating of data elements contained in other files to those inserted by MSPD management permits a quantitative monitoring of program and personnel performance.

Conversion. Transcription personnel in the City Computer Facility receive the above listed data elements on hard-copy input forms. Subsequently, the information contained in these documents is directly converted to machine readable language for entry into the various information files and related processes. The data elements from OIC files are already machine amenable and require no conversion for purposes of the AIC.

This in turn facilitates the transmittal of data elements from interfacing files and subfiles into the AIC.

Outputs. The four files in the AIC are designed to support MSPD administrative decision making through the analysis and retrieval of time and/or event triggered information. Time-triggered information is output on a predetermined basis to meet routine reporting and analytical requirements. Event-triggered information is output on a demand basis which is predicated on a specification.

We see that the SIF outputs information intended to assist MSPD administrators in their efforts to improve their relations with other surrounding jurisdictions. The PSF supplies information designed to aid the police administrator in formulating beat plans and manpower allocations. Also, it has a capability for immediately transmitting information about the present on-duty of off-duty location of an MSPD employee.

Further, the EIF outputs a general review of the environmental responses being made by the department to community changes. The administrator is thus provided with a means for quickly comparing previous techniques and results with those presently in use. In addition, the status and findings of special research and planning activities are reported. To summarize, we have learned that the EIF provides the MSPD with environmental inputs or indicators of existing and emergent community needs which supplement those derived from general community planning and the broader socioeconomic system. The MIF first generates a managerial outline for subsequent organizational analysis and evaluation. Second, the file is responsible for filling in the outline by automatically selecting appropriate data from the interrelated files in the AIC and OIC. Both outline and content are then output either on a time-triggered or on an event-triggered basis. There are essentially two interrelated time-triggered reporting requirements: (a) external—city and criminal justice and (b) internal—police department.[37] Figure 7 presents for the reader a general illustration of AIC information processing. Further, Table 3 provides a description of time-triggered information reporting requirements.[38] Not listed for us is the event-triggered (exceptional) information because it stems from special and singular requests.

[37] Internal security dictates which police data are shared with exogenous information systems. As an example, the number, location, and types of juvenile offenses can appropriately be given to the recreation department. The criminal justice subsystems are entitled to the names, addresses, case dispositions, and so on, of the juvenile offenders.

[38] Output reports described as basically fulfilling external user requirements are also used by the Department for internal purposes.

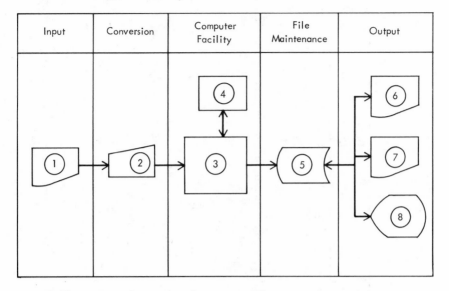

1. Time-triggered input based on receipt of supportive, maintenance, environmental, and management data. 2. Data converted to machine-sensible language for entry into processor. 3. Computer facility programs. 4. Master file update. 5. System files: supportive, personnel, environmental, and management. 6. Information retrieved according to predetermined time periods for reporting purposes. 7. Information retrieved in response to an inquiry for special analytical correlations. 8. Information retrieved immediately in response to an inquiry for information concerning a specific event or person.

Source: Municipal Systems Research, *A Pilot Study of a Municipal Civil Defense Information Subsystem*, Quarterly Technical Report Number 3 to the Office of Civil Defense, Department of the Army, Washington, October 1967. This figure was prepared by Paul M. Whisenand, Research Associate, Municipal Systems Research, School of Public Administration, University of Southern California (Los Angeles: Municipal Systems Research, 1967), Vol. 3, Sec. 8, p. 67.

FIGURE 7. **Administrative Information Component: Processing**

TABLE 3. **Management Information File–Reporting Requirements: Time-Triggered (Automatic) Data Output**

Output Report Title	Originating Source of Data	User Requirement Distribution	Frequency	General Information Reported
FBI Return A	APIS–OIC Information Files	FBI, Chief of Police	Monthly	Information relating: (1) the number and type of offenses reported or known, and (2) the number of offenses which are unfounded, actual, cleared by adult arrest, and cleared by juvenile arrest.
FBI Supplement to Return A	APIS–OIC Information Files	FBI, Chief of Police, bureau commanders	Monthly	Information relating: (1) the type and value, (2) the type and number of offenses against property as compared to values, (3) the type and number of larceny offenses as compared to values, and (4) the location and number of automobiles stolen and recovered.
FBI Return C	APIS–OIC Information Files	FBI, Chief of Police, bureau commanders	Annually	Information relating: (1) the number of persons charged (arrested and summoned or cited), (2) the number and type of case dispositions, and (3) the number of traffic arrests and citations.
FBI age, sex and race of persons arrested 18 years of age and over	APIS–OIC Information Files	FBI, Chief of Police	Annually	Information relating by type of offense, the age, sex, and race of offenders arrested 18 years and over.
FBI age, sex and race of persons arrested under 18 years of age	APIS–OIC Information Files	FBI, Chief of Police, bureau commanders	Annually	Information relating by type of offense, the age, sex, and race of offenders arrested under 18 years of age.

Report	Source	Distribution	Frequency	Description
State Department of Justice, felony, crime and clearance	APIS–OIC Information Files	State Department of Justice, Chief of Police, bureau commanders	Monthly	Similar to FBI Return A.
State Department of Justice, adult felony, arrests	APIS–OIC Information Files	State Department of Justice, Chief of Police	Monthly	Information relating: (1) adult felony offenses, (2) sex of the offenders, and (3) case dispositions.
State Department of Justice, juveniles arrested	APIS–OIC Information Files	State Department of Justice, Chief of Police, bureau commanders	Monthly	Similar to preceding report except all (felony and misdemeanors) offenses are included.
National Safety Council	APIS–OIC Information Files	National Safety Council, City Manager, Public Works Department, Planning Department, Chief of Police, all bureau commanders, Traffic Division Commander, Traffic Division Supervisor	Annually	Information relating: (1) the types and causes of traffic accidents, (2) traffic enforcement activities, and (3) a comparison with earlier periods.
City Manager Summary of performed police services	APIS–OIC Information Files APIS Environmental Information File APIS Supportive Information File	City Manager, all city department heads, Chief of Police, division commanders	Monthly	Information relating: (1) a summary of performed police services and staff activities, and (2) a comparison with earlier periods.
City Manager/Chief of Police performance-accomplishment analysis	All APIS Files	City Manager, Chief of Police, bureau commanders	Monthly	Information relating: (1) crime, traffic and general police services performed in relation to predetermined performance goals, objectives, and standards, (2) structural activities performed in relation to predetermined structural goals, objectives, and standards, (3) changes of over 10% and (4) comparisons with earlier periods.

369

TABLE 3. (Continued)

Output Report Title	Originating Source of Data	User Requirement Distribution	Frequency	General Information Reported
Traffic events	APIS–OIC Information Files	City Manager, Public Works Department, Planning Department, Chief of Police, bureau commanders, traffic division commanders, traffic division supervisors	Monthly	Information relating: (1) traffic accidents, (2) enforcement activities, and (3) miscellaneous traffic events, and (4) traffic workload analysis.
Location and type of performed and called-for police services	APIS–OIC	Planning Department, Chief of Police, bureau commanders, division commanders, division supervisors	Monthly	Information relating: (1) the types of performed services by time, day, reporting district, and census tract, (2) the types of called-for police services by time, day, reporting district, and census tract, and (3) comparison with earlier periods.
Performed police services for juveniles and young adults	APIS–OIC Information Files	City Manager, Recreation Department, School District, Chief of Police, Uniform Bureau Commander, Uniform Division Commander, uniform division supervisors, investigation bureau, investigation division commanders, investigation division supervisors	Monthly	Information relating performed police services for juveniles and young adults (18–25 years of age).
Performed police service: fire related	APIS–OIC Information Files	Fire Department, Chief of Police, Uniform Bureau Commander, uniform division commanders	Monthly	Information relating performed police services which are connected to fire protection.

Report/Transaction	File	Recipients	Frequency	Information Relating
Police department personnel transactions	APIS Personnel Status File	Personnel Department, Chief of Police, all bureau commanders, all division commanders, all division supervisors	Daily	Information relating changes in assigned personnel and their position.
Police department financial transactions	All APIS Files	Finance Department, Chief of Police, all bureau commanders	Weekly	Information relating: (1) past, present, and predicted status of program accomplishment, plant use, and equipment life, and (2) data elements of use in the citywide PPBS.
Disaster preparedness and emergency operations	APIS Personnel File, APIS, Environmental Information File	City Manager, Disaster Preparedness Department, Chief of Police, all bureau commanders, all division commanders, all division supervisors	One per 8-hr shift	Information relating: (1) present operations status, and (2) existing and predicted disaster emergencies.
Location and type of performed police services: criminal justice users	APIS-OIC Information Files	Involved Court District, Involved Parole Office, Involved Probation Department, Involved District Attorney, Involved FBI Field Office, Involved State Department of Justice Field Office, adjacent local police departments	Monthly	Information relating: (1) performed police services by time, day, reporting district and census, and (2) comparisons with earlier periods.
Special reports on demand	All APIS Files	Requesting User, Chief of Police, Administrative Service Bureau Commander	As needed	Information dependent on request. Based on departmental approval, external and internal users can query the APIS for needed information. Such requests, depending on the type of interface and information subsystem configuration, are either handled automatically or through manual search. After repeated special requests for the same information from a particular requesting subsystem will

371

TABLE 3. (Continued)

Output Report Title	Originating Source of Data	User Requirement Distribution	Frequency	General Information Reported
				result in the output being changed to an automatic mode. The APIS data base and program capacity for unique aggregations and output of data is sufficiently flexible to make an effective response to nearly all inquiries. Therefore, the APIS changes as new information reporting requirements are ascertained and those in existence are modified by the agency and external subsystem users.
Exceptional occurrences	APIS–OIC, Information Files, APIS Environmental Information File, APIS Supportive Information File	City Manager, Chief of Police, all bureau commanders, all division commanders	Immediate	Information relating occurrences of special interest to city government in general and the police department in particular.
Uniform crime reports	FBI Information System	All police personnel	Quarterly Annually	Information relating statistics concerning the national crime pattern.
State Department of Justice crime reports	State Department of Justice Information System	All police personnel	Quarterly and Annually as Generated	Information relating: (1) statistics concerning the statewide crime pattern, and (2) special studies and research reports.
City Management activities	City Management Information Subsystem	Chief of Police	Monthly	Information relating: (1) programs accomplished, initiated, and planned by priority, and (2) important present and future city government and community events of relevance to the police department.

Public Works Department: traffic engineering activities	Public Works Information Subsystem	Chief of Police, all bureau commanders, all division commanders, traffic division supervisors	Monthly	Information relating present and planned changes in traffic, engineering streets, and highways.
Planning Department activities	Planning Department Information Subsystem	Chief of Police, all bureau commanders, all division commanders	Monthly	Information relating: (1) all present and planned changes in land uses, and (2) changes in industrial and residential patterns.
City Clerk activities	Business license fee	Chief of Police, all bureau commanders, all division commanders	Monthly	Information relating all present and requested business permits that are pertinent to possible police services.
Personnel Department: update of police department personnel	Personnel Department Information Subsystem	Chief of Police, all bureau commanders, all division commanders	Daily	Information relating all changes in the position and career development of police personnel.
Finance Department: update of police department budget	Finance Department Information Subsystem	Chief of Police, all bureau commanders	Monthly	Information relating: (1) present expenditures and remaining unspent balances relative to, program objectives, (2) comparable figures for past quarters and years, and (3) projected expenditures for forthcoming period.
Civil Disaster Preparedness and Emergency Operations Department	Civil Disaster Preparedness Information Subsystem	Chief of Police, all bureau commanders, all division commanders, all division supervisors	One per 8-hr shift	Information relating: (1) present citywide operations status, (2) potential disaster emergencies, and (3) if required, alternative disaster solution approaches.
Recreation and Parks Department	Recreation and Parks Information Subsystem	All bureau commanders, all division commanders, all investigation personnel, all uniform personnel	Monthly	Information relating: (1) identification data on potential youthful and young adult offenders, and (2) existing or possible problem areas.

TABLE 3. (Continued)

Output Report Title	Originating Source of Data	User Requirement Distribution	Frequency	General Information Reported
Fire Department	Fire Department Information Subsystem	All bureau commanders, all division commanders, all division supervisors	Monthly	Information relating: (1) identification data on suspected arsonists, (2) high fire danger areas, and (3) monthly summary of fire responses.
Local School District	School District Information System	All bureau commanders, all division commanders, all investigation personnel, all uniform personnel	Monthly	Information relating: (1) planned events requiring police involvement, (2) existing and potential problem areas and (3) flagrant violators requiring school discipline.
FBI Local Field Office Activities	FBI Information System	Chief of Police, all bureau commanders, all division commanders	Monthly	Information relating: (1) activities performed in or nearby the city by type, time, day, reporting district and census tract, and (2) comparisons with previous periods.
State Department of Justice	State Department of Justice Information System	Chief of Police, all bureau commanders, all division commanders	Monthly	Information relating: (1) activities performed in or nearby the city by type, time, day, reporting district, and census tract, and (2) comparisons with previous periods.
State Parole Division	State Parole Information System	Chief of Police, all bureau commanders, all division commanders	Monthly	Information relating: (1) activities performed in or nearby the city by type, time, day, reporting district and census tract, and (2) comparisons with previous periods.
County Probation Department	County Probation Information System	Chief of Police, all bureau commanders, all division commanders	Monthly	Information relating: (1) activities performed in or nearby the city by type, time, day, reporting district, and census tract, and (2) comparisons with previous periods.

County District Attorneys' Office	County District Attorney's Information System	Chief of Police, all bureau commanders, all division commanders	Monthly	Information relating: (1) activities performed in or nearby the city by type, time, day, reporting district, and census tract, and (2) interpretation of recent legal decisions and statutes.
State Department of Corrections	State Department Corrections Information System	Chief of Police, all bureau commanders, all division commanders	Monthly	Information relating: (1) the release into or acceptance of offenders from or nearby the city.
Superior and Lower Courts	State Court Information System	Chief of Police, all bureau commanders, all division commanders	Monthly	Information relating the status and disposition of offenders from or nearby the city.
Adjacent local law enforcement agencies	Other local law enforcement information system	Chief of Police, all bureau commanders, all division commanders	Monthly	Information relating: (1) activities performed in or nearby the city by type, time, day, reporting district and census tract, and (2) comparisons with previous periods.
Officer's monthly activity summary	APIS–OIC Information Files, APIS Environmental Information File, APIS Supportive Information File	All division commanders, all division supervisors	Monthly	Information relating activities performed by individual officers.
Patrol monthly activity summary	APIS–OIC Information Files, APIS Environmental Information File, APIS Supportive Information File	Uniform Bureau Commander, Patrol Division Commander, Patrol Division	Monthly	Information relating: (1) performed and called-for police patrol services in detail, and (2) workload analysis.

TABLE 3. (Continued)

Output Report Title	Originating Source of Data	User Requirement Distribution	Frequency	General Information Reported
Detective monthly activity summary	APIS–OIC Information Files, APIS Environmental Information File, APIS Supportive Information File	Investigation Bureau Commander, Detective Division Commander, Detective Division Supervisors	Monthly	Information relating: (1) performed police detective services in detail, and (2) workload analysis.
Juvenile monthly activity summary	APIS–OIC Information Files, APIS Environmental Information File, APIS Supportive Information File	Investigation Bureau Commander, Juvenile Division Commander, Juvenile Division Supervisors	Monthly	Information relating: (1) performed police juvenile services in detail, and (2) workload analysis.
Equipment and plant status summary	Purchasing Department Information Subsystem	Chief of Police all bureau commanders, all division commanders	Monthly	Information relating current status of police equipment and buildings.
Police personnel status summary	Personnel File Department Information File	Chief of Police, all bureau commanders, all division commanders	Monthly	Information relating: (1) all changes in human resources, and (2) training activities.
Environmental activities	APIS Environmental Information File	Chief of Police, all bureau commanders, all division commanders	Monthly	Information relating in detail all environmental activities.

Supportive activities	APIS Supportive Information File	Chief of Police, all bureau commanders, all division commanders	Monthly	Information relating in detail all supportive activities.
Anticipated police services to	APIS–OIC Information Files, APIS Management Information File	Chief of Police, all bureau commanders, all division commanders	Monthly	Information relating predicted police services to be performed in the following month, 3 month, and 12 month periods.

Source: Municipal Systems Research, *A Pilot Study of a Municipal Civil Defense Information Subsystem*, Quarterly Technical Report Number 3 to the Office of Civil Defense, Department of the Army, Washington, October 1967. The above table was prepared by Paul M. Whisenand, Research Associate, Municipal Systems Research, School of Public Administration, University of Southern California (Los Angeles: Municipal Systems Research, 1967), Vol. 3, Sec. 8, pp. 68–78.

12

POLICE-COMMUNITY RELATIONS

The mutual advantages of a friendly relationship between the people of a community and their police force should be widely understood and more fully appreciated. The success of a police force in the performance of its duties is largely measured by the degree of support and cooperation it receives from the people it serves. It is of paramount importance, therefore, to secure for this department the confidence, respect, and approbation of the public. The cultivation of such desirable attitudes on the part of the public is dependent upon reciprocal attitudes on the part of this department.[1]

Each year as fiscal budgets and plans of action are being developed, there is a striving to justify the need for additional police personnel. Administrators are continually faced with rising crime rates, increases in called-for services, and a concomitant reduction in free patrol time—time to do the crime prevention that one hears so much about. Eventually, in all justification messages, the ratio of policemen to population is in some manner cited. While such arguments are postulated in a variety of ways, the population-policeman formula

[1] Los Angeles, California, Police Department Memorandum, 1963.

invariably boils down to three things: the ratio average of cities of similar size, the existent ratio in one's own city, and the desired ratio.

Perhaps there is no one ideal formula, but every police administrator would like to reach what he considers to be an optimum. Without public support, there could be no optimum. The police are not an occupational force and the community is not the enemy. The majority of both subscribe to similar values, similar goals. Unfortunately, this does not always guarantee majority support, especially the kind that requires more effort than mere lip service.

It is inconceivable that any community could financially afford adequate police service without substantial citizen support. True, at present a relatively small percentage of the citizenry does not support the police. This small percentage, however, is not evenly distributed among the total population; it is generally concentrated for the most part in areas predominantly populated by minorities who for certain reasons, real or imagined, view the police as antagonists.

This is not to say that the police who serve in white middle-class neighborhoods are free to ignore the problem, for they are not. The relationship that exists between the police and any community served is not to be regarded lightly.

Without the support of its citizens, a city police force in *any* ratio is not likely to be effective.

There has been a tendency in the past at least to primarily identify community support with citizen-police cooperation, with crime prevention, and perhaps even with the absence of verbal and physical assault. As we become more conscious of the criticalness of attracting high-quality young men and women into the police service, however, as well as retaining them, other facets become graphically apparent. The President's Commission on Law Enforcement and Administration of Justice put it this way in its 1967 report:

> Hostility, or even lack of confidence of a significant portion of the public, has extremely serious implications for the police. These attitudes interfere with recruiting, since able young men generally seek occupations which are not inordinately dangerous and which have the respect and support of their relatives and friends.
>
> Public hostility affects morale and makes police officers less enthusiastic about doing their job well. It may lead some officers to leave the force, to accept more prestigious or less demanding employment.[2]

[2] The President's Commission on Law Enforcement and Administration of Justice, *Task Force Report: The Police* (Washington, D.C.: Government Printing Office, 1967), p. 144.

The development of community support through the conscious improvement of police-community relations has shown itself not to be just one more front office idea to take up the field officer's time. Rather, it emerges as a prime target in the survival of not only police departments but entire communities where people can live, work, and play — in confidence and harmony.

The awareness of the importance of a good public image is not new, even to this century. Sir Robert Peel, the father of modern law enforcement, gave recognition in the early 1800s to the concept that the manner in which the police were viewed was likely to influence the degree of cooperation that they were likely to receive. He emphasized as a principle of police organization that "no quality is more indispensable than a command of temper; a quiet determined manner has more effect than violent action."[3]

In spite of the rich inheritance from Sir Robert Peel and the legion of able police administrators who followed, attempts to gain greater community effectiveness through formalized police-community programs were many decades arriving. While the need for police-community cooperation has been well recognized since those early times, apparently events as drastic as those occurring during the civil unrest of the 1950s and 1960s were needed to bring into focus the critical need for such formalized programs.

In this chapter it is our intent to develop support for the hypothesis that *police-community relations* are the crucial link, the difference between cooperation and noncooperation, interest and disinterest, respect and disrespect, and, finally, police success and police failure. We will explore a number of innovative programs and will also approach the question of training which we believe to be most paramount in any community relations program. For in the end it is not the philosophy of a chief alone that will motivate his officers to effective police-community relations, but rather their own understanding of the problem and their own commitment to the program and to the community.

POLICE-COMMUNITY RELATIONS VERSUS PUBLIC RELATIONS

Earlier police texts have generally dealt with the relationship between the police and the community as primarily being one of "public relations." One such listed the following as goals for a public relations program;

> *Public Understanding*. This is primarily an educational goal. It

[3] Attributed to Sir Robert Peel.

presupposes that an informed citizenry is basic to effective law enforcement.

Public Confidence. This is primarily a psychological goal. It involves the building of citizen trust and respect for the policemen and police department.

Public Support. Such support may take many forms such as compliance with the law, assistance in police investigations, and backing of measures to improve the police service.[4]

These goals are still valid, of course, but it must be recognized that there are major differences in *public relations* as compared with *police-community relations* programs where goals have been formulated as follows:

1. To encourage police-citizen partnership in the cause of crime prevention.

2. To foster and improve communication and mutual understanding between the police and the total community.

3. To promote interprofessional approaches to the solution of community problems, and stress the principle that the administration of justice is a total community responsibility.

4. To enhance cooperation among the police, prosecution, the courts, and corrections.

5. To assist police and other community leaders to achieve an understanding of the nature and causes of complex problems in people-to-people relations, and especially to improve police-minority group relationships.

6. To strengthen implementation of equal protection under the law for all persons.[5]

Public relations is essentially a one-way communication program embracing the concept that people are more likely to support those things that they understand. *Police-community relations,* on the other hand, involve two-way communication with the specific intent of bringing about change and modification. This change is desirable on the part of not only the public but the police as well.

The need for an active *public relations* program has not diminished with the formalization of police-community relations. If anything, the priority of its importance to the total law enforcement program is even greater than in earlier years. The police are continually called upon to perform many tasks, the results of which often take on negative overtones, especially when overshadowed by half truths and

[4] Institute for Training in Municipal Administration, *Municipal Police Administration,* 5th ed. (Chicago: The International City Manager's Association, 1961), p. 476.

[5] Paul M. Whisenand, *Police Supervision—Theory and Practice* (Englewood Cliffs, N.J.: Prentice-Hall, Inc., 1971), p. 277.

conjecture by the uninformed or the ill informed. Therefore, much clarification is needed and can best reach the greatest number of people in the most expedient manner through an active public relations program.

It must be recognized, however, that successful organizations are those that are flexible enough to accommodate changing needs and to change themselves. Recognizing the need for change is the first step in the process, and this recognition is accomplished through feedback. The best feedback is often the most direct, and in this case it involves the bringing together of active members of the police department and active members of the community in a two-way communication situation. Obviously, there is a certain amount of *public relations* in *police-community relations*, a communication of the kind of goals and responsibilities held by the police and the method by which they are most likely to be accomplished. On the other hand, with two-way conversation the police learn something of how they and their actions are perceived and, if they are properly alert, how they can better attain certain goals in a more acceptable manner.

Patrol-level officers and citizens in their own neighborhoods are the two most basic or primary elements in the relationship that exists between the police and the community. Obviously, there are many kinds of policemen and equally numerous publics. Some officers instinctively know how to communicate effectively in a diversity of situations. And, too, some publics have always respected the police. Numerous studies show, however, that in too many clusters, especially in the lower socioeconomic groups and the police who serve them, there is little effective communication and little change by either side to accommodate needs of the other.

THE HANDLING OF POLICE-COMMUNITY RELATIONS PROGRAMS

Police-community relations are handled in a variety of ways depending upon a number of factors, such as the department's size, the available manpower, and the orientation of staff-level officers, especially the chief. And in some departments they are simply not handled at all. The President's Commission on Law Enforcement and Administration of Justice indicated that most police agencies were keenly aware of serious community problems but were slow to institute programs to confront them.[6]

Traditional belief in the police service has been that the *complete policeman* can do and will do all jobs. "Every policeman is a community relations officer" has been espoused by many police ad-

---

[6] President's Commission, *Task Force Report*, p. 150.

ministrators. In the organizational structure of the police department, the idea that police-community relations are everyone's job most often leads to the *job* being accomplished by no one. "Although, ideally every man on the force should indeed be a community relations officer, he also has a full-time job of patrol or investigation. What is in effect every officer's business can wind up being no one's business."[7]

We are not indicating that because policemen have other full-time assignments and that because they are busy they are free to ignore their individual and personal role in reducing negative and building positive community attitudes toward the police. Rather, we are observing, along with others, that the importance of community support is too great to be looked upon as simply an adjunct to other duties. Therefore, if a police-community relations program is to be successful, responsibility for its direction, coordination, and implementation must be formalized.

In smaller departments, formalization may be in the form of a single person and in some cases even half of one officer's time. We are aware of the staffing constraints on smaller police departments but still must point out the inherent shortcomings of an assignment that receives only part of a man's time. Generally speaking, there is no equitable way to divide an officer's time in half, for there is no logical way to insure the point at which he can drop one function and pick up another. The probable result will be that at best one of the jobs will suffer, and there is a risk that neither will achieve expectations.[8]

Small police departments typically have had to make do with part-time court liaison officers, part-time pistol range masters, part-time lab men, and so on. Perhaps these have enjoyed a measure of success and could be pointed to as examples of why a part-time police-community relations coordinator might be expected to perform equally well. We would counter with two observations: First, these other functions are close-ended in that they can most often be programmed for a specific time and place. Police-community relations, on the other hand, are open-ended and ever changing, and the coordinator must be available at all times. Second, we would gamble that the other "part-time" jobs are in fact not operating at a desirable level, but rather at an acceptable level, considering other priorities, which of course small departments must always consider. Police-community relations, especially in the more sensitive communities, cannot be

[7] *Ibid.*

[8] For an excellent discussion of staffing for effectiveness, we suggest viewing Peter Drucker's training film, *Staffing for Strength* (BNA Films, Division of the Bureau of National Affairs, Inc., Rockwell, Maryland).

considered in the same light. Otherwise, the program will tend to become a lip service program at best.

Some larger departments, more able to specialize, have tended to have one central police-community relations unit that covers all the police divisions, precincts, or area offices, while others have appointed one or more officers in each division. Typically they report directly to the division commander and operate autonomously in terms of the total organization.

Both designs are capable of producing a level of desirable results, but both are restrictive to some degree. The umbrella unit handling all police-community relations from one central point is likely to develop standard programs not properly modified for specific neighborhoods.

> The task of building strong police-community relations is different with each population group. In one case, it may be a matter of translating a general endorsement into concrete assistance to the police in preventing crime, obtaining adequate salaries, and the like. In minority communities, the effort must begin at a more basic level with a frank exploration of the attitudes and practices which cause hostility on both sides.[9]

And too, there is a need for feedback and training by the police-community relations unit to the precinct or division, which may be difficult to achieve since it is not responsible to the area commander.

On the other hand, police-community relations officers assigned to individual precincts or divisions and who are not coordinated by a central unit are likely to produce fragmented programs, some even in conflict with one another.

CENTRAL CONTROL

The necessity for a formal organizational entity's having primary responsibility for police-community relations cannot be overstated. Departments with totally fragmented police-community relations programs have generally not gotten the job done, or the results have not measured up to the investment of manpower and effort.

To realize the best of two worlds, then, it is essential that each division, precinct, or geographical designation have its own police-community relations unit, which in turn has a concomitant relationship to the central or headquarters police-community relations unit. The central unit sets general program guidelines, interprets and translates departmental policy, and generally is responsible for the coordination and communication between all police-community relations

[9] President's Commission, *Task Force Report*, p. 150.

units. The individual police-community relations units in turn are expected to transmit programs into action and to adapt them to the individuality of the area served.

The formalization and implementation of a police-community relations unit, or units, does not, however, insure the attainment of necessary goals. The President's Commission on Law Enforcement and Administration of Justice observed that

> Too often such units have been regarded by the rest of the department as the sole repository of the responsibility for good community relations. The activities of the units are not well known in other parts of the department and have rarely affected the activities of individual officers or substantially influenced departmental policy in such police activities as field interrogation, recruitment, assignment of personnel, and integrated patrols.[10]

Observation of numerous police-community relations programs has led us to conclude that there must be understanding and support by the departmental majority if such programs are to enjoy a respectable measure of success. In addition, each departmental member must also understand the positive relationship good police-community relations have to his individual job. It appears that this understanding and support is most likely to occur in those departments that involve their regular operational personnel in addition to the police-community relations specialists. Two excellent examples of this philosophy, the Los Angeles Police Department's Basic Car Plan and the Covina Police Department's more modest Coffee Klatch Program, will be discussed later in this chapter. In both cases patrol car officers, through the coordination of the police-community relations unit or coordinator, operate directly with citizen groups in their respective patrol areas or beats and are in the best possible position to relate their philosophy to the real world.

ELEMENTS THAT DETRACT FROM POLICE-COMMUNITY RELATIONS

The very existence of a police-community relations unit surprisingly enough will be threatening to some segments of both the community and the police department. Regardless of the unit's title, regardless of its goals and good intentions, some at least will perceive a sinister or negative motive.

At the community level, there is a need for confidence and freedom of expression. By virtue of his presence, the police-community relations officer will learn a great deal about the community, and

[10] *Ibid.*, p. 151.

rightly so, since his is a training as well as a communication function. Care must be taken, however, to insure that he is not called upon to consciously seek intelligence-type information. Obviously, intelligence is necessary for some departmental operations. On the other hand, "if a community relations unit deliberately engages in intelligence activities, many citizens—and particularly those already suspicious of the police—will refuse to participate in its activities."[11]

The point being made is that the formal organization should recognize that sincerity, trust, and mutual respect must exist between the community and the community-relations officer and should make every attempt not to compromise this relationship.

Conversely, the police-community relations officers are bound to learn a great deal about the conduct of other departmental members. If the department in general perceives the police-community relations unit as covert, that it is in reality an "internal affairs unit" searching for police misconduct, or at least investigating police misconduct coming to its attention, dysfunctional suspicion will arise.

While the police-community unit is the source of a great deal of information, the information should be primarily utilized for training and bringing about understanding and change in the broadest, most positive sense.

The police-community relations officer must not be placed in a compromising situation in the community. It is only reasonable that he likewise should not be compromised in his own department.

THE SPAWNING OF POLICE-COMMUNITY RELATIONS

In recent years we have witnessed a surge of interest in and implementation of police-community relations programs. Three factors appear to be major contributors:

1. The 1967 report of the President's Commission on Law Enforcement and Administration of Justice
2. The 1968 report of the National Advisory Commission on Civil Disorders
3. The infusion of federal funds through the Law Enforcement Assistance Administration and its local state agency counterparts

The President's Commission on Law Enforcement focused on the general problem of police ineffectiveness. The Commission on Civil Disorders became more specific and more dramatic because of the many immediate instances of violent disorder. Together they set

[11] *Ibid.,* p. 153.

the direction; federal funding became the vehicle. Of course all police-community relations programs have not required or received federal funds. Generally speaking, however, it was difficult for most police agencies to justify specific funds for an activity that seemed to
have little relationship to the accepted traditional police activity and
produced such intangible results. Today, however, the need for such
programs is well established and the implementation of new programs
is an almost daily occurrence.

KINDS OF POLICE-COMMUNITY RELATIONS PROGRAMS

Police-community relations programs generally fall into two categories: First and most easily recognized is the formalized police-
community relations precinct or area unit. Second is the myriad of
support programs, and it is on these programs that this section of the
chapter will focus.

Support programs more commonly known by such titles as the
School Resource Officer Program (Tucson, Arizona), Ride Along Program (Los Angeles County District Attorney), Bicycle Safety Program
(National Safety Council), Crisis Intervention (New York City), Coffee
Klatch Program (Covina, California), and Basic Car Plan (Los Angeles,
California). Many prefer acronyms, such as P.A.C.E., public anti-
crime effort (Monterey Park, California). All are vitally important and
for a number of reasons, not the least of which is that they tend to involve the greatest number of police officers.

Regardless of the title or the area of special emphasis, each
program is aimed at opening communication links with some specific
element of the community, and each has an ultimate goal of reducing
conflict and obtaining voluntary cooperation and community support.
Perhaps the most important single element is that each program
places its officers in direct contact with the public in a nonthreatening situation where it is hoped that each will learn something positive about the other. Our own belief is that as police officers become
more personally involved in police-community relations programs,
the other desirable organizational traits will follow. For example, as
we stated in earlier chapters, a man must be "self-actualized,"
must feel that his work has meaning if he is to reach his potential. If
an officer is alienated from those he serves and only uses his job for
performing specific assigned functions for eight hours and then es-
capes back to his own world, he is not likely to perform optimally.

We are reminded of an interview with a veteran eastern police
officer who had worked the same particularly difficult ghetto beat for
ten years. After listening to his incredible description of a typical tour

of duty, we inquired as to how he had retained his stability. His answer was simple. "I just tell myself that I'm a zoo keeper. I go to work in the zoo for eight hours and then I go home." Obviously some people do need to be insulated from man's inhumanity to man, but a policeman who needs to be so insulated is not likely to offer much hope for those he serves. How much more rewarding his job would have been if he could have been personally involved, and how much better for his department had he had a personal mission.

Holyoke, an Example of Involvement and Awareness

Reemphasizing a need for personal development, one looks to the various federal programs that take Americans abroad to assist in the development of other nations. It would be unthinkable to send our representatives on such missions without thorough training and indoctrination in the culture, values, and language of the nation or district to be visited. The reason is obvious; if inadvertently our representatives offend or misunderstand the native culture, they are not likely to be effective in their mission. And yet daily we send white middle-class-oriented police officers into neighborhoods where the culture and the value system are equally foreign and where the language is either completely different or the words are similar but have totally different meanings. Obviously, under these conditions a police officer's effectiveness is severely impaired and he may do irreparable damage to police-community relations. In their 1968 report, the National Advisory Commission on Civil Disorders observed that

> If an officer has never met, does not know and cannot under-
> stand the language and the habits of the people in the area he
> patrols, he cannot do an effective job. He deprives himself of
> important sources of information. He fails to know those persons
> with "equity" in the community, home-owners, small business
> men, professional men, persons who are anxious to support proper
> law enforcement—and thus sacrifices the contributions they can
> make to maintaining community order.[12]

We would add that he is also likely to unnecessarily offend those people in whose area he patrols and inadvertently turn away the very people he is attempting to serve. It would seem incongruous that any formal police-training program could omit this most elementary base upon which the success of police-community relations is so dependent.

[12]Otto Kerner, *Report of the National Advisory Commission on Civil Disorders* (Washington, D.C.: Government Printing Office, 1968), p. 160.

An interesting and viable positive example of this hypothesis is the Holyoke, Massachusetts, Police Team Project. In the Ward 1 Model Cities area of Holyoke, a police team consisting of one captain, two sergeants, and twelve patrolmen, all of whom are volunteers, is responsible for a 235-acre inner-city neighborhood with a population consisting of 60 percent French Canadian descent, 21 percent Puerto Rican, and 16 percent black. This is a storefront operation and the team is located centrally in the area served. The team is a highly sensitized group of men whose members carry and display identification credentials printed in both English and Spanish. An important facet of the program design, in addition to its police methodology, is its focus on studies in human relations, with particular emphasis on the language and the traditional culture of those races residing in the team area. The team works closely with all elements and actively seeks advice and assistance of citizens through:

> —creating an extremely casual "front" by working out of a storefront office connected to a restaurant, by wearing blazers instead of uniforms and by driving unmarked cars;
>
> —setting up a community relations council made up of six citizens and three police officers who meet regularly and have enlisted a crime and delinquency task force of 17 citizens to carry out the prevention programs agreed upon by the Council. Both citizen groups represent a cross-section of the entire Model Cities area in terms of ethnic, racial and age makeup;
>
> —hiring a Neighborhood Liaison Specialist who communicates the community's information and program needs to the police team and the team's crime control goals to the citizen task force; and then develops innovative programs for uniting the needs and goals of both;
>
> —hiring four community service officers who work side by side with the team and are involved in all law enforcement duties except making arrests (they also represent a cross-section of the community);
>
> —organizing community activities (coffee hours, socials, school lectures, etc.) as a technique to improve police-community relations, to "get the kids off the street," and to improve relations among ethnic and racial groups in the area; and
>
> —working closely with Model Cities representatives who have already developed contacts with citizens since January, 1968.[13]

Upon interviewing team members, we were impressed with the

[13] Robert H. Quinn, Report by the Committee on Law Enforcement and Administration of Criminal Justice, *Holyoke's Police Team: New Roles for Police, Citizens* (Massachusetts, March 1971), p. 1.

perception and personal depth that had been developed in a relatively short period of time. Simple techniques such as when to sit or when to remove one's coat to reduce tension and unnecessary threat when present in the Puerto Rican household have obviously brought amazing results. This was but one example of a myriad of skills relating to cultural awareness that these men had apparently acquired in the early stages of the team project as they began to *understand* their clientele.

Team members work in plain clothes or blazers. They handle all normal police activities in the model area to conclusion, assuming roles normally reserved for detectives, traffic officers, and the like. The team works closely with community service officers recruited from the community who have been especially helpful in overcoming language barriers and reducing tension in difficult situations.

The field training in the project has been supervised by Professor Raymond Galvin of the School of Criminal Justice, University of Minnesota, and Professor John Angel of the School of Criminal Justice, University of Michigan.

In a March 1971 report the Massachusetts Committee on Law Enforcement and Administration of Criminal Justice stated that "although the Police Team has only been training since October and operational since December 1970 it is obvious that it has dramatically changed a few very traditional and sensitive relationships—between police officer and citizen and between patrolman and his superior officers."[14]

Before leaving this section we must again look to the Holyoke Model Cities program for an example of positive attitude change. As we have previously stated, members of the most victimized race are apparently the most hostile toward police. Although they are the most victimized, they are also the least likely to report such victimization to the police. In contrast, the Holyoke Team in its 235-acre inner-city model area has experienced a sixty-case, or 300 percent, rise in reported crimes in its first three months of existence.[15] (The rise in reported crimes should not be confused with or equated as a rise in actual crimes committed.)

Obviously a new kind of communication, a new feeling of confidence, is developing. Perhaps a major factor in the attitude change is the involvement of seventeen citizens of the community who serve as a police advisory committee and who have had a major role helping the police understand a culture that is so different from their own.

[14] *Ibid.*
[15] *Ibid.*

Ride Along Programs

Throughout the country many law enforcement agencies are encouraging young citizens to "ride along" with their policemen during regular duty tours.

The ride along concept was primarily initiated in an effort to improve communication and understanding between youth and the authority structure, especially law enforcement. High school students are given the opportunity to observe firsthand the daily routine of police officers, such as handling calls on narcotics problems, disturbances, and traffic accidents, issuing citations, and writing reports.

A second function of the program is to give officers an opportunity to converse with young people in a nonthreatening situation. Typically, patrol-level officers talk with teen-agers in negative situations, when perhaps neither the policeman nor the teen-ager is at his best, or at least not perceived in the best light. A great deal of understanding can develop in a rather short time under different circumstances. The teen-ager can ask questions about "those other cops," and the policeman can find out that every teen-ager with long hair is not a "wise guy."

Interestingly enough, a number of years before "ride along" became popular, one small West Coast city initiated a similar program. The riders were primarily citizens of all ages who had complained about specific officers' attitudes in traffic cases. The complainants were invited, nearly cajoled, into riding for an afternoon or an evening. Whenever possible, they were placed with the officer who had been the basis of the complaint. While the beginning of such rides may have been somewhat traumatic for citizen and officer alike, the results were excellent, most often ending with a much better understanding by both parties and actually bringing about a noticeable behavior change in some officers.

Traditionally, riding in police cars by persons not under arrest had been discouraged for years on the basis of liability or unnecessary time consumption, or simply because of the unwillingness of administrators to take a chance. It appears now that the "ride along" risk is minimal when compared with the gains to be achieved in terms of support for the police.

Family Crisis Intervention

Like the Ride Along Program, Family Crisis Intervention can be classified as a police-community support program. Perhaps somewhat differently in that Family Crisis Intervention provides a much needed service, but beyond that it, too, offers an opportunity for community members to view policemen in a positive nonthreatening role. And policemen in this role learn a great deal about the values and mores of those they serve who may be different from themselves.

In 1967 the original Family Crisis Intervention Unit was implemented by Dr. Morton Bard in the New York City Police Department. The two-year program was accomplished under a Law Enforcement Assistance Administration grant to the City College of New York.

Eighteen highly motivated patrolmen were selected from volunteers for the month-long specialized training. After the training, the members operated in uniform, around the clock, and performed all regular police functions. Their primary responsibility, however, was to respond to family disturbances anywhere in their precinct. They were supported by individual and group professional consultations. An integral part of the program was the utilization of referral agencies.[16]

To deal with family disturbance (crisis) problems realistically and effectively, Family Crisis Intervention Unit officers are expected not only to restore order and prevent injury but also to assist the disputants in finding lasting solutions to their own problems—solutions that will eliminate the need for repeated police involvement. The approach to these disturbances should thus be that of problem solving—usually by referral—and crisis management, and not necessarily that of arrest and prosecution.

It should be stated that this program has not attempted to develop the police officer as a social worker or a psychologist, but rather to enhance his professional competence as a working policeman. "Police are untrained and ill-equipped to *treat* psychological and social pathology. It is not, moreover, the purpose of this Program to make them so. Officers can be competent, however, to *identify* a vast range of ills— health problems, social hardships, housing problems, employment difficulties and mental illness—all of which, when they lead to turmoil, have been too broadly categorized as 'family disputes.' "[17]

> Intervention in the family fight has been presented as an underrated, rather neglected police function, but one that holds much promise for crime prevention as well as for community mental health and family welfare. Selected and trained police Family Crisis Intervention specialists, supported by other professions, can also gather basic data leading to identification of violence-

[16] Morton Bard and Bernard Berkowitz, *Law Enforcement and Science and Technology*, ed. S. I. Cohn (U.S.A.: Port City Press, Inc., 1969), II, 565–67.

[17] *Family Crisis Intervention Program*, Information Bulletin (Oakland, Calif., Police Department, January 18, 1971), p. 1.

prone individuals and situations. Such specialists, keenly aware of human sensibilities, may afford a new avenue for improvement in the crucial area of police-community relations.[18]

Since 1967 Family Crisis Intervention Units have been instituted in core cities across the United States as a valid extension of regular police service. The growing number of such programs attests to the support by prominent police chiefs, such as Chief Charles Gain of the Oakland, California, Police Department, to Dr. Bard's 1967 prediction that "such specialists, keenly aware of human sensibilities, may afford a new avenue for improvement in the crucial area of police-community relations."[19]

The Basic Car Plan—A Large City Approach to Working Officer Involvement

The Los Angeles Police Department has established a program aimed at "providing more effective police service by establishing a closer relationship between the policeman and the people he serves."[20]

Primarily, the Basic Car Plan is an effort to overcome the anonymity that typically develops between the policemen and the community as officers are rotated and assigned to various districts, various beats, and special details.

The methodology is to establish basic car districts whose boundaries are clearly defined. Nine men, consisting of one lead officer, five senior officers, and three officers with less experience, are assigned to each district. Three of the officers are assigned to each of three watches. Additional cover cars are deployed during peak workload hours and are superimposed on the basic car plan.

The lead officer has primary responsibility for coordinating the activities of those assigned to his basic car district. The nine officers meet on a monthly basis with neighborhood block representatives constituting the basic car area. The purpose of the meeting is to provide valuable dialogue between officers and citizens.

We are especially impressed with this concept in that it tends to "repersonalize" the police service. Policemen have a firsthand opportunity to discover the strong and weak points of their daily activities and to receive the kind of feedback that is likely to produce a more flexible adaptive work style.

[18] Bard and Berkowitz, *Law Enforcement and Science*, p. 567.

[19] *Ibid.*

[20] *Basic Radio Car Plan*, Information Bulletin (Los Angeles, Calif., City Police Department, 1970), pp. 1–5.

The following material is extracted from the Los Angeles Police Department's *Basic Radio Car Plan* information bulletin:

Objectives   The Basic Radio Car Plan is a means of attaining the primary police goals of helping society prevent crime by improving community attitudes toward police, providing stability for the Policeman on the street and generating in him a proprietary interest in his "beat," and better knowledge of the police role.

Workload study   A Basic Radio Car District profile folder was prepared for each district. Information included is: current crime problems, wanted suspects, crime maps, problem locations, names and addresses of V.I.P.'s living in the district and any other information that would assist the officers in knowing their district. This folder is kept current and passed from watch to watch. The lead officer is responsible for ensuring that the folder is kept current.

Personnel selection   The selection of officers to participate in the program has been accomplished by utilizing the knowledge of all uniformed supervisors. Personnel selected for assignment to the Basic Car Plan was predicated on many factors: Length of Service, Department Ratings, Reputation, Personality, Personnel Complaints, Partner Compatibility, Education, Hardships, Training Officer Experience.

Training   Conference leadership training for all personnel assigned to the Basic Radio Car Plan is a necessary factor in the success of the program. Each lead officer and number one senior officer on each watch has attended a three day Conference Leadership Course prepared by Training Division. The remaining team members have had one day of conference, leadership training with follow-up training to be accomplished on the division level.

Selection of community representatives   An integral part of the Basic Radio Car Plan is selecting and organizing the community representatives to meet and effectively communicate with officers. The Division Commander, assisted by the Community Relations Officer, contacted key community leaders to request their assistance in the selection of an Advisory Committee which was composed of residents who represented the Basic Radio Car Districts in the Division. The goals of the committee were to select a representative from each block in the division. The block representatives were organized into groups by radio car district, and regular monthly meetings between the officers and block representatives were established. Divisional detectives, existing Police-Community Councils, entrance oral board members, Community Relations Administration, and other resources were utilized to assist in the selection of community participants. The membership of the community representatives was weighed heavily in favor of bona fide residents of the concerned district.

Monthly meetings Once each month the nine man Basic Radio Car team meets with the district representatives. The purpose of the meeting is to give the individual citizen and officer an opportunity to participate in mutual discussion concerning police problems. This is facilitated by dividing the meeting into discussion workshops following the general meeting. Each officer acts as a workshop chairman. Supervisory personnel do not normally attend the meetings. Officers wear the basic uniform when participating in the meetings.

The lead officer presides over the meeting and makes the necessary preparations for an interesting and informative program. All resources of the Department are used to accomplish this goal. Specialists (e.g., Detectives, Narcotics Officers, Traffic, etc.) used as resource persons are contacted by the lead officer.

The meeting with the community representatives is preceded by a briefing during which the agendum and program are finalized. The nine radio district team members and the team advisor (Sergeant) attend. The Watch Commanders may also attend.

A debriefing session follows the community meeting, for the purpose of completing an evaluation report. The report is reviewed by the team advisor and several copies forwarded to the Division Commander to be distributed at his discretion. One copy is retained by the concerned "A" Unit team.

It is the responsibility of the lead officer of the Basic Radio Car Unit to maintain direct communication between all team members of his Basic Radio Car on all watches. The lead officer makes himself available for problem discussion with individual team members of his unit on other watches, and to disseminate information received from the team advisor. The lead officer is a coordinator and performs a staff function. He does not act as a supervisor.

A Summary of each lead officer's evaluation is included in the Commander's weekly activities report.[21]

Nothing in the Basic Radio Car Plan detracts from the typical responsibilities of regular supervision. It can be anticipated, however, that the sharing of leadership responsibility with lead officers is likely to have a positive impact on their development as decision makers and as future upper rank leaders.

And, finally, it seems to us that this program genuinely seeks to involve the community in its proper crime prevention role and to consider the personal needs of young officers by offering a greater degree of autonomy and opportunity for self-actualization.

[21] *Ibid.*

The Coffee Klatch (A Small City's Approach to Working Officer Involvement)

Smaller suburban communities as well as their larger core-city cousins have need to develop viable relationships between the patrolman and the citizens he serves. One city's approach is the "Coffee Klatch."

In Covina, California, each patrolman is responsible for holding at least one Coffee Klatch monthly in some citizen's home located in his assigned beat. The meetings are designed to provide a vehicle for dialogue between policemen and small neighborhood groups of citizens, normally husband and wife teams totaling about twelve people. The meetings are coordinated by a community relations officer, who is also responsible for necessary training and orientation, and for the development of supportive information.

The program is developed around five policemen who are assigned on a twenty-four-hour basis to each patrol beat. Each beat is about one mile square. Basically, the idea is to invite a few couples from a given neighborhood to an informal evening get-together for coffee and conversation, bring into the group the police officer responsible for patrolling that particular neighborhood, and afford him the opportunity to present his department's viewpoints on law enforcement in the community. Over a friendly cup of coffee, the assembled couples are given an opportunity to ask questions, to make known their personal expectations regarding efficient law enforcement, and to air their own gripes about the service.

Getting couples to open their homes and invite neighbors in for the informal coffee klatches proved to be no great obstacle. Original meetings were arranged by members of the Junior Women's Club. Acting as hostesses, they made preliminary arrangements for the initial get-togethers in their own neighborhoods patrolled by Covina officers.

When apprised of a scheduled meeting, the police department arranges for advance delivery of coffee, cookies, and movie projection equipment to the host's home by a police aide (cadet). Everything is in readiness when, at an appointed time, the beat officer, on duty and in uniform, arrives for his coffee klatch session.

The host introduces him to each individual present, and in turn, the officer distributes attractive personal business cards bearing his name and other pertinent information. He encourages each member of the group to call him by his first name, pointing out that it is imprinted on his card.

The officer, armed with up-to-date police information developed for this specific neighborhood, speaks to the guests about the problems and events that are occurring on their street. Through friendly, informal discussion he encourages response from the group.

Next he presents a short movie, which portrays typical home burglaries. He follows with a discussion on crime prevention in the neighborhood, pointing out how each citizen can become personally involved in crime prevention.

The officer talks about his own role in the community. He encourages questions and attempts to answer each one intelligently and sincerely, carefully avoiding negative overtones that might indicate any form of defensiveness on his part.

Offering himself as a personal contact between law enforcement and citizen, the officer invites each individual to call him personally if any future questions or problems arise in which he can assist. He invites comments, including complaints, and makes it clear that he will welcome any opportunity to discuss them. He lets it be known that he is personally concerned about establishing a mutual relationship that will strengthen the sometimes critical feedback procedure, and he promises prompt and correct answers to all future questions, stating that his replies will be fed back no later than the following day.

Before leaving the coffee klatch the officer assures each couple that he will be continuously interested in hearing their suggestions, or their doubts, about his own job performance or that of a fellow officer on the beat. He reiterates that their street is also his street and that their concerns are his as well.

Before taking part in the program, each policeman is given substantial training in communication skills. Special emphasis is placed on the avoidance of defensiveness when receiving negative feedback. It appears that policemen inherently feel the need to defend the actions of other policemen, often without sufficient information but rather based upon some prior personal experience.

This particular portion of the training utilized role playing and the assistance of a local little theater group. The program for developing officers' empathy for people who are different from themselves will not be discussed here but will be thoroughly covered in this chapter's lesson plan case study, for it was an important preparatory ingredient.

In retrospect, the program has not presented the anticipated problems of getting willing participation by the officers. Instead, holding down the number of meetings per officer per month has become a concern, since each klatch represents a substantial investment in time, normally two to three hours. Interestingly enough, it is the officers themselves who are initiating the oversupply of klatches.

Police-Community Relations

Both the Los Angeles and the Covina models tend to maximize the field patrol officers' involvement. Both programs provide a continuing education and development opportunity which in turn gives assurance that as neighborhoods and communities change, the policemen themselves will be changing as well.

TRAINING FOR POLICE-COMMUNITY RELATIONS STAFF AND FOR MAXIMUM FIELD SUPPORT

Generally speaking, the key to any police-community relations program is the understanding and enthusiasm brought to it by the police participants. Since these factors are not always present, they must be developed.

It would be unrealistic to expect every policeman to instinctively understand the importance of his role in police-community relations or to have a natural empathy for the various publics he serves. And each public, each population group, represents a different task in building strong supportive relationships. In each of the previously discussed models, special training was an important element of success.

It has been demonstrated in various pre-1965 studies that in most cases police preservice academy training had not devoted sufficient hours to the study of people, of community relations. This void is being dramatically changed in many areas, primarily because of subsidized training programs such as those required by the California Commission on Peace Officers Standards and Training, and similar bodies in other states.

Apparently there is still a need for greater attention to continuing in-service training in this area. Officers assigned specifically to police-community relations units should also have a greatly reinforced training program, for it is they who will set the tone for field officers to follow.

The President's Commission on Law Enforcement and Administration of Justice observed that police-community relations officers "need special training in such fields as the psychology, culture, and problems of minority groups and the poor, the dynamics of crowd behavior, the history of the civil rights movement, and the attitudes of various segments of the public toward the police."[22]

We are in agreement with the commission but would add to their admonition by observing that while classroom-type learning is helpful, police administrators who provide field-learning experiences in the ghetto and the barrio are likely to experience more

[22] President's Commission, *Task Force Report*, p. 156.

significant, more lasting results. By submerging policemen, who are not acting in their capacity as policemen, into the respective cultures, a great deal of learning will take place that cannot be found in text-books.

We are reminded of our experience in a recent ghetto workshop in which the participants were predominantly black probation and social workers. An example under discussion was that of poor language understanding by a white female elementary school teacher in a totally black school. The young teacher was well motivated and well liked, though somewhat naïve. At the close of class one day, a black fifth grader waited until the students had departed. The youngster approached the teacher stating, "Teacher, the shit's gonna fall." The teacher, taken aback at such language, marched the sputtering youngster off to the *white* principal's office where he spent the next hour, for, after all, "Children shouldn't use such language." The "shit" was indeed going to fall, and did. With some personal risk, but sensing an ally, the black youngster was trying to tell his white teacher that a gang fight was about to take place. A more appropriate reaction by the teacher would have been to inquire, "How big is the pile and where is it going to land?"

The point is, as we stated earlier, the words may be a part of the English language, but that does not guarantee that they will have white middle-class meaning. We are not suggesting that the police-man should alter his vocabulary to a great degree, but he should under-stand what is going on around him, for an important part of effective communication is *effective listening*. This kind of earthy learning is not easily taught; it must be experienced. A learning program such as this is not without some risks, especially in terms of administrative peer group understanding. The potential for long-range effectiveness, however, should appeal to the more modern creative leader.

Obviously, this submersion into a culture should be supervised by professional trainers, preferably behavioral scientists, who can guide the program and, perhaps more importantly, prepare the participants for the experience.

Familiarity in this type of training has led us to believe that laying a proper foundation for field experiences or real life role playing (sometimes referred to as the "reversal-of-roles technique") is likely to bring about a more rapid, more significant transition. The behavioralist continues to play an important role during the training period, which may last for several days, by bringing the participants together from time to time to discuss and share experiences. Finally, the behavioralist must assist the participants in summarizing and evaluating the training experience so that it may be a guide for those who follow.

CHAPTER SUMMARY

One continues to hear the rhetorical query of those policemen who still remain rigidly connected with yesterday's system: "How soon can we get the baloney over with and get back to doing police work?" But who is to say what form modern police work will take? Certainly policemen for decades have shown concern that "some people would like to make us into social workers." Perhaps it seemed so, but most rational people realize that someone must enforce the law; at least enforce it with someone else. And yet one must consider the potential of a Family Crisis Intervention Unit that may reduce felonious assaults and homicides resulting from family disturbances in a high-risk area by as much as 25, 50, or even 75 percent. Who is to say that this is not crime prevention in its purest form? And who can place a true value on taking a youngster for a ride in a police car, or spending an evening with a group in some citizen's home? Is the cop on campus really changing student attitudes, and does it really make any difference whether or not policemen communicate effectively with the community, especially the minority community?

We submit that these questions are not questions at all, for the answers are apparent. These programs are capable of changing attitudes, both within the police service and within the community. The degree of change becomes the challenge for creative police administrators. And that degree of change is decidedly proportional to the philosophical commitment of the administration, coupled with commitment, support, and skills from the highest-ranking officer to the newest recruit.

In this chapter we discussed several models, and there are scores of others with which many readers are familiar. Models are cited, for they are most often examples of successful programs. Models are developed for specific times and places, however, and while these ideas as such are transferable, we suggest that they are seldom applicable in their entirety to other situations without modification. The growing number of needless model translocation failures has led us to offer the following paragraphs as a caution.

In a West Coast suburb of Los Angeles stands a relatively new and imposing United States Post Office building. It is moderately appointed and typically functional in the traditional sense. We are told that its design was conceived and executed in the East, to eastern taste; that it is not atypical but rather patterned after a very carefully developed functional model. Obviously, the processing of mail is sufficiently similar in all parts of the country. Post offices in the West have the same mission as those in the East, cope with the same problems, are governed by the same general rules and philosophy, and accommodate materials of similar shape and design.

Therefore, why shouldn't a model developed in the East be applicable to the West? Why, in effect, should designers of postal buildings be expected to "reinvent the wheel"? As one examines this imposing building, one must be impressed at the ability of its designers to so adequately blend the functional and aesthetic qualities, from its rooftop to its basement coal chute. *Coal chute!* A rather strange appendage, considering that coal is not a common fuel in the West. Natural gas is delivered directly from its point of origin to the point of consumption through a permanent pipeline. A simple turn of the valve delivers whatever quantity is needed. A closer investigation reveals that in fact the heating unit is fueled by natural gas. Why then the coal chute?

The point of this vignette is simply to suggest that while model building and model transferring (a sharing of ideas) are a part of modern management, one must always be alert for the coal chutes.

Each situation has its own peculiarities which must be taken into consideration when applying the solution to another time and place.

LEARNING EXERCISE

Altering behavior patterns, actually bringing about dramatic change in attitudes, is perhaps the most challenging aspect of training. In training policemen to be effective, to communicate effectively with all the publics they serve, the challenge becomes even greater when one considers the preponderance of daily negative experiences that must be overcome.

The following learning exercise is a limited case study of such an effort. In it the reader should discover for himself the impact of role playing as a training technique. The role playing becomes a more critical element when only the principals, in this case the police, are aware of the exercise. All other participants are real world people in real world situations.

Since the completion of this innovated training project, the California State Bureau of Corrections has adopted a similar program for its new employees. It has also been implemented in a number of other police agencies with varying degrees of success. Once again, we must point out that caution must be exercised in adopting someone else's model *in toto.* "Operation Empathy" was developed for a particular time and place and is obviously not applicable in every situation.

The reader should perceive from the case study that a great deal of classroom work, of emotional and skills preparation, was accomplished prior to the more dramatic field exercises. And, of course, the dedication and enthusiasm of the program directors, which in turn was generated in the participants, cannot be overlooked as a factor of success.

COVINA

Located twenty miles from downtown Los Angeles, California, is the city of Covina.[23] Incorporated in 1901, it has a population of thirty-one thousand, with a growth potential of eighty thousand. It encompasses eight square miles and provides schools for twenty-two thousand students, many of whom live in the surrounding unincorporated area. It is a middle-class bedroom community possessing excellent retail stores, professional offices, and industrial parks. Covina has enjoyed a history of competent city councils and since 1951 has embraced the city manager form of government. Two city managers have served during that time. Both have made certain that all the elements necessary for creative management were and are present. Each department head is encouraged to be self-actuated, and each is secure in the knowledge that he has the right to be creative and to fail.

The Problem

Many communities have particular elements present that provide a wealth of experience for their police officers. Others, such as Covina, do not. They are not called upon to provide answers to ghetto problems, for there are no ghettos. While some long hair is in evidence, no hippies per se are about. Police departments in these cities are normally small, providing minimal specialization, with no place to transfer or hide the incompetent. Most cities like Covina provide proper, even superior, training, but certain experiences are simply not available. Police managers in these cities are faced with an unusual responsibility—providing a special kind of training that might happen naturally in other more congested areas and continually looking for ways to reinforce concepts and values that may never be tested, except during some unforeseen crisis. And, too, these same managers, charged by the President's Crime Commission with the responsibility for recruiting better-educated young men, must find new ways to humanize and de-routinize police work while increasing services and making better use of available resources. If they do not, it is doubtful that better-educated self-activated young men will be content to remain in the service.

OPERATION EMPATHY—PREPARATION FOR THE CHANGING POLICE ROLE

Is it necessary for policemen to empathize with those they serve and those they arrest? Some have said that policemen must remain aloof in order

[23] From a paper prepared for the Second Annual Law Enforcement Science and Technology Symposium, Chicago, 1967.

to approach situations unemotionally. Well, empathy is not sympathy, but it does provide a policeman with needed communication links. And, too, should policemen in a predominantly white community understand the ghetto, the barrio? Or as communities begin to change, will there be a special role for policemen in understanding the differences in others? Can a policeman learn about jails by being a jailer or about hippies by observing from a scholarly distance? And, finally, how are we perceived by those who come under our purview, especially those who feel powerless?

To answer these questions and at the same time integrate a leadership team-building, participative management exercise, the Covina Police Department enlisted the aid of two behavioral scientists, Dr. Kent Lloyd and Dr. Kendall Price. The department of fifty members was evenly divided into two sections. A retreat (two days and one night) launched the "program" which continued one day each week for eight weeks and was climaxed by two field exercises. Obviously, the program created difficulties in scheduling, court appearances, and the like, but these were overcome by the shared desire for success. During the retreat and weekly sessions, new communication channels were opened and employees at every level (sworn and unsworn, male and female) began to develop a new awareness of individual responsibility for a successful organization. Ongoing monthly feedback meetings were developed for all who wished to participate. These proved somewhat threatening to the chief at first, since people began to feel free to criticize operations, procedures, and just about everything else; however, he too went through a growth period, gradually finding a different kind of security in knowing that a real team had emerged. (This "team," incidentally, has brought about quite a number of changes, most of which have resulted in improvements. Those that did not were returned to the drawing board or discarded.)

The Jail Experience

At the completion of the training sessions, all participants spent two days and one night in the large, thirty-mile distant Riverside County Jail of Sheriff Ben Clark. With the exception of Sheriff Clark, his correctional chief, and the under-sheriff, no one was aware of the pseudoprisoners. Teams of four and five were "booked" on phony burglary and forgery charges, "to be held in transit," a not uncommon practice. The "prisoners" were fingerprinted, mugged, booked, deloused, issued jail clothing, and placed in large one-hundred-inmate tanks. The degradation of the booking process had its effect. Finding oneself in a cell with 100 bunks and 110 prisoners compounds the problem, especially when the only available floor space is in the "head." A great deal was learned about the jail subculture in which the prisoners themselves exercise certain controls over each other. For example, a prisoner never calls to a guard for help, regardless.

Many experiences and anecdotes were cited upon release, some serious and some humorous. Cell participants agreed that while they wouldn't volunteer to return to jail, none would have missed the experience. Even officers who had previously served as jailers in a large county jail before their Covina employment stated that they had gained a complete new insight—from the prisoners' point of view. When all had gone through the experience, participants met with jail personnel in what began as an uncomfortable setting. (This critique was insisted on by Sheriff Clark.) The atmosphere improved as the meeting progressed, and the jailers themselves agreed that the exercise was productive. In addition to understanding more about who goes to jail, who remains there, for what reason, and who really runs the jail, it was hoped that there would be an elimination or at least a decline in the "contempt of cop bookings";[24] there has been, to the delight of the investigators who had spent countless hours in clearance and release processing of prisoners.

The "Skid Row" Experience

The second field exercise of Operation Empathy was to infiltrate "skid row" in a large metropolitan city. Cops became "bums" for the experience, wearing clothes purchased in pawn shops along the "row." For additional realism, they did not bathe or shave for two days before their visit. Female employees were excused from this exercise for obvious reasons; men participated in teams of two.

The Problem

Policemen, like others, tend to lump people into neat little boxes and treat them accordingly. It is easy to see a "kid" and treat him the way "kids" are supposed to be treated—or females—or subordinates—or superiors— or wives—or longhairs—or blacks or browns. Most of us deny this tendency, but simple observation proves otherwise. Some obviously do this less than others, but the truth remains that it is easier for most of us to treat people as groups as opposed to the thought process required to treat people as individuals.

The men spent a great deal of their time on skid row, with the real bums. Each time patrol cars or foot patrolmen passed by, they were confronted with negative remarks about the police. Not one "skid row habitué" could remember being personally abused by the police or had even observed such abuse. Nevertheless, all *knew* that "police look for chances to abuse, arrest, even shoot bums." (It seems that even bums are guilty of lumping individuals into groups and of knowing truths that are not always true.) The pseudobums were treated shabbily by many "normal" citizens, especially shopkeepers, because everyone *knows* that bums are dishonest, bad for business, and have no feelings. They were ordered to leave middle-class cafés and were followed by clerks in retail stores. They were ordered to "move on" when they stopped to observe a sick woman lying on the sidewalk, although other onlookers were permitted to remain. They began to feel powerless.

No attempt has been made here to cover all the significant experiences; however, one that is quite representative and relevant to the desired goals concerns a young sergeant, Tom Courtney (recently promoted to lieutenant). At dusk, in a nearly deserted downtown parking lot, Tom and his partner had

[24]*Contempt of cop bookings* is a term used by policemen to describe arrests that result from a policeman-arrestee communication breakdown (the "wise guy" who refuses to identify himself in a high-crime area because he thinks the cop is acting like a "wise guy") rather than for a specific crime. The arrestee is most often released the next day when cleared by the detective division.

just about decided to head for their pickup point. For the "hell of it" Tom decided to polish off one of his props, a "mickey of wine," normally wrapped in a paper bag and carried in the coat pocket of the more affluent bums. As Tom tipped up the bottle, two uniformed policemen appeared and did something Tom himself had done many times. Tom was commanded to turn around and place his hands on the building wall for a search. (Like all of our pseudo-bums, Tom had been instructed not to reveal his true identity under any circumstances, since that would have brought the exercise to a halt.) Tom's almost involuntary reaction was to identify himself as a policeman. "I'm a cop, if you'll check in my inside coat pocket you'll find my badge and I.D." "I've heard everything now," returned the officer. After some pleading, Tom's identity was established and both men were released. Later Tom was asked why he "blew his cover," spoiling it for others who were to follow. "I thought I was going to be shot," remarked Tom. It was established that the policeman did not have his revolver unholstered, did not push Tom around, or did not even raise his voice. The most negative recollection was that the policeman "did not smile." Tom had simply been conditioned by his experiences. A glimmer of how and perhaps why people react negatively toward policemen begins to come through, especially when one feels powerless.

Operation Empathy has been praised by some and damned by others as "foolish," "nonproductive," and "that Communist-type sensitivity training"; some felt "that the policemen who participate would be emasculated, wouldn't want to make arrests, and would be overly sympathetic with their clientele." None of the negatives ever came true. Arrests have gone up, assaults on officers have been reduced to near nonexistence, and complaints against officers have been greatly reduced. It is interesting to note that officers hired since "Empathy" have picked up a great deal from their experienced peers but still have more communication problems, are more often assaulted, and sustain more damaged uniforms.

New Experiences

Other dimensions were added, such as placing policemen in existing picket lines operating in front of so-called lewd movie houses in a large neighboring city and attending "love-ins" as hippies.

At the movie houses, the legitimate marchers were delighted at the influx of new converts and readily provided placards with such innoxious statements as "Anyone entering this movie is a pervert."

What possible good can come of such an exercise? For one thing, a new understanding of the "silent language." As policemen arrived, as they routinely do at picket lines, they emerged from their cars and then reached back inside to obtain batons (nightsticks) which were then holstered in baton rings. The policemen-marchers had done the same thing innumerable times, and yet when questioned later each had the same perception, "I thought I was going to get hit with that thing." They knew better but still felt "something" as the policemen made a show of obtaining their batons. (Lesson—get out of the car fully equipped. Do not call attention to weapons unnecessarily.)

At "love-ins" it was interesting to observe working police officers from a different viewpoint, and especially to become aware of the tremendously volatile mixture when hippies, motorcycle gangs, and police come together. Innumerable lessons were gained, including a bruised set of ribs by one "hippie-captain." (Covina exercises involve all ranks.)

When a short time later a love-in came to conservative Covina, thirty-five hundred hippies and others spent a rather dull day by the standards of love-ins visited.

As with most such events, there was advance publicity (the *Free Press* and the like), and Covina police had sufficient time to plan. Involved in the planning, in addition to the police, were hippie leaders and "Hell's Angels," a representative motorcycle gang. One hundred hippies became policemen for the day while regular policemen melted into the crowd undercover as hippies, for the felony type work. The hippie monitors put down one problem after another throughout the day, any one of which could have exploded if uniformed policemen had been in the crowd, and as a consequence they were less busy than usual.

Operation Empathy, a success by any terms, was viewed by the department as an "Alternative to Flexing Police Muscle." Thirty-five hundred hippies is not a great number when one considers the huge rock festivals that are becoming so prevalent; but in a center-of-town ten-acre park, bordered by a major hospital on one side and the older, wealthy residential district on the other, it becomes a rather uncomfortable responsibility. Incidentally, the decision to handle the problem in this manner was a group one, brought about when one policeman said, "This is what we've been training for. Let us do it our way." Obviously, a confident city manager and city council were essential to the opportunity for success.

13

THE POLICE MANAGER
AND THE FUTURE:
Coping
with Organizational Tremors

Even if you're on the right track you'll get run over if you just sit there.[1]

and

. . . the roaring current of change, a current so powerful today that it overturns institutions, shifts our values and shrivels our roots. Change is the process by which the future invades our lives, and it is important to look at it closely, not merely from the grand perspectives of history, but also from the vantage point of the living, breathing individuals who experience it.[2]

and

The most common cause of executive failure is inability or unwillingness to change. . . The executive who fails to understand this will suddenly do the wrong things the wrong way—even though he does exactly what in his old job had been the right things done the right way.[3]

[1] Will Rogers.
[2] Douglas McGregor, *The Human Side of Enterprise*. See also W. R. Rhodes,
[3] Peter F. Drucker, *The Effective Executive* (New York: Harper & Row, Publishers, 1966), p. 58.

407

Writing a textbook is not the easiest or simplest chore that one can tackle (at least it is not so for the authors of this book). All the chapters preceding this, the final, chapter caused us the typical amount of frustration, intellection, and perspiration that we are certain other authors commonly experience in their pen-to-paper efforts. This chapter, however, generated a heightened sense of anxiety and confusion. *Anxiety* because much has been written about the future. Why create a chapter when a multitude of books on the subject exist? *Confusion* because with the numerous approaches that can be taken (theoretical, empirical, descriptive, prescriptive, and so on), What is best for the few pages devoted to this subject? Where do we begin? End? What do we include? In due regard for these questions, we were immediately tempted to continue with the above quotations until we felt that enough had been said. We chose instead to establish and adhere to the following criteria: (1) brevity, (2) focus on the *process* by which we are accelerated into the future, and (3) say whatever is necessary to convince you that the police manager must prepare himself for constant and massive adaptations to the changes that are an integral part of the future. Let us start by rereading the introductory quotations—note the third one!

Another point and an explanation of one of the above criteria appears useful before pushing onward. First, we want to state that a variety of background materials were investigated before producing what you will be reading. The third item, in particular, forms the foundation and direction for this chapter. Hence, we call your attention to (all are footnoted elsewhere): (1) Warren G. Bennis, *Changing Organizations*, (2) Daniel Katz and Robert L. Kahn, *The Social Psychology of Organizations*, and (3) Alvin Toffler, *Future Shock*. Second, as mentioned earlier, the following pages examine the process of adapting to change, that is the steps by which we can most effectively reach tomorrow. We are saying, in essence, that the future is responsible for causing accelerated changes that require a greater degree of human adaptability. Without it, we are in danger of technological and, most critically, human breakdowns. Clearly, the manager in his role of maintaining an *adaptive* organization is in a key position to either foster or resist the necessary human and organizational changes that permit continual successes rather than repeated dismal failures. Toffler, in turn, cautions us:

> This is the prospect that man now faces. Change is avalanching upon our heads and most people are grotesquely unprepared to cope with it.[4]

[4]Toffler, *Future Shock*, p. 14.

This chapter discusses (1) the evolution of rapid change as it relates to the future, (2) the dimensions of the change process, (3) management and the necessity for a flexible stance toward the future, (4) strategies in developing a capacity for constant renewal, and (5) a learning exercise. In each instance our focus is on the people-ware or human "bent" as it pertains to change. The degree to which you, after completing this chapter, think, predict, and take action on future events, is the *major indicator of its impact and effectiveness*.

COPING WITH CHANGE: EVOLUTIONARY DESIGNS

Again, the point to be made is a simple one: Habitual thought patterns can have the effect of insulating parts of a system from desirable environmental challenges. Changing these thought patterns can present serious problems to the evolutionary designer. For example, if your habitual thought patterns are focused upon yesterday's technical challenge (How can we build a bigger bomb and a faster delivery system?)—if you persist in viewing problems of systems design through the filter of this technical challenge alone—it is perhaps inevitable that the systems you design will be unresponsive to changing challenges of goal statements focusing upon the values of human integrity and survival. Of course, all this may be good or bad. One presumably should always be free to root for the values of either the beauty or the beast.[5]

Perhaps the distinguishing feature of every age or society is the amount of change or "pace of life" that it is experiencing. For example, the pace of life in Samoa is overtly different from that in downtown New York. Even within a nation one is able to discern considerable differences among regions (the rural South as compared with the industrialized Northeast) and groups of people (women's lib versus keep them barefoot and pregnant, or the omnipresent generation gap). Finally, there are individual differences in that one person enjoys a faster pace while another (same age, values, desires, etc.) is repelled by it. In general, however, we are witnessing a world that is being compelled to cope with accelerated change. Our life is becoming faster whether we like it or not!

While complex and worthy of extensive review, the reasons for rapid change are covered in short fashion. The three primary forces stimulating increased speeds of change are technological, knowledge, and expectations (or hardware, software, and peopleware). The first two stimulators feed on *themselves* and *each other*. Because technology and knowledge make more technology and knowledge

[5]Robert Boguslaw, *The New Utopians: A Study of System Design and Social Change* (Englewood Cliffs, N.J.: Prentice-Hall, Inc., 1965), p. 152.

possible, as we can see if we look for a moment at the process of innovation. Technological innovation has three stages, linked together into a self-reinforcing cycle: (1) the creative idea, (2) its practical application, and (3) its diffusion through society. The process is completed, the loop closed, when the spread of technology and knowledge embodying the new idea, in turn, helps produce new creative ideas. Today there is evidence that the time between each of the steps in this cycle has been shortened. These new ideas and tools are put to work much more quickly than ever before. The time between original concept and practical use has been radically reduced. And this leads to our expecting situations, products, and theories to last for a shorter period of time. Basically, many now expect greater temporariness as a part of their life. We thus learn not only how to adapt quickly, but to actually expect it as a normal characteristic of the modern world.

The evolution of our interest in change extends back to man's first *awareness* of his environment's manifesting certain newnesses. Seasons, movement of stars, changing of the tides, and other natural phenomena were recorded in the first scratchings on the interiors of our ancestors' caves. Once recognized, man started *coping* with these and other changes in order to reduce physical risks and improve the pleasure that he might derive from his life. When he reached certain points, man would make the immediate and necessary adjustments to survive. Next, our forefathers found that they not only could, but should, anticipate events. Hence, we found ourselves planning for change.[6] To this planning for change we have introduced the most sophisticated tools and concepts known to man—computers, operations research, statistics, behavioral science findings, and so forth.

To the planning process has been added of late an expanding interest in measuring the amount of existing change for (1) a comparison of the speed of different events and (2) a foundation from which to predict the speed of future changes. One example of a scientific endeavor to capture the rate and impact of change whether a nation is changing is reported as follows:

> Social changes in Turkey over the last two decades have
> contributed to a breaking down of older styles of bureaucratic
> behavior. The changes can be summarized in terms of the prob-
> lems confronting the administration in 1956 and 1965. In 1956,
> the Turkish administration was struggling with social and polit-

[6] For articles on this subject, see Warren G. Bennis, Kenneth D. Benne, and Richard Chin, eds., *The Planning of Change* (New York: Holt, Rinehart & Winston, Inc., 1962).

ical change, and the atmosphere was highly politicized. The conflict was between bureaucrat and politician, each representing different social groups. Although these conflicts had not been completely resolved by 1965, significant progress had been made. In 1965, technical change seemed to be posing a major problem to the administration. New organizational structures and increased demands for experts rather than generalists were transforming the bases of power and status within the Turkish bureaucracy.[7]

A review of the above quotation might cause one to speculate about the possibilities of such an analysis ever being conducted within a police department. An observation on our part concerns the police facility (formerly called headquarters—even the name has changed). The late 1940s saw a rather unattractive and very old structure being used as the police facility. The 1950s brought into being a number of somewhat more attractive blockhouse-appearing buildings. In the 1960s the new police facilities were constructed in accordance with modern, eye-appealing, structural designs, which included considerable *glass*. During the late 1960s, unfortunately, a few militants sought to damage police buildings. Obviously, glass walls and windows became the target of bombs and bricks. Therefore, we are currently witnessing the structure of the 1970s being designed with aesthetic features, but hidden behind the glass facade are bricks and mortar, and within the walls the more vulnerable and high-risk targets (communications and data processing) are well protected. On the surface we want to look "pretty," yet all the while having a tough skin and strong insides. Although referring to the measurement of modernism, the following statement holds true for "changism":

> The overriding consideration of a strategy for scientific analysis of modernism is the level of specificity we desire: the more specific the behavior and social status we wish to analyze, the more we need consider the possible variations in the content and development of modernism, as well as the modalities.[8]

Furthermore, Churchman warns us that

> My bias is to look for the fiber of the system, the structure that ought to hold it together. This approach amounts to saying that we require an explicit moral base for measuring social

[7] Leslie R. Roos, Jr., and Noralow Roos, "Administrative Change in a Modernizing Society," *Administrative Science Quarterly*, 15 (March 1970), 77.

[8] Allan Schnaiberg, "Measuring Modernism: Theoretical and Empirical Explorations," *American Journal of Sociology*, 76 (November 1970), 420.

change. Far more important than "agreement of experts" is the moral prescription which says that our measure should be based on a policy of moral universality—everyone to count as an end—and not a means only—a deep analysis of how people are affected by the difference the measure will make.[9]

Finally, we have arrived at a point, a point that encompasses the previously described stage, of *total* or systemic programs devoted to continuous renewal for continuous innovation and change. Gardner writes:

> Over the centuries the classic question of social reform has been, "How can we cure this or that specifiable ill?" Now we must ask another kind of question: "How can we design a system that will continuously reform (i.e., renew) itself, beginning with presently specifiable ills and moving on to ills that we cannot now foresee?"[10]

The most recent major response to the human need for planned organizational change is in the expanding emphasis on organizational development (OD). The three primary objectives of OD programs are, where deemed appropriate, to (1) change attitudes or values, (2) modify behavior, and (3) induce change in structure and policies.[11] Significantly, a few police departments have been experimenting with various OD approaches. The learning exercise at the end of the chapter depicts one such endeavor. Other such efforts can be found in many of the police crisis-intervention training programs. We foresee that by the time you read the printed words in this text, OD programs will be present in a large number of police departments. We will defer further comments until later.

THE CHANGE PROCESS

> Emphasis on process—and the complex interweaving of continuity and change—plays havoc with old fashioned conceptions of liberalism and conservatism. As Peter Drucker has pointed out, in a world buffeted by change, faced daily with new threats to its safety, the only way to conserve is by innovating. The only stability possible is stability in motion.[12]

[9]C. West Churchman, "On the Facility, Felicity, and Morality of Measuring Social Change," *The Accounting Review*, 46 (January 1971), 34–35.

[10]John W. Gardner, *Self-Renewal: The Individual and the Innovative Society* (New York: Harper & Row, Publishers, 1963), p. 5.

[11]Robert T. Golembiewski, "Organization Development in Public Agencies: Perspectives on Theory and Practice," *Public Administration Review*, 29 (July-August 1969), 367.

[12]Gardner, *Self-Renewal*, p. 7.

Yes—we must emphasize the process and not the ultimate product. This is so because of the collapsing life expectancy of a product or an idea. Perhaps the most outstanding example of this phenomenon is the so called relevance of this book. We would be the first to admit that the ideas contained herein have a limited usefulness. What merit the text possesses or lacks should be assessed on its ability to stimulate the reader into accepting constant change as "stability in motion." Consequently, the need arises for a *process* the assists us in equally adapting to the rate and the direction of change. The learning exercise in the chapter on planning is one part in building an appropriate process. Others are described later on in this chapter. This section seeks to impress upon the reader the thinking of Alvin Toffler. In summary form he posits that the process for coping with change must:

- Recognize the sharp break with the past
- Allow for the accelerative thrust provided by technology and knowledge
- Account for a more rapid pace of life
- Deal with always greater *transience, novelty* and diversity
- And, in due regard for the above challenges, keep in mind our human and institutional limits of adaptability
- Finally, understand that the future (not the past) determines the present![13]

Therefore, we are confronted with the building and maintaining of an all-inclusive process which can read the future for present-day answers to present-day problems. The question of our survival hinges on such a process. Furthermore, the manager—in this case the police manager—holds a major share of the responsibility for creating the process!

THE POLICE MANAGER: A CHANGE AGENT

In a society based on large scale organization, the saviors will mostly be public executives, for it is they who bring people together in organizations to make things happen in the public interest.

It used to be that somebody else defined the public interest—the administrator was a nonlethal gun for hire, but the direction of change was set by some boss or bishop, or by groups of political generals or generalist politicians. But nowadays the public executive sets his own direction and makes his own policy.[14]

[13] Toffler, *Future Shock.*

[14] Harlan Cleveland, "A Message for Apocalyptists," *Public Administration Review*, 31 (January-February 1971), 78.

The problem for the police manager, in short, is not how he can take control of the changes he himself institutes—but how to avoid concentrating on change where it is easy (in science and technology) and neglecting change where it is hard (in the social institutions)—and to control and channel and give ethical content to the new technologies. The question and a partial answer to it is posed as follows:

> How can local governments apply science and technology to improve urban life rather than make it unbearable or at least unpleasant? Somehow science and technology have to be put to work for local governments in a positive way instead of leaving these governments to their own devices to cope with the adverse spin-offs of technology applied for the advancement of only one small segment of society.
>
> Consequently, one of the first—and probably the most important—things that needs to be done is to give local officials some mechanism through which they can identify the kinds of assistance they need, clearly define their needs, and then help them learn where to find ways to meet them. The development of new technologies is currently not as important to local governments as the development of advisory mechanisms geared to make local officials familiar with existing technology. Unless cities know what they are looking for and how to express that knowledge, the hopes for assistance from modern technological developments are likely to be empty ones.[15]

The rest of the answer to the above query is, first, to insure ourselves that the *public* interest is reflected in the process and, second, to insure ourselves that we have capable managers who are (1) willing to construct and operate a change process (of which the above mechanism is one part), (2) "interested" in the public interest, and (3) ready to make changes within themselves. In stressing the importance of the last requirement, Peter F. Drucker asserts:

> The most common cause of executive failure is inability or unwillingness to change with the demands of a new position. The executive who keeps on doing what he has done successfully before he moved is almost bound to fail.[16]

Most progressive police managers (and police educators) today are deeply concerned with the problem of developing managerial strategies appropriate to the changing conditions. The word *change* is no longer even a buzz word. It has become part of our every-

[15] A. Lee Fritscher, "Organizing for Science and Technology," *Public Management*, 53 (February 1971), 4.

[16] Drucker, *The Effective Executive*, p. 58.

day language. Police are continually working on the problems of how to develop a flexible organization that can move with changing requirements and can be "proactive" (influencing the environment) rather than reactive. Police managers are seeking ways to establish a work climate in which increasingly complex decisions can be made by people with the information, regardless of their location in the organization. Police managers are looking for ways in which increasingly complex technologies can be managed and in which people who have an ever higher sense of freedom and autonomy can be encouraged to want to stay and work in the organization. They are doing all these things (that is, the effective ones are) in addition to fulfilling their more traditional responsibility of organizing for *efficiency.* The search for ways of concurrently increasing collaboration among the members of organizations and at the same time increasing the rationality of decisions occupies many hours of management time and many chapters in management books. In summary, then, "Mr. Police Manager," you have an obligation to create a change process that provides your organization with a capability for constant self-renewal. And, at the same time, you must subject yourself to the demands of the process.

SOLUTION ONE: ORGANIZATIONAL DEVELOPMENT

To repeat a position taken at the onset of this chapter—our focus is on the *human* side of the *organization.* Thus, the solutions examined in this section are limited to those activities that "we" can take within our "police organizations" as "police managers" to cope with or control change. Also mentioned earlier, other devices and techniques not only can, but should, be used in sustaining the change process. The two strategies or solutions discussed below contain, however, the majority of the tactics associated with planned human and organizational changes. It is necessary to recognize that there is no one best way to change; rather, the change process needs to be systematically tailored to organizational goals and individual human purposes. Finally, our focus remains on the change process, with little attention given to the outputs. Briefly, the two solutions are organization development (internal orientation) and environmental participation (external orientation).

To begin with, organizational development (OD) is a

planned,
organization-wide,
managed

process to
improve organization *effectiveness* by
either coping with or controlling *change* with
behavioral science knowledge.

Again, the threefold mission of OD is to change attitudes and values, modify behavior, and thereby induce change in *people, structure,* and *policies.*

Before describing the tactics, it should be mentioned that OD, while beneficial, is not a panacea for avoiding the crash and crush of change. The omnipresent legal constraints, human resistance to change, procedural habits, and encrusted policies are not easily beaten down. Numerous studies have been, are being, and will be conducted into properties of an organization that either hinder or facilitate change. One study, for example, reported that an organization that had a high degree of job codification was susceptible to programmatic changes.[17] Clearly we cannot separate the individual from his organization or view the organization as being comprised of some kind of living mass. Hence, we come full circle to once more realizing that any OD effort must be total and must be targeted for both the person in singular form and the persons in corporate form. If nothing else, the above ought to impress upon one that change is difficult to achieve. Moreover, *sustained* change is even more difficult!

The tactics or methods of OD are team development, intergroup relationships, goal setting and planning, and education.[18] In general, the four methods are based on the same set of activities that, in combination, constitute the OD process. The activities and overall process are shown in Figure 13-1. Remember, the OD process is not the only way to change a police department; however, we do believe it is (in conjunction with the second solution) the most effective means for doing so at the present.

Team Development

A fundamental assumption is that the organization, as it does its work, does it through a number of work teams of different kinds. The teams may be "family" groups, that is, police manager and subordinates. They may be colleague or peer groups, such as all the middle-managers division. They may be technical teams, such as

[17] Jerald Hage and Michael Aiken, "Program Change and Organizational Properties: A Comparative Analysis," *American Journal of Sociology,* 72 (March 1967), 503–19.

[18] These four methods are drawn from Richard Beckhard, *Organization Development: Strategies and Models* (Reading, Mass.: Addison-Wesley Publishing Company, Inc., 1969).

the total personnel function or the data processing function. They may be project teams, with members from a variety of functions (e.g., data processing, traffic enforcement, and advanced planning) brought together for some specific activity. They may be the topman-agement.

Almost all organization-wide planned-change efforts have, as one of their early targets of change, the improvement of team effec-tiveness. A number of types of activities are used for helping teams do this. Some of these are focused on the "interactions" of the team, such as the development of the team's working relationships or the team's problem solving skills. Some are focused on the *tasks* of the team and have an action-planning or a goal-setting emphasis. Re-gardless of the specific focus on task or relationships, there is usually a spillover into the other area. A team-building activity explicitly designed to plan the team's work efforts in the subsequent year will probably also consider the processes of the group and the re-lationships of its members. If an activity is designed to focus on the relationships of the people in a group, it will probably also look at the group's goals and plans for work.

Team-building activities usually include three interrelated steps: collection of information, feedback of the information to the team, and action planning from the feedback. These steps take different situations but are a common characteristic of most team-building activities whether focused on relationships or work tasks.

Team-improvement activities frequently take place in a setting removed from the police department so that the members of the team can be away from day-to-day pressures. This type of work requires a pace and emphasis different from that required in the normal oper-ation of the team.

There is also a learning component in the activity. Members of the team are interested in, and to some degree committed to, learning while they work. The learning may be addressed to working better together or to setting better goals. Whatever the objective, the mem-bers of the team see, as a relevant output, that the *team learns to func-tion more effectively* and, incidentally, that *members* learn how to function more effectively with their personal styles. Hence, both the individual and the group stand to gain from this activity.

Intergroup Relationships

One of the major problems affecting organization effectiveness is the amount of energy expended in inappropriate competition and fighting between groups that should be cooperating. Because of the

FIGURE 13–1. A Simplified Model of Findings/Hypotheses Underlying the Typical OD Program

---

Basic Premise: When individuals can meet their own needs while meeting organizational needs, output will be qualitatively and quantitatively best.

An individual's basic needs center around *self-realization* and *self-actualization.* The former involves a person seeing himself as he is in interaction with others, with the goal of increasing the congruence between his intentions and his impact on others. Self-actualization refers to the processes of growth by which an individual realizes his potential.

An individual whose basic needs are satisfied does not seek comfort and security; rather, he *searches for work, challenge, and responsibility.*

An efficient organization will develop an appropriately shifting balance between *institutionalization* and *risk-taking.* The former refers to *infusing with values* the activites of the organization, so as to elicit member support, identification, and collaboration. Risk-taking is necessary in *innovating* more effective ways to deal with existing activities, and in *adapting* to environmental changes in society, market technology, and so on.

An organization's successful balancing of institutionalization and risk-taking will depend upon
—the increasingly complete *use of people* as well as nonhuman resources
—the development and maintenance of a viable balance between *central control* and local initiative
—fluid lines of *communication,* vertically, horizontally, and diagonally
—decision-making processes that solve problems that stay solved without creating other problems.

Satisfaction of both individual and organization needs will be facilitated by, if such satisfaction does not in fact crucially depend upon, *skill and competence in interpersonal and intergroup situations.*

An individual's growth and self-realization are facilitated by interpersonal relations that are *honest, caring, and nonmanipulative.* Hence the reliance on

Organizational "family" teams are exposed to sensitivity training, with the intention of *increasing trust and responsibility* that can be applied directly to solving organizational issues, and with the intention of *decreasing*

418

FIGURE 13-1. (Continued)

of individuals with no past relationships. Such training is a managed process of gaining experience with attitudes and skills for inducing greater openness about positive and negative feelings, attitudes, or beliefs. Such openness leads to greater trust and reduced risk in communicating in the "stranger" group, and is intended to suggest possible transfers into other environments.

the risk in being open in interpersonal and group situations. Skill and competence in interpersonal and intergroup situations can be increased in sensitivity training groups composed of strangers, but the real test is the application of such learning in life-relevant situations. Such application will require that substantial numbers of organization members learn appropriate interpersonal skills, as well as that they internalize a set of values which support and reinforce such learning.

Persons in groups which develop greater openness tend to *identify strongly* with other members and with the goals of the group.

Groups characterized by strong identification with members and goals become *increasingly capable of dealing with issues* facing their members, and hence increasingly *capable of influencing their environment* in desired ways.

Groups whose members identify strongly and who can influence their environment are likely to be effective *reinforcers of decisions about change.* Such groups also can provide *emotional support* necessary to sustain required changes in the values, attitudes, or behaviors of their members.

Used with the permission of the *Public Administration Review.* Robert T. Golembiewski, "Organization Development in Public Agencies: Perspectives on Theory and Practice," *Public Administration Review,* 29 (July–August 1969), 369.

very nature of organizations, there are bound to be conditions where if one unit achieves its goals, it frustrates the achievement of some other group's goals. Competition for rare resources is a continuing condition and one that must be constantly managed. If the reward system in an organization is such that it requires people to meet their goals but sets conditions over which they have no control and then punishes them for not meeting their goals, the system tends to produce frustration and a great deal of job dissatisfaction. Unfortunately, this is a rather common organization condition. And, regretfully, police departments are not free from its weakening effects.

A common and very successful means for reducing harmful

competition is to bring two competitive groups together and request that they independently list all the grievances that they have about the other group. They are also asked to list all the items that the other group may be citing as their grievances against them. They then exchange lists without conversing. Each group evaluates the other's list and establishes priorities for mutual discussion. Finally, they are brought together to create a single agenda for tackling one problem area at a time.

Goal Setting and Planning

One of the major premises underlying OD efforts and much managerial strategy today is the need to assure that organizations are managing toward goals. Healthy organizations tend to have goal setting at all levels. As a cornerstone of their practices, *individuals* engage in systematic performance improvement and target setting; *groups and teams* periodically and systematically set work goals and plans for achieving them; the *organization* as a whole engages in systematic goal-setting activities. Let us consider the third type of goal setting for a few moments. It has been used by a number of organizations and is now becoming more of interest to the police organization. The top management of the department sets departmental goals for service, performance, organization growth, manpower, and so forth. Each unit down to the bottom level independently sets its own goals with the knowledge of, but not the restriction to, the departmental goal at this time. These unit goals are fed to the top of the organization, which then looks at the discrepancies between the departmental goal and the sum of the unit goals. If there is a discrepancy, this is noted, and an analysis of the incompatibility is sent back to the system; all units are then asked to develop a strategy for closing the gap. From this second set of goals, the final departmental goals are formulated.

The results of a goal-setting endeavor are contained in Figure 13-2. While entitled "Chief Dyson's Seventeen Goals for the Dallas Police Department," it is actually a misnomer. Chief Dyson is quick to point out that the goals are the product of a collective effort that involved many middle and all top police managers in the Dallas Police Department. When describing the group dynamics that ensued during the goal-setting exercise, those included revealed that improved group relationships and team solidarity also developed. Not given in Figure 13-2 are the required semiannual reports from the managers in "Actions Taken" and "Achievements." In other words, not only are the goals expressed, but the managers must seek to accomplish them. Chief Dyson is, therefore, in a position to manage his managers by their results.

FIGURE 13–2.   **Chief Dyson's Seventeen Goals for the Dallas Police Department**

1. Obtain community involvement in crime prevention through voluntary citizen support.
2. Develop aggressive programs to prevent organized crime from moving into Dallas.
3. Develop aggressive programs to cope with the juvenile delinquency problem in Dallas.
4. Develop programs to effectively cope with the vice and narcotic problems in Dallas.
5. Obtain denial for repeat bond offenders.
6. Achieve a maximum response time of 3 minutes from citizen's call to police to arrival of beat officer.
7. Obtain maximum effectiveness in deployment of police officers.
8. Obtain maximum effectiveness through use of available technology.
9. Obtain a high level of internal inspection to achieve maximum effectiveness.
10. Achieve a high level of recruiting proficiency in order to attract superior quality applicants in sufficient numbers to staff the Department.
11. Enhance the image of the police officer and improve morale.
12. Improve decision-making through expanded use of staff work and by bringing all levels into the planning process.
13. Optimize the effectiveness of the police information system.
14. Open up channels of communication within the Department—up, down, and across.
15. Prepare personnel for more responsible positions.
16. Conduct long-range planning with emphasis on budgeting, operational and administrative systems, new concepts in police work, advanced technology, crime prevention, traffic supervision, and development of human resources.
17. Conduct planning and coordination with other agencies for the improvement of the criminal justice system.

Source: *Program for Individual and Departmental Effectiveness* (PRIDE), (Dallas, Tex.: Dallas Police Department, 1971), p. 2.

Education and Skills Acquisition

Although individual learning and the development of skill and ability are not the primary targets of an OD program, they are still part of the target. Some specific skills and abilities are more relevant than others for achieving the kind of organization effectiveness and health toward which OD efforts are aimed. Some of these developmental programs are (1) interpersonal competence (e.g., ability to cope with conflict), (2) problem solving (e.g., decision-making clinics), (3) goal setting (e.g., performance improvement), (4) planning (e.g., predicting the future), (5) understanding the processes of change (e.g., analysis of behavioral research findings), and (6) system diagnosis (e.g., enhancing analytical ability).

SOLUTION TWO: NEW ORGANIZATIONAL FORMS

The preceding solution centers on one or two individuals (the person), on three or more (the group), and on hundreds (the organization). This solution considers the need for new and better ways of organizing the persons who comprise departments so that they will be more adaptive to change. By way of a preface, we wish to inform the reader that we (1) will *not* offer our concept of the one best way to organize for change and (2) do not believe that bureaucracy is dead or dying.[19] In regard to statement one, we will concentrate on the characteristics (not structure) of a flexible organization. Statement two is in answer to those who are having fun with titles. The bureaucracy of yesterday and today was and is a formal organization. Both had or have a set of authoritative relationships, rules, regulations, written policies, rationality, and impersonality. We believe that future organizations will also possess these properties. The manner in which they are established and enforced, however, will be drastically changed. And the frequency with which they change will be extremely fast. We will find ourselves—that is, if we want to be capable of rapid adjustments to environmental demands for changes —creating *temporary* and *open* structures.[20]

Temporariness—Ad Hoc Designing

Temporariness in the "organizing" of our police organizations holds much in the way of a hope for constant structural renewal. The problems of the police department will be solved by *groups* of relative strangers who represent a set of diverse professional skills. The groups will be comprised of organic rather than mechanical models; they will grow out of the response to the problem rather than static positions. The function of the police manager thus be-

---

[19]Examples of opposing prognostications can be found in Warren G. Bennis, "Beyond Bureaucracy," *Trans-Action*, 2 (May 1965), 31–35; and Robert D. Miewald, "The Greatly Exaggerated Death of Bureaucracy," *California Management Review*, 13 (Winter 1970), 65–69.

[20]Warren G. Bennis, *Changing Organizations* (New York: McGraw-Hill Book Company, 1966), p. 12.

comes that of coordinator, or "linking pin" between various project groups. He must be a man who can speak the diverse languages of research and who can relay information and mediate among the groups. Police personnel will be specialized, not vertically according to rank and role, but flexibly according to skill and professional training. Adaptive, temporary systems of diverse specialists solving problems, linked together by coordinating and task-evaluative specialists, in organic flux, will gradually modify the bureaucracy that we know today.

Let us first note the term *specialists*, for it connotes professionalization. Temporary organizations will most frequently require employees with professional capabilities and training. More and more we observe within police departments, personnel—sworn and civilian —who are statisticians, chemists, programmers, pilots, psychologists, accountants, and so on. And, professionals possess dual loyalty: to the organization and to their profession. One example of this two-part loyalty is currently found in those police officers assigned to the juvenile unit. Often they belong to a professional association of juvenile officers which seeks a certain level of commitment to its ideals and goals. Police managers must develop a capacity for directing professional policemen who are divided in their loyalty to professional values and organizational goals. Job mobility (transferring from one police department to another) will serve to strengthen the allegiance to the "permanence" of the profession as compared to the "temporariness" of the organization. Hence, the rise of the professions means that modern large-scale organizations are being heavily infiltrated by men who have an entirely different concept of what organization is about and an entirely different image of their own relationship to it. This can have far-reaching consequences in the way the organization is run, as anyone familiar with the administration of aerospace firms and hospitals can testify.

Next we should study the phrase "problems. . . solved by groups." When the group process of decision making is used properly, discussion is focused on the problems to be solved. Communication is clear and adequately understood through overlapping group memberships. For example, the member of a patrol team may also serve as a member of a training requirements team; furthermore, the supervisor of a patrol team is also a member of the supervisory team. Thus the really important issues are recognized and dealt with. The atmosphere is one of "no nonsense," with emphasis on high productivity, high quality, and low costs. Decisions are reached promptly, *clear-cut responsibilities* are established, and tasks are performed rapidly and productively. Because of good communications, confidence and trust pervade all aspects of the relationship. The group's or the team's capacity for effective problem solving is maintained by examining and dealing with group processes when necessary through OD sessions.

It is essential that the group method of decision making and management *vision* not be confused with committees that never reach decisions or with wishy-washy, common-denominator sort of committees about which the superior can say, "Well, the group made this decision, and I couldn't do a thing about it." Quite the contrary! The group method of management holds the police manager fully responsible for the quality of all decisions and for their implementation. He is responsible for building his subordinates into a group that makes the best decisions and carries them out well. *The police manager is accountable for all decisions, for their execution, and for the results.* And, he is so (or soon will be) within an organizational framework that is consistently rearranging itself.

Openness: Increasing Representativeness and Participation

Traditional organizational theories have tended to view the human organization as a closed system. This tendency has led to a disregard of differing organizational environments and the nature of organizational dependency on environment. It has led also to an overconcentration on principles of internal organizational functioning, with consequent failure to develop and understand the processes of feedback which are essential to survival.[21]

The open-system approach to organizations is different from commonsense approaches, which tend to accept popular names and traditional ideas about basic organizational properties and to identify the purpose of an organization in terms of the goals of its founders and leaders. The open-system approach, on the other hand, begins by identifying the repeated cycles of input, transformation, output, and renewed input which comprise the organizational pattern. Organizations as a special class of open systems have properties of their own, but they share other properties in common with all open systems. These include the importation of energy from the environment, the throughput or transformation of the imported energy into some product form that is characteristic of the system, the exporting of that product into the environment, and the reenergizing of the system from sources in the environment. To put it in other

[21] Daniel Katz and Robert L. Kahn, *The Social Psycholgy of Organizations* (New York: John Wiley & Sons, Inc., 1966), p. 29.

terms: input, processing, output, and feedback. If a police organization is to be successful, all four properties must be operating effectively and in coordination.

More than ever before the four properties of input, processing, output, and feedback are dependent on enhanced environmental representation within their boundaries, and vastly improved programs for internal participation. Representativeness and participation are two key reference points for sensing and moving toward pending changes. In regard to representation, it is in the air everywhere. People have a perceptible interest in being represented in the *administrative agencies* of the government.

> Political democracy, by incorporating larger and larger numbers in social decision making, facilitates feedback. And it is precisely this feedback that is essential to control. To assume control over accelerant change, we shall need still more advanced—and more democratic—feedback mechanisms.
>
> The technocrat, however, still thinking in top-down terms, frequently makes plans without arranging for adequate and instantaneous feedback from the field, so that he seldom knows how well his plans are working. When he does arrange for feedback, what he usually asks for and gets is heavily economic, inadequately social, psychological or cultural. Worse yet, he makes these plans without sufficiently taking into account the fast changing needs and wishes of those whose participation is needed to make them a success. He assumes the right to set social goals by himself or he accepts them blindly from some higher authority.
>
> He fails to recognize that the faster pace of change demands — and creates—a new kind of information system in society: a loop, rather than a ladder. Information must pulse through this loop at accelerating speeds, with the output of one group becoming the input for many others, so that no group, however politically potent it may seem, can independently set goals for the whole.[22]

Obviously there is no "one" best way to increase the clientele's representativeness in its administrative units. Of paramount consideration, however, is the hope for decentralization of services. By simply placing those responsible for *serving* close to those being *served*, the possibilities of influencing and being influenced are heightened. The so called bassic car plan, or team policing, is designed to provide greater representation. Out of representation grows support for the agency and its goals. To the insecure or marginally qualified police manager, the acceptance of external ideas and expressed needs is threatening. The professional police manager

[22] Toffler, *Future Shock,* p. 421.

will invite greater community representativeness in the policy decisions of his department. Not only will his organization be more
susceptible to the *right* changes, but he will also find that his ability
to manage the members of the department is significantly improved![23]

The importance of participation can be best understood by the
reader's reflecting for a moment on those situations in his workaday
world where decisions were made *for* him and not *by* him. One could
only predict reduced commitment to the fulfillment of such decisions. It is unfortunate that more police managers do not allow
their personnel some *share in the making of decisions that affect
them* (e.g., what sidearm to wear; helmets, soft hats, or no hats; long-
or short-sleeve shirts, and the rest).

> Whatever its scope, the possibility of the employee influencing
> his broad work environment tends to pay off in increased output
> and heightened satisfaction. Indeed, management has but limited
> choice in the matter. It can attempt to mesh the norms of the in-
> formal group with the goals of the formal organization or it can
> thrust its head into the proverbial sand by neglecting the need for
> participation.[24]

To paraphrase one sage commentator, over two thousand years ago
we put *participation* in the religion that has come to dominate the
Western world. Two hundred years ago we put this essential element
in our political and social structure. We are just beginning to realize
that we ought to put participation in police organizations as well.
A final caveat on participation, participative programs must be imbedded in a system of compatible structure and techniques, not
superimposed on some more or less hostile system. Next, participative
techniques must be delivered from careless misuse as well as from
wrongful manipulation, and this poses a delicate practical problem.
The general requirements are quite plain, however. Participative
techniques must really give as well as get. They must do more than
"create a sense of participation," and they must reward and reinforce
the substantial participation of the police employee.

We now close the above concern for and emphasis on OD,
new organizational forms, and the need for planned organizational
change with the following thoughts and challenges. The changes
that we have mentioned or hinted about, complex and difficult as
they are, are necessary. Our current police departments, effective

[23] For additional thinking on this subject and representation in general, see Herbert Kaufman, "Administrative Decentralization, and Political Power," *Public Administration Review*, 29 (January-February 1969), 3–14.

[24] Robert T. Golembiewski, *Men, Management, and Morality: Toward a New
Organizational Ethic* (New York: McGraw-Hill Book Company, 1965), pp. 227–28.

as they have been in the past, are at this moment on the edge of failure. The impersonality of the large police organization, the sharp horns of our immediate dilemma between quality and numbers, the unwillingness of our clients, the citizens, to accept much longer the rigidities of our present police organizations—all combine to force change upon us. *Let us make these changes as they should be made, voluntarily and with careful planning, rather than wait to have them forced upon us, and let us establish a police tradition of not being afraid of something new.*

LEARNING EXERCISES

The following learning exercises are from the Menlo Park Police Department in California.[25] The reader is requested to forgive the citation of precise salary figures, which will appear obsolete when read. Incidentally, one of the authors of this book joined a city police department in 1957, thought he was being well paid at $440 per month, and even started to raise two of his three children on this salary—with money left to save. In any event, the reader is now presented with the outcome of an OD program. The inclusions are in chronological sequence.

UNIFORM EXPERIMENT AND ORGANIZATION DEVELOPMENT

In April 1970 the *Police Chief* published a five-month interim report on the Menlo Park Police Department blazer uniform experiment. We continue to receive inquiries about our experiment and we have had numerous requests for a final report.

One problem in preparing a uniform experiment report is that the change to soft-wear blazer is only part of a two-and-one-half-year organization development program that began in the summer of 1968. A second problem is to make the report credible because the statistical data to be presented are in many ways extraordinary.

To help the reader with a perspective of the Menlo Park Police Department, the following background and brief review of the interim report is presented.

Menlo Park is a heterogeneous community of thirty thousand located on the San Francisco peninsula and is adjacent to the city of Palo Alto and Stanford University. Our 20 percent black population has a median age of nineteen years, and the community has experienced disorder in the past few years.[26] After a prototype experiment with two patrol officers,

[25] The learning exercises are selected from materials furnished by Chief "Vic" to the *Police Chief*. See the pertinent monthly journal issues during 1970 and 1971.

[26] We had our first full year (1970) without a black community disturbance since 1966.

a lieutenant and the chief of police, the entire police department (forty-eight personnel) switched to a green blazer uniform in August 1969. The motorcycle officer was the only exception to the change because the traditional motorcycle uniform is designed to protect if there is an accident.

A five-month comparison study between 1968 and 1969 showed a 50 percent reduction in assaults on officers, an increase in traffic citation production (+78 percent), and a reduction of not-guilty pleas by defendants. We also had a great many questions about safety, and loss of authority and identification, from citizens and police.

Initially a great deal of peer pressure was brought to bear on the officers from other police department personnel. Some officers did not like their new image and left the department.

In addition to the blazer, all officers are equipped with a utility bag that holds a baton, zip-in jumpsuit, and gas mask. A three-quarter-length coat was issued for wear during cold or moderately inclement weather. The jumpsuit is worn during very bad weather or for prolonged traffic control. (Menlo Park does not have any fixed traffic posts.)

January 1, 1971, marked the eighteenth month of the experiment. The questions of identification have not proved out. We have had only three minor incidents where the identity of the officer was questioned. They involved an elderly lady, a young lady, and a man under the influence of alcohol. The year 1970 showed a 29.1 percent decrease in assaults on officers, and we have not had a *lost time* assault on an officer in a blazer. During the six months preceding the experiment, five officers were briefly hospitalized after being assaulted in the old blue uniform.

The FBI crime trend report for the first nine months of 1970 shows a 13 percent national increase in Part I crimes for cities in the 25,000–50,000 population category. At the end of the calendar year 1970, Menlo Park showed a 02.5 percent Part I crime decrease. Rape was 27.2 percent, robbery–31.4 percent, aggravated assault–38.1 percent, burglary–8.9 percent, and auto theft–4.4 percent. Our only Part I increases were murder (2 compared to 0 in 1969) and theft (over $50–+31.2 percent).

Police departments in reality have little control over assault cases, but we feel the decreases in burglary, robbery, and auto theft can be attributed to department programs. During 1970 we used special patrol in high-crime-rate areas. Our field interviews increased 177 percent (1969–304, 1970–844). It is worth noting that we did not have one complaint of a mishandled interview. This indicates active *courteous* police can interact with citizens without causing hostility. We feel the soft-wear blazer helps us in these contacts.

Our 1970 traffic flow increased by approximately 750,000 vehicles, but our injury accidents only increased by four (1969–105, 1970–109). We attribute this to our 54.8 percent increase in moving citations (1969 –3,915, 1970–6,050) and 104 percent increase in equipment citations (1969–648, 1970–1,323). Parking citations increased 38.7 percent (1969 –13,246, 1970–18,382).

With all of the increase in production we also increased our patrol mileage by 19.6 percent. This represents 62,025 additional patrol miles with the same number of vehicles as 1969. In more graphic terms, it represents an extra *two months* of patrol service when compared to the 1969 average of 31,000 miles a month.

We have learned that a three-quarter-length topcoat is not functional for patrol work, and we are changing to a more practical three-quarter-length jacket that is green in color. A shirt and tie are worn with this jacket, and the identification is a badge on the left breast. This jacket will be worn during late evening or early morning hours when it is too cold for the blazer. We are also looking for a new blazer that has a full reinforced lining and heavy duty stitching.

The trauma of change is past. We like the blazer and so does the public. Approximately five hundred police departments across the United States have developed some form of blazer program. We believe this is part of a transition from blue-collar worker to white-collar professional.

We began our organizational development by establishing new promotion requirements in September 1968. At that time our city personnel board set January 1, 1972, as the effective date for requiring sergeants to have an AA degree prior to promotion, and lieutenants will be required to have a bachelor's degree or a State of California Advanced Police Officers Standards and Training certificate.

Next we changed the work schedule to one of rotating days off, giving officers two consecutive three-day weekends out of every five-week period. Shift rotation is accomplished twice a year and coincides with area college semester breaks. There is no seniority preference in shift rotation. The city of Menlo Park paid tuition and cost of books up to nine units each semester.

For in-service training we set every Friday aside as a training day, all officers reporting one half hour early for work. The first Friday of the month consists of shooting on the department range. At the end of the shooting day an International Association of Chiefs of Police Training Key is given to each officer for review during the week. On the second Friday, the first key is reviewed with the shift supervisor and a second training key is distributed. On the third Friday, a video tape presentation is made on the subject matter of the two keys. These video tapes are prepared by department personnel who are assigned on the basis of expertise and interest in a given field. On the fourth Friday we test on the subject matter of the month.

We have not altered this in-service program during the past two years. We do occasionally have video tape presentations during the week on special problems as they arise.

All staff officers were enrolled in various supervisor and management programs by the department. We now have graduates from middle management programs from California State College, Long Beach; University of California, Santa Cruz; San Jose State College; and from the University of Santa Clara Graduate School seminar series on municipal management.

The management of the department was deliberately decentralized, and participative management became a department goal. Staff meetings now have published agendas and minutes. Anyone in the department can put an item on the agenda. A patrol officer who is the president of the Police Officers Association sits in and participates in all monthly staff meetings. The Officers Association formed at the suggestion of the chief of police and the representation of the association is an invitation and not a directive.

Staff meetings at this point are in fact problem-solving sessions and not a meeting to receive directives from the chief of police. It is interesting to note there is no hierarchy order of seating in staff meetings.

In the fall of 1969 the department published and posted a "Theory Y"[27] policy statement, i.e.: We believe

1. The expenditure of physical and mental effort in work is as natural as play or rest.

2. External control and the threat of punishment are not the only means for bringing about effort toward organizational objectives. Man will exercise self-direction and self-control in the service of objectives to which he is committed.

3. Commitment to objectives is a function of the rewards associated with their achievement.

4. The average human being learns under proper conditions, not only to accept but to seek responsibility.

5. The capacity to exercise a relatively high degree of imagination, ingenuity and creativity in the solution of organizational problems is widely, not narrowly, distributed in the population.

6. Under the conditions of modern industrial life, the intellectual potentialities of the average human being are only partially utilized.

This drastic change in police management style was not accomplished easily. It required constant attention from a dedicated staff and a lot of psychological adjustment on everyone's part. Some men rejected the management change like those who rejected the uniform change and left the department.

We believe we have stabilized at this point. The department is at full strength for sworn personnel with an active list, and we also have a large number of unadvertised-for applications to be processed if we do have an opening.

We believe the approach in our policy statement works because we see many officers working on their own time without remuneration on cases they have interest in. There is not a nine-to-five working attitude, and a survey of the department by the group from the Stanford Graduate School of Business reported the officers feel they are part of a vanguard organization and that the officers receive satisfaction from their expanded responsibilities.

The motivation of the department is also indicated by the following statistics. During 1970, 85 percent of sworn personnel attended college, attaining an average of nine semester units. Department personnel also attained three Advanced Police Officers Standards and Training certificates, six Intermediate Police Officers Standards and Training certificates, and eight vocational Police Science teaching credentials.

In June 1968 we did not have any Police Officers Standards and Train-

---

[27] Douglas McGregor, *The Human Side of Enterprise.* See also W. R. Rhodes, "Behavioral Science Application to Police Management," *Police Chief,* May 1970.

ing certificates above the basic level. We had one teaching credential, and one person with a college degree. We now have four Advanced and nine Intermediate Police Officers Standards and Training certificates. We have seven college degrees (AA and Bachelor's), and nine more officers will qualify for AA degrees. Our average number of college units has risen from twenty-one to fifty.

In the two-and-a-half-year development we also had strong emphasis on community relations and community involvement. We feel our IACP Crime Check Program that involved a mailout to every citizen on crime prevention, our ride-along program that involved four hundred juveniles and adults, four hours each, and school education programs all have contributed to the statistical successes mentioned at the beginning of this report.

On January 26, 27, and 28, 1971, the chief of police, two lieutenants, and six sergeants, along with the community resource officer, the traffic officer, and the president of the Officers Association, spent a three-day department seminar at the Asilomar Conference Center in Pacific Grove, California. The department now has a written philosophy, a team concept with a definition and new defined working relationships and job role descriptions. The sergeants and lieutenants indicated they wanted to change their titles in addition to their job role description and now call themselves police operations managers and operations directors respectively. The development of this three-day seminar will be the subject matter of a final organization development report that will be submitted to the *Police Chief* when it is complete.

Victor I. Cizanckas
Chief of Police

ORGANIZATION DEVELOPMENT

Organization development has been the subject of many management articles and books in recent years. It is usually discussed in connection with profit-making organizations and rarely associated with public service agencies. Organization development, or OD with a police department is almost unheard of.

Our department began such a program in 1968 and it is more than "an effort to manage all of a company's resources, including its management style and behavior in relationship to each other."[28] It is in many ways finding one's self. It is admitting work is not only rewarding and challenging, but it is also fun. It is also the realization that not all people can adjust to a management style that calls for self-direction, little supervision, and freedom to participate and express one's own ideas. Organization development is also unpleasant. It produces trauma, uncertainty, and discomfort while you are building, changing, and waiting for results. It also takes time! You cannot say we will try human and organization development for a month or two

---

[28] Marvin R. Weisbord, "What, Not Again! Manage People Better," *Think*, p. 2.

and see if it works. The real rewards and dividends take years.

Our two-and-a-half-year program resulted in many statistical successes in crime reduction and service production. It also brought about a philosophical change, new working relationships, and new ideas about the structure of a police department and the job roles of the people in the organization.

We decided to formalize and work out what we had accomplished in a three-day seminar at the State of California Conference grounds located at the Asilomar in Pacific Grove, California. This seminar took place on January 26, 27, and 28, 1971. The participants included the chief of police, two lieutenants, six sergeants, our traffic inspector, community resource officer, and a patrol officer, the president of the officer's association. Our city manager also participated during the second day of the conference.

With the exception of the traffic inspector, all of the participants had been involved in formal management training programs during our two-and-one-half-year development period.

The chief of police took the role of conference coordinator, and our first step was to write down everything we wanted to discuss. Next we established a priority of subject matter that looked like this.

ASILOMAR OBJECTIVES

1. Department philosophy
2. Job description
3. Distribution of manpower
4. Reorganization
5. Team concept
6. Career development
7. Training
8. Program cutback
9. Burglary suppression
10. Accident prevention
11. Motorcycle disposition
12. Community relations
13. Reserve program
14. Uniform changes
15. Reporting procedures
16. Selected equipment

This report deals with the first six items and community relations.

All participants decided we could not proceed without a basic philosophy to guide us. This is what developed.

MENLO PARK POLICE PHILOSOPHY

The Menlo Park Police Department is a municipal multiservice organization designed to provide better living and safety for citizens.

Recognizing it must relate and respond to community needs that are dynamic and constantly changing, the department is pledged to recruiting talented personnel who are committed to their fellowman and are free from color and economic bias.

While rejecting an authoritarian approach to problem solving, the department is continually involved in enforcement, prevention, and education programs designed to control and reduce crime and traffic accidents. The department commits itself to its employees and will make every effort to provide a work atmosphere conducive to personal and career development.

Ultimately we hope to provide quality police service at minimum cost to the citizens we serve.

As we examined existing working relationships and job roles, it became apparent that we were in fact team policing. We defined a team as a problem-solving police unit that utilized available skills and expertise in a coordinated effort to meet organization objectives. We also acknowledge a *group* responsibility for all police services and activities. We removed our dispatchers from staff services division, changed their title to communications officers, and then made them a team member. We kept our investigation division intact, but we assigned a particular detective to each team as a resource. What finally emerged as a team system is shown in Figure 1.

Next we eliminated two-man units and adopted a *zone* policing concept that will allow greater flexibility and utilization of team personnel. Basically this system calls for a two-zone rather than a four-beat plan. Each zone has two or more units and one additional unit (police agent) acts as a floating unit between zones. This system will also eliminate excessive reports for one officer. It will in fact balance case loads and reduce overtime report writing.

Next the group eliminated the titles sergeant and lieutenant, replacing them with police operations manager and an operations director. (See Figure 1.) Brief job descriptions and 1971 salary schedules for team personnel are as follows:

Operations Director—$13,248–$16,104[29]

Plans, directs, and coordinates the activities of a police service division. Innovates and generates programs designed to meet organization objectives. Is an adviser to the chief of police and may act in that capacity in his absence.

Police Operations Manager—$11,724–$14,244

Develops, trains, and coordinates a police service team to provide community protection and services. Conducts surveys and researches special needs of the community. Generates programs that will accomplish organizational goals. Exercises budget control, and as a member of a management team continually analyzes department philosophies, objectives, and programs. Makes recommendations for change.

[29] All salaries are built on a three-and-one-half-year, five-step progression.

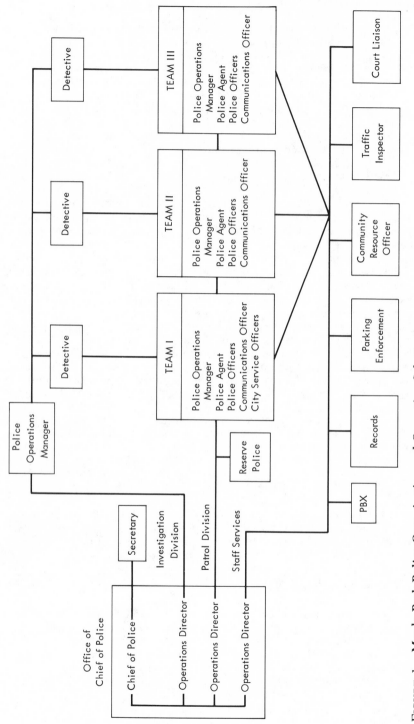

FIGURE 1. Menlo Park Police Organization and Operating Schematic

434

Detective—$11,172-$13,572

Conducts general and criminal investigations, acts as resource to a police service team providing training and investigative expertise. Acts as a member of a major case investigation team. Gathers and disseminates intelligence information.

Community Resource Officer—$11,172-$13,572

As a member of staff services he coordinates efforts to establish a working relationship between the community and police service teams. Provides information and programs to citizens groups and schools. Develops and implements community relations programs. Evaluates overall department community relations efforts.

Traffic Inspector—$11,172-$13,572

As a member of staff services, he is a resource to police service teams and the office of the chief of police. He is an ex-officio member of the City Traffic Commission. He coordinates and participates in major injury accident investigations. Prepares monthly accident data and citation ratios for use of police operations managers.

Police Agent[30]—$10,632-$12,924

As a member of a police service team provides expertise to team members, assists in accomplishing objectives, acts in capacity of police operations manager in his absence.

Police Officer—$10,128-$12,312

As a member of a police service team, he protects life and property and assists the city in an overall effort to provide better living and security for its citizens. Answers calls for assistance and service. Conducts criminal and general investigations. Helps develop and maintain positive interaction with the community. Maintains an awareness of police service needs and developments.

Communications Officer—$8,244-$9,896

As a member of a police service team, he coordinates team activity and makes assignments at the general direction of a police operations manager. Operates various types of communication equipment. Assists in communication training of de-

[30]Appointed by chief of police after two years of service showing high proficiency and maintenance of three units of college each semester with *B* average.

partment personnel. Provides information and assistance to
the public through personal and telephone contacts.

City Service Officer — $6,684–$8,224

As a nonsworn member of a police service team, conducts residence checks for citizens who are vacationing, reports city
ordinance violations for processing. Does radio and parking
control relief work.

The conference group developed burglary suppression and accident
reduction programs that will be tried during the coming year. We also put
together the following policy statements.

CAREER DEVELOPMENT

The Menlo Park Police Department has a strong active interest
in the personal development of all of its employees. Therefore it will make every effort to provide a working atmosphere
that invites and encourages personnel and career growth. The
city will support this commitment through monetary assistance
in college programs and the scheduling of training and education
programs for all personnel.

COMMUNITY RELATIONS

It is our responsibility to develop community involvement,
support, and confidence in its police service.
We believe the only way to achieve this goal is through a total
organization commitment to all community relations programs.
We also believe every personal contact should be as positive
and helpful as circumstances allow.
We feel if we fail in this commitment, ultimately we will
fail completely.

We left the Asilomar with a feeling of accomplishment, a commitment
to what we developed and a positive feeling about the future of the Menlo
Park Police Department.

Victor I. Cizanckas
Chief of Police

INDEX